PR   ON

J   LF

"Mar

"It is   ; the game.'
My fri   f brilliance,
depth,   context is
'changi

— N   *Kingdom*

"You   ooks of the
new   tern and
Wes   eat Birth
that   pensable
read   of evolution

"I   d in your
han   rever not
only   postmeta-
phys   k is mag-
nific   be one of
the   lique Self
brings together East and West in a higher integral embrace of stunning implications.
Unique Self is a pivotal step toward an authentic Enlightenment. First laid out by

Marc in his academic articles on 'The Evolutionary Emergent of Unique Self, A New Chapter in Integral theory,' it appears here for broader public, for the first time in full-developed form, in this volume."

— Ken Wilber, Author of *A Brief History of Everything*

"Dr. Marc Gafni has written a brilliant book, *Your Unique Self*, which I believe is essential reading. *Your Unique Self* articulates a bold evolutionary, spiritual, philosophy that calls every individual to realize their Unique Self and give their Unique Gifts in an evolutionary context. Gafni, together with his colleague Ken Wilber, is a bold visionary and a catalytic voice for the newly emergent World Spirituality movement, which combines the best of premodern, modern, and postmodern insight. I highly recommend this book."

— John Mackey, CEO of Whole Foods
and Chair of Center for World Spirituality

"With exceptional brilliance and an awakened heart, Dr. Marc Gafni speaks to all of us who are interested in the evolution of consciousness. His teachings on the Unique Self enlightenment are essential for the next stage in our evolution. They have emerged from his direct experience and I highly recommend them."

— Michael Bernard Beckwith, author of *Spiritual Liberation:
Fulfilling Your Soul's Potential*

"Marc, a fellow drinker at the holy taverns has written a fine, fine book. Kabbalists say a Day of Tikkun (evolution, soul-repair) is coming. There are great stories here from the Hasidic masters and from Marc's own life, honoring the unique soulmaking that has brought you to this moment. This beautiful book will deepen that astonishing mystery and awaken you to the individual beauty of your path."

— Coleman Barks, author of *Rumi: The Big Red Book*

"*Your Unique Self* is a great read. As is obvious from even flipping through its pages, Dr. Marc Gafni not only understands the material, but also has lived it. The book is both thorough and fun, and will provoke deep thoughts. I meant to scan it on vacation and ended up reading it cover to cover in one sitting. It's a book that is worth many readings. It will both fascinate you in its insights and annoy you that you haven't read this book until now."

— Dave Logan, PhD, New York Times #1 bestselling co-author
of *Tribal Leadership;* former Associate Dean, USC Marshall School of Business

"Dr. Marc Gafni's teaching on the Unique Self radically evolves the way we understanding and realize enlightenment. He is a great teacher of both heart and mind. His penetrating depth, practicality, and heartfelt charisma will change your life."

— John Gray, author of *Men Are from Mars, Women Are from Venus*

"This is a coherent, comprehensive and amazing book from an amazing mind on a challenging topic. Using the concept of the "Unique Self" as the essential reality behind all forms of the self, the author succeeds in integrating not only the historical East-West polarities regarding the nature of the self, the variables of spiritual practice and the meaning of enlightenment, but also the antinomies between psychotherapy and the spiritual traditions. His redefinition, extension and integration of the core meanings of healing, wholeness and the self will expand the consciousness of all readers. I compliment the author's intellectual and spiritual achievement and recommend it to all travelers on the journey to enlightenment."

— Harville Hendrix, PhD, author of *Getting the Love You Want: A Guide for Couples*

"I am usually stingy with superlatives because their meaning has been so diluted by overuse, but I cannot control myself regarding this book—it is truly brilliant. It offers an engaging and erudite corrective to the tendency in the spiritual community to disdain personal uniqueness and worship transcendental oneness, as well as the striving to rise and remain above the ego and the material world. Instead, Gafni says go ahead and transcend, but then reclaim your uniqueness on the other side of transcendence and bring your unique enlightened consciousness back to this world with you, and use your unique gifts to change it for the better. It would be entirely accurate to say that Internal Family Systems and Unique Self are overlapping models that recognize each other's insights while each excels in its own domain. The integration of these two models fosters a creative synthesis that is nothing short of revolutionary in its implications for healing and transformation."

— Prof. Richard Schwartz, founder of Internal Family Systems. Author of *Internal Family Systems Therapy*

"*Your Unique Self* has a core idea of considerable importance that could change the way spiritual transformation is understood and inaugurate a whole new level in the InterSpiritual dialogue."

— Cynthia Bourgeault, Christian theologian, author of *Mary Magdalene*

"At this historic moment, our human mind is passing the border towards a new consciousness. Marc Gafni is far enough ahead of most of us to articulate insights he gained beyond that borderline. Yet, like all great teachers, the author becomes transparent. Here is an invitation and a great opportunity to listen—not to Marc Gafni, but to *Your Unique Self.* Thus this book becomes an indispensable travel guide into the realm of a vast new consciousness."

— Brother David Steindl-Rast, Christian theologian. Author of *Belonging to the Universe: Explorations on the Frontiers of Science and Spirituality,* coauthored with Fritjof Capra and Thomas Matus

"Marc Gafni's brilliant intellect and spiritual passion make him a force to be reckoned with. His deep knowledge and advocacy of Abrahamic mysticism, coupled with his inspired vision of a World Spirituality, offer a unique and significant contribution to the evolution of our understanding of God, religion and Spirit in the 21st century."

— Andrew Cohen, founder of EnlightenNext. Author of *Evolutionary Enlightenment*

"Marc Gafni's overflowing heart and transmission of the Unique Self teaching profoundly moves me. Dr. Marc holds the lineage energy of the great Hasidic masters of Kabbalah, which he brings with him into the visionary initiative of Center for World Spirituality. There is little doubt in my mind that *Your Unique Self* will become one of the classic texts that forms the World Spirit vision that our world needs so deeply. This is a book and a teacher that we all very much need."

— Lama Surya Das, author of *Awakening the Buddha Within: Tibetan Wisdom for the Western World* and founder of the Dzogchen Meditation Centers

"I've never met anyone so talented at what he does and passionate for his work as Marc Gafni. He is simply spellbinding. He awakens people's grasp of the ungraspable better than any spiritual teacher I've ever known. He is a true artist. A creative genius. To not experience his transmission as a teacher in this lifetime, whether in person or through his writings, would be a tragedy."

— Kristen Ulmer, world-renowned top ranked professional extreme skier and sports coach

"Marc Gafni's *Your Unique Self* is the great invitation to live a meaningful life that we have all been waiting for. This book is especially for anyone who has ever wondered if they have a unique calling or purpose in life. The answer is YES and you are well on your way to learn how to live a life of infinite creativity, passion and possibility. The next step of the journey is to read this brilliant guide to discover WHO YOU ARE and WHAT YOU ARE here to uniquely experience, express and expand on behalf of the whole."

— Paul Taylor, CEO, Global Citizen Consulting; former Global VP, The Coca-Cola Company

"*Your Unique Self* could only have been written by someone who passionately lives his own uniqueness. Marc Gafni is a brilliant teacher and heart master with a rare capacity for empathy and a gift for creating community. This book contains the essence of his teaching on what it means to live from an enlightened life from a ground of one's own personal uniqueness. A truly ground-shifting book, it offers a perspective on personal transformation that integrates insights of traditional and postmodern wisdom. Reading it can change your understanding not only of your own path, but also of what it means to live a life of inner contemplation and transformative service in the world. This is a book that deserves to become a classic."

— Sally Kempton, author of *Meditation for the Love of It*

"Dr. Marc Gafni's writing eloquently demonstrates the essentially mental—and futile—conclusion that there ever could be separation between 'I' (oneself, me) and 'Presence' (no-I, unity). Both 'I' and 'unity' are radiant refractions of the infinite mystery of beingness conscious of itself. I salute and support his expression and recognition of the uniqueness of each in all."

— Gangaji, author of *Hidden Treasure: Uncovering the Truth in Your Life*

"*Your Unique Self* represents a truly planetcentric mysticism that provides a powerful way of integrating the enlightenment traditions of the pre-modern East and the modern West. It has been easy for spiritual traditions to embrace profound states of Kosmoscentric consciousness, but they have often neglected to include the developmental capacities to take perspectives thereby falling short of an emancipatory worldcentric articulation. Marc Gafni's teachings on Unique Self provide the first sophisticated and mature expression of this 'unique' integral position. *Your Unique Self* ushers in an exciting new chapter in Integral Theory building on the most widely applied meta-framework on the planet and extending it into new contexts of embodied enlightenment."

— Sean Esbjörn-Hargens, PhD, co-author of *Integral Ecology* and editor of *Integral Theory in Action*

"No one book has inspired me to cherish myself, respect others and have hope for both this country and this world more fully than *Your Unique Self*. With insights as sharp as a knife and words that hone its blade, Rabbi Gafni holds before us the mirror of our unique selves and the molecular, spiritual, internal and external paths we might explore to enhance that uniqueness. An extraordinary future classic. *Your Unique Self* gives my unique self shivers."

— Warren Farrell, PhD, author of *Why Men Are the Way They Are and The Myth of Male Power*

"What I love about *Your Unique Self* is that among the nondual traditions, it stands alone in its conviction, demonstration and celebration of our uniqueness. It does not ask us to sacrifice our individuality in the service of the highest truth, but rather to become fully ourselves in order to be of greatest service in the world. Marc Gafni backs his vision with brilliance, passion, humor, personal integrity and a life lived in dedication to articulating a world-changing dharma."

— Mariana Caplan, PhD, author of *The Guru Question: The Perils and Rewards of Choosing a Spiritual Teacher* and *Eyes Wide Open: Cultivating Discernment on the Spiritual Path*

"Gafni's work on Unique Self is utterly essential reading for everyone who wants to step into the fullness of their being."

— Richard Barrett, Chairman and Founder of the Barrett Values Centre, author of *The New Leadership Paradigm* and *Love, Fear and the Destiny of Nations.*

"Unique Self is a truly important book which can potentially take the conversation between psychology and spirituality to the next level. The crossroads of so many psychotherapies is facilitating the differentiation of self, moving beyond the false self that fears the disappointment of others, and opening the full capacity of the human to be intimate. This book integrates in an original and important way Eastern and Western spirituality in a way that provide therapists and their clients with critical new tools and insights for the assault on self hatred that blocks integration internally and confidence and competence externally."

— Dr. Mark Schwartz, Clinical Director, Thought Leader in the Fields of Eating Disorder, Trauma, Sexual Addiction, Clinical Director, Castlewood Treatment Centers, Former Clinical Director, Masters and Johnson

YOUR
UNIQUE
SELF

ALSO BY MARC GAFNI

Soul Prints
The Mystery of Love
The Erotic and the Holy **(audio)**
Soul Print Workshop **(audio)**
Radical Kabbalah: The Enlightenment Teaching of Unique Self and Nondual Humanism, Vol. 1
Radical Kabbalah: The Wisdom of Solomon, Vol. 2
Reclaiming Uncertainty as a Spiritual Value (Hebrew, Safek)
Re-Defining Certainty (Hebrew, Vadai)
Lillith: Re-Reading Feminine Shadow (Hebrew, with co-author)
First Steps in Judaism

Forthcoming:

World Spirituality Based on Integral Principles (with Ken Wilber)
The Dance of Tears and Rosh Hashanah: Towards an Integrally Informed Judaism
On the Erotic and the Holy (with new material and primary source footnotes)
Soul Prints: Living Your Story (with new material and primary source footnotes)
Integral Religion: The Dance of Certainty and Uncertainty
Integral God (with co-author)
Actualize: A User's Guide to the Universe (with co-author)
Answering the Call (with co-author)
Shadow (with Sally Kempton)
Wounds of Love (with Sally Kempton)
Beyond Venus and Mars (with Warren Farrell)
Beyond Twelve Steps (with Lori Galperin)
Word Spirituality Practice Guide (with Tom Goddard)
Pleasure Rewoven: Addiction Undone (Towards an Integral Vision of Recovery)

Trilogy of Sex, Love and Eros
  Seven Levels of Sexing
  Seven Styles of Love Relationship
  Seven Laws of Eros
  (English Version with Annie Lalla)
  (Dutch Version with Leon Gras and Sujata van Overveld)
Unique Self, Dutch version, expanded *(with Mauk Pieper)*
Soul Prints, Dutch Version *(with Chahat Corten)*
Eros and Nondual Humanism (Academic)

Forthcoming Works on World Spirituality, Unique Self or Marc Gafni's teachings:

The Rise of World Spirituality (Joe Perez)
The Enlightenment of Fullness: Marc Gafni Reader (Ed. Dr. Heather Fester)
Loving Your Way to Enlightenment: Marc's Teachings on "Outrageous Loving"
  (Chahat Corten)
Teachings from the Holy of Holies {365 days of Wisdom Teachings} (Elizabeth
  Helen Bullock)
Letters to my Students (Kathleen J. Brownback)

MARC GAFNI

YOUR UNIQUE SELF

THE RADICAL PATH TO PERSONAL ENLIGHTENMENT

On the Democratization of Enlightenment,
Self beyond Ego, the Personal beyond the Impersonal,
the infinity of Intimacy & Individuation as Enlightenment

© 2012 Marc Gafni
© 2012 Foreword and Afterword by Ken Wilber

Published 2012

Book design by Kathryn Lloyd and Lisa Kerans
Crafty Coyote Book Design

Cover art by FeaturePics.com, Pedro Rebelo

Printed in the United States, the United Kingdom and Australia to minimize shipping distances and reduce the negative impact on our environment. Lightning Source has the following environmental printer Chain of Custody certifications: Forest Stewardship Council™, Sustainable Forestry Initiative®, Programme for the Endorsement of Forest Certification™.

ISBN 978-1-4675-2277-9

1. Spiritual life. 2. Self-actualization (Psychology)—Religious aspects.

For my friend, brother and
"Giga Pandit" to so many, Ken Wilber

For Eytan, Yair, Zion, and Rachel

For my beloved friends and colleagues,
Metuka Benjamin, Diane Hamilton, and Dalit Arnon,
incarnations of the divine feminine integrity who held me
in the narrow places, especially in the first years after.

For my students who have received the transmission
of this "Torah," and are living it in their lives.

For beloved Sally Kempton, whose
integrity and radiance inspire.

For Mariana Caplan, divine mother of Zion,
ally, love, and founding partner in
The Center for World Spirituality.

CONTENTS

Foreword by Ken Wilber xix

A Note to the Reader xxi

Preface xxiii

Introduction xxvii

PART ONE

Chapter 1   The Great Invitation of Your Life 3

Chapter 2   The New Enlightenment of Unique Self 7
             Being God's Verb. 8
             God Is Having a Marc Experience 9
             The God of Unique Self 9

Chapter 3   Two Visions of Enlightenment and
             Their Higher Integration in Unique Self 15
             Two Images of Light 16
             The Biology of Unique Self 18
             The Democratization of Enlightenment 21
             Answering the Call 22
             Enlightenment Is Sanity 24
             Unique Self Is Not a Concept 28
             Enlightenment Is Not Impersonal 28
             The Personal Face of Essence 28

Chapter 4   **Eight Stations on the Road to Unique Self** **31**

Station 1: Pre-personal Self. 31

Station 2: Separate Self: Level One Personal 32

Station 3: False Self. 33

Station 4: True Self—Classical Enlightenment 34

Station 5: Unique Self—The New Enlightenment:

    Level Two Personal 37

Station 6: Unique Shadow 40

Station 7: Your Unique Gift 41

Station 8: Unique Vow, Unique Obligation 42

The Five Great Awakenings. 44

    Ego Awakening: Pre-personal to Personal Awakened Self 45

    The Awakening to the Unity Principle 46

    Awakening from Separate Self to True Self 46

    Awakening from True Self to Your Unique Self 47

    Evolutionary Unique Self Awakening 47

Three Clarifying Notes on the Eight Stations. 48

A Short Recapitulation of Unique Self Doctrine 48

Stations of Self (chart) 54

Chapter 5   **The Evolutionary Integration of Eastern and Western**
Enlightenment: The Essential Discernment between
Separateness and Uniqueness **55**

The Insight and Mistake of the East 56

The Insight and Mistake of the West 58

Are You Special? The Distinction Between

    Separateness and Uniqueness 60

Nothing Exists A-Part or A-Lone 63

The Evolution of Buddhism and Christianity:

    Unique Self, Sex, and Suffering 65

Unique Face and Original Face 68

Your Unique Letter and *The Truman Show* 69

Chapter 6   **Ego and Unique Self** **71**

Twenty-Five Distinctions between Ego and Unique Self . . . 71

    Special or Not Special. 72

Action or Reaction 72

Imitation or Originality 72

Satisfaction or Greed 73

Enough or More 73

Ego Story or Unique Self Story 73

Joy or Fear 74

Open Heart or Closed Heart 75

Eros or Grasping 75

Authentic Freedom or Pseudofreedom 75

King or Servant 76

Victim or Player 76

Betrayal or Loyalty 77

Authentic Friendship or Pseudofriendship 77

Bigger or Smaller 77

Yes or No 77

Justice or Injustice 77

Responsibility or Excuse 78

Paradox or Splitting 78

Past or Present 78

Special Relationship or Open as Love 79

Love or Fear 79

Eternity or Death 80

Pleasure: Delusion or Divine 81

Ego Story or Unique Self Story Reloaded 82

Ego Points to Unique Self 84

Chapter 7 **Personal and Impersonal** **89**

Recognizing the Place of Ego 93

The Impersonal Appears as Personal 94

Choice 96

Sex and Love 96

Relationships 97

Shadows of the Personal and Impersonal 98

Shadows of the Personal 99

Shadows of the Impersonal 99

The Unfolding Dance of Alignment 100

Personal and Impersonal Sex 102

Personal and Impersonal Love 103

    Intimate Communion 105

Teacher and Student 105

Unique Self Is a Quality of Presence 108

PART TWO

Chapter 8   **Unique Self and Evolutionary Spirituality.** **113**

Two Tastes 114

    The First Taste 114

    The Second Taste 114

The Evolutionary Context of Unique Self:

    Nothing to Something 115

    The Sexual Context 116

Evolution Is the Mechanism of the Mystery 117

Being, Becoming, and Unique Self 120

Your Evolutionary Yes 122

Evolution: Personal and Impersonal 124

Chapter 9   **Evolutionary Spirituality Reloaded** **127**

The Whole Is in the Part 128

That Which Is Above Depends on You:

    The Whole Needs the Part 128

God Needs Your Service 130

Chapter 10   **True Self and Unique Self, Parts and Wholes Reloaded** . . **135**

Right Relationship between Part and Whole 135

Love, Fear, and the Evolution of God:

    The Whole Is Evolved by the Part 137

    Conflict 141

    Ethics, Values, and Extremism 141

Individual or Community, Autonomy or Communion . . .143

The Part Needs the Whole 146

The Puzzle-Piece Teachings 147

Chapter 11   **Eros and Unique Self: The Eros of Living Your Story** . . . **151**

The Four Faces of Eros 156

    The First Face of Eros: On the Inside 156

    The Second Face of Eros: Full Presence 158

    The Third Face of Eros: Longing and Desire 160

    The Fourth Face of Eros: Wholeness and Unique Self. 161

Eros, Death, and Unique Self 163

Eros and Pseudo-Eros 164

PART THREE

Chapter 12   **The Story of Story: Only Half the Story** **171**

The His-story of Story 171

Expand Your Story 173

The Grace of the Story 174

The Loss of Memory 175

The Great Story of Evolution and the

    Democratization of Enlightenment 176

    The Shift 177

Not All Stories Are Equal. 178

Five Movements against Story 180

The Denial of the Story Is a Primary Source of Evil . . . 182

Chapter 13   **Sacred Autobiography** **185**

Mispar—Our Clarion Call 187

Unique Self Story 189

Appreciating Each Other's Purple Trees 189

Don Juan Meets Dovid of Lilov 191

Recovering Your Story 192

The Lost Thread 192

Wrong Turns and Leaking Buckets 194

Chapter 14   **Unique Self and Loneliness** **199**

Exile 200

Levado 201

A Family Myth I Share with My Son 201

PART FOUR

Chapter 15 Love and Unique Self **207**

Love Is a Verb 208

Love Is a Perception-Identification Complex 211

Love, Being, and Becoming 212

The Perception of Love Creates a New Reality 213

Liquid Love—To See the Future in the Now 214

The Secret Is in the Eyes 215

Self-Love 216

The Three Faces 217

Self-Love Is Not Narcissism 219

Chapter 16 Joy and Unique Self **221**

The Joy of Depth 223

From Daimon Comes *Eudaimonia* 224

A Paradigm Shift in Understanding Joy 224

Choosing Joy 225

Chapter 17 Shadow Integration and Unique Self **227**

Greater Is the Light That Comes from the Darkness . . . 230

Lost in the Darkness 231

Greater Is Wisdom Than Folly 233

The Shattering of the Vessels 234

Befriend Your Darkness 234

The Teachings of the Blood 236

Walking in the Dark—From Demon to Daemon 239

Unique Self and Unique Shadow 241

Chapter 18 The Ten Principles of Unique Self Shadow Work **245**

1. Shadow is your Unique Self distortion. 245

2. Your story includes both your True Self
   and Unique Self. 246

3. Any part of your story that you do not live,
   lives in darkness. 246

4. When unique light is trapped in shadow,
   it does not remain static. 247

5. When unlived life stagnates and devolves,
    it reemerges as shadow qualities. 247
       Unlived Passion 249
       Taking Anger into Account 250
       3-2-1-0 of Shadow 251
6. You feel the full depth of the goodness and aliveness of your
    life only when you are fully living *your* full story. . . 252
7. Shadow is a lie about your Unique Self. Shadow is a lie
    about your essential identity. 253
8. Shadow integration does not mean to integrate
    shadow qualities. Shadow integration does mean to
    reclaim your unlived life that is in darkness. 254
9. Joy is your life energy. Joy is a by-product of
    Unique Self living. 254
10. The technology for shadow integration is love. Shadow
    integration effects a transformation of identity. Love is the
    evolutionary force that transmutes shadow to light. . 256
Heart of Darkness 256

Chapter 19   **Shadow and Unique Self Reloaded:**
             The Alchemy of Love 263
Shadow and the Eight Tenets of Love 264
The Way of the Dragon 265
1. Love is a perception. 265
2. Love allows for shadow to be held in the larger
    context of your enlightened Unique Self. 265
3. Being loved is being seen. 266
4. In the safety of being seen and held in love,
    you can engage your shadow without the need
    to hide, deny, or project it. 266
5. It is the divine feminine, in self or other,
    that holds you in the gaze of love and catalyzes
    your transformation. 266
       Holding Heart Meditation 267

6. Without the loving gaze of the divine feminine,
the pain of your shadow would be impossible to hold
in your first person. 270

    The Gentleman 270

    The Beadle's Wife 274

    To Not Grow Up 276

7. Shadow and shadow qualities are both personal. . . 277

8. Love gives you hints that show you how to follow
Unique Shadow back to Unique Self. 278

    On Envy's Poison 279

Transformation of Identity 282

The Only Possible Path 282

PART FIVE

Chapter 20 Sex and Unique Self 287

1. Vital Sexing 288

2. Separate-Self Sexing 288

    Separate-Self Sexing—A Deeper Look 290

    Empty Wisdom 291

3. Pleasure Sexing 292

4. True Self Sexing: Impersonal 294

5. Unique Self Sexing: Personal 299

6. *Tikkun* Sexing or *Bodhisattva* Sexing. 303

**Chapter 21 Evolutionary Intimacy:
The Seven Laws of Unique Self Encounters** 309

1. In every Unique Self encounter, each person holds
a piece of the other's story, which must be returned
to the other in order for both to be complete. 309

2. To have a Unique Self encounter, you have to make
authentic contact in the present. 310

    The Pain Trance 312

    Staying in the Present 313

    To Walk in the Wide Places 314

    Staying in the Symptoms 316

3. Labels obstruct contact. 317

4. You never know. 319

5. Unique Self encounters create evolutionary We Space. . 321

6. To engage in a Unique Self encounter, you must
   stay open as love through the pain. 323

7. Unique Self encounters require not only integrity
   but evolutionary integrity. 326

PART SIX

Chapter 22 Parenting and Unique Self **329**

The Job of Parents 330

Letting Alone—Like Soil for the Soul 331

Can I Make My Children Happy? 332

Early Voices 334

Tradition? Tradition! 335

Chapter 23 Malice: The Denial of the Unique Self Encounter . . . **337**

Malice Is Painfully Private, Publicly Dangerous 339

The Murder of Christ 342

The Evil Eye 343

Chapter 24 Death and Unique Self **347**

Response One: Pre-personal 348

Response Two: Personal 349

Response Three: Transpersonal 352

Chapter 25 Say Yes **357**

Epilogue: Unique Self, World Spirituality and Evolutionary We Space . . .**363**

Afterword by Ken Wilber. **389**

Appendix I Evolutionary Love **403**

Three Core Perspectives. 409

On the Nature of Evolutionary Love 413

Evolution in Second- and First-Person Perspectives . . .415

Cellular Love in Human Beings 416

Appendix II **Core Recapitulation and Unique Self** **419**

Appendix III **Unique Self and Wounded Self** 421
    Evolutionary We Space 423
    The Wounds of Love or the Idolatry of Hurt 424
    Lying About Your Hurt to Support Your Ego 426
    Facing Through the Fear of Death 430
    God Is More Than Physical, Not Less Than Physical;
      More Than Personal, Not Less Than Personal 431
    It All Depends on You Personally 433

Appendix IV **Between Unique Self and Authentic Self** **435**

Acknowledgments **439**
Integral Afternote. **441**
Notes **443**
Index **489**
About the Author **501**
    Unique Self Scholars Project **503**

FOREWORD BY
KEN WILBER

DR. MARC GAFNI'S INTEGRAL UNIQUE SELF TEACHING IS SEMINAL. What you hold in your hands is a radically exciting and ground-breaking book that will change forever not only how you think about enlightenment, but how you understand, from a post-metaphysical perspective, the very nature of human life itself. The Unique Self work is magnificent, and it belongs among the "great books." It offers what may arguably be one of the most significant contemporary evolutions of enlightenment teaching. Unique Self brings together East and West in a higher integral embrace of stunning implications. Unique Self is a pivotal step toward an authentic Enlightenment.

The teaching in this book has been evolved primarily by Marc Gafni for over three decades and draws from his own realization, insight, and the enlightenment lineage in which he stands. In Gafni's reading of this lineage, brilliantly articulated in his three-volume opus, *Radical Kabbalah: The Enlightenment Teaching of Unique Self, Nondual Humanism and the Wisdom of Solomon*, (forthcoming) which I read in several highly excited nights, Unique Self is a nondual realization of Unique Perspective. This realization expresses itself both as the Unique Perspective on a text and as the Unique Perspective of the realized individual—what Gafni terms, in Lainer's thought, the Judah Archetype, whose perspective is a unique incarnation of unmediated divinity and therefore overrides all previous text, including even the Torah itself. In essence, the realized individual, whose True Self has been disclosed, expresses that True Self through his or her

Unique Perspective—what Gafni originally termed "Unique Self." Hence, what Gafni calls the nondual humanism of Unique Self is rooted in this equation, in my wording: True Self + Perspective = Unique Self.

Unique Self brilliantly articulates the idea that within each of us is a post-egoic nondual realization of unique perspective, a unique incarnation of unmediated divinity. The Unique Self re-inhabits all the natural capacities of the human body-mind and all its multiple intelligences. It embraces its capacity for math, for music, for introspection, for love and interpersonal connection—all the talents and capacities given to human beings—without dismissing the True Self, the One Spirit condition that connects us all. Unique Self drenches and permeates the entire system of what is known as Eastern and Western forms of enlightenment.

The full crystallization of this New Enlightenment/Unique Self teaching that Dr. Gafni initiated, in which he and I have partnered, emerged through a series of many important dialogues that we had over nearly a decade. Through these dialogues, a highly significant new chapter in Integral Theory has emerged. These conversations were coupled with intensive discourse that Marc and I had with other leading Integral Spiritual teachers and thinkers, including, initially, Diane Hamilton in a catalytic role and later Sally Kempton. World Spirituality based on Integral principles is an entirely new lineage—a trans-path path. Unique Self models the emergent World Spirituality based on Integral principles in that it includes all the good stuff of previous paths, but adds a whole new level of emergence. *And that is something that is extraordinary, historic, and not to be denied.*

A NOTE TO
THE READER

WELCOME.

THIS SHORT NOTE IS TO HELP YOU EASILY NAVIGATE THIS BOOK.
Please do not skip this note. It will guide you through the book.

There are two different ways to read this book. Let's call them Track One
and Track Two. The first track is simply to follow the order of the chapters. The advantage of this approach is that Part One and Two unpack the
core enlightenment teachings that ground the rest of the book. However—
and this will be important for readers primarily interested in the practical
application of these teachings—you can also choose to take another road
through the book. Read the first three chapters, which will take you about
one hour. Then, skip directly to Parts Three, Four and Five, which contain
the chapters immediately applicable to your day-to-day life. These are the
chapters on sacred autobiography, living your story, love, shadow, sexing,
joy, evolutionary relationships and much more. Once you've read these,
you can circle back and read the core framework teachings on Unique Self
enlightenment in Parts One and Two, which will add profound depth to
your understanding and embodiment of the latter part of the book.

Each part of this book deals in depth with a different dimension of
Unique Self:

Part One lays down the core teaching or model of Unique Self enlightenment.

Part Two places the Unique Self model in a larger evolutionary context
and unpacks a global vision of what it means to live your "evolutionary
Unique Self."

Part Three teaches you what it means to live your story and incarnate the infinite dignity of your sacred autobiography—or a Unique Letter in the evolving cosmic scroll.

Part Four deploys the Unique Self teaching toward a radical re-understanding of Love, Joy, and Shadow in our lives. The sections of love and the two chapters on shadow are key as they significantly evolve our understanding of shadow integration, which is presently an essential but profoundly misunderstood dimension of the spiritual path.

Part Five offers a critical new understanding of sexuality and relationships in light of Unique Self. The section on sexing presents a new map of six forms of sexing, which re-orients and deepens the sexual in a significant way. The chapter on Unique Self encounters outlines seven principles of evolutionary Unique Self meetings, and it re-visions the essential nature and skill of all relationships.

Part Six deploys the Unique Self model in relation to parenting, malice, and death in a way that fundamentally changes our understanding of all three. And finally, the Epilogue places the realization of Unique Self in the context of the emergence of a Global Spirituality based on Integral principles.

Please use the table of contents and index. They are very detailed and will be helpful to you in identifying a particular topic you are called to or in finding a particular section after you have finished your first reading.

Last, there is a footnote section in the back that is particularly important for those interested in Integral Theory as it relates to Unique Self. If you are not a theory person or an academic intellectual type just skip the footnotes. You do not need footnotes to get the point of the book. However, for those of you, myself included, who love footnotes, know that the footnotes contain academic and intellectual citations as well as deeper dives into the sources, the intellectual history of Unique Self, and the broader context of the conversation.

PREFACE

*On the Enlightenment of Fullness, Individuation
beyond Ego, Democratization of Enlightenment
and Living in a Personal Evolutionary Context*

UNDERLYING THE VISION behind democracy is the recognition that every individual has dignity, adequacy and worth.

Western Enlightenment:

This democratic understanding of the worth and standing of the individual lies at the core of what the West calls enlightenment. The Western idea of enlightenment, rooted in the great vision of the Biblical prophets, is generally understood to have entered mainstream consciousness through the political democratic movements of the mid 18th century. Western enlightenment is primarily concerned with the democratization of political power. This signified a quantum leap in the evolution of consciousness. For the Western enlightenment introduces a new structure stage or level of consciousness sourced in the recognition of the individual as an irreducible self-validating essence. The original emergence of human rights was rooted in the ontological dignity of the separate self. All ethics virtue and responsibility welled from the affirmation of the irreducible value of the separate self. The suffering imposed by the mythic levels of consciousness, which refused to grant dignity and rights to the individual outside the particular contexts of church, tribe, state or empire, was overcome in this realization of the Western enlightenment. The separate self-individual became an independent locus of value, adequacy and dignity. Western enlightenment was seen as the path beyond suffering.

It was not long, however, before Western individuality was cut off from its sources in essence. For this evolutionary movement of spirit paradoxically coincided with the emergence of a narrowly materialistic view of reality. This flatland view took root within the Western psyche. The individual lost the sense of being an expression of essence, and began to experience herself as "separate self", what some referred to as a skin-encapsulated ego. Individuals began to be seen as but an expression of their personal, social and psychological conditioning. The infinite inner dimension of the individual was reduced to the individual as a bounded and hopefully balanced ego structure. Democratic human rights were won but their source in infinite individual depth was lost. Individuality was exiled into the separate self and personal essence was reduced to ego identity. This opened the door to the lost, dislocated experience of the contemporary human struggling, often vainly, to find his or her place in the larger context of Eros and essence.

Eastern Enlightenment:

Classical enlightenment, sometimes called Eastern enlightenment because it was greatly emphasized in the East, is about the individual merging into the greater one. The appearance of separate self is an illusion, which must be overcome as the individual realizes that are really not separate at all but part of the one. The Buddhists call this form of awakening, the enlightenment of emptiness. This view holds that emptiness actually contains all, but in the all there is virtually no recognition of the individual's irreducible uniqueness. This opened the door to the West's dismissal of classical enlightenment as irrelevant. The individuality of ego and separate self, which Western enlightenment viewed as essential to human dignity and rights, was viewed by the East as the source of all suffering. The goal of Eastern enlightenment is moving beyond the grasping ego and desperately seeking separate self by attaining a state of consciousness in which the illusion of separateness was dissolved in the greater one. This path of classical enlightenment is seen as the path beyond suffering.

Unique Self Enlightenment:

Unique Self enlightenment brings the Eastern and Western understandings about enlightenment together, into a higher Integral World Spirituality embrace. Based on series critical distinctions that I unfold in this volume, a new evolutionary vision of enlightenment begins to emerge. Unique Self enlightenment is based on your commitment to transcend separate self into the one, even as you realize that essence sees through your unique perspective, i.e. Your Unique Self. Unique Self enlightenment is what I have called the Enlightenment of Fullness. It begins with the recognition that every individual is both part of the one and uniquely incarnates the personal face of Essence, or God.

Because it is based on the irreducible uniqueness and hence value and dignity of every individual as an expression of essence, Unique Self opens the door to the potential democratization of enlightenment. That does not mean that everyone is enlightened in the same way—or that there is no hierarchy of qualitative distinctions in every person's level of enlightenment. Quite the opposite. Enlightenment always is Unique. Enlightenment always has a perspective, your perspective. But it does mean that enlightenment is a genuine option and therefore genuine invitation and even delightful obligation for every individual.

Aligning with your Unique Self is the change that changes everything. Awakening to your Unique Self fundamentally shifts your worldview, your purpose, and your internal experience of your self, your relationships, your sexuality, your shadow, and the way you love. Unique Self enlightenment relocates you in a larger evolutionary context. It enacts in you new leadership ability, and fosters your capacity to form relationships that are both unique and evolutionary.

In contemporary culture where scientific materialism is the default world view of so many, truth is too often regarded as accessible only in the form of purely objective scientific information. In this view truth must be verifiable through the third person empirical and logical methods of the hard sciences and mathematics. This modern view of reality is true but partial; that is, it has an incomplete understanding of truth. In reality there are three perspectives and not one. These might be rightly described as first, second and third person views of reality. Science favors the knowledge that results from a third person perspective. This is reality as observed from the outside. Relationships yield knowledge from a second person perspective. Meditation and all forms of introspection yields knowledge from a first person perspective. Each perspective yields its own truths. The truth of every perspective is then verified by the validity tests appropriate to that perspective. For example, one verifies the distinction between the internal experience of love vs. infatuation through a number of internal introspections (checking the nature and quality of your own feelings) and second person inquiries (talking to trusted friends) that would be irrelevant if the goal were to verify a mathematical equation. Unique Self is hinted at in third person through the uniqueness of the cellular signature of every individual. In second person, love is a Unique Self perception. Love is the faculty of perception that reveals Unique Self. In first person, Unique Self is primarily accessed as an enlightened experience of Self. Unique Self shows up as the personal face of essence living in you, as you and through you. In first person one experiences the self as an irreducible and unique expression of Self. This is what I have called Unique Self. That is the first person view. To awaken to your Unique Self is to be lived as God, which, in truth, means to be lived as love.

INTRODUCTION

WHEN I WAS SIXTEEN, my teacher at seminary school, Pinky Bak, died. I was very close to him. Pinky was for me somewhat of a cross between a big brother and surrogate father. I came from a painful first thirteen years of life, and he felt who I was beyond the trauma. He said to me, "You have gifts to give. Your life is valuable. You are needed." He was the first one who invited me to believe in the possibility of possibility.

Pinky was thirty-two when he died. He fell down right next to me in the middle of a rollicking religious holiday party. As was his custom, he was dancing like a wild man—ecstatic, alive, on fire, and contagious. He half looked up for a moment and said, "Go on without me. I will get up in a second." He then died instantly of a brain aneurysm.

I was numbed with shock and my heart was broken. Later that week, the dean of the school asked me to give the eulogy on behalf of the student body, because everybody knew that I was very close to Pinky. The auditorium was packed. I was lost in grief because my teacher had died, and scared out of my mind because I had never talked in public before. But as I walked up to the podium, something happened. It was like a window from heaven had opened up. In my talk, the words flowed out effortlessly from a place beyond me. They felt like wings, lifting and falling, carrying us all to a place where pain was not king, and broken hearts were healed. I spontaneously promised—not knowing where the words had come from—to pick up the baton that Pinky had dropped, to become a teacher of wisdom in the world. It was done.

The place was silent when I finished. Not silence of absence, when there are no words left to cover over the emptiness. Rather, it was Silence of Presence, when words are insufficient to hold the fullness of a moment. Although at the time I could not name the quality, this was my first genuine experience of Eros, of not only praying to or beseeching God, but also of knowing that I was part of, not separate from, the larger divine field. In a moment of Eros, what I call in this book the Unique Self had shown its face. My Unique Self had shown its face. As it often does, it had made itself known in a peak moment.

And so began, at age sixteen, my calling as a teacher. As is often the case, however, my ego then partially hijacked my Unique Self revelation. I was, on the one hand, sincerely committed to teaching, sharing, and even evolving the wisdom of my lineage, but mixed with that sincere and sacred intention was an egoic need that used my speaking and teaching skill to cover up an aching emptiness. My childhood pain had not been healed or addressed. Instead, I had contained it, tucked it away in some supposedly safe place. This, I believed, was what a good person is supposed to do. I barely remembered where I had stored the container.

So public speaking and teaching, for which I had a gift, welled up from mixed places in my consciousness—from a pure instinct to express the good, but also from an isolated, vulnerable ego, passionately yearning for the wave of embrace and affirmation that came from the public's response to my teaching. At that point in my life, my need for a home and for the aliveness of public recognition unconsciously affected key decisions I made, but in very disguised and subtle ways. The good and sincere intention was so strong that I did not detect the ego's bad advice insinuating itself.

My false core sentence at the time was probably "I am not safe." Your false core initially emerges to cover the pain of alienation and the shock of apparent separation. You then develop a false self to soothe the pain of the false core.[1] The false self is precisely the personality that you unconsciously deploy to hide, deny, or fix your false core. The paradox of the false self is that it usually reflects much that is true about you. The problem is that—at least in part—the false self is motivated by the ego's neediness and not by the authenticity of your Unique Self. The false self is false in the sense that it is not sufficiently motivated by the deeper truth of your own gorgeous and authentic being.

So if my false core sentence was "I am not safe," then my false self at that time probably sounded something like this:

> I am a rabbi, committed to outreach to unaffiliated Jews. I am filled with love, passionately committed, creative, and brilliant. I give my life to God. I serve my people and the tradition. Everyone is beautiful. I am committed to seeing only the beauty in people. If I just love people enough, I can do anything and take care of anything that comes my way. If I love people, they will feel loved by God. No one could possibly betray or distort my love.

Of course, none of this was fully articulated or even conscious. My false self was true, partially. But it was clouded by the ego's neediness.

I was asleep.

Part of what kept me asleep was—paradoxically—the depth of the teaching, the sincerity of my intention, and my sense of the innate goodness of myself and others. All of this was real, but it was happening at an early stage of egoic unfolding, when I was still, at least in part, identified with my false self. Since part of my energy was running in a false self track, it ultimately could not sustain itself. The false self may well be telling the truth about your beliefs and intentions. But since it rests on top, and is motivated to hide, deny, or heal the false core sentence "I am not safe," it never connects with the ground of your being and is therefore never stable or secure. I was headed for a series of dramatic train wrecks, with no idea that they were coming.

Evolution beyond Ego

In order to genuinely move beyond ego, beyond the false self—or even more precisely, beyond exclusive identification with ego—you need authentic and sustained contact with the transcendent, with the intention of facilitating your own evolution. You also need rigorous and unflinching self-inquiry, which includes some process of sustained shadow work. Prayer, chanting, contemplative study, and meditation are *part* of the path. In my early years, as for many young teachers, they were my entire path. But beware of parts pretending to be wholes. These paths may not be enough for you. They were not enough for me.

As I moved from my twenties to late thirties, my separate egoic self began to clarify through a mixture of chant, intense sacred study, and deep pain. By my early forties, the clarification process was becoming more intense and dramatic. But I still was not sufficiently clarified in the full realization of my enlightened Unique Self. Events then took place in my life of such pain and proportion that I almost died of heartbreak.

My own genuine mistakes and misjudgments provided a seemingly plausible cover to enable betrayal, public distortion, falsification, power plays, and behind-the-scenes malice. Whatever was not clarified in my person gave a hook to the projections of others, and my world came tumbling down. Held in the burning furnace of false complaints and public humiliation, by grace, I somehow remained alive. But for a full year, I could barely breathe. Not more than a half hour would go by without my heart welling up with tears. I was not able to utter the words of prayer. Only with great pain could I chant, and that very rarely. The visceral heaviness of my heart virtually stopped my life force several times a day. Enduring the pain of sudden rupture from all I held dear, and the insanity of *National Enquirer*-like poisonous lies on the Internet,[2] for which there is little recourse, were more than the small egoic self of Marc Gafni could hold. The only analogy I can think of that holds the pain of that time is something like the pain of losing the ones closest to you and then being falsely accused of their murder.

All of this came together as a gift of terrible grace.

I was forced to fully step out of my story. Out of my pseudo story. Out of my ego. Out of my small self. It was simply too painful a place to live.

All the spiritual work of the past twenty-five years came to my aid. But it was grace, known by many names, that shattered all vessels and cracked me open to a new level of light and love.

For the first time in my life, I found a place inside of me in which it was totally OK if I never taught again. I was able to locate myself outside of my gifts. I did not even know if I would be able to keep them. I was so cracked open that, for a long period of time, sitting in a rocking chair on the porch of some small house seemed like pure bliss. Pain, moments of loving, involvement in details of the world, spaciousness, taking refuge in the Buddha, and flashes of intense enlightened awareness all burst in at regular intervals, always expanding and often dissolving my small self into profound ecstasy.

This went on for almost three years. And as time passed the vessel expanded.

I spent many hours in the first year after the tragedy reading Psalms, by myself or together with my friend Dalit. "Reading" is not quite the right word for what I did. It was more like intense wracked sobbing while reading the text as prayer.

I felt the psalmist and his God close to me, holding me, understanding it all, and lifting me up. And the gifts came back. At some point, I began teaching again, but from a more spacious place, a wider place. The meeting with nonexistence had worked me. The knot of the heart had been untied.

Yet it is not over. Knots can tangle up again very quickly. I untie the knots every day anew.

Something, however, had shifted in a way that is virtually indescribable. It was, on the one hand, slight, modest, small, almost unnoticeable. And yet it was everything, All-That-Is—grand and glorious beyond imagination.

I had experienced in a new way the depth of transformation that is possible when the ego opens up in sweet surrender to the luminous love-light of the One. Only then, after stepping beyond identification with ego—or more accurately, being thrown out of ego—was I able to take the next step. To truly live from Source as Unique Self, passionately committed to evolutionary manifestation, yet increasingly unattached to the results of my effort. There was no choice. There is never really a choice.

So how do you live as Source? How do you allow your self to be lived by love as a force for healing and transformation? Not by leaving your story behind, but by entering the full depth of your story. Not your ego story—but your Unique Self story. It is on this essential distinction that your enlightenment and very life pivot.

This book speaks dangerous words. Dangerous to your sense that you are small; to your feeling that you are alone and invisible; to your belief that you are worthless, inadequate, or bad; to your belief that you are too much or not enough.

I invite you to listen dangerously.

As William Blake writes, "No bird soars too high if he soars with his own wings."[3] What it means to soar with your own wings is the New Enlightenment teaching of Unique Self, which I am honored to transmit to you in these pages.

PART ONE

CHAPTER ONE

THE GREAT INVITATION OF YOUR LIFE

EVERY PERSON IS RESPONSIBLE for their own awakening. In the same way every generation is responsible for its own evolution of consciousness. There is a covenant of partnership between generations. Each generation commits to contribute its own unique insights to the ongoing transformation and evolution of consciousness. At its core, consciousness is love—*the evolution of consciousness is therefore nothing less than the evolution of love.* If you then realize that God is synonymous with love, you begin to understand that the *evolution of love is no less than the evolution of God. God is the infinite. The infinite is the intimate. God is the infinity of intimacy.*

To be awake is to be a lover: alive, aflame, and open as love.

Therefore, at its heart, to be a lover means to be willing to participate in the transformation of consciousness.

Consciousness = God = Intimacy = Love.

Love is the spiritual technology operating through you as the expansion and transformation of identity itself. Enlightenment is no less than the ultimate transformation of identity, permanently widening and deepening the radius and depth of your love.

I come from a tradition of evolutionary mysticism. Evolution is the creative impulse inherent in the kosmos, to unfold toward ever higher levels of complexity, consciousness and goodness. The great teaching of my mystical lineage, confirmed by my own realization, is that the motive force of evolution is love. To awaken is to know that, as Dante put it, love moves the sun and other stars. As the new biology and physics are beginning to implicitly suggest, love is the interior kosmic force that animates and drives the evolutionary impulse. Love is the strange attractor, the allurement that holds the Uni-verse together. Alfred North Whitehead said that evolution is really the gentle movement toward God by the gentle persuasion of love.[1]—and sometimes far from gentle.

This book intends to unfold the teaching of Unique Self. What is your Unique Self? Unique Self is the individualized expression of the love-intelligence that is the very Eros of evolution and that lives as you. To realize your Unique Self then is your contribution, your gift, to the evolution of love—which, as we have already seen, is no less than the evolution of God. It would therefore be fair to say that to awaken as your Unique Self is to participate in the future of God. It is no small thing to participate in the future of God.

This book is written as a serious book of enlightenment teaching, as a passionate love letter and as transmission of love from me to you.

This is not a book of spiritual information. Instead, it is designed to give you a transmission that can shift your consciousness. This shift can bring many gifts to *your* life and make *you* a gift to the life of All-That-Is.

You could keep your distance and read from a safe place. Or you could say, "I am here. I am ready to undergo a momentous leap in my own personal evolution. I am willing to engage in the work of self-creation. I am ready for a transformation of identity. I am ready to leave my small self behind. I am ready to recognize my true self, incarnate my Unique Self and live as the evolutionary force of love."

This book speaks dangerous words. I invite you to listen dangerously. Dangerous words means dangerous to your sense that you are small, to your feeling that you are small, to your feeling that you are alone and invisible, to your belief that you are inadequate or bad, to your belief that you are too much or not enough.

One of the great Unique Self mystics, Isaac Luria, taught that every person has an obligation to write their own letter in the kosmic scroll. *This means that the ultimate purpose of your life is to bring forth and live the unique expression of love-intelligence and life force that can only be manifested by you.* In other words it means to incarnate what I call your Unique Self.[2]

Unique Self is partially foreshadowed in several spiritual traditions, West and East, and the teaching of Unique Self woven from three distinct strands.

The first strand consists of the intimations of Unique Self teaching found in some of the great spiritual traditions, such as the Kabbalistic citation from Hebrew mystic Isaac Luria in the previous paragraph.[3] I have also found important intimations of unique self teaching in Sufism, mystical Christianity, Kashmir Shaivism, and even Vajrayana Buddhism.

The second strand is the pivotal insight of modern and postmodern wisdom streams,[4] which posits understanding of "perspective" as the core element of reality.[5]

The third strand is my own lived recognition and realization, born of practice and grace. These arose in introspection, study, conversation with colleagues and radical immersion in the transmission of the Unique Self lineage masters. All of these together helped birth the evolutionary emergent that I call Unique Self.

An evolutionary emergent is an idea whose time has come. It always comes at a time when the world can no longer live without it. It sits atop all that has come before, yet it adds something undeniably new. *This book is an invitation for you to understand, realize and practice Unique Self in the story of your life—for all of this is just words, until we learn it in the stories of our own lives.*

CHAPTER TWO

THE NEW ENLIGHTENMENT OF UNIQUE SELF

WHAT DO WE MEAN BY UNIQUE SELF? Your Unique Self is not merely ego or personality. It is the essence that lies beneath and beyond your personality. More precisely, it is the personal face of essence. It is the unique God-spark living in you and as you. *Your Unique Self is the infinite love-intelligence, which is All-That-Is—living in you, as you, and through you.*[1] The higher your level of consciousness, the more fully you are able to realize your Unique Self.

And Unique Self is revealed and realized throughout your life, in moments of flow and grace, regardless of your level of consciousness. Yet it is only after you have begun to move past the grasping of your separate self ego, and realized your nature as indivisible from the infinite, unqualified field of consciousness, that Unique Self is revealed as the full and stable realization of your enlightenment.

In other words, there's a process involved in the New Enlightenment of Unique Self. You first realize that you are part of the seamless coat of the Uni-verse. *You then realize that the Uni-verse is seamless but not featureless—and that you are one of its essential features.*[2] *You see that you are irreducibly unique, and therefore irreplaceable as a unique expression of All-That-Is.*

You realize that your personal existence, your being, is utterly distinct, worthy, and needed.

Unique Self is the enlightened realization that you are both absolutely one with the whole, and absolutely unique. You are more and more free from the contractions of your personality, even as you experience yourself as personally engaged in the great evolutionary unfolding of consciousness.

Realizing your Unique Self will fundamentally change the way you understand virtually every facet of your awakened life. Once we've engaged the core teachings of Unique Self, we will look separately at how these teachings fundamentally reconfigure and dramatically re-vision our understanding of love, joy, shadow, sexuality, parenting, death, relationships, loneliness, evolutionary spirituality, malice, ego psychology, and the integration of East and West.

Your Unique Self is God's love-signature written all over you. God loved you so much, He personalized himself as you. You are the individualized heart and mind of God. This is your Unique Self.

The creative process that mysteriously moves from nothing to something is the God-impulse. To live as your Unique Self means to align yourself with that process, with the ecstatic evolutionary impulse that initiated the kosmos, with the ecstasy of God, which re-creates all of reality in every second of existence.

Are you ready to respond to this invitation, to offer yourself to the infinite love-intelligence that wants desperately to show up in the world through and as you?

Then keep on reading . . .

Being God's Verb

The God you do not believe in does not exist. By "God" I mean All-That-Is, in all of its infinite and personal faces—the love-beauty that initiated and animates All-That-Is. That love-beauty wants to see with your eyes, touch with your hands, and love with your heart. Big Heart, the Tao, the Great One, the Universal Mind—by whatever name—wants to come into its fullest expression of being as each and every one of us. For this to happen, you have to be willing to hear the call of the evolutionary impulse of the kosmos beating personally in you and as you.

You are God's verb. To be God's verb, you do not need to leave your small separate self ego behind. You only need to leave your *identification* with your small self ego behind. You will then be able to identify with the unlimited and unfathomable mind of God, coming into its own by manifesting through and as you.

Are you tired of feeling trapped in the maze of your own self-contraction? Of being a side effect in your own life? Are you tired of your constant reaction, which creates your constant contraction? Are you tired of feeling like little more than a living cluster of habits and preconditioned reactions? Or are you here to survive in your physical body? I hope not, because you will not. Or to get rich or get famous? I hope not, because as mama said, "You can't take it with you."

You are here to be the poem that only you can be. You are here to sing the song that only you can sing. You are here to be the Unique Presence of Being and Becoming in the world that no one else but you can be. *To live aligned with the highest intention of God, allowing God to live you.*

God Is Having a Marc Experience

When I live my Unique Self, then God is having a Marc experience. When my oldest son lives his Unique Self, then God is having an Eytan experience. The same is true for you. When you live your Unique Self, God is having a "you" experience. God is devastated when Marc, instead of living the great mythic story of Marc, tries to be John or Rob.

This causes what the kabbalists call the "Exile of God."

The great realization of Western mystical consciousness is that God "desires" a Marc experience. Something is evolved in the Godhead when you live your Unique God-spark by incarnating your Unique Self. God is delighted, what the kabbalists called Sha-a-'Shua, the eros of divine pleasure. It is the divine pleasure in the evolution of God, catalyzed by the awakening of Unique Self.

Reveal yourself. Manifest your mystery through your Unique Self.

The God of Unique Self

God is not merely without but within the system. God *is* the system, the infinite living, intelligent depth of the system. God is the Suchness and ground of all Being. In Alfred North Whitehead's wonderful phrase, "God is the seamless coat of the Uni-verse," of which we are all a part. To awaken to the stunning realization, power, and responsibility of your Unique Self, you must remember that "seamless" does not mean "featureless." Every Unique Self is a particular feature of the Uni-verse, a particular letter in the kosmic scroll, a distinct and gorgeous manifestation that is both a part of the whole, not separate from the whole, absolutely necessary for the whole, and not so swallowed up by the whole as to lose its distinct nature.

All the great traditions tell us about two selves: a "true" self, and a "false" or "fallen" self. Your everyday ordinary self is known as the separate self. Your false self is a distorted or unhealthy expression of your separate self. This might involve a distorted self-understanding due to false core sentences or belief structures. For example, "I'm not safe," "I'm not good," or "I'm not enough" are false core sentences that unconsciously filter our perception of reality.[3] False self also expresses itself in one's identification and "stuckness" in their typology. The Enneagram, for example, does not tell us who we are, but rather precisely who we are not. The Enneagram essentially maps the pattern of navigating egoic reality that the separate self may have developed in order to overcome the shock and pain of separation.[4]

Even after we clarify the distortion of our false self and access our healthy separate self, a fundamental distortion still remains in place. This distortion is the illusion that our separate self is all that we are. From this perspective, our separate self is also our false self in that it is our limited identity with our personality or ego—it is the cluster of needs, drives, memories, fears, and expectations that you typically refer to as "me." It is a painfully finite self, born into the illusion of separation. It is a life cast in shadows, like a prisoner in Plato's cave.[5]

But while your false self is trapped in time and therefore destined to die, your True Self is eternal. It is the infinite Spirit within, the effortless expanse of awareness behind all your experiences. It is forever unblemished by the pains and ecstasies of time, for it exists completely outside of time.

The overall number of True Selves in the Uni-verse is one. Whenever someone realizes their True Self, that person is literally in a state of at-one-ment, communing with the infinite singularity of Being. There is only One. However—and this is the central realization of Unique Self—the One True

Self shows up differently through every pair of eyes. *In the old enlightenment, True Self was understood to erase all distinction. In the New Enlightenment, we realize that enlightenment always has a perspective.*[6]

Human beings used to think we were directly engaging reality as it is. This is why every spiritual system thought that it owned the truth, that it was seeing reality itself. But this was only half true. At some point, we began to realize that there is no reality without perspective. To put it another way, reality itself is fundamentally constructed from perspectives.[7]

In the old, dominant paradigm, we assumed that perception was a faculty that showed each of us the same picture and revealed the True Nature of things. In the new paradigm, we understand that our perspective is like the pair of glasses through which our vision takes place. Wear red-tinted glasses, and the world is bathed in red. Wear Christian-tinted glasses, and see Jesus in your meditations. Wear Hindu-tinted glasses, and see Shiva or Kali in your meditations. Wear Buddhist glasses, and see everything as empty. Wear Jewish-tinted glasses, and see all of reality as an apparition of the Shekhinah.

The new paradigm is in-formed by the deconstructive insights of philosophers from Hume to Kant to Saussure and everyone who wrote in their wake, by relativity, Heisenberg's uncertainty principle, the new physics and biology, by multiculturalism, and more.

The recognition that every culture— and indeed every individual—holds a Unique perception of the world is an evolutionary emergent.[8] Our conclusion, however, is not that of the post-modern deconstructive thinkers who were among the champions of this insight. Deconstruction wrongly assumed that when perspective is revealed to be part of the process of meaning making, there is no longer any real meaning. Rather, when we understand perspective, we understand that every culture and every great tradition of spirit has its own Unique Self. Perspective reveals a plenitude of meaning and not a dearth or death of meaning. All cultures perceive essence, but each unique perspective gives a particular resonance and cast to essence. Loyalty to one's religion and culture is not, therefore, (as modern and post-modern fashions sometimes suggest), primitive or fundamentalist. It is rather partially true, in that it is how my culture is intuiting essence. The pre-modern mistake was the failure to realize that every religion has a particular perspective, and therefore not to realize that no religion can claim that its intuition of ultimate truth is the only truth. Now that we understand that every great tradition and culture perceived essence through a particular perspective, we can avoid the tragic mistake of deconstructing the traditions as meaningless. Instead, we understand that every tradition is a particular perspective, a particular instrument in the symphony of spirit that is indeed making sacred music. All of the perspectives come together to create a symphony. And at that point, there is the possibility that the followers of each tradition can begin to realize that their particular religion is not the music but an instrument of the music.*

In Judaism, Christianity, Hinduism, and Islam, Unique Self might be expressed as the Unique perspective and radiance of your eternal soul. In Buddhism, Unique Self would manifest as the unique perspective and radiance of your enlightenment; in Hinduism, as the state of open-eyed *samadhi*.[9] Yet for all of these, the same evolutionary equation holds true:

$$\text{True Self} + \text{Perspective} = \text{Unique Self}[10]$$

Every evolved culture and every evolved individual may realize Unique Self when True Self awakens to its Unique Perspective. An early expression of this equation is sourced in premodernity in the great teachings of the kabbalists. For these masters, the sacred text of the Torah is the word of God. Yet, paradoxically. in Hebrew mystical teaching a human being who is deeply grounded in True Self while fully incarnating his or her own uniqueness, also speaks the word of God. Human insight, however, is considered the word of God and, given the status of Torah, only when it derives directly from the clarified unique perspective of a human being who is connected to the ground of true self. In this radical teaching the supreme identity between the human being and the godhead is only realized through the paradoxical portal of radical human uniqueness. Irreducible uniqueness, the full inhabiting of unique perspective or voice, is revealed to be an absolute quality of essence. In modernity and especially in postmodernity, the early realization of the kabbalists in regard to the primacy of perspective takes center stage. There is an emergent cultural realization, placed front and center in Integral Theory, that perspectives are foundational. But in postmodernity, perspectives have too often been used as the key tool of postmodernity's deconstructive project. The sentence used to deny all truth is, "That's just your perspective."

The kabbalists foreshadow our post, postmodern World Spirituality reconstructive project. Nothing is true, says postmodernity, because everything is contextual. For the kabbalist, the opposite is correct. When you fully inhabit your unique perspective you become Source. You not only speak the word of God, you incarnate the word of God. World Spirituality based on Integral principles, including the first principle of Unique Self, understands that Uniqueness reveals essence through a particular prism creating not a dearth of truth, but a magnificent kaleidoscope of truth. Every authentic insight deriving from Unique Perspective is true but partial. No part is reducible to the whole but no part stands alone. It is this insight of Unique Self that is the foundation of the great reconstructive project, which is Spirit's Next Move.

Your Unique Self expresses itself in your drive to reach your limitless potential. It is your authentic desire to move beyond your exclusive identification with your small self, and to realize something *within* you that is both unique to you and infinitely *larger* than you. In this process, the first step is to dis-identify with your small self, your ego, and identify with the larger field of existence. You understand that you are part of a larger whole.

The ego that we are referring to here is the tendency to identify all that you are with your body-mind personality. It is like the story of the biker who irrationally picked a fight with someone who touched his bike. When pressed afterward to explain himself, he said, "When you touch my bike, you touch me." This is precisely the overreach of your ego when it claims to be the fullness of your identity. In this sense, the ego is an expression of your false self.

Classically, enlightenment is the move from false self to True Self. The motivation to dis-identify with your egoic false self is the evolutionary impulse of love.[11]

Evolutionary love is not an emotion but a perception.[12] It is the capacity that allows you to perceive your own True Nature as far more vast, stunning, and spacious than your "skin-encapsulated ego." Love realizes that your small self is not isolated, alienated, and alone—it is a spark in the inferno of love and evolving consciousness that we sometimes call God.

It is the force of evolutionary love that drives you to trance-end your separate egoic self and move toward union with the whole.

However, the realization that your separate self is one with the whole is a *stage* on the journey, not its endpoint. The New Enlightenment moves one step beyond classic enlightenment. In the New Enlightenment, you realize that the spark is not merely absorbed in the larger light. Even as the spark dances in the roaring flames of heart-melting and searing divinity, it does not lose its unique character. As identification with separate self disappears, your clarified individuality, your Unique Self, appears. ***The dross of grasping separateness is burned away so that the luminous character of your unique light can shine resplendent.***

This is the realization of what I am calling the New Integral Enlightenment. Since we now realize that all perception, even the realization of True Nature, has perspective, we now realize that True Self never appears without Unique Self.[13] This is the realization of Unique Self. It is the realization that:

> Your enlightenment has a perspective.
> Your perspective.
> Your Unique Self.

CHAPTER THREE

TWO VISIONS OF ENLIGHTENMENT AND THEIR HIGHER INTEGRATION IN UNIQUE SELF

THROUGHOUT HISTORY, when the sages and mystic philosophers have looked at consciousness, two very different understandings about the self have contended with each other for dominance. Each has termed its understanding of the self "enlightened." The first conception is that of classical mystical consciousness. This view understands the separate self—or ego—as being essentially false and the source of suffering, while proclaiming impersonal consciousness (often called True Self, or Inner Self) to be the essence of your True Nature or identity.

While this view is often correctly identified with classical nondual Eastern teaching, it is not limited by geography. True Self has gone by many signifiers, including *rigpa* in Tibetan Buddhism, *mochin degadlut*, or Expanded Mind in Kabbalah, *antar atman* (Inner Self) or *tat* (That, as in the aphorism *tat tvam asi* "Thou Art That") in Hinduism, and Christ Consciousness in Christianity. This realization of the True Nature of self is what is classically termed "enlightenment." It has also been called self-realization (Shankara, Abulafia), Liberation (Ramana Maharshi), or being awake, the state the Buddha famously attained under the Bodhi tree. This understanding about the True Nature of self that I am calling "classical enlightenment" is indeed true.[1] But it is also partial.

The second understanding, which also calls itself enlightened, makes almost the directly opposite claim. This teaching, which flowered in the West during the so-called Age of Enlightenment in the mid-eighteenth century, asserts that your personal, separate self—your identity as a distinct individual—is your essential nature. This is seen by Western enlightenment thinkers such as Hobbes, Locke, and Rousseau as the basis of all human rights and responsibilities. Thus, the Western enlightenment conception sees the failure to recognize the autonomy of each individual as the source of all suffering. This is the core understanding behind almost all of Western psychology.

The understanding of self as the large, impersonal Ground of Being suggested by mysticism is either ignored, denied, or deemed irrelevant and even immoral by the Western enlightenment conception. As with the nondual understanding of the self, the Western enlightenment conception is true but partial.

The recognition of Unique Self transcends and includes the true but partial insights of both visions of enlightenment, and for the first time in the history of consciousness allows a higher Integral embrace of both.[2] In Unique Self enlightenment, you recognize and realize your nature as indivisible from the larger field of consciousness, even as you know yourself to be an absolute unique expression of True Self, unlike any other. True Self always looks out through a unique set of eyes, which reveals a radically one-of-a-kind and special perspective. In this way, you transcend the limitation of separate self while affirming the autonomy, value, and infinite dignity of your Unique Self.

True Self + Perspective = Unique Self

Two Images of Light

In the old scientific paradigm, light was thought to be of one quality and nature. In the old paradigm of awakening, to be enlightened was to be absorbed in the unqualified field of light, which is one. In the new science paradigm, we realize that every beam of light vibrates at its own unique frequency. To be enlightened, then, means to consciously live the radiance and purpose of your singularly unique frequency of light. This is the core teaching of the New Enlightenment.

Classical enlightenment, the old enlightenment, viewed uniqueness as the enemy. The belief was that your experience of uniqueness would obscure the realization of your identity with All-That-Is. That ego or separate self is something to be surrendered, pushed aside, utterly dissolved in the timeless Absolute. There is an element of truth to this—the ego must be *trance-ended*. You must end the trance of the ego.

You will always experience yourself in part as a separate self—that is as it should be. If you did not, you would be psychotic or otherwise deranged. What you need to trance-end is your exclusive identification with your egoic separate self. For it is your sense of being, but a skin-encapsulated ego, that creates the sense of suffocation, fear, and drabness that passes as your life. This fundamental error in identity is the root of virtually all suffering. Your disconnection from your larger context, and the aliveness it holds for you, gives birth to every form of egoic grasping and addiction.

But the ***ego contains within it more than a glimmer of truth.*** As we'll see later, the ***ego bears gifts that require clarification.***

Clarification takes place through contact with the transcendent, resulting in the revelation of the larger whole of which the separate self ego is but a part. The gifts of the ego, which are the intimations of your infinitely valuable uniqueness, can then flower in your higher realization as Unique Self.

We must love and nourish our egos, not destroy them altogether. Ego prefigures and points toward Unique Self.

We are wholes unto ourselves, as well as parts of even larger wholes. To be part of a larger whole does not mean to be so absorbed that you lose the unique nature of your part-ness. You can fully engage in deep communion and even union with the divine, even as you retain the integrity of your uniqueness.

Once you can transcend exclusive identification with ego, realize True Self, and celebrate your Unique Self, you are at the portal to your full enlightenment. ***Once you shatter the tyranny of the ego's dream, even as you awaken to your unique calling of radical love, beauty, and obligation, you begin to live as source, naturally manifesting your deepest authentic desire.***

Your Unique Self is your birthright. In your Unique Self, you begin
to live as Source, carrying the evolution of love and the transformation of
consciousness one generation forward. It is from this place that you discover
your ultimate purpose in living, where you remember your most sacred
vows, taken long before you were even born—promising to bring as much
love and light as you possibly can to a world that is so desperately in need
of your extraordinary gifts.

The Biology of Unique Self

Unique Self expresses itself in all dimensions of reality.* It begins at the base
atomic level of matter, or what the Buddhists call form: "Physical atoms each
have their own specific energy signature. Similarly, assemblies of atoms radiate
their own identifying energy patterns. So every material structure in the uni-
verse, including you and me, radiates a unique energy signature."[3] And, "Each
atom is unique, because the distribution of its positive and negative charges
coupled with its spin rate generates a specific vibration or energy pattern."[4]
Ascending the great chain of being from matter to body, we come to what we
might call the biology of Unique Self. To be clear, I am not suggesting that
this is evidence of the enlightenment teaching of Unique Self in the formal
sense. Rather, it suggests an expression of Unique Self on a biological level.
Human beings used to think that consciousness was a higher level of reality
than the material plane of matter. We now realize that this is not quite true.
It is more accurate to say that every human event has an interior and exterior
face, an inside and an outside expression. The outside viewed through the
third-person mechanisms of science and empirical verification is matter. The
inside, accessed through introspection and other forms of internally directed
forms of knowing, is consciousness.

So we would naturally expect uniqueness, which appears at the interior
level as the awakening of your unique consciousness, to also appear at the
exterior plane, the level of form. Looking specifically at biology, we see that
of course uniqueness does appear in biology in highly dramatic and unmis-
takable ways. *Every single human being is biologically unique, with a*

---

*See page 389 for a theoretical afterword which clarifies this usage of the term Unique Self in rela-
tion to its more classical usage in referring to a structural stage of developmental consciousness
and to the unique perspective of the enlightened state of True Self.

unique molecular and cellular signature. The cellular signature is comprised of two distinct dimensions of uniqueness, which together comprise what we might fairly call the Unique Self perspective of a cell.

One type of molecule that exists in a cell is the DNA molecule. DNA is the star of genetic research, and its double-helix structure contains the objective biological codes of Unique Self. This, however, is but one dimension of the unique complex cellular signature that comprises every human being. There are a host of other factors that interpret the DNA. It is these factors and not the objective genetic information that have the most impact on the actual life of a person. That is, it is the prism or perspective through which the genetic information is received that makes virtually all the difference.

This is the object of study of perhaps the most dynamic field in molecular biology today—epigenetics, which literally means "control above genetics." These factors include at least two major components. The first is a host of environmental factors that interact with the cell. This is what has often been referred to as "nurture as opposed to nature." As biologist Frederik Nijhout writes, "When a gene product is needed, a signal from the environment, not an emergent property of the gene itself, activates the expression of the gene."[5] The second factor is the proteins in the cells:

> By far the single most important component of living organisms is the proteins. The body's proteins are the essential building blocks of life. Our cells are in the main an assembly of protein building blocks. So one way of looking at our trillion-celled bodies is as protein-run systems deploying over 100,000 different kinds of proteins.[6]

The proteins contain identity receptors that receive environmental signals, and together they are the prism or perspective through which the unique DNA of an individual manifests in the world. In effect, you might say that the proteins are the hermeneutic prisms of the DNA. The DNA together with the proteins and the environment comprise the perspective of a cell that forms the core of cellular uniqueness. It is in the interaction between the unique proteins, the unique DNA, and all of the environmental variables that what might be called the Unique Self perspective of a cell is formed.

Clearly, uniqueness from this biological perspective is much more than mere social or psychological conditioning. Rather, uniqueness is the cellular reality of life. The core building block of life is the unique perspective of a cell that is formed by a number of diverse factors, including DNA, the environment, and the unique structures of the proteins and their receptors.

Proteins are utterly unique, very much like a puzzle piece. When the protein puzzle-piece "encounters a molecule that is an energetic and physical complement, the two bind together like human-made products with interlocking gears."[7] And, "The meeting or binding that takes place between the receptor protein and a resonant molecule is described by biologists as a lock and key."[8] Cells possess a unique "tuned" receptor protein for every environmental signal that needs to be read. Receptor proteins are the way the cell "perceives the environment." One scientist described receptor proteins as "units of perception."[9]

Each unique cell's set of identity receptors is located on the cell membrane's outer surface, where they act as antennae downloading the complementary environmental signals. "These identity receptors read a signal of self, which does not exist within the cell" but comes from the cell's unique reading of the "environmental signals."[10]

The analogy offered by Robert Lipton compares the human identity to the image on the screen of a television set. But your image does not come from inside the television. "Your identity is an environmental broadcast that was received via an antenna that is downloading the complementary environmental signals" to the antenna, much as the self-identity receptors download signals from the environment. Let's say that one day your television blows. Your image is no longer on the screen, but your Unique Self has not disappeared. All you need to do is "get another television set, plug it in, turn it on, and tune it to the station you were watching before the picture blew out . . . The physical television in this analogy is the equivalent of the cell. The TV's antenna, which downloads the broadcast, represents self-identity receptors that download the environmental signal."[11]

It is the perspective of the cell, formed in large part by the interaction of the identity receptors with the environment and DNA, that expresses the Unique Self. *The evolutionary realization that the core structures of Unique Self are rooted in the very cellular level of human being-ness suggests that Unique Self is not merely an elite expression of enlightenment, but is, at least in potential, an awakening that is possible for every human being.* This is but one more indication that it is time for a radical democratization of enlightenment.

The Democratization of Enlightenment

It is time for a radical democratization of enlightenment.

It used to be that enlightened living was for the elite. The few great lovers, saints, and sages throughout history reminded us that something more was possible, that there was a better way to live, that joy and overflowing love could and did exist, at least for some, as the animating essence of everyday life.

This tiny elite of subtle and evolved minds and hearts held alive for all of us the possibility that human beings could genuinely realize a transformation of identity, that they could truly evolve from their small constricted egos into spacious, dynamic, enlightened beings.

In days gone by, we relied on this elite to guide our world. Today, that age has passed. The old elite no longer has the power to guide us. We can no longer hope that in some room somewhere, in the halls of spiritual power or the inner chambers of an ashram or temple, there are holy, wise people upon whom we can rely for our salvation.

In a globally interconnected world, one person acting alone or a small group of ignorant individuals has the ability to literally destroy humanity. This is a pointing-out instruction by the universal love-intelligence. Said simply, reality is telling us something that we desperately need to know. The lesson is clear. For better and for worse, the age of ruling elites, be they spiritual or political, is over. ***Democracy is the evolutionary unfolding of love-intelligence in our era. It began with the democratization of governments.*** Now it must move to the democratization of enlightenment. This is the enlightenment of your True Self beyond personality and ego, which then expresses itself in the full glory and power of your Unique Self. The Unique Self principle is an implicit potential in the genetic source of consciousness. To show up in life means to show up as your Unique Self. In order to show up, you must both grow up and wake up. Unique Self enlightenment is to grow up to your highest possible level of development in which you spontaneously inhabit the full power of your unique perspective. Unique Self enlightenment is also to wake up beyond exclusive identification with ego to your higher identity as True Self, an indivisible part of the larger conscious whole. Every human being is radically unique. Every human being is part of the One True Self.

Enlightenment is a genuine possibility, and therefore a sacred obligation, for every single person. You are not obligated from without. You are obligated in love by your own highest possibility.[12]

The disciples of one master liked to explain this radical Unique Self principle with a story:

> A precocious child was convinced that the king was not as wise as people claimed. And so he set out—as young people are wont to do—to prove his point. He came before the king with a question. "Sire," he said with great audacity, "it is said that you know the future and can answer any question posed. Well, I have a question for you." The assembled court gasped at his insolence. But the boy went on. "I have in my closed hand a butterfly, sire. Tell me, is it alive or dead?"
>
> The boy thought to himself, "If he says 'alive,' I will simply squeeze and kill it, and if he says 'dead,' then I will open my hand and let it fly away."
>
> The sage was silent for a moment, even as the room grew very silent. When he finally spoke, it was with the gentlest voice the boy had ever heard. "My son," said the king, "whether the butterfly lives or dies depends on you."

It depends on us. On each and every one of us uniquely.

Answering the Call

Once you understand at the very cellular level of your being that your uniqueness is not a historical accident but an intentional expression of essence, then you realize that enlightenment is a genuine option for every human being —including you! The living universe took 13.7 billion years of intentional evolution to manifest the new and original evolutionary potential of your Unique Self. When you realize this, and remember that your Unique Self is

God having a *You* experience, everything in your essential experience of life changes.

Once you understand that your uniqueness is not the haphazard result of your cultural, social or psychological conditioning, but that all of these are necessary conditions for the emergence of the personal face of Essence that is You, your essential experience of life transforms. You move from having a desperate need to escape your life to the radical embrace of your life.

When this happens, fate is transformed to destiny. Every detour becomes a destination. Desperation becomes celebration. Grasping becomes purposeful action and resignation becomes activism. The contracted smallness of your frightened suffering self becomes the expanded joyful realization of Your Unique Self. At such times you know that the irreducible uniqueness of every awakened human being is a sign that reality actually invites, and even lovingly demands, your enlightenment. Reality yearns for a full and authentic expression of your uniqueness, for you to live in the world as God's verb. Unique essence, living in you, as you and through you, is the essence of enlightenment.

It is from this place that you answer the call of Unique Self. It is from this place that you give the world your desperately needed unique gifts, those charismatic endowments that arise from your Unique Self. This is what I mean when I talk about Unique Self enlightenment. This is what it means to answer the call.

Unique Self enlightenment is a genuine possibility and therefore a responsibility for every human being. For there is no separation in essence. Every unique expression of essence is part of the seamless coat of the universe. Seamless, but not featureless. So, we could say that failure to clarify the contours of your Unique Self is not a failure of the contracted ego but a failure to love God. For to love God is to let God see through your eyes. Through the unique perspective of essence which is You. And remember, the god you don't believe in doesn't exist. God is the eros of evolution—the love intelligence and love beauty—that animates and drives all of existence to higher and higher levels of complexity, consciousness and love.

Realizing Your Unique Self and giving your Unique Gifts, as we said at the outset, is the evolution of love that is the evolution of God upon which the future of God depends. There are two key steps involved.

Firstly, you clarify your realization to know that you are not a separate self but a True Self, inseparable from the All.

Secondly, you realize that your True Self has a Unique Perspective. **True Self + Perspective = Unique Self.** Your Unique Self is able to address a Unique Need that can be addressed by no one else in the world that ever was, is or will be, other then you. No one has the capacity to address this unique need in the way that you are able to do. This is your Unique Gift.

In sum, your obligation and joy in being alive is to clarify your Unique Perspective, realize your Unique Self and give your Unique Gift. This is how you Answer the Call. Transforming your awareness of self to Unique Self-consciousness is the change in your life that changes everything.

As we have already seen, democratization of enlightenment, therefore, does not mean that everyone is enlightened, but rather that a full expression of authentic unique essence is a genuine possibility and therefore a genuine expression of love-obligation for every living being. In other words, awakening to your Unique Self it is the joy and responsibility of answering the call.

Enlightenment Is Sanity

The future of our world depends on your enlightenment. A genuine shift in your consciousness will effect a similar shift in the consciousness of many of the people with whom you come into contact, and will spread enlightenment in ever-widening circles. The ease and urgency of enlightenment is contagious and exhilarating.

This transformation of consciousness is serious business. It is also an urgent, ecstatic, contagious, absolutely necessary, gorgeous, and delightful business. It is no more or less than the transformation of your identity.

Enlightenment means no more and no less than sanity.

To be enlightened is to know reality. To know reality is to be sane. The core of your reality is your identity. A correct understanding of your identity is core to your sanity and joy.

One old Aramaic text states, "Anyone who sins has been seized by a spirit of insanity." In the original, "to sin" does not mean to be bad. It means literally to miss the mark. Modernity threw the word "sin" out of our vocabulary because it was hijacked by all sorts of fundamentalist communities who used it to make the body evil. We threw it out because it became associated with teenage masturbation and failure to assent to particular dogmas and doctrines. But now we need to reclaim the core meaning and space of insight held by this word. To sin is to miss the mark, to not properly understand the nature of reality. Sin is a form of ignorance, a false or partial relationship to reality. Ignorance is not realizing you are in a forest, because your attention is fixated on one tree.

The experience of sin is the feeling that things are not holding together. As Yeats wrote,

> The falcon cannot hear the falconer;
> Things fall apart; the centre cannot hold;[13]

To be enlightened means to be sane: so-called normal consciousness is insane. "Normal" consciousness rooted in the grasping ego produces suffering. "Normal" consciousness killed 100 million people in the last century. That is not normal. "Normal" consciousness is insane. To be sane is to be in right relationship with yourself and with all of the larger frameworks and contexts in which your self lives and breathes.

One of the simplest definitions of sanity used in the psychological literature is to know who you are. To be sane is know your identity, to recognize your name. For example, if I tell you that my name is Ken Wilber when my name is really Marc Gafni and I insist on being called Ken Wilber, there is a fairly good chance that I am more than a bit insane. Clearly, I don't know my true identity.

But the distance between the identity of Marc and Ken may be less wide than the distance between my experience of myself as a separate, skin-encapsulated ego-self, and the experience of my True Self. From the place of True Self, I am able to access much more than my limited personal power, knowing, creativity and love. Rather, all of the power, knowing, creativity and love in the universe flow through me. When I see from the place of True Self, there is no reason for me to be jealous of you, to lash out at you or to do anything other then love you as myself. In some sense, you *are* myself. The pathological competition, the grasping and violence produced by contraction are deconstructed in the emergent glory of True Self. Instead, you access a spacious sense of peace, joy and harmonious equilibrium with all other expressions of being and becoming on the planet. The world literally becomes a different place. These are the gifts of what has classically been called enlightenment.

So here is the great question. If enlightenment is so great, why isn't everyone seeking it? If enlightenment is the answer to our suffering, if it actually delivers on all of its wildly amazing promises – which it does – why is the world not lining up for intensive enlightenment studies?

Some enlightenment teachers explain that this is because of the clever obfuscations of the ego, which does everything in its power to avoid its own death. In other words, since the ego does not want to die, it attaches you to a narrow identity as a small self. Other teachers say that the work of practice required to liberate into True Self beyond ego is simply too demanding for most people. Still other teachers may blame the seductions of culture and society, which so entice you with their pseudo-comforts that it is hard to free yourself from the game.

All of these explanations certainly carry some weight. But at the core of things the problem is not with the seekers of enlightenment. Instead, there is a core defect in the way classical enlightenment is being presented.

The teaching of classical enlightenment often points to a state that, at its core, appears boring, dislocating and alienating. It is dislocating because it leads a student to ask, quite rightly, "If I give up my separate self-ego identity, then who am I?" Many enlightenment teachers respond to this natural question by pointing out that it comes from the voice of the ego. In other words, they imply that once you're enlightened, it doesn't even arise. The price for enlightenment, as they say in the Zen tradition, is " Die to separate self!"

In one sense, that is true, But it is also partial. If enlightenment meant only disappearing into the undifferentiated oneness of True Self, it would seem to deny the sacred dignity of the individual. And besides, (as many seekers intuit), it would be boring. The sense of creative edge, vitality and becoming that are the ground of our aliveness would be lost in the beingness of it all. If to be enlightened means to lose "me", then it becomes irrelevant to most of the world.

Unique Self enlightenment teaches you how to lose "me" at the level of ego only to reclaim a higher and deeper "me" at the level of Unique

Self. The Unique Self enlightenment teaching points out that to be enlight-ened—to know who you really are, your true identity—is not merely to recognize True Self, that which is only One (the total number of True Selves is, in fact, only one!) Rather, unique self enlightenment demands that you move beyond your separate self to True Self, *while understanding that the realization of True Self is the ground for the awakening of your Unique Self.* As an individual, you correctly sense that the source of your dignity and value is your irreducible uniqueness. And, the Unique Self teachings confirm that enlightenment is not a loss of individuality. It is the reclaim-ing of your infinite individuality as the unique expression of Essence that lives as you. **To be enlightened means to realize your True Nature as an utterly unique perspective and manifestation of consciousness.** It is to live at the energized edge of your evolutionary creativity and your capacity for becoming that is both indivisibly part of the greater One, and, at the same time, ecstatically You. This is sanity. This is what it means to live in a larger context as an evolutionary lover. This is enlightenment. This is your true identity. Enlightenment and sanity are one.

To be enlightened means to realize your True Nature as an utterly unique perspective and manifestation of consciousness.

To be enlightened means to be in love. Sometimes agonizingly, some-times blissfully, but always in love. To be enlightened means to be living a life of ecstatic expression, aligned obligation, and unique meaning and fulfillment. Enlightenment is the life of pleasure, for the enlightened person knows how to discern between pleasures. There is no greater plea-sure, even when painful, than your enlightened life manifesting as your Unique Self.

In Sanskrit, *dharma* means something like "truth," "law," and "path." When you access the truth of Unique Self, the individualized law of your life reveals itself, and the path that is only yours to walk opens up and welcomes you.

When you realize the dharma of Unique Self, your relationship to love, malice, sex, joy, pleasure, relationships, parenting, ethical failures, jealousies, anger, all forms of acting out, death, reincarnation, heartbreak, and the very purpose of your life on earth will all evolve dramatically.

A realization of your Unique Self shifts everything, as you begin for the first time in your life to live and generate as Source.

Unique Self Is Not a Concept

Unique Self has been pointed to by Sufis as essence or the Diamond Body. It has been alluded to in Buddhism as the Eternal Drop, and by Hindus as the Inner Self *(atman)* or inner God.

Kabbalists call it Soul Root, and for some it is the personal manifestation of the Absolute. It is the lure of your own hidden being and becoming. It is the movement from personality to essence.

Personality is, in part, the pseudo-story you tell to make sense of the pain of your existence. Personality is not bad. It is both necessary for you to navigate the world and an essential stage of your development. Moreover, in personality are glimmerings of your Unique Self. Unique Self is found when you get beneath and beyond your personality.

Personality should not be confused with the personal. We seek to move beyond the personality, but not beyond the personal. *Unique self is your personal response to the call of the transpersonal.*

Enlightenment Is Not Impersonal

The goal of the New Enlightenment is not impersonal. You do not disappear in your enlightenment. You begin for the first time to appear, for your enlightenment takes on a perspective held for God only by you.

You harbor a greater life than you know. Give your little, private, convulsive, reactive self a rest in order to find the greater Self that is there.

In Unique Self practice, you allow yourself to become available to the extraordinary capacities beyond your imagining that you contain. You gain access to knowing beyond your experience. You are connected to perceptions and practices far beyond the capacity of your small self.

To recognize your unique qualities is simply to be present to what is.

Unique Self is the unique feeling, a personal knowing, of your full presence.

The Personal Face of Essence

Some mystics refer to Unique Self as *ani atzmi*, best translated as "Essential Self." Essential is that which is most substantial and real. Essence is what makes something what it is. The wonder of your irreducible uniqueness is your essence.

Would that you could
know yourself for a time.
You will be shocked by your delight.
—RUMI

The Persian poets Rumi and Hafiz wrote their verse to recall you to your essence. Essence is your enlightened state expressed in its Unique form. Your Unique Self is not an object. It is the personal face of essence. To realize your essence is to realize your enlightenment. ***Let yourself be seduced by essence, and your life in all of its passing moments becomes filled with glory.*** Unique Self is not a mental construct or a concept: the Unique Self is the fullest flowering of your humanity and the blooming of your divinity. It is both the omega point and the dynamic purpose that drives us toward realization.

Unique Self is a direct manifestation of who you are. It is also your gift to the world. Your expression is unique, and if you block it, it will never exist through any other medium. If you do not realize your Unique Self then all that only you can and must offer the world, all that the world needs from you, will be lost.

In Unique Self practice, you allow yourself to become available to the extra-ordinary capacities we each contain. You unleash extra-ordinary possibilities beyond your imagining. You gain access to knowing beyond your experience. You are connected to perception and practices far beyond the capacity of your small self. It is the individuation of your Unique Self that is the main task of your life.

You are the only perfect expression of what and who you are. So you might as well be yourself. In any event, everyone else is taken.

Too often, people never quite recognize themselves, because they are busy trying to be something or someone else. There is great shock and delight at self-recognition. Unique Self practice begins with a simple recognition of basic qualities of your Unique Being and Becoming. Unique Self is not a reaction. It is the spontaneous expression of Self being Unique.

The willow is green, flowers are red.
—ZEN SAYING

CHAPTER FOUR

EIGHT STATIONS ON THE ROAD TO UNIQUE SELF

THERE ARE EIGHT DISTINCT STATIONS in the evolution of identity on the path to your Unique Self. You will recognize them as you encounter them on your journey. I will now outline the stations to give you a view of the whole picture. Do not worry about fully understanding each station as you read it for the first time. The meanings and contours of the key stations will become clear as we explore them over the course of the book.

Station 1: Pre-personal Self

The first station appears at the beginning of life, before you have developed a sense of your personal separate self. In individual development, this is the station of the infant who is not yet individuated from their mother or environment. However, this pre-personal station doesn't disappear completely after infancy; it remains with us and reappears later in life in different forms. It is, for example, the station of someone who loses their autonomy and sense of identity in an abusive cult or lynch mob or someone caught in the group-think of politically-correct victimology. Falling in love also requires you to move—at least for a time—from the clear boundaries of the personal to the fusion of the pre-personal. It is for this reason that Freud, in his less romantic moments, viewed falling in love as regressive. Deeper insight reveals that this "falling" is an absolutely necessary, if temporary, first station of love. It gives the lover a temporary glimpse into what might be possible. In the next station, boundaries snap back into place as the personal reasserts itself. This is the station where lovers must decide if they are willing to stay and do the work. If all goes well you then evolve to station three, true love, when the infatuation of fusion is transmuted into the ecstasy of union. But the initial infatuation with another is one of the places, long after infancy, in which the pre-personal reappears in our lives.[1]

Station 2: Separate Self: Level One Personal

In this station of development you move from the pre-personal to the first personal stage of human development. This is when the personality, sometimes referred to as the ego, or separate self, comes online. The formation of personality and ego is a wonderfully healthy and necessary stage. You learn to experience yourself as a separate entity among many other separate entities, with your own boundaries and identity. The separate self is born. You feel joy at your success and frustration at your failure. At this station, the distinction between your false self, True Self, and Unique Self does not yet appear.

In this station you are wonderfully caught up in the glory of your story. In the best expression of this station, you are not thinking about your story; you are simply living it. There is great potential depth at this level of consciousness, expressed in part by a direct and unflinching recognition of what is. *There comes a time when, in order to grow, you need to get over the fantasy of your idealized life and start recognizing the story of your life for what it is.* You embrace your life in all of its complexity, ecstasy, and pain. You can bear it all, and you delight in it all, because it is your life. And in claiming your life as it is, you start to feel something deeply right about it and about yourself. There emerges in you a willingness to take absolute responsibility for everything that happens in your life. You are fully identified with your story. You are a player in your life and not a victim of its circumstances.

Many teachers like to say, "You are not your story." They are right, but only partially. They fail to distinguish between the ego story and the Unique Self story. But there is also great wisdom in this first level of the personal, the station of ego and personality. The ego *prefigures* the Unique Self. And as we shall see, there are many important stations through which you must still evolve toward your full depth and enlightenment. In the next stages of development, you will need to first clarify your story and then to dis-identify with it, in order to return to your ego story at a much higher level of consciousness, the level of Unique Self. While first glimmerings of Unique Self appear at this level of separate self, it can only fully be realized when ego gets over itself.

Station 3: False Self

False self is the unhealthy form of separate self. In this station, you take an essential step in the transformation and evolution of your identity. It is here that you begin to consciously deploy what Freud called the observing ego. Your ability to see the inner structure of your personality comes online. As you separate and look at the story of your life as an object, its contours and patterns begin to become clear to you. You begin to recognize some of the core beliefs that have defined and sometimes deformed your life. Certain core mind-sets start to stand out. You see that you have a particular way of fixing your attention, of stabilizing yourself with familiar and deeply held beliefs.

In this station, the essential practice is that of "making subject object": Just as we get settled in the story of who we are, something amazing, something startling happens. We see that we have been telling a story. The entire narrative that we have formulated, the one that we have become so accustomed to, so comfortable with, slips from our subjective experience and becomes an object, an artifact. Remember Robert Kegan's insight: the subject of one level of development becomes the object of the next level of development. The understanding of this stage of the journey is based in part on the pioneering work of the great psychologists Robert Assagioli, Oscar Ichazo, and others, which reveals how the fixation of attention, which creates a false sense of self, is the very mechanism that prevents us from uncovering our deeper nature. Your fixation is the particular prism through which you see the world, the way in which, very early in your life, your attention fixated into a very particular pattern. This fixation of attention into a particular slant of seeing will naturally produce a distorted picture of your identity, which is your false self. Your false self is the unhealthy and distorted expression of your separate self.

Your false self fixation often expresses itself in a sentence or series of sentences: "I am not safe." "I am not enough." "I am bad." "I am too much." You live inside your sentence. *You need to step outside of your sentence in order to genuinely realize your True Self.*

The model of the Enneagram type describes another kind of fixation. It is a distorted pattern of perceived meaning upon which you fixate early in your life, which then shapes and determines your experience of reality.

Recognizing these patterns, trance-ending them, and deploying them skillfully is the next critical step in your evolution. *To walk toward your enlightenment, you must recognize your fixations, break their hold on you, and cleanse the doors of your perception.*

To recognize your false self, you must first see it. This is the process of making subject—your false self—into object; your false self becomes an object that you can see and therefore change.

The discernment of the observing ego allows you to take the first steps out of your false self into your real life. You still identify with your separate self, but without the distorting smoke and mirrors of your false self.

Station 4: True Self—Classical Enlightenment: Impersonal

In this station we make the momentous, freeing leap from the personal to the transpersonal. This has been called by some the liberation from the personal and the great realization of the impersonal. It would be more accurate to say that it is liberation from the ego personality, which is only level one of the personal. This level of the personal is transcended only to reappear in clarified form at the level of Unique Self, but first we must realize our True Selves.

We are ready and even yearning to evolve beyond our separate-self ego. We are no longer able to adhere to an identification with self that is painfully limited. The space beyond the story, the awareness beyond the fixations of attention, and the contracted conception of self now become the foreground instead of the background. This is the classical stage of ego dissolution. You realize your True Nature. Your identity shifts from your separate-self ego to your True Self. You move to trance-end your personality and identify with your essence. This is the change that changes everything.

Sometimes this dissolution occurs spontaneously, sometimes through overwhelming pain or extreme fatigue; at other times, it emerges as the fruition of years of dedicated study and practice. Yet even at this stage of development, the ego does not disappear. Rather the ego is freed from its own narcissism and becomes an ally. You never evolve beyond ego. You evolve beyond your exclusive identification with ego.

As you begin to dislodge from your exclusive identification with the separate self, as you become disillusioned, you may be fearful or anxious, longing for the old, solid ground of your narrow identity. At the same time, your growing sense is that you are part of an infinitely larger context, that you are part of the "seamless coat of the Uni-verse."

Understand that this is not a one-time event, but a continuous process of death and rebirth at each and every moment.

At this station, you engage in spiritual practice in order to dislodge your identity from the hell of separation, and you begin to realize your identity as the eternal Witness, as Big Mind/Big Heart, as the effortless spacious awareness behind this moment and every moment. You recognize your profound interconnectedness with others and the world. You realize that you are part of the larger field of love, intelligence, and creativity underlying All-That-Is. You reach beyond time and taste eternity, stepping out of the stream of past, present, and future, consenting to the full presence of the unchanging Now.

Two Notes on True Self

The first note concerns one's level of True Self-realization and the relationship between True Self and Unique Self. Clearly there are different levels of True Self-realization. Our evolution beyond exclusive identification with ego is an ongoing process, and it is fueled by regular practice. Many people have glimmerings of True Self-realization at several different times in their lives and then remain faithful to the lived memory of that experience. (In fact, one definition of faith could be "living with fidelity to those moments when you authentically realize the true nature of your self and the universe"!)

All this means that levels of True Self-realization vary greatly from person to person. It is fair to say, however, that there is a direct relationship between the level of your True Self-realization and the clarity of your

Unique Self awakening. The more deeply you know your True Self, the more you can be sure that your experience of a distinctive self-sense is at the level of Unique Self and not merely the grasping of ego. The more experiences of True Self you have, especially if you ally them with certain practices (witness practice, surrender practice, and others), the more you are able to discern between the voices of your child-ego and the experience of self that comes from true alignment with the divine in you.

The second note concerns the nature and method of True Self-realization. If you can only realize True Self by attaining the ultimate realization of Buddha, and if Unique Self comes online only after one has attained that level of True Self-realization, then only a very few people could ever realize Unique Self. That would make Unique Self-realization practically irrelevant for most human beings. Yet we know that True Self is accessed through many different means, not only through a nondual realization, born of first-person meditative practice, as in the classical Zen *kensho* or Hindu *samadhi*. Realizing True Self can happen through non-meditative experiences like prayer, ecstatic dance, spontaneous visionary experience, or even during a tennis game or a car accident. A sense of being enmeshed in and intertwined with invisible lines of connection that link all of reality may be accessed through direct contact with many forms of the transcendent, including contact with personal, second-person forms of the divine such as Christ or the divine mother. You can access glimmerings of True Self in the course of living for a higher social purpose or artistic vision, or by incarnating values like service and kindness. For example, my grandmother was a profoundly awake woman who experienced herself as selflessly committed to the highest good of all beings, and connected to all beings. Her compassion was vast, and her consciousness was full of God-awareness. She never meditated or had a non dual satori realization in her life. Indeed, she never heard of meditation. Her major formal spiritual practice was praying, reading psalms, and absorbing the laws and stories of the great Jewish masters, along with the ritual practices of Jewish teaching. All of this served to produce in her what can only be described as an enlightened consciousness, which had profoundly trance-ended separate self. There are many like her, who have had enough experience of contact with True Self to be able to awaken to their Unique Self, and to discern the difference between Unique Self and ego.

Station 5: Unique Self—The New Enlightenment: Level Two Personal

At the fifth station you witness the emergence of Unique Self. The personal comes back online at a higher level of consciousness. You realize that your True Self is not merely an indistinct part of a larger unification, but expresses itself uniquely, and that you have a unique role to play in the evolutionary unfolding. *The personal face of your True Self is your Unique Self.* You are able to consciously incarnate the evolutionary impulse toward healing and transformation that initiates, animates, and guides reality. No one else in the world can respond as you can to the unique need of *All-That-Is*, that is yours and only yours to address, and the place of your full liberation and power.

Awakening to your Unique Self has been called the "Pearl beyond Price" by the Sufi adherents, or "*ani* after *ayin*" by Kabbalists. It is alluded to as "Kosmic Consciousness assuming individual form" in the *Yoga Vasistha* of Hinduism.

Unique Self is not just another subtle disguise of the ego.

Not in the least. Unique Self is rather the personal face of True Self. Unique Self is the antidote to the grasping of ego. In one moment you are fully alive, dynamically reaching for love and manifestation, and yet you are willing to let go of any attachment in the next moment. Your ego is still present, but you have moved beyond exclusive identification with your ego. The ego points toward Unique Self. Your Unique Self, which begins to reveal itself at the level of personality, comes to full flower only after freeing itself from the grasping of ego through genuine and repeated experiences of ego clarification and trance-ending. Unique Self appears gradually and in direct proportion to the level of egoic clarification and trance-ending. Unique Self also shows up fleetingly in peak experiences in conjunction with parallel appearances of True Self. An example of this might be a moment of "flow" or an Eros experience, sometimes called "being in the zone," when ego temporarily drops, and a felt or even lived experience of Unique Self becomes temporarily available to the person.

In classical enlightenment, we move from an experience of ourselves as a-part, to a felt experience of ourselves as an indivisible expression of the larger oneness, where the sense of the part dissolves and the wholeness even momentarily overwhelms our sense of distinction. And then, in a subtle shift of emphasis, we evolve to an even deeper depth of realization. At this station, we begin to experience ourselves as the part again, but from the place of vast awareness, we realize that the part is not separate. We realize that we are not a separate but rather a unique part of a larger whole. And you realize that whole living in you, in part. ***Your awakening or enlightenment has a perspective that is held only by you.***

True Self + Perspective = Unique Self

This stage is hinted at in the Tenth Oxherding picture in Buddhism, one of ten snapshots of enlightenment. In the tenth picture, the man walks back to the marketplace—and I would add "in order to offer his Unique Gifts and to perform the unique *bodhisattva* obligations that can and must be fulfilled by him alone."

Evolutionary Unique Self

It is not enough, however, to awaken only to your Unique Expression of True Self. As we will unfold in more depth in Chapter 8, there is a second critical dimension of awakening that is essential to Unique Self-realization. I received a direct transmission of this second dimension of Unique Self enlightenment from my lineage teachers who are best described as evolutionary mystics.

Isaac Luria, the teacher of my teachers, the great evolutionary mystic of the Renaissance period, taught that every action that a person takes must be with the explicit consciousness and intention of *tikkun*. *Tikkun* is best translated as the evolutionary healing and transformation of all of reality. Every action must be invested with evolutionary intention. In Luria's language it must be *leshem yichud,* meaning for the sake of the evolutionary integration and transformation of all of reality.

Said simply in the language of the evolutionary mystics themselves, to awaken to your Unique self is to "shift your perspective." The way the evolutionary mystics say it is simply to shift your perspective from "your side" to "God's side." To the evolutionary mystics, to awaken means not necessarily to have a profound mystical state experience in which you feel all of being living in you; rather, to awaken is to dramatically, yet simply, shift your alignment. To no longer align with your will, but with God's will.

We do not mean God here in the old mythic sense of the ethnocentric God who created the world in six days and is anti-science, vengeful, and anti-humanity. By God, Luria refers to the evolutionary process of unfolding which drives and animates the kosmos on every level of existence. God's will is the will of the kosmos. God is what Aurobindo refers to in his great work *The Future Evolution of Man* as the evolutionary imperative or what has been more recently renamed as The Evolutionary Impulse* *It is the creative force of the kosmos, which is, intends, and moves All-That-Is toward healing and transformation. It is the evolutionary impulse that lives in you, as you, and through you.*

To awaken to your Unique Self means to awaken to the impulse to evolve, which is the divine creativity surging in you at this very moment, reaching toward the good, the true, and the beautiful. To awaken to your Unique Self is to realize—as the evolutionary mystics taught us—that you live in an evolutionary context. To awaken to your Unique Self is to realize that your True Self is not static. When we thought that the divine field was an eternal absolute, then naturally we felt that the realization of True Self was the awakening to your unqualified eternal, absolute, and unchanging consciousness. The evolutionary mystics, however, from Luria to Schelling to Kook to Aurobindo, awakened to the evolving nature of spirit. As we moved into modernity and Darwinian science, the contemporary evolutionary mystics realized that their initial insight into the evolution of spirit applied not only to spirit, but also to the evolution of the biosphere, of the physical world. As my teacher Abraham Kook writes, "all of reality"—matter, body, mind, soul, and spirit—"is always evolving." To be a mystic is to know something of the interior face of the kosmos. The novice knows today what only the most advanced souls knew five hundred years ago, that evolution is the inner mechanism of mystery.

For example, Renaissance mystic Isaac Luria and his school of Kabbalists had a deep knowing of the inner evolutionary process of spirit. They knew through deep mystical contemplation that the awakened human being was actively and consciously engaging in the evolution of all of reality. In their more audacious nondual formulations, these evolutionary mystics, writing in the 16th century, realized that *man is responsible for the evolution of God.*

*Barbara Marx Hubbard, Conscious Evolution: Awakening our Social Potential, 1998

They understood and clearly articulated that the specific privilege and wild responsibility of the human being is to awaken to conscious evolution. And, these very evolutionary mystics are the original inspiration for the core teaching of Unique Self. This is substantively different than what my colleague, Andrew Cohen, calls Authentic Self. For Authentic Self in his teaching is an "awakened impersonal function." By contrast, Unique Self is the personal after the impersonal and is characterized by irreducible uniqueness.

In this broader evolutionary mystical context, it is possible to say simply that in the awakened Unique Self, evolution becomes conscious of itself. It is the awakened Unique Self feeling the imperative of evolution consciously alive in herself that is therefore called to give her Unique Gifts for the sake of the evolution of all of reality. So, the Unique Self in full realization might be more accurately termed the evolutionary Unique Self. The awakened Unique Self who has evolved beyond exclusive identification with ego is constantly being called by the evolutionary impulse. Indeed, it is in consciously aligning his Unique Self will with the evolutionary will of the kosmos that the human being is pulled beyond ego to True Self, and then to the personal face of True Self—Unique Self. One does not escape ego by awakening to the evolutionary Unique Self. Ego is always present. However, by identifying with the infinitely larger context of the evolutionary Unique Self, the limited identification with ego is gloriously trance-ended.

(For a graphic representation of these stations of consciousness, see the chart at the end of this chapter, page 38.)

Station 6: Unique Shadow

In the post-enlightenment experience, there are still layers to be shed. Even when we are most expansive, most identified with All-That-Is, small pockets of identity are kept out of our awareness, although they are experienced quite directly by everyone around us. You simply can't see them directly, even though recognizing them would free up your energy and directly facilitate a more powerful and beautiful expression of your Uniqueness. This is what is called, both in some of the great traditions and in modern psychology, your shadow.[2]

Learning to recognize and do shadow work is one of the challenges of the full journey of Unique Self. Although shadow work begins at the level of separate self, the full completion of your shadow work is directly connected to your realization of Unique Self. The common understanding of shadow is the negative material about your self that you are unable to own in your first person. This negative material—your jealousy, pettiness, fear, rage, brutality—is understood to be generic. The same core material is said to show up and be repressed into shadow, to a greater and larger degree, by everyone. This is a true but highly partial understanding of shadow.

In Unique Self teaching, we evolve the shadow work conversation and realize that shadow is not generic—shadow is intensely personal. This is a critical evolutionary unfolding of our understanding of shadow.

Your personal shadow is your Unique Shadow. Your Unique Shadow is your dis-owned Unique Self, the unavoidable result of a life yet unlived. Shadow is not merely your repressed negative material. Shadow is your dis-owned, denied, or distorted Unique Self. Your Unique Self and your Unique Shadow are a double helix of light and dark coiled into the patterns of becoming.

Remember William Blake's teaching on wisdom and folly: "If the fool would follow his folly, he would become wise."[3] In precisely the same way, you can follow the path of your Unique Shadow back to your Unique Self.

You can almost learn more about yourself through your darkness than you can through your light.

Station 7: Your Unique Gift

The obligation that wells up from your evolutionary realization of Unique Self is your responsibility to give the gifts that are yours alone to give, gifts that are desired and needed by the rest of creation. Every human being has a particular set of gifts to offer in the world. Your Unique Perspective gives birth to what I call your Unique Gift.

The ability to offer this gift freely and fully depends on your ability to free yourself of limiting and false notions of who you are, and to instead identify with your larger service. And beautifully, when this happens you are also able to allow others to be fully who they are as Unique Beings: complete, whole, and specific. This is one of the litmus tests of whether you are in Unique Self or in ego, whether you are able to joyously recognize and affirm the Unique Self of others without feeling that they are taking something that is yours.

Your Unique Gift is the particular contribution that you can make to the evolution of consciousness, which can be made by no one else who ever was, is, or will be. Both the overwhelming desire and ability to give your Unique Gift is a direct and spontaneous expression of your Unique Self-realization. Your Unique Gift, whether public or private, is your divine evolutionary gift to All-That-Is. It is the very face of God, the unique face of evolution alive and awake, in you, as you, and through you.

Some of our gifts are modest, private, and intimate; some are larger than life and have dramatic impact in the public sphere. Some of our gifts are actively given; others emerge from the very uniqueness of our being and presence.

This last point is subtle but essential. Unique Self contains in it something of the old idea of "answering the call" that is essential in Kabbalah and Protestant theology. But it is much more than that. Your Unique Self expresses itself in your Unique Being as well as in your Unique Becoming. Unique Self might have a public face, but it can also be utterly private. A hermit may live Unique Self no less than the president of the United States.

Station 8: Unique Vow, Unique Obligation

In the Buddhist tradition, the *bodhisattva* is one who seeks Buddhahood through practicing noble action. The *bodhisattva* vows to postpone his or her complete awakening and fulfillment until all other beings are awakened and fulfilled.[4] In Kabbalah this same archetype is called the Tzadik. The determining factor in their actions is compassion, deployed by utilizing the highest insight and wisdom. The realization of Unique Self may be regarded as *bodhisattva* activity, the unique manifestation of wisdom and guidance. The Unique Self *bodhisattva* vow is an expression of evolutionary joy and responsibility, even as it is a commitment to the fulfillment of your evolutionary obligation.

Many of us recoil when we hear the word "obligation." We identify obligation with arbitrarily imposed limitations set by the church or state that suffocate the naturally free human being. Let's inquire for a moment what obligation might mean at a higher level of consciousness, rather than the obligation imposed by an authority external to you. This inquiry yields the deeper truth that obligation is the ultimate liberation. Obligation frees you from ambivalence and allows you to commit 1,000 percent to the inherent invitation that is the Unique Obligation present in every unique situation.

Obligation at this level of consciousness is created by the direct and clear recognition of authentic need that can be uniquely addressed by you and you alone. For example, let's say you are stuck on a lush tropical island with another person. There is abundant food. The problem is, due to a physical ailment, this person is unable to feed herself. Are you obligated to feed her? Most people would agree that in this situation, you have an absolute obligation to feed her. Why is this so? It is based on what I call the fivefold principle of authentic obligation.

First, there is a need.

Second, it is a genuine and not a contrived need.

Third, you clearly recognize the need.

Fourth, you are capable of fulfilling the need.

Fifth, you realize that you are uniquely capable; the need can be uniquely addressed by you and you alone.

The combination of these five factors creates your Unique Obligation to give the Unique Gift that can be given only by you in this moment. Generally we cringe at the word obligation. We commonly understand obligation to be the opposite of love. In the original Hebrew, however, love and obligation are the same word. Authentic obligation is a natural by-product of authentic love.

Every true obligation is sourced in love. Unique love creates a Unique Obligation to give your Unique Gift. While most of our gifts address more subtle hungers than food, there is no person who does not possess Unique Gifts that respond to unique needs. From a non dual perspective, it is your Unique Gift that creates your Unique Obligation. To live your Unique Self and offer your Unique Gift is to align yourself with the evolutionary impulse and fulfill your evolutionary obligation. *The realization of your Unique Self awakens you to the truth that there is a Unique Gift that your singular being and becoming offers the world, which is desperately needed by All-That-Is, and can be given by you and you alone.* There is no more powerful and joyous realization available to a human being. It is the matrix of meaning that fills your life and is the core of your Unique Self enlightenment.

The Five Great Awakenings

Another way to understand the core of these stations is through the prism of what I call the Five Great Awakenings.

A shared understanding, revealed by so many systems of knowing, whether pre-modern, modern or post modern, is that we are asleep and need to wake up. But the fact that we are asleep is not an accident. It is not a cosmic mistake. Rather, it is the intentional nature of the living kosmos that we earn our attainment, as well as its by-products of joy and fulfillment, through the process of waking up. Everyone agrees: we need to wake up. The disagreement in culture, however, is this: In what way are we asleep, and consequently, in what way do we need to wake up? Each stream of culture, including psychology, spirituality, evolutionary theory and more, answers this question differently. Moreover, there are significantly different answers within each of the aforementioned streams. More confusing still, each one focuses on one form of awakening as the key to liberation, fulfillment, or some other great good of humanity, but ignores other forms of awakening.

As Integral philosophy wisely points out, no major stream of knowing is smart enough to be entirely wrong. Each claim in regard to the essential nature of the desired and required human awakening is true, but partial. The problem starts when a partial claim to truth claims to be the whole story. When parts pretend to be wholes, as we shall see, the result is cancer in the body or the body politic. But when we integrate the major streams of insight and view them as complementary, we realize that there are in fact five great awakenings in the journey of a human lifetime. All are necessary. Each form of awakening addresses a different level of reality, that is to say, a different way that humans have of being asleep. Each gives a different gift. Each requires a different process to awaken. Together, they might be seen to be an accurate map of the human journey that we are invited into at birth. Taken together, they might be said to point towards the core intention and purpose of our lives.

Although the numbering system is somewhat different, these awakenings closely approximate the map described in the eight stations that we have just unfolded. When we use different mapping systems, the number of levels or stages or stations nearly always differ, even in the best maps of spirit. Below, I will briefly correlate the two maps. But if you read closely, it becomes clear that they are covering the same ground.

So, what I share with you below is a very brief view of the Five Great Awakenings. It recapitulates, in different form, the journey to awakening we have just outlined. These Awakenings may serve to sharpen the contours of the Eight Stations in your mind and deepen their roots in your heart and spirit.

Each of these levels of awakening creates a deeper and more expanded sense of identity and consciousness. Each level of awakening takes place both within humanity as a whole and within every individual human being. Ontogeny recapitulates phylogeny.

1) Ego Awakening: Pre-personal to Personal Awakened Self.

The first great awakening takes place when the human being emerges from the slumber of immersion in the Great Mother. At the dawn of human existence, a separate sense of self has not yet emerged. Instead, the self was, to varying degrees, identified with nature and the immediate environment, with no sense of an individuation. At this level, there is no sense of larger frameworks of time beyond the immediacy of the present moment or the present day. So, the first level of awakening is to a separate self, or Level One Personal. You experience this awakening in your life in the beginning of your journey, as your baby self awakens to an individuated identity as a separate self-ego. This is the move from the pre-personal to the personal. It might also take place when you free yourself from any pre-personal context, such as a cult or a family system, that subsumes individual emergence.

One expression of this awakening crystallizes in Hebrew mysticism, which affirms the human being as a homo imago dei, a separate dignified self, rooted in the divine, and possessed of infinite dignity, value, and adequacy.

Once you have firmly stabilized your realization of separate self, you need to fully claim your story and your life. You need to clarify the true nature of your story and step out the limiting beliefs and distorted narratives of your false self. I call this the Awakening of Ego.[5] This is a stage of awakening. The ego is not merely a level to move beyond. It is a level to awaken. This is the first expression of a full integral enlightenment. It requires that all the parts of the self, all the voices, all the sub-personalities, be given their place. The protector, wounded child, controller, seeker, competitor and all other parts need to be seen with compassion and recognized for the gifts they give. It is only this recognition, which will allow the parts to let go of their attempt to pathologically hijack the whole. Once each part or voice is given its place and recognized, it more naturally takes its place in the larger whole and releases its destructive and pathological expressions. Shadow in the sense of any disowned parts of your consciousness needs to be surfaced and appropriately integrated. All of this is part of awakening to your separate self. On the Eight Stations map, this awakening takes place as part of Stations One, Two and Three.

2) The Awakening to the Unity Principle:

This is an awakening to the Absolute, the eternal divine principle, which is the ground of being. This takes place when you awaken to the reality that this unified principle, the organizing principle of the kosmos, holds you. If you are a theist, you might see this as the arms of the Great Mother or Great Father holding you. You may awaken to the unity principle and then realize that you are in the arms of the Mother, or held by the Father-God. Or you may waken into the arms of God and then realize that she is the Unity Principle. This awakening begins in Station Two. As you evolve, however, in Stations Three through Eight your personal relation to the ultimate deepens in quality and depth.

3) Awakening from Separate Self to True Self:

This awakening is classically called enlightenment in the great spiritual traditions. It is possible to awaken to the unity principle and still experience yourself as a separate self. You can be in the arms of the Great Mother and still be in separate self. The awakening to True Self is the awakening described in the texts of classical enlightenment, where you realize not only that there is a unity principle, but that the unity principle is one with you. You realize that infinite no-thingness is who you are. This is the recognition: "I am part of the All, not separate form the ground of being. All the love that inheres in All-That-Is flows through me and incarnates in me." This awakening is a realization of the Absolute, the eternal divine principle, which is the ground of being living in you, as you, and through you. At this level, the human being at her core is realized as identical with the spacious ground of All-That-Is, incarnate as the essence of all life. This is the Supreme identity that is the secret teaching of all the great traditions. In the Eight Stations, this takes place at station four.

4) Awakening from True Self to Your Unique Self.

The fourth great awakening is the realization of your Unique Self, when you awaken to your identity as a radically singular expression of the single One. You realize that you are not only the process, but also the personal face of the process; you realize that God is having a You experience. You know that you incarnate a unique emanation of All-That-Is, with unique gifts to give to, the evolutionary process itself. You follow your unique shadow back to your Unique Self when you realize that your shadow is simply your unlived, or distorted, unique Essence. You recognize that awakening as Your Unique Self is the essential joy, obligation, delight, awesome privilege, and responsibility of your life. You commit to express your Unique Gifts. This is the great vow of your life. In the eight stations model, this level corresponded with stations five, six, seven and eight.

5) Evolutionary Unique Self Awakening.

The fifth great awakening is also an awakening to the ground of being. However, this time, the ground of being is understood to be constantly evolving. You awaken to the fact that you are living in an evolutionary context. You realize that the context is alive and conscious. This is an awakening to the divine nature of the evolutionary process. In some sense, it is an awakening of the process itself. The Unique Self awakens to his or her nature as evolution, as a unique expression of the evolutionary impulse. In this awakening, you realize that the evolutionary impulse lives in you, as you, and through you. You understand that your heart is identical with the evolving heart of the kosmos, that the heart of the kosmos beats as you and through you.

This is the level where you become an evolutionary mystic. This happens as you realize your identity with the impersonal creative energy of the divine, which has been called the evolutionary impulse.[6] Once this realization awakens as you, you live with evolutionary integrity, giving your unique gifts. Holding this infinitely wider context makes it easier for you to work with your shadow. Your contraction naturally expands. Evolution becomes conscious of itself and advances through the awakening of your Unique Self.[7] In the eight stations model, this corresponds with Stations Five, Six, Seven, and Eight.

In the best possible scenario, each level of awakening transcends and includes the previous rung of consciousness. The levels of development may happen in a different order than described here, but to freeze at any one level creates shadow—shadows of the personal and impersonal.

A Clarifying Note on the Eight Stations

Finally, it is important to understand that these stations and levels of awakening are not necessarily linear. The path is more mysterious and paradoxical than can be conveyed in simple, neat categories. For example, you might, as I did after my teacher Pinky's death, catch a powerful—if temporary—hit of Unique Self or True Self, even while your center of gravity is still at the station-two ego level. And conversely, you may have experiences of false self even after you have realized some significant level of enlightenment. Your Unique Shadow may attempt to hijack your best intention right after an experience of profound open heart and awakening. The pre-personal may appear to seduce you when you are convinced you are firmly rooted in True Self. Finally, it is important to note that the ego never disappears, even at the highest levels of consciousness. What disappears is the *identification* with the ego. So while these stations usually unfold one after the other, they also zigzag, skip levels, reverse direction, and may take all sorts of unexpected turns.

A Short Recapitulation of Unique Self Doctrine

(For advanced theory students. For the rest of us, skip this section and go directly to the next chapter.)

In conclusion of this chapter I offer a brief recapitulation of the core of Unique Self doctrine. The Unique Self teaching evolves and qualifies the classic enlightenment teaching of many of the mystical traditions. The Unique Self-realization, which began to emerge with my Soul Print teaching (1986), has been a key lodestone in the dharma that I have tried to share in the world. In the last years 2003-2012) an intense and delightful friendship and dharma dialogue with Ken Wilber further evolved and clarified the teaching within the context of Integral Theory. In the last ten years (2002-2012) the Unique Self teaching, has challenged and evolved the way enlightenment has been understood and taught in many, if not most, contemporary Western contexts. Many realized teachers, passionately committed to evolving truth, have encountered the Unique Self teaching, recognized its insight, and audaciously incorporated it into their own dharma.

The enlightened state, in the classic Eastern enlightenment traditions, is your awakening to the one True Self. The total number of true selves in the world is one. True Self is the realization of reality—which exists unconsciously in every state and in every level of consciousness—that there is only one True Self and every being has that True Self as it own essence. Awaking is when your unconscious reality of True Self becomes our conscious identity. You are enlightened when you have the shocking realization that your True Self is the True Self. You then further evolve to realize that the same is true for every other sentient being. You realize at the same time that your True Self is utterly one with everything that is, everything that ever was and everything that ever will be. The sensual knowing of this truth is what is usually referred to as enlightenment.

Enlightenment practices and processes teach you how to open the eye of the spirit and realize the truth that your essence is your True Self. You are aware of your body, your emotions, your thoughts, but you are not exclusively identified or defined by them. You are the consciousness that holds them and in which they arise. You are True Self. The more profound the enlightenment the more clear, powerful and stable the realization of True Self.

What we have added with the Unique Self doctrine is that your awakened True Self is not the same as anyone else's awakened True Self. This is a key truth that many of the great Eastern traditions, which have almost entirely dominated enlightenment teaching in the Western world, simply did not understand. They thought that your True Self and my True Self are simply the same. They understood True Self (or its awakened creative state, which have been called Authentic Self or Evolutionary Self) as fundamentally impersonal. My True Self and yours are therefore essentially interchangeable. Whatever uniqueness you might have is ultimately a function of your ego or your "cultural, social and psychological conditioning".

What Unique Self realizes in its genuinely evolutionary unfolding of True Self, is that every True Self sees from a different perspective. Every True Self sees through a unique perspective. Once you understand that perspectives are foundational there is no way to escape this truth. Perspective is not less than but it is much more than merely your conditioning. Perspective is a property of your essence. While the same True Self exists in every one of us, each of is awakened as True Self from a radically unique perspective. Each one of us has a personal perspective that is irreducible. Unique Self thus insists that enlightenment is ultimately not at all impersonal. Rather, Unique Self reveals the radically personal nature of enlightenment. For the classical enlightenment traditions enlightenment was the realization of the emptiness that is empty of all personal dimensions. I call this the enlightenment of emptiness. The new enlightenment of Unique Self is the realization of the radically personal nature of your True Self, which is your Unique Self. For this reason I have called Unique Self enlightenment the Enlightenment of Fullness.

Your Unique Perspective forms your Unique Self. This is the unique expression not merely of your manifest self but also of your unmanifest self. This is what the Hebrew mystics called Ayin and the Buddhists called sunyatta or emptiness. (This is why we deployed the term Unique Self instead of soul. While some texts refer to soul as I am using Unique Self, see for example, some passages in Gafni, *Soul Prints,* 2001. Other classical mystical texts refer to soul as the spiritual substance of separate self. Soul is thought in this usage to be the unique expression of your manifest self.) Unique Self, however, transcends and includes this understanding of Soul, for unique self is the infinite and irreducible uniqueness of both your manifest and un-manifest self. You un-manifest essence, which was there before the big bang, is unique as it always looks out through a unique set of eyes. Your enlightenment has perspective. Your perspective.

Your perspective is the source of the irreducible dignity of your individuality. Your perspective creates your unique insight. Your unique insight creates the unique gifts of being and becoming that you have to bring to the world. The radical and irreducible uniqueness of your gifts is precisely what creates your Unique Obligation to give those gifts. You have a unique responsibility to give those gifts because they are yours and yours alone. There is no one else in the world that ever was, is or will be that can give those gifts.

The failure to realize Unique Self undermines the recognition of the infinitely special nature of every human being. It is only such a recognition that prohibits you from using another human being as merely a means for your end. To love a human being is therefore to recognize their Unique Self and support its emergence in the world.

Unique Self like True Self always exists. Unique Self only fully grows up into itself after awakening to some level of True Self and after evolving to higher levels of developmental consciousness. After I unfolded the core of the Unique Self teaching I was exposed to a plethora of developmental models, which confirmed that it is at the more evolved levels of consciousness—beginning at about World Centric and progressively deepening—that Unique Self is naturally and spontaneously experienced. At these higher levels of consciousness your True Self-consciousness awakens to its Unique Perspective of the world. So while Unique Self, like True Self, is present all the way up and all the way down in every stage and state of sentience, it comes online spontaneously as the natural property of the higher reaches of developmental consciousness.

Enlightenment then can be properly understood as having two distinct steps. The first step is waking up and the second step is growing up.

The first step is when the human being wakes up to their state of being fully identified with True Self. The realization that True Self—your awakened conscious knowing that the living essence of all that is, lives in you, as you and through you—is step one.

Step two is when True Self grows into the realization of its irreducible uniqueness. In growing up you realize that what you thought was your identity at the level of separate self-consciousness was an illusion. Your ego claimed that all sorts of expressions of self, which are illusory and fleeting, are your core identity. These might include your wealth, social status, physical prowess and the like. When you liberate those illusions of self into the realization of True Self you wake up.

You grow up when you reclaim every part of you, including the unique properties of your separate self, as an expression of your unique perspective. The natural and spontaneous experience of your unique perspective comes on line at the higher levels of developmental consciousness.

Pause for a second to review how we are deploying some of these terms. A state of consciousness, be it a mystical, orgiastic or drunken, is attained through free grace of practice. It is transitory and not stable. In a mystical state you feel in first person the true nature of your expanded identity. A level is not an awakened state but a structure stage of developmental consciousness. The simplest example might be the movement of moral consciousness to expand your circle of love from your self, to your tribe, to the whole world, including all human beings, and then even beyond. These expanding circles of caring, concern and love are often labeled ego-centric, ethnocentric and World Centric. Each is a distinct structure of consciousness that once you realize you virtually never lose.

Unique Self-Realization becomes a natural, spontaneous and stable expression of self at the higher levels of developmental consciousness beginning around the World Centric stage. Beyond the World Centric stage is where states and levels (sometimes called stages) arise together. This level of consciousness has been called Kosmoscentric. At this level one's circle of love includes not only human beings but all sentient beings and not only in the present but also all past and future. In parallel, in Kosmoscentric consciousness at its more evolved stages, you awaken to your real identity as True Self.

At Kosmoscentric consciousness the movement of waking up happens together with growing up as well. Growing up at Kosmoscentric occurs when you make the ultimate shift in perspectives. You move, as it were, from the human to the divine perspective. You become God's perspective. But not in the sense of being absorbed in the undifferentiated source. You do not become indistinguishable oneness or divinity. Rather, you shift to God's perspective through growing up fully into your Unique Self that is grounded in your unique perspective. When your unique perspective wakes up and grows up into itself, a new emergent quality of divinity that never was before comes into being and becoming. God has evolved.

God evolves as and through the awakening of your Unique Self. This particular quality of essence that awakens in you when you fully grow up is your unique perspective that births your Unique Self. This is the radically personal face of both enlightenment and evolution.

When you grow into Kosmoscentric consciousness you become fully aware of the larger evolutionary context of ever emerging source, which seeks to awaken in you as you and through you. Your awakening as

Evolutionary Unique Self is source's evolutionary awakening to itself. Through you and only through you can a unique set of gifts be given to reality, gifts that are not extra or ornamental, but gifts which are desperately needed and passionately desired by all.

Paradoxically Unique Self also implies relationship. Irreducible uniqueness creates the face of the other that yearns to recognize and be recognized. Mutual recognition is realized in the face-to-face relationship. For Unique Self the paradoxical encounter with the second person of God is not dogma, but realization. Sufi master Rumi and Hasidic master Levi Isaac of Berdichev do not "believe" in the personal god. Rather, they know and taste the personal face of essence. Unique Self is paradoxically the unique expression of God in the first-person, what the Upanishads called, Thou Art That, known in Buddhism as I Amness, as well as God in the second-person, the unique face-to-face encounter of other with Source. At the same time Unique Self incarnates God in the third person, the conscious and unique expression of the evolutionary impulse, God having a You experience. Therefore, it would be most correct to say that in Unique Self-realization the three faces of God incarnate in paradoxical unity.

Stations of Self

Evolutionary Emergent of Unique Self
(Level Two — Personal)

- The New (Integral) Enlightenment—Personal and Impersonal
- Personal face of Essence
- Personal face of Impersonal
- Personal Incarnation of the Evolutionary Impulse
- Seamless but not Featureless
- True self + perspective = Unique Self
- Individuation beyond ego
- Being and Becoming
- Aware of living evolutionary context
- Evolution awakens as Your Unique Self
- Catalyst for the Evolution of God
- Give Unique Gift
- Unique Gift not distorted by Ego Fixation
- Second Tier Obligation
- Joy of Unique Obligation
- Obligation = Love
- Respond to Unique Need
- Trace Unique Shadow back to Unique Self
- Boundary, No Boundary

True Self
(Awakening State — Impersonal)

- Classical Enlightenment (Impersonal)
- Seamless Coat of the Universe
- Oneness without perspective
- Beyond illusion of separation
- Being
- One with all arising forms in gross, subtle and casual
- Aware and indivisible from larger context of essence
- Beyond exclusive identification with ego
- No evolution beyond ego
- Transcend and include ego
- No-boundary consciousness
- Impersonal Enlightenment

Personality - Separate Self - Ego / False Self
(Level One — Personal)

distortion / clarification

- False self is the unhealthy version of separate self
- Pre-enlightenment
- Requires false self clarification processes such as shadow integration
- Enneagram Fixation
- Healthy Ego Strength
- Positive Identification with Ego
- Good boundaries

Pre-differentiated Ego
(Pre-personal)

- Stage before ego individuation
- Or after pre-personal regression
- Example: babies and cults

CHAPTER FIVE

THE EVOLUTIONARY INTEGRATION OF EASTERN AND WESTERN ENLIGHTENMENT

The Essential Discernment Between Separateness and Uniqueness

PERHAPS THE GREATEST MISTAKE in the evolution of human spirituality was the failure to properly distinguish between separateness and
uniqueness. This simple statement is the result of many years of meditation on Unique Self and the reading of countless classic and popular texts
that all confused separateness and uniqueness, each in its own way. Once
this realization dawned on me, I could see that one of the great intractable
problems standing in the face of human evolution could be resolved. The
knotted contradiction between the major types of human spirituality are
easily unraveled, opening the door to a higher Integral embrace of enlightenment. This acknowledgment of the difference between separate and
unique in turn allows us to move one vital step closer toward the emergence
of a genuine translineage dharma and world spirituality.

The core contradiction lies between the dominant motifs and moods of Eastern and Western spirituality.

Each suggests a different path—paths that are, to a large extent, mutually exclusive. Both are right and both are wrong. Or to put it another way, each one has a piece of the story, but each thinks its respective piece is actually the whole story. ***When a part pretends to be a whole, pathology of some form is invariably produced.*** Moreover, Eastern and Western spirituality each make a critical mistake based on an essential confusion between separateness and uniqueness.

Each side in this dharma combat, which has spanned the generations, is motivated by pure and holy motives. Each, with its teachings and practices, seeks the highest expression and flowering of human love and goodness. Each, with its teachings and practices, wishes to end suffering. Yet each made the same mistake, in the opposite manner.

The Insight and Mistake of the East

Eastern spirituality by and large rightly sees the separate self as an illusion. The realization of this illusion comes from profound spiritual practices like meditation, which work to open the eye of the spirit. Not only is the separate self exposed as an illusion, it is also the root source of most human suffering. Fear, death, terror, and cruelty in virtually all of its forms can ultimately be traced back to the illusion of the separate self. It is for this most powerful and compelling of reasons that the East devoted an enormous amount of energy to dispelling the illusion of the separate ego self.

In realizing that the separate self is an illusion, the East made a mistake: it confused separateness and uniqueness. The axiomatic assumption in many Eastern teachings—both ancient and modern—is that to transcend the separate self, you must leave behind not only the illusion of separation, but also the apparent experience of uniqueness.

Much effort was directed to demonstrating that what seemed to be unique and particular was in fact common and universal, and what seemed to be personal was actually impersonal. There was great truth in some of this teaching, and it clearly brought immense spiritual depth and some measure of peace to many.

And yet the core teaching did not take root among the masses. The problem was not simply that the masses were lazy, stupid, or in lower states of consciousness, as some teachers told us. The deeper problem was that the masses felt that the teaching violated their basic sense of the necessity, desirability, and dignity of uniqueness. The problem was—and is—that uniqueness will just not go away. The majority of people correctly feel that to surrender their uniqueness would be to surrender their life force, as well as their personal value and dignity. The personal is, by its very nature, *unique.* The dignity and value of the personal derive directly from its uniqueness.

You can have a powerful and authentic experience of your own specialness even after the dissolution of your ego. Many Eastern teachings try valiantly to explain this away by telling you in many different ways that your lingering experience of uniqueness or specialness is merely evidence that you have not yet evolved beyond ego.

But you, and many like you, know in your deepest place that this is simply not true. You experience the reality of your specialness and uniqueness not as an expression of ego, but as a glorious expression of your truest nature. *You understand that the seamless coat of the Uni-verse is indeed seamless, but not featureless. You understand that your uniqueness is the highest expression of God looking out from behind your eyes and taking in your uniquely gorgeous perspective and insight.* You must move beyond your separate self, even as you must embrace and affirm your uniqueness beyond ego. Because the East demands that you throw out your uniqueness as part of dispelling the illusion of the ego or the separate self, you correctly rebel against this dharma. You intuitively affirm the value of the personal. To you, impersonality feels like a violation of the very quality of humanness that you hold most dear.

You feel your uniqueness as a deep truth. So you reject the dharma of the East, and while trying to salvage your uniqueness, you cling to your separate self. Ironically, the failure of virtually all Eastern approaches to spirituality to make this essential distinction between uniqueness and separateness undermines the ability of the discerning heart and mind to receive the great dharma of the East. It is for this reason that the Eastern teachings that have been disseminated throughout the Western world have ultimately failed to break out of a very small and elite audience, and have not had a genuinely transformative impact upon mainstream culture.

Of course the East is half right. The illusion of an isolated ego, the separate self, really is the source of virtually all suffering. The confusion between separateness and uniqueness in Eastern teaching has paradoxically caused the rejection of Eastern teaching in the West. The West has essentially ignored the Eastern call to evolve beyond separate-self ego, and most of humanity has remained stuck with ego and all of its attendant horrors.[1]

The Insight and Mistake of the West

Conventional Western spirituality, like the spirituality of the East, is motivated by love and the desire to end suffering. However, the West came to essentially opposite conclusions about how to achieve this same result. The West saw the affirmation of human individuality as the greatest good of the human spirit. Western spirituality asserted that our rights and relationships are rooted in the dignity of the separate self. It is the separate self that is in relationship not only with others but also with God. Communion with the divine rather than absorption into the One becomes the good of spiritual practice.

It is the great divine gift to affirm human adequacy and dignity through the very encounter between humans and God. For humans to be addressed in this encounter, their distinct otherness as a separate self apart from God must be affirmed and supported. In other words, our relationship with God requires some degree of separation. *Two parties can only meet in love and mutuality if they are separate.* We are both overwhelmed by the presence and at the same time affirmed by the presence as a separate other. In the revelation of the infinite, the finite is held in love, nourished and challenged at the same time. *Our individuality becomes the source of our dignity. Moreover, it is in our individuality that we find our ability to love, to act in compassion, and to take responsibility for our destiny.*

For one who is wholly merged with the infinite, there is no Encounter. If there is no Encounter, then there is no love, no dignity, and no responsibility. If there is no other, then we cease to be a moral agent and a lover. With the total annihilation of the personal comes the end of personal responsibility. If human beings are not separate selves with individual rights and responsibilities, then there is neither good nor evil. It becomes virtually impossible to distinguish between what is below and what is beyond. Good and evil imply relationship. When there is an identity of subjects, when humans and God are one, when we are truly submerged in a condition of *tat tvam asi* ("Thou Art That"), there can be no relationship. Where there is no relationship, there is no love, no good, and no evil.

The miracle of We comes only from the union of I and Thou. What is love without an I and a Thou? Ethics, goodness, and judgment are meaningful only in the realm of the personal. They have no place in a Uni-verse of no-selves.

For all of these very noble reasons, the West insisted on the reality of the separate self. However, Western spirituality made the same great mistake as the East, but in the opposite direction. The West essentially confused separateness and uniqueness. Western teachers wrongly assumed that all the virtues of love and relationship required the dignity of individuality in the form of a separate self. This is simply not true. All the goods and virtues of love, relationship, compassion, responsibility, and all the rest can be had through the Unique Self. There is absolutely no need for the separate self. *The Unique Self, as we have shown, emerges in its full splendor only after the separate self has been trance-ended.* You can experience the full dignity, responsibility, and joy of individuality by recognizing your uniqueness. Uniqueness does not require separateness.

The result of this colossal mistake in Western spirituality has been that your intuitive spiritual desire to evolve beyond exclusive identification with your ego—to transcend your separate self—has been thwarted and even ridiculed by Western spiritual teaching. Your desire to reach for the transpersonal was stymied because it seemed like you needed to reject the personal to get there. The Western deification of the personal blocked the gateways necessary for your enlightenment. Your heart knew this was wrong. You knew you needed to transcend your separate self, but you did not know how to do it without losing the critical moral and relational virtues of the personal. So you remained stuck in the personal, unable to find a path beyond yourself.

For both East and West, drawing a correct distinction between separateness and uniqueness allows for a powerful evolution of their respective teachings. This crucial dharmic distinction allows for a higher and Integral embrace of these seemingly disparate teachings, which split the world of spirit into two warring camps.

The Unique Self is the pivot point for this translineage spiritual break-through, which allows for the evolutionary integration of these two teachings.

For the West, the Unique Self is the source of human dignity, love, obligation, and destiny. At the deepest level, you know that your Unique Self is not your separate self. Your separate self is an illusion, though you remain a unique strand in the seamless coat of the Uni-verse. *Spiritual practice moves you to realize your essential enmeshment with the larger reality, even as you retain the dignity of your distinction.* Uniqueness is the source of this dignity, as well as your sense of intimacy.

For the East, the realization of Unique Self is equally critical. It is precisely the recognition of the Unique Self that allows for the transcendence of the illusion of separate self without the wholesale rejection of individual specialness and uniqueness. You are able to fully embrace the call to evolve beyond separate self and ego, even as you affirm and embrace your Unique Self that emerges from your Buddha nature.

For both the East and the West, higher translineage integration can be achieved. A genuine evolution of spirit can be accomplished. The full glory of meditative realization and classic enlightenment is redeemed and recognized as the first major step. In the second step, the full glory of individual dignity is realized in the post-egoic Unique Self.

Are You Special? The Distinction Between Separateness and Uniqueness

One of the most confusing things to people on a genuine spiritual path is the utter denial of specialness. You have an experience that you are special, but you are told by spiritual teachers and books that if you experience yourself as special, you are still stuck in ego. So you work really hard to get rid of the feeling of being special. But it is always there, lurking in the corner just beneath the surface of your spiritual posturing. This makes you feel like an impostor and fraud. On the one hand, you are having intense spiritual experiences during regular practice and living your compassion in the world. On the other hand, the lurking feeling of specialness makes you feel like your realization is false and fraudulent. "Special" is often used interchangeably with "unique." To think you are special is to think you are unique, which is radically rejected by most spiritual teachers on the contemporary scene.

One well-known spiritual teacher speaks of what she calls the illusion of uniqueness. She says time and again in her teaching of impersonal enlightenment that there is "no such thing as a unique spiritual experience." This is precisely wrong. The deeper the spiritual experience, the more unique it becomes. Your enlightenment always has a perspective. The very essence of enlightenment is the liberation of your unique perspective from the prison of voices not your own.

A second example of this rejection of specialness as being anti-spiritual is *A Course in Miracles*. Below is a citation from one entry entitled "The Pursuit of Specialness":

> *The pursuit of Specialness*
> *Is always at the cost of peace*
> *You are not Special*
> *If you think you are*
> *And would defend your specialness*
> *Against the truth of what you really are*
> *How can you know the truth*
> *Specialness always makes comparisons*
> *It is established by a lack seen in another*
> *The pursuit of Specialness*
> *Must bring you pain*[2]

The conclusion of the section is that specialness is but an illusion that needs to be forgiven, and dispelled through forgiveness.

A Course in Miracles is a significant and profound teaching. And yet in both examples and in the larger teachings that they represent, the same two mistakes are made. First, there is a complete conflation of uniqueness or specialness on the one side, and separateness on the other. They are all taken to refer to the same thing. Now, it is true that the assertion of specialness is one of the favorite tactics through which the consciousness of separate self attempts to ward off the terror of its own inevitable death and dissolution. From this perspective, specialness is indeed an illusion of ego to be overcome in order to gain the peace and joy that come from a realization of your True Nature, the realization that you are not separate or alone but an indivisible and eternal expression of the seamless coat of Uni-verse. However, from a perspective of Unique Self, of course you are special. That is precisely what it means to be a Unique Self. Your utter uniqueness is precisely what makes you special.

The second confusion in the teaching that blithely rejects specialness is the failure to distinguish between different stages on the spiritual path—what are often referred to as levels of consciousness. For example, as we pointed out in Chapter 2, ego and Unique Self represent two distinct levels of consciousness.

When you are operating from the level of ego, your feeling that "I am special" is the ego's delusion. The ego's feeling that "I am special" is based on something unreal. Seduced by the significance of this truth, enlightenment teachers who stress dis-identification with ego will often mistakenly conflate personal-specialness with ego-specialness, and therefore wrongly reject specialness and personal uniqueness altogether.

Eastern-influenced teachers of evolution beyond ego correctly point out that most of the experiences that you feel are special and personal are really, at their core, shockingly impersonal. You think, for example, that all of your sexing is intimate and personal to you, when in fact much of your sexing can be said to result from a vast, impersonal sexual current that courses through you and everyone else on the planet.[3] Or, to take another example, you think that these details of your life are all very special, personal, and fascinating, when in fact they are very common, ordinary, and even banal. Ninety-five percent of your waking thoughts are dedicated to reviewing details of old stories and worrying about how new stories will play out. You get lost in personality, and miss essence. Much of what you thought was personal is actually impersonal.

This move beyond the obsession with the personal helps you to wake up. You evolve from separate self to True Self. You begin to realize that you are in fact not an isolated or separate part, but rather you are part of the whole, of All-That-Is. Once, however, you have had that realization or even a glimmer of that realization, the personal will begin to come back online at a higher level. At this point, your Unique Self, your feeling of specialness, reemerges, but this time in a far more clean, clear, and crystalline form. As my lineage master, Mordechai Lainer of Izbica, taught, when you evolve beyond ego, your uniqueness/specialness does not disappear; it becomes clarified. At the Unique Self, you reconnect to your specialness with the stunning realization: You are special! You are unique!

There are many differences between egoic specialness and Unique Self specialness, which emerges in moments of evolution beyond exclusive identification with ego. But one distinction stands out as a surefire litmus test that will always allow you to distinguish between egoic and Unique Self specialness: specialness at the level of ego is always at someone else's expense. If I am special, that means that others are not. This is the level of ego that *A Course in Miracles* was referring to in saying that specialness exists only by comparison.

However, specialness at the level of Unique Self is of a different order of reality. Unique Self specialness is an authentic realization of overpowering joy. I am special, and so are you. Each of us has a Unique Self. We are not equally talented, wise, sensual, or compassionate. But paradoxically, we are all special, each in our own infinitely unique ways. *In the enlightened identification of your Uniqueness, you realize your specialness, which is a wondrous and gorgeous expression of your very enlightenment.* It is paradoxically this very realization that opens you up to fully perceive and delight in the specialness of others.

Nothing Exists A-Part or A-Lone

Though your surface experience may tell you that you are a separate fortress behind impenetrable walls, the demand for sanity invites you to move from surface to depth, to know the truth of your reality. Depth is the opposite of surface. *The delusion is not that you are an individual, but that you are an isolated individual.*

Consider: In the last twenty-five years, an enormous amount of serious scientific investigation has been done into what is called nonlocal distance healing, the ability of a person at some great distance to effect healing. Verified effects range from protecting red blood cells to impeding the spread of cancer to lowering blood pressure, and much more. These experiments reveal that we are not discrete units but rather interconnected, nondiscrete "unities." Like a network of rivers that interweave along their way back to the sea, we are fully woven into each other. We are therefore naturally able to traverse all the frontiers of separateness—including even space and time.

Consider: Physics has for years been speaking about a nonlocal Uni-verse. One of the leaders in this work was Irish physicist John Stewart Bell. Bell showed that if distant objects have once been in contact, a change in one causes an immediate change in the other. It is irrelevant how far apart they are. Even if they're separated to the opposite ends of the Uni-verse, the connection is not broken. Enlightenment teachers have forever told us that there is a deeper level of consciousness available when we allow ourselves to let go of our separateness, even as we delight in the uniqueness so necessary for both creativity and responsibility.

Consider: Quantum physicists have described a world of subatomic particles within which everything exists as a kind of energy soup. Brain science has shown us that our experience of separation is actually a function of the left brain and the neurological system. The right brain perceives an original wholeness, which the left brain then splits into parts. The brain creates a "me" by creating separate "pictures" of reality, when in fact there are only densities of energy.

These are but three of the millions of hints toward wholeness that the objective Uni-verse winks at us in every moment.

There is autonomy—the free choice you have at key moments in your life. There is Uniqueness—the experience of your Unique Self. There is independence—from the delusion that tells you that you live a-part from the wholeness of the Uni-verse.

But there is no separate self.

We are, in the words of kabbalist Luria, "cut from the same cloth and hewn from the same quarry, even as we each have an utterly unique soul expression and soul destiny."

The great Buddhist way of describing this is the story of the water and the wave:

> Two waves flowed toward shore. The larger wave was extremely depressed, while the small wave peacefully moved along.
>
> "If you could see what I see from up here," said the large wave to the small wave, "you would not be so happy."

"What do you see?" asked the small wave.

"In not too long, we will crash into the shore, and that will be the end of us."

"Oh, that," said the small wave. "That's OK."

"What, are you crazy!?"

"I know a little secret that tells me that it's OK," said the small wave. "Would you like me to share it with you?"

Our large-wave friend was both curious and suspicious: "Will I have to pay a lot of money to learn it?" he asked.

"No, not at all."

"Will I have to do *zazen* for thirty years in the lotus position?"

"No, not at all," said the small wave. "Really, the whole thing is only eight words."

"Eight words!!! Then, tell me already!"

The small wave said, ever so gently, "You are not a wave. You are water."

To which the Unique Self mystics add, "And you are also a Unique, beloved, and irreplaceable wave."

The Evolution of Buddhism and Christianity: Unique Self, Sex, and Suffering

There are those who teach that the goal of enlightenment is to move beyond this world. The possibility that divinity could fully incarnate in the world of form is thought to be either impossible or limited to a few idealized figures. In the Buddhist version of this teaching, the ultimate goal is to find the infinite spaciousness, the formless, unmanifest void. In the Christian form of this teaching, our sight is set on *Civitas Dei,* the city of God, which can be arrived at only by leaving the city of man behind.

But if we look a little more closely, we see that these goals are not really possible, tenable, or even desirable. These weaknesses, which appear in both the Buddhist and Christian versions of this teaching, are rectified and evolved by the teachings of Unique Self, which are already implicit but not yet clarified in their classical texts.

Christianity, under the influence of incomplete readings of Plato, sought to escape the world, this sticky place of sin and suffering. Sexuality is the symbol of the dangers of this world-incarnation. It may be expressed, but only if absolutely necessary. So teaches Paul in the Corinthians. Paul writes, "If they cannot contain let them marry, for it is better to marry than to burn."[4] To burn in hell or to burn with the fullness of human desire—these were considered by most Christian commentaries to be pretty much the same thing. Jesus Christ is immaculately conceived in the Virgin Birth, so that divinity is not sullied by sexuality. Certainly, then, the priest could not be allowed to tarnish divinity with sexuality. So the priests in the early church were required to be celibate, liberated from the stain of sex. In this early Christian teaching, humans lack the adequacy, dignity, and power to redeem themselves. Human suffering was redeemed only in the appearance of the immaculately conceived God-human Jesus Christ, a one-time event. In early Christianity, there was only one Unique Self, and that was Jesus Christ.

In the evolution of Christianity, the realization gradually emerges that, while suffering can indeed be redeemed in Jesus Christ, the historical or mythological Christ is not the only source of redemption available to us. In fact, the story of Christ is the story of *you*—you become the Christ when you realize your Unique Self. There is Marc the Christ, and Tami the Christ, Mariana the Christ, and you the reader—Your Name the Christ and Your Child's Name the Christ.

> Reb Zushya of Onipol, mystical master, was found crying on his deathbed.
>
> "Why are you crying?" his students asked. "You who were so pious—what do you have to regret or fear?"
>
> Reb Zushya of Anipol responded, "If they ask me at the bar of judgment why I was not a teacher like Moses, I will have an answer. If they ask me why I was not devout like Elijah, I will have an answer. But if they ask me why I was not Zushya, to this I will have no answer."

This is the great teaching of Unique Self. There is only one . . . and you are it. There is only one Zushya, and he was it. Your Unique Self is desperately needed and passionately desired. You need and desire it; the world needs and desires it; God needs and desires it. This is the holy trinity of Unique Self.

Some level of pain continues to exist in this world of form. And it will remain while humankind continues to evolve. In that evolution, we will begin to devote our capacity and consciousness to healing the world of pain with every breath. However, suffering, the experience of meaningless and unnecessary pain, is immediately redeemed and healed through the realization of your Unique Self.

How does your Unique Christ Self redeem suffering? *When the **who** of suffering becomes clear, then you can bear almost any* **how.** *When you realize that the particular pain you feel is an intrinsic part of your passion and presence, part of your path and purpose, then it becomes somehow livable—even joyous.* The pains and the joys of existence are felt to an almost unbearable degree, but you do not become lost in them. You find pain and joy *within you*, rather than finding yourself *in pain* or *in joy*. This is the incarnation of Jesus Christ that is to be realized in every person.

One wonderful young Christian theologian, Rollie Stanich, with whom I have shared the Unique Self teaching, wrote to me of his vision of an evolved Christianity, in which Jesus was an incarnation of the Unique Self principle that waits to be realized in every person: Rollie wrote of Isaiah who speaks movingly of God's immanence and presence as us, expressed in our Unique Self: "I will never forget you, my people; I have carved you on the palm of my hand." Through the perspective of Jesus the Unique Self, Christ was given sight. With the nails of the crucifixion, our names too— our Unique Selves—are carved on the palms of the hands of Christ.

And when Christ beheld his mother, and the disciples whom he loved— who represent all those who seek Christ—from the cross, looking upon them with limitless love, it truly could be said that he had his Father's eyes. Unique Self is to be, as Rollie wrote, "something beautiful for God." In an implicit Unique Self statement that takes a moment (if not a lifetime) to reconcile, Meister Eckhart says: "The eye through which I see God is the same eye through which God sees me; my eye and God's eye are one eye, one seeing, one knowing, one love." To have the gift of being is to hold a unique perspective; to have the gift of human being is to hold a unique human perspective—through the same eye, the same seeing, we are invited to behold and to be God.

Jesus, we are told, gave sight to the blind. But in a miracle of equal magnitude is that, *Jesus gave sight to Christ.* In the emergent language of Unique Self thought, Jesus is True Self plus perspective. "Jesus lets God see through his eyes. God's perspective was enriched immensely, immeasurably, through the eyes of Jesus; never was humanity seen—and thus loved—as from the cross," wrote Rollie. "This is how Unique Self inspires me to unpack my own Christian teaching. In Christian celebrations of the Eucharist, the minister holds up the consecrated bread and repeats the words of Jesus at the Last Supper: 'This is my body, which will be given up for you. Do this in memory of me.' To give one's body and one's very self is the most intimate of gifts—'There is no greater love.' To take the priceless gift of our human perspective, and then to offer our perspective to the divine, that the divine might see the world through our eyes, touch the world with our hands, and love the world with our hearts, is to do, as Mother Teresa so said, 'something beautiful for God.'"[5]

Unique Face and Original Face

Theravada Buddhism, often called the first "great turning of the wheel," launched a fierce attack on the separate self, calling it the source of all suffering. Any expression of Uniqueness was seen as clinging to the separate self. The goal was the realization of No-Self. The Theravada teaching of No-Self is the dominant teaching in most enlightenment schools and teachings on the contemporary spiritual scene in the West.

The only problem with this is that it is not true, and hopelessly confusing to the genuine seeker. This was pointed out by no less a figure than the great Buddhist sage Nagarjuna.

Nagarjuna was the great founding teacher of Mahayana Buddhism, "the second great turning of the wheel," who took it upon himself to thoroughly expose the great fallacy in the earlier Theravada teaching.[6] As the classic Mahayana text, the *Heart Sutra*, says, "Emptiness is form, and form is emptiness." Emptiness, the ground of all Being, animates all form, and form is but a unique manifestation of emptiness. All human beings are part of this Ground of Being, and can feel their actual participation in this ground through the right practice of meditation. This infinite, open, pure emptiness—called the Original Face, unmanifest spirit, Godhead, I AMness, nirvana, *ein sof, ayin,* or *sunyatta*—by whatever name, is beyond any particular idiom or expression. It is pure Being. When the world gets too crazy, you can "take refuge in the Buddha," surrendering to the pure emptiness of the formless.

In the words of the famous Zen koan, "What was your Original Face before your parents were born?" It is to this Original Face that the Hebrew wisdom tradition points when it mandates the spiritual practice of *bittul hayesh*, nullifying your illusory identification with the world of manifestation and identifying yourself with the mystery of pure Being.

What the New Enlightenment adds, based only in part on Nagarjuna, is that the pure spacious formless never exists in our consciousness outside of the framework of form. ***There is no Original Face without a Unique Face.*** There is no consciousness, no perception, and no awareness without form—and form is always Unique. In a very real sense, form is not composed of atoms or molecules or "stuff" of any kind—it is composed of perspectives.[7] Form in its highest expression becomes conscious and therefore responsible for its unique perspective. We may both be looking at a vase, but we will each maintain a perspective on the vase that is utterly unique. Every person is a Unique Self, which means that every person has an absolutely Unique Perspective on reality.

Your Unique Letter and *The Truman Show*

For instance, in the mythic teaching of ancient Hebrew mysticism, the calligraphy of your Unique Letter in the kosmic scroll is determined by the particular angle at which you were situated in relationship to the revelation at Mount Sinai.[8] Sinai, in the great Hebrew myth, is the portal through which the Infinite discloses itself in love through the medium of a sacred text. Based on one's distinct angle in relationship to the mountain—one's Unique Perspective—perceptions of the revelation vary. Your perspective forms the Unique Calligraphy of your letter in the Torah, the kosmic scroll. This is an ancient version of the New Integral Enlightenment teaching of true self and perspective—Unique Self.

There is a wonderful movie called *The Truman Show* in which the main character, Truman, thinks he is living an ordinary life, but in reality he and all the people in his life are actors in a globally televised show. The subtext of the film plays with the themes of enlightenment, the shocking process of waking up to the True Nature of your reality.

The movie almost got it. However, it suffered from the same mistake as early Christianity. There was only one Truman in the film, just as there is only one Christ in early Christianity. When we are truly awake, we realize that the world is really something like six billion interlocking *Truman Shows*. Each of us is the absolute unique star of our own *Truman Show*—but at the same time, we are all co-stars, supporting actors, minor characters, and extras in one another's shows. Your *Truman Show* is nothing less than your own globally broadcast and kosmically significant unique life story.

A few years ago, I saw a wonderfully long, obscure film by Claude Lelouch.[9] Though never explicitly mentioned, it was very much a film about falling in love. As the film followed three generations in just three hours, we were not quite sure where we were being led. All of those strange and random scenes, however, built to the very last moment of the story, when a young man and woman meet "by accident" on a plane. We realize that what appears to be a chance encounter has in fact been planned by the Uni-verse for three generations. A seemingly meaningless story has suddenly flourished forth with stunning significance. Everyone in the movie was present—from one perspective—in order to create the conditions necessary for the dramatic moment of their chance encounter.

The significance and intentionality invested by the Uni-verse in your Unique Story is life affirming beyond imagination.

CHAPTER SIX

EGO AND UNIQUE SELF

ONE OF THE MOST IMPORTANT DISTINCTIONS that we have pointed out is the difference between ego and Unique Self. As I've stated, they represent two very different levels of consciousness. At the level of ego, you must let go of the illusion of specialness. At the level of Unique Self, you must embrace the infinite gorgeousness of your specialness, and the obligation that it creates for you to give your deepest Unique Gift in the world. Unique Self, which is your Unique Perspective, creates your Unique Gifts, which in turn creates your Unique Obligation to offer your gift.

This entire linked set of unfolding realizations is predicated on the discernment between Unique Self and ego. This discernment is essential to prevent ego from hijacking Unique Self. So what we need to do at this point is deepen our grasp of that discernment, which is all-important for the realization of your Unique Self enlightenment.

Twenty-Five Distinctions between Ego and Unique Self

To live a successful life of realization, power, and genuine attainment, you must be able to discern between expressions of your separate self or ego and your Unique Self. In the following section I will draw a number of distinctions between Unique Self (station five) and ego, which I refer to in the eight stations as separate self (station two). The purpose of these distinctions is to serve as pointing-out instructions that will help you make the discernment between ego and Unique Self in your own first-person experience. The ego and Unique Self dualities that I offer below are—like all dualities—not ultimate.

Reality is nondual and far more fluid and complex than this set of dualities. Nevertheless, to develop into your enlightenment, you must begin with essential discernments between these different qualities of ego and Unique Self. The ability to spontaneously access these discernments is an essential step toward your Unique Self enlightenment.

1) Special or Not Special

Your ego thinks that you are special because you are better or worse than other people. Your Unique Self knows you are special because you are yourself. For the ego, "special" means "better than." For your Unique Self, "special" or "different" means distinct and free from any comparison or point of reference. Your specialness is your spontaneous experience of your essence.

2) Action or Reaction

Ego reacts. Unique Self acts. Your ego is constantly in reaction to outside stimuli. It never thinks a spontaneous thought. It rarely acts because it is moved to do so by a freely arising thought or desire.

Unique Self is moved to action by the power and joy of its own authentic original impulse.

3) Imitation or Originality

Ego imitates. Unique Self is original. Your ego is trapped in imitation. For the ego is, by its very definition, in limitation. Limitation leads to imitation. So the ego is always living the life of limitation based on imitation, which leads to mindless competition. Your ego is in constant competition, which leads to compulsive comparison and dissatisfaction. Originality, which is a quality of Unique Self, freed from the tyranny of comparison, is by its nature both urgently creative and self-satisfied.

Your ego never thinks an original thought. Originality emerges from your Unique Face, which is evoked by contact with your Original Face. "Original Face" is the Buddhist way of describing the experience of sustained contact with the eternal, transcendent Ground of Being. Originality gives birth to action beyond reaction. Your Unique Becoming emerges from your immersion in Being.

4) Satisfaction or Greed

Your separate self is driven by greed. Greed is not the want of anything specific. Rather, it is insatiable want that creates perpetual anxiety. Insatiable want is a structure of the egoic mind, which seeks more and more identity enhancers to confirm its existence. Satisfaction and ego are opposites.

Give the ego everything, and it will not be satisfied. Give the Unique Self anything, and it will be grateful and satisfied. Satisfied, not resigned. Satisfaction emerges from the fullness of whatever the moment brings.

Satisfaction comes from contact with Being and from doing your radical, intense best in the world of Becoming without attachment to outcome. ***Being is all one, so any moment of Authentic Being gives infinite satisfaction.*** Becoming is an expression of the evolutionary impulse and not merely of the egoic drive to achieve. So for Unique Self, your very best is always good enough. For your ego, your very best is never good enough. This is why the ego is the source of all your suffering. It always wants more to fill its greed.

Greed, however, is not a root evil. At its core, greed is your ego's distortion of a quality of essence, the quality of pure infinite desire. Infinite desire is the natural expression of the endless creativity of essence. It is this quality that creates constant yearning, especially the yearning to grow, to create. This yearning, however, lives in paradoxical harmony with satisfaction.

5) Enough or More

Your ego thinks that there is never enough to go around. It always needs more to feel like it exists at all. Your Unique Self knows that it is enough. Your Unique Self knows that there is enough to go around. ***Your Unique Self strives for more, not to fill the emptiness but as an expression of the fullness of its being—bursting forth as the evolutionary impulse of the kosmos.***

6) Ego Story or Unique Self Story

Enlightenment requires your ability to discern between your ego story and your Unique Self story. Your separate-self egoic personality has needs. It wants to make itself feel secure. So your ego tells you a story about yourself that makes you feel safe, valuable, and worthy. The inability to feel safe, valuable, and worthy is a devastating experience for the ego, one it will ward off at virtually all costs. So the ego hijacks everything that happens to you, and everything that you do, into a story about its own goodness, value, and worth. The ego has a simple if ingenious mechanism for doing this. It disguises its ambition, its drive for power, or its insecure grasping, and converts them into narrative material that supports its own positive self-image. This is how the separate-self ego story develops. It is this story that teachers of True Self correctly tell you to leave behind when they say, "To be enlightened you must let go of your story."

One of the places in which you can see with naked clarity the mechanisms deployed by the ego to disguise its primal needs and present them as a "good story" is your dream life. To move beyond the ego's story, you must be able to look at the story from the outside. You must wake up and identify the true root cause of your experience in the dream that has been disguised by the ego as *story*. One simple example, which highlights the hidden dynamics of the ego's deceptive narrative, occurs when you awaken from a dream and you realize that its elaborate story, which climaxes in you urinating, is really the ego's story. The literary ego weaves a narrative tapestry when really what is happening is that you just need to urinate. That is a great relief and a great realization.

This is an essential part of the process of enlightenment or awakening. What you are essentially doing is dis-identifying with your story or perspective, and then taking a perspective on your perspective.[1] You are letting your story become an object, so that you can see it and understand the root motivations and dynamics that are really at play in your story. When that happens, there is space for your more authentic story to arise, which reflects not the grasping of the separate-self ego but the utterly resplendent uniqueness of your Unique Self. This is your Unique Self story.

7) Joy or Fear

The Unique Self is in joy. Joy is the natural by-product of living your Unique Self story. The ego is rarely happy and often plagued by an underlying feeling of fear, deadness, or depression. The happiness that the ego does experience is of a heavier and less richly textured quality than the joy of the Unique Self. The joy of the Unique Self is lighter and freer, often verging on the ecstatic.

8) Open Heart or Closed Heart

When the ego's heart breaks, then the heart closes and contracts. *When the Unique Self's heart breaks, the heart opens through the pain into greater love.* For your ego, the interior face of the kosmos is at best a concept. For Unique Self, the interior face of the kosmos is the infinity of intimacy.

9) Eros or Grasping

The ego is not erotic. Unique Self lives in Eros. To live in Eros means to live with fullness of presence and with a felt sense of wholeness. It is to yearn urgently and ecstatically, without grasping and to experience interiority, the feeling of being on the inside. This is the experience of Unique Self. The ego lives with the feeling of always being on the outside. It fragments, grasps, and never shows up fully present to other. Unique Self lives in Eros.

10) Authentic Freedom or Pseudofreedom

Your ego is a slave that wants to be free. Freedom is the quality that we call autonomy. Your ego, however, understands and experiences freedom/autonomy as freedom from external influence. Only then does ego feel free to do what it wants. *Unique Self is free. Unique Self understands and experiences freedom as the freedom to live your Uniqueness and give your deepest gifts in the world.*

When you feel yourself demanding your egoic freedom, stop for a moment and feel into it. Do not cover over the emptiness that lies at the root of your desire for freedom and autonomy. Feel into the emptiness. Feel into the hole.[1]

For example: Perhaps you are in a relationship that you want to leave. You are chafing to get out of the relationship. But as you contemplate this, stay in the discomfort that you can palpably feel—which lies at the root of this desire. For now, do not give the feeling words. Instead feel the quality of the vacuity and emptiness that arouses the desire.

If you stay in it long enough, the emptiness will begin to fill up with being and presence, with your Unique Being and Presence.

What happened?

You have discovered that the root of your desire to be free from another was your disconnection from your own personal essence, your Unique Self. When your Unique Self filled the hole, the desperate desire you felt to leave the group—or the marriage or the job—faded away. That does not mean that you should necessarily stay in the marriage or the job. It does however mean that you will make the decision from a grounded place of full presence as your Unique Self, and are therefore far more likely to make the right decision.

11) King or Servant

Ego is the servant pretending to be a king. You are avoiding stepping into your Unique Self for fear of being a king. Your ego thinks it is God but does not really believe it, so your ego insanely tries to make itself the God it knows it is not. *Your Unique Self knows it is God, so it acts in the world with majesty, audacity, and grace.*

12) Victim or Player

In your ego, you cling to every petty detail of your story. You never let go of any of your wounds. Your mantra is "I hurt, therefore I am." Therefore, your ego can never wholeheartedly forgive. If it does, the ego's forgiveness is a tactic, not a sacrament. Your Unique Self forgives freely without giving up your own truth.

From the evolutionary context of your Unique Self, you realize that you have a Unique Gift to give to All-That-Is. You are animated, driven, and drawn by that larger vision and obligation. This allows you to place your wounds in a larger perspective. *Your Unique Self is not a victim. It is an audacious player in the Great Story of the evolution of consciousness.* This larger perspective allows you to begin to let go of the story of your wounds. As it is replaced by the greater story of your Unique Self, delight and obligation begin to emerge.

From the place of your Unique Self, you are able to intuitively balance your outrage at injustice with an intuition about when to give up being right and move on. Because you are able to give up being right without giving up your core identity, it becomes infinitely easier to forgive.

13) Betrayal or Loyalty

The ego betrays. The Unique Self is loyal. When you are in your ego, and things go bad, you are willing—in your fear—to betray virtually anyone. Your ego is easily identifiable by the shallowness of its integrity. If you live in Unique Self and things go bad, you find your way, through thick or thin, to a deeper center of spirit.

14) Authentic Friendship or Pseudofriendship

When you are in ego, you might help friends who are successful and even friends who are down, as long as it does not threaten your position. But you are not capable of truly delighting in your deepest heart in a friend's large success. *When you are in Unique Self, your deepest heart delights in your friend's success, even if there is nothing in it for you at all.*

15) Bigger or Smaller

When you are in ego, people feel smaller when you walk into the room. They feel invisible before you. The result is that they feel depleted and in danger. *When you are in your Unique Self, people feel bigger when you walk into the room.* They feel seen by you. They feel your desire to love and give to them.

16) Yes or No

Your ego is always contracting and saying, "No." Even when your ego says, "Yes," it is only because it is afraid to say, "No." *Your Unique Self is always expanding and saying, "Yes."* Even when you say, "No," it is only to make room for a more authentic "Yes."

17) Justice or Injustice

The ego is angry at what is done to it. It very rarely feels the same outrage at what is done to someone else. The Unique Self is not merely outraged against injustice done to its own person; it is hurt and outraged by any and all injustice. The ego often fights large causes of injustice as a way to bolster its grandiosity. *Unique Self fights the battles of injustice in its own backyard, even when there is potential collateral damage to its own power and status.*

18) Responsibility or Excuse

The ego very rarely takes substantive responsibility. When the ego attempts to take responsibility, it creates a painful, virtually unbearable contraction in the self. So the ego becomes the master of the excuse. *The Unique Self is able to take responsibility spontaneously, lightly, and with full gravitas.* The Unique Self holds with equal measure of gravitas and ease its own responsibility and its rightful anger at injustice. Usually, the ego advises the other person to "take responsibility," while the ego itself wallows in the real and imagined offenses that it has suffered.

19) Paradox or Splitting

The ego is always splitting. It always sees dualities, and it cannot hold paradox or complexity. For the ego, others are either enemies or friends. Actions are either good or bad. The separate-self ego has a very hard time stably holding perspectives other than its own for extended periods of time. The Unique Self can naturally hold paradox. Contact with the transcendent within the large field of divine reality allows for the holding of opposites. *Sacred outrage and equanimity live in paradoxical harmony within the Unique Self.*

20) Past or Present

The ego lives in the past, thinking it is the present. Therefore, the ego unconsciously confuses past with present. The ego is unable to create intimacy, which means meeting each other in the fullness of the present moment. To make real contact, you must be personal and present. Only the Unique Self can make contact. *For the Unique Self, the present moment consciously includes the past and anticipates the future.*

The ego confuses the past and the present. When you are confused—thinking you are present in the present while you are actually lost in a past trance—you are unable to act effectively, lovingly, or powerfully in the situation that you are in. And the past remains always unhealed. Several years ago a friend and board member of my organization called me, angry at not being included in a particular email loop. Her anger was full of intensity and flaming aggression, which was vastly disproportionate to the ostensible exclusion from the email loop. I considered asking her to resign from the board, as this was not the first time such an overreaction had occurred. Of course, what was coming up was not her present exclusion, but a very old sense of being excluded. She held this sense of being left out from her early childhood as a girl with four brothers who were better loved by their father. This inability to discern the past from the present has made her unable to effectively navigate her professional or personal world, because she is always prone to dramatic overreactions that undermine many key relationships. The Unique Self does not confuse the past with the present. When the past comes up in the present, the Unique Self recognizes it for what it is: the past coming up in the present.

The Unique Self then uses the present moment to heal the past. The Unique Self recognizes that the patterns of the past have no true foothold or power in the present.

21) Special Relationship or Open as Love

Your ego always seeks the "special relationship"—in the egoic sense—to cover the pain of your emptiness, and thinks the "special relationship" is better than all the rest of your relationships. The Unique Self does not limit love to one person, even though the traditional definition of marriage or a committed relationship can limit you to one partner at a time. *The Unique Self lives open as love in the world.*

22) Love or Fear

The isolated ego is the root cause of murder, war, and virtually all human suffering. The ego feels its own fragility, its limits, and its ultimate powerlessness. As a result, the ego grasps for ways to assert power and experience aliveness. This causes the acting out of all forms of shadow. When you deconstruct your mistaken identity with the separate-self ego, and instead identify with your distinct path in the seamless quilt of the Uni-verse, the fear dissipates and the love returns. When the contraction of ego uncoils, your Unique Self experiences all of the good—personal love, responsibility, compassion, ethical action, activism, and all the rest—that you previously thought was accessible only through your assertion of a separate self.

The choice between personal love and immersion in True Self is a false choice. There is no contradiction between them whatsoever: The West—motivated by love and the desire to end suffering—affirmed the separate self because it thought this was the only way a person could gain the goods of the encounter, namely personal love, responsibility, contact, intimacy, accountability, compassion, and care. This was a mistake; all of those goods may be realized through the encounter between two Unique Selves who are not separate from each other, but consciously part of the same seamless coat of the Uni-verse. ***Personal love does not require two separate selves.***

23) Eternity or Death

The ego strives for immortality it can never achieve, and therefore displaces its grasping for eternity onto projects of control and conquest. The Unique Self experiences authentically what the ego longs for mistakenly—namely the recognition that it is divine and therefore eternal.

This distinction is essential and therefore deserves a brief clarification. The separate self emerges at a certain stage of human history and at a certain stage in the development of the individual human being.[2] As the sense of separate self solidifies, so too does the terror of death. The person feels correctly that death is wrong, that they should not have to die. They feel that they are eternal and should live forever. They are right. The core intuition of immortality could not be more correct. But locked as they are in separate-self ego awareness, they mis-apply that core intuition in two ways.[3]

First, because they are utterly identified with the ego, they apply their intuition of immortality to the egoic separate self. They think that the ego will live forever. Second, because they are identified with the now-eternalized ego, and yet at the same time are gripped by the fear of death, which is oblivion to the ego, they seek all sorts of Viagra-like identity enhancers. They make the finite goods of the world into infinite goods. Money, surplus goods, power, accumulated pleasures—all become identity enhancers for the ego. Their purpose is to give the ego a felt sense of its immortality. But since the ego is not immortal, all of these death-denying immortality projects are doomed to failure.

Even though the ego does make these two essential mistakes, the ego's intuitions are not wrong. When the mistakes are corrected at the level of Unique Self, the truth behind those intuitions can emerge. After you disidentify with your separate self, your Unique Self appears as a distinct and indivisible part of the eternal one. It is in your Unique Self that you realize your immortality. The Unique Self expresses correctly the mistakenly applied, but inwardly correct, intuition of the ego.

24) Pleasure: Delusion or Divine

Money, power, and pleasure, when experienced at the level of ego, appear separate from the divine field and trap you in the clutches of grasping and striving. When experienced from the level of enlightened consciousness, money, power, and pleasure are expressions of your Unique Self touching the divine. Pleasure from the place of Unique Self is experienced as a divine caress reminding you that the world is sane and good. Ego pleasures feel narcissistic, and solidify the coiled contraction into small self. They never satisfy; you are constantly driven to get more and more, and someone else's pleasure makes you feel your own lack. *The same pleasure experienced from the consciousness of Unique Self expands your heart and consciousness into the love-intelligence, love-beauty, and love-pleasure of All-That-Is. You are satisfied by even the simplest pleasure, and you delight in the pleasure of others.*

Similarly, power and money grasped by the ego seek to support the false belief of the separate self that it will live forever. Power and money are used to accumulate goods you do not need, and to acquire superficial control over others in order to assure yourself that you are valuable and worthy. Money and power experienced from the consciousness of Unique Self are gracefully and skillfully deployed with delight for the greater good of all beings.

Separate from the divine field, money, pleasure, and power appear as foolish and even grotesque identity enhancers for the ego. This becomes radically apparent whenever we encounter death. The ego is confused. It fails to discern between separateness and uniqueness, and so the goods of existence are hijacked to serve its own impossible goal of survival—separate from the larger field of love-beauty-pleasure-intelligence from which it was never separate and never can be separated.

Correct intuitions that are hijacked and misapplied by the ego are contextualized and reclaimed at the level of Unique Self. These include eternity and the finite goods of the world, the goodness of pleasure, the divine aspect of power, and more. All of these are reclaimed without grasping at the level of Unique Self.

25) Ego Story or Unique Self Story Reloaded

Your egoic story can be taken away by the circumstances of life. Your Unique Self story can never be taken away from you.

Ego can be taken away from you. Unique Self can never be taken away from you.

This realization was driven home to me years ago in a pivotal moment. It was a sweltering Thursday morning in Salt Lake City. Three weeks earlier, my life had come to a careering crash. This was caused by a combination of circumstances that included my personal misjudgments or mistakes, and other people's misjudgments or mistakes. It was all driven by behind-the-scenes, masculine shadow, expressed in a strange combination of malice, ignorance, cowardice, and corrupt political maneuverings. False complaints had been made about me, directly encouraged by interested parties; and adversaries, playing on the hysteria and fear that envelop these kinds of events, had made sure—at least for a time—that there would be no forum set up to allow for any kind of due process, or even to hear and check both sides of the issue. Close colleagues and others in my circle, to whom I had given my heart and life energy consistently over many years, had turned away from me. Most were driven by fear, confusion, ignorance, weakness, and self-projection, with a very few of the hidden players motivated by the darker drives of power, jealousy, and legacy. As far as I knew at the time, I might never teach, write, or even see my friends again.

I was not at all sure that my body would survive the trauma. The brokenheartedness I felt was so fresh that I could barely function. The phrase "broken heart" is no mere metaphor. I felt the brokenness jutting out of my chest, feeling that at any moment I would explode into death from the raw pain of it all. Love and loyalty, the deep, abiding commitment to the best and most beautiful in another through whatever life throws at you, is what I stake my life on every day. The experience of love's betrayal was so intense for me that it literally took my breath away. My vocation as a teacher and fierce lover who tried to receive and honor the Unique Self of everyone who came his way seemed dead, trampled in the mud of false complaints and malice-driven rumors. I felt there was no way back to my path.

That morning, I was scheduled to meet with a law firm in downtown Salt Lake City that would help me determine my actions in response to the false complaints. I was staying with a friend some distance from downtown, and I had no car or any sense of direction in the city. I thought I would take a bus from the mountains to downtown.

Having cried most of the night, I pulled myself together and left the house around nine in the morning for my meeting at ten. But when I got to the bus station, it turned out that the next bus wouldn't come for two hours. I had no cell phone, not much cash, and no American credit card. As I stood there, feeling totally lost, realizing that I wasn't going to make it to the meeting, I said to my heart, "My unique calling has been to receive people in the fullness of their beauty and to reflect back to them in radical love their goodness and greatness. How can I do that now?"

At that moment, a car slowed down by the bus stop, and the driver motioned for me to get in. I was confused. Why is this car stopping, and who is this woman motioning for me to get in? As I approached the car, a slightly plump fiftyish woman, with very lovely yet ordinary features and thick graying hair, leaned out and said to me, "I woke up this morning knowing that I had to leave for work early. I knew there was something I had to do, but I did not know what. Now I know. I need to take you wherever you need to go. Don't worry—I have plenty of time. Hop in."

I was more than amazed at this small act of kindness from a random stranger. I rejected the dark thought that perhaps she was a serial murderer, thanked her, and stepped into her car. We began driving toward downtown, quite a distance from where she had picked me up. I asked her name, which she reluctantly gave me, and then, my heart's curiosity naturally aroused, I started to ask her about herself. Slowly, bit by bit, she began to tell me her story. Before I knew it, we were both lost inside the lining of her story. What a story it was! About a husband who had left her and having to raise three kids by herself. About her private but epic, tragic struggles with her boys. It was a story of love and betrayal, a story of love won and love lost, of a profound kind of pain and courage. It was a story that would have opened the most contracted heart. For the rest of the car ride, I forgot about my own pain, and lived and breathed inside her Unique Self story.

About forty-five minutes later, we arrived at the law offices. As she pulled over to the curb, still finishing her story, we were lost and found together on the inside. My heart was blown wide open by her goodness, her depth, and her heroic beauty in the face of so much suffering. My heart told me at this moment that there was only one real set of questions I needed to answer every day of my life: "Are you in love? Are you in love with the unspeakable beauty that lives in every person? Can you receive that beauty and give it back to every person you meet?!"

As she pulled to the curb, she was crying profusely. I had a tear rolling down my cheek, and I was not even sure why. She was a Mormon woman raised on the tradition of the tabernacle, high priest, and temple, and her next words came out of the context of her tradition. She looked at me and said softly, "Who are you? Are you the high priest in the temple? No one has ever listened to me like that and made me feel so beautiful."

Now, we were both crying for different reasons. As I thanked her and stepped out of her car, I realized that everything was going to be OK, even if it did not turn out well. I knew that while my ego could be crushed and my dignity debased, my Unique Self could never be taken from me. I could, wherever I was, hear and receive people's stories and remind them of their wonder and beauty. Nothing could ever stop that from happening. My Unique Self was inviolate. Everything else would find its way.

In the end, I did find my way back to my vocation—teaching, loving, and writing in the ways that have always delighted my soul. But on that day, I realized that the expression of Unique Self is not confined to what you do in public. It is not dependent on optimal life circumstances. Ego depends on these things, but Unique Self always finds a way to flourish. It is wonderful when life conditions meet you and support your most glorious manifestation. *You never know when the mystery of fragility will again intrude on your life. You do know that the apparent unfairness of the world can never take your Unique Self away from you.*

Ego Points to Unique Self

Ego is not the villain. All you ego-busters can sit down. *Your ego has wisdom to offer you. Ego holds truths that in their clarified form belong to Unique Self. The core truths of Unique Self are distorted by your ego's fear, contraction, and shadow.*

The personal story I told in the preface with which this book began is an example of how the ego points toward Unique Self. It is worth your going back to reread it in this light. What allows qualities that show up in ego to be reclaimed at the level of Unique Self is sustained contact with the transcendent, which shifts your perspective and opens the space beyond fear to do the genuine work of clarification and healing. In this book, I have called contact with the transcendent True Self, the realization of your essential nature.

Ego is pre–True Self.

Unique Self is post–True Self.

Or at least, post some glimmering of True Self, as True Self may show up in a flow experience or in other glimpses of authenticity. It is critical to note again at this juncture that, while True Self-realization is the stated goal of most classic enlightenment practices such as meditation and chanting, contact with your True Nature may also be awakened through ethical practice, personal suffering or joy, transpersonal depth psychology, or other similar paths. After authentic contact with your True Nature—or at least a sustaining glimpse of it—garnered by any of these modalities or others, the gifts of ego can be harvested at the level of Unique Self. I will deploy the Enneagram method of typology to make this point.

Below are two examples of how ego points to Unique Self. Specifically, these examples include the gift of loyalty and committed activism, and the gift of passionate ecstatic entry into the invitation of the moment. Glimmerings of these gifts appear at the level of ego, are clarified by contact with the transcendent through genuine psycho-spiritual work, and reappear with grace at the level of Unique Self.

One of the simplest ways to see the gifts of the ego, and how the ego points toward Unique Self, is through the classic typology of the Enneagram. Let me say a few words about the Enneagram so that you can see how the gifts that show up in distorted form at the level of ego can reappear in clarified form at the level of Unique Self. Stated simply, the Enneagram divides people up into nine basic separate-self personality types. Of course, from the Unique Self perspective every person is a type unto themself. Nonetheless, clear, broad classifications are helpful pointers in the right direction. Each Enneagram type is driven by a particular form of egoic contraction. In each type, the ego contracts in a very particular way, which produces a particular personality type, which has specific expressions of shadow and acting out.

While there may be some disagreement among the various schools of the Enneagram and their proponents, in all of them there is a clear evolutionary progression from the former fixation and ego-trap of each personality type to what becomes, through growth and integration, a positive expression of that personality type.

From the perspective of the New Enlightenment, you would say that this very same Enneagram type, when clarified and refined, reappears as what we are calling Unique Self. It is expressed in the Unique potentialities and gifts that this person might have to give, which are identified in their specific Enneagram type. The enlightenment teaching, which is a through line in these pages, is that this evolutionary transformation takes place through contact with the transcendent, with glimmerings of True Self, which then allows the egoic properties to be clarified and reclaimed at the level of Unique Self. These are the great gifts of ego that point toward Unique Self. It is through this method that the shadow of your Enneagram type becomes the radiance of your Unique Self.

Example one: The basic primary egoic strategy for self-contraction of the Enneagram seven type, sometimes called "the epicure" or "the enthusiast," is to avoid pain and their own core wounds. The seven type can become terribly narcissistic and shallow in pursuit of fun, excitement, and distraction. On the less wholesome end of the spectrum, this can lead to serial, never-ending, shallow romantic relationships, and oftentimes to addiction and premature death. On the healthy end of this same spectrum, the seven has overcome the fixation with fun, excitement, and surfaces, and has done depth work, confronted the primal wound, embraced their own shadow, and transmuted this repressed darkness into light and wisdom. The seven who has done this work then re-embraces enthusiasm, and sustained and repetitive passionate engagement with life, potentially becoming a model of radical, delighted, and even ecstatic existence in a way that is not dependent on external life circumstances.

Example two: The basic, primary egoic strategy for self-contraction of the Enneagram six type, sometimes called "the loyalist," "the trooper," or "the devil's advocate," is not avoidance but fear. Their unhealthy strategy for dealing with this basic primal fear is often paranoia and vicious projection of the internal demons onto others, or in the reverse, their strategy is an extreme form of people-pleasing that often involves a wholesale abandonment of principles and integrity. The type six is powerfully loyal, and in the service of that loyalty often abusive and damaging. The evolved version of these same qualities tends to produce courageous warriors for the sake of noble ideals who model service and almost unshakable strength, humility, and commitment to the cause of the good. The inner work of the six type is to confront the terrors within and without. In doing so, they are able to realize their own true essence beyond the fear and the terror that consciously or unconsciously plagued them in the past. In the most evolved case, they realize that their own True Self is none other than the source and wellspring of true faith and goodness. The thus-realized type six accesses deep reservoirs of power and courage, becoming valiant, serene, and self-directed. The ultimate Unique Self expression of the type sixes who have faced their fears and transmuted them into a vibrant faith in life are the good knights and the fearless loving leaders who appear in the times of our greatest peril and need, rallying us by their example of courage and selfless service.

CHAPTER SEVEN

PERSONAL AND IMPERSONAL

AT THIS POINT WE WILL REENGAGE the core distinction between Eastern and Western consciousness through a different prism. The prism is the distinction between the personal and impersonal. This window into Unique Self enlightenment will add a level of powerful depth and nuance to understanding why Unique Self is so critical, both for your life and for the evolution of consciousness.

There are two grand types of human beings living inside of you. As we shall show, they are integrated in higher embrace only in the consciousness of Unique Self. The first type we might call personal man, and the second type we might call impersonal man.[1] In the following entry, I will try to evoke for you in the broadest of brushstrokes an internal image of both of them. Each speaks with a different voice. Each means something very different when they talk of enlightenment. Each one is in some real way offended by the position of the other.

Personal man views that which is impersonal as being offensive. For him, the personal is sacred, and anything that is impersonal or depersonalized he experiences as a form of sacrilege. He views impersonal understanding of spirit as an "escape from reality." He views people engaged in the pursuit of the impersonal as being *inhuman* in their sensibilities. Even as he embraces the objectivity of science, he fears its depersonalization. Sanity for him is defined by personal integrity and equilibrium. His life centers on the world he lives in. He values that world, and enjoys his life in it. The healing and transformation of the world is his noble endeavor. Feeling that he has a home in the world is one of his primary values. It is absolutely core to his sense of self. Being productive and creative are crucial for his self-worth. He experiences himself as a unique, separate being with rights and responsibilities. He is a social being who exists in relation to others. His center of gravity is located in himself, his loving and responsible relationships, and his place and contribution to the world. When he talks of enlightenment, it is to these values that he refers.

These precise understandings of human beings and their place in the world lie at the center of the Western social and political movement that emerged in the late eighteenth century. The movement was naturally called the Enlightenment. Essential to this worldview is the dignity and adequacy of the separate individual. Its chief recent contribution to humankind is psychology, whose major focus is to help the separate individual self live a free, functional life of satisfaction, happiness, and dignity.

The personal man is also majestic man. He surges forward to conquer and settle the world. He roots himself spiritually in the great ancient Western traditions of spirit—from the Bible to Plato. He responds to the biblical imperative "Fill the earth and conquer it." He considers the unexamined life to be inferior, so he engages in introspection and self-examination. He believes in his ability to heal and transform the world. He seeks to create an orderly and fair society that supports the full flowering of human grandeur and goodness.

The second human type we have called impersonal man. Impersonal man finds the personal offensive. Not only offensive, he finds the personal to be radically limiting. He views attachment to the personal as the source of all suffering. He believes that to know reality is to move beyond the surface experience of the personal and to align with the deep structures and processes of impersonal reality. His experience born of practice is that impersonal awareness is the true core of the human being. He also lives in the world. But for him the world is illusory, because it is impermanent.

For him, enlightenment means something entirely different than it means to personal man. For impersonal man, enlightenment means the realization of his True Self as unqualified awareness. At its core, this means realizing the illusory nature of the separate self. The contraction and limitation created by the illusion of separate self is released in the radical freedom of enlightenment. For him, the ego is the great obstacle, which stands in the way of true wisdom, bliss, and compassion. He sees that so much conflict is rooted in the inability to evolve beyond ego. He distinguishes between surface structures like ego, which are personal and illusory, and depth structures like awareness, which are impersonal and real.

He aligns himself with the impersonal impulses of spirit coursing through him. His ecstatic impulse is toward even more expansive freedom and transcendence. He is gripped by the urge to merge with the eternal principle that underlies all of reality. He yearns to trance-end. At these times, he may be referred to as transcendent man. At other times, he is moved to align himself with the ecstatic God-impulse of evolutionary unfolding. He is gripped in these times by the urge to emerge and evolve. At these times, he might be referred to as evolutionary man. In both cases, however, he is called by the impersonal. The personal simply gets in the way.

For impersonal man the personal is often confused with personality. Impersonal man, who sometimes goes under the name "transpersonal man," seeks to liberate the human being from the coiled contraction of the separate self. Impersonal or transpersonal man seeks to free man from the bondage of fear and self-referential pettiness that traps personal man in the confines of his own strivings.

For the first time in history, a critical mass of humanity is no longer bound by the particular understanding of culture, religion, and spirit into which it was born. We are able to dis-identify from any one understanding, and get a much broader view of the entire range of human stories and understandings. It is only from this new place that we are able to discern the distinct perspectives of personal and impersonal man. *We have evolved to a point where we can take a perspective on perspectives.*

Personal and impersonal man each tell a different human story. Each holds a partial truth as the whole truth. Each plays the music of spirit on a different instrument, using different tones and notes, just as the system of Indian ragas uses a different scale from the classical European system of music.

Each of these voices exists inside every one of us. It is from the diversity of tones and notes that new and gorgeous music is created. *Right relationship between personal and impersonal man is the very core of enlightened consciousness.*[2]

Here is the key. *For the first time in the history of consciousness, we have evolved to a place where the higher integral embrace of both these human types is possible through the Unique Self.*

The source of the conflict between personal and impersonal man is precisely the confusion between separateness and uniqueness that we have made explicit in the Unique Self teaching.

For personal man, the dignity of the personal is the central value and experience. It is the glory, wonder, and power of the individual that moves and inspires him. However, he often confuses his ego with the Unique Self. Or, said differently, he confuses level one personal with level three personal. Personal man correctly sees in the ego a glimmering of something noble and good. The ego or the separate self (level one personal) holds the promise of the infinite value and dignity of the individual. The ego or the separate self introduces the glory of human goodness, choice, and accountability. As the person becomes a separate personal self, the person becomes a moral agent capable of enormous good precisely because they are capable of enormous evil. It is in the encounter between separate selves that human holiness, dignity, and ethics are realized. It is in the encounter between two separate selves that human love is born.

For personal man, the response to the terror of death is a life *well lived*. Imagine yourself before the bar of justice at the end of life—well pleased with your life choices, knowing that you did your best. And knowing that when you made a mistake, you did everything you could to correct it. You will find that in this state of consciousness, that of a life well lived, you have absolutely no fear of death.

A life well lived means two distinct things for personal man. First, a life *well lived* means that the goodness, compassion, and ethical mindfulness lived in his very particular life give it value and worth. Moreover, his spiritual insight acquired through rigorous practice and grace reveals to him that there is ultimate accountability, and that through karma or divine justice, all scales are righted. In that sense, a life well lived reflects itself on the scales of justice and in the good karma created. No small accomplishment. Second, a life *well lived* means having lived the right life by responding to the call of its very particular and special destiny. Giving his Unique Gifts and fulfilling his Unique Obligation fill his life with purpose, meaning, and joy.

All the goods of being human are, according to personal man, derived from his ego, which in our usage is synonymous with his separate self. Human rights, relationships, love, responsibility, and achievement are thought by personal man to derive from the individual dignity of the separate self. Personal man does not understand that his separate self is not necessary to attain the goods of being human. Indeed, his ego keeps him locked in separation, self-contraction, competition, hatred, and violence. He does not understand that the ego is but a foreshadowing of the Unique Self. *The Unique Self is fully realized only after the ego relaxes its death grip on the personal.* He can trance-end his separateness into his Uniqueness. He is a distinct part of the larger whole.

For impersonal man, the noble goal of all spiritual life is the ability to heal the suffering of humanity by transcending the egoic contraction of the personal. He recognizes that it is only by moving beyond the separate ego self that human beings realize the bliss and joy of their True Nature. It is only by aligning with the larger contexts of eternity and evolution that we experience our life as true and good.

But impersonal man confuses the ego with the Unique Self. He believes that the move beyond separateness is also, by necessity, a move beyond uniqueness and specialness. So he rejects the personal, which is always special and unique. He fails to distinguish the level one personal of personality, ego, and separate self from the level two personal of Unique Self. As a result, most of the Western world rejects this teaching. For the evolutionary intuition of virtually all of humanity today is that the very dignity and purpose of our existence is tied to our specialness and Uniqueness.

Recognizing the Place of Ego

It is true that the confusion between ego and Unique Self is still rampant in the world. But the evolutionary goal for humanity is realized not by stamping out the ego, but from recognizing its place. In other words, ego is not only a contraction of the vastness, as the Eastern spiritual traditions correctly point out. Ego is a crucial step on the road to Unique Self. We never leave the ego behind. Rather, we trance-end our exclusive identification with ego. Some of the more evolved Western mystical traditions explicitly understood this; most did not. This realization on a global scale is the precise next step in our evolution.

Just as personal man clings to his identification with the separate self and embraces ego as himself, the impersonal man, who is motivated by love and the desire to end suffering, rejects the ego totally. He forgets that the ego points toward Unique Self. He views evolution beyond ego, and the awakening of the impersonal human creative capacity, as the omega point of human authenticity.

This understanding, because it violates our intuitively correct yearning to realize post-egoic uniqueness and specialness, will always be rejected by most of humanity. Moreover, because of its impersonal nature, it becomes a major obstacle to intimacy and authentic encounter between individuals. *Intimacy and authentic contact between individuals are always the result of a genuine encounter between Unique Selves who incarnate the life force of the impersonal, seamlessly merged with the intimacy of the personal.*

In order to realize Unique Self enlightenment, you must go through three levels of consciousness, as stated in Chapter 4. First, you emerge from the pre-personal to the level of separate self, or ego. Second, you move beyond this first level of the personal, and recognize the impersonal nature of the life force moving in you and as you—from which you are not separate. This is the realization of essence or True Self. Third, you undergo a momentous leap in your evolution, as the Unique Self comes fully online, once again reasserting the primacy of the personal. But this time you are not experiencing the personal at the level of ego or personality, but as the personal face of essence.

Unique Self is ultimately and infinitely personal. The infinite is the intimate. Unique Self is not merely ego writ large. Unique Self incarnates the infinity of intimacy,[3] which is the personal heart of the kosmos. Unique Self realizes himself and herself as an expression of the infinite, though that is the essence of All-That-Is. It is the pure intimacy at the heart of everything.

The Impersonal Appears as Personal

At the level of ego, you take everything personally. The first step in moving beyond ego is to realize that almost nothing is personal. So much of what you think of as personal is really common to all—in other words, impersonal. It is happening to everyone in just the same way, and has nothing to do with your authentic uniqueness or distinction.

Most of what you do at the level of ego is a reaction. Virtually everyone has the same kind of reaction to the same stimuli of attraction, desire, seeking, fear, survival, and all the rest. So, to move beyond ego, stop taking things so personally. You need to realize that it is not personal.

However, at the level of Unique Self, the personal comes back online. In Unique Self consciousness, you are engaged in being or becoming, which wells from your singularity and uniqueness. You are responding to the unique clarion call of your life. At the level of ego, you engage a creative project or new job in order to advance your status in the world. You are motivated by reaction, to other people in your field, to the imagined or real threats to your security, and to your own sense of emptiness. From the place of Unique Self, you engage the exact same project, but this time you are motivated not by your emptiness but by your fullness. You are called by your own authentic desire to manifest your unique evolutionary creativity, and you have an intense and gorgeous desire to be a beneficial presence in the world. The core of your life is based on action, not reaction. At this level, it all becomes personal again, but from a free and spontaneous place instead of a desperately constricted and grasping place.

To realize Unique Self, you need to be able to distinguish between these two experiences of Uniqueness. One is authentic uniqueness, and the other is just ego and personality, a set of reactions and side effects disguising themselves as your Unique Self. ***To get to your personal Unique Self, you need to move beyond the personal illusion of the ego's personality.*** You do this by carefully considering your life until you realize that, just as the elements and most of the processes of your body are shared by all mammals, much of the desires and needs that you experience as personal and unique to you are expressions of impersonal forces. You let go of the illusion of being your limited personality, and embrace the impersonal realization of True Self.

After that, the realization of the higher-level personal of Unique Self, which is characterized by a full integration of the personal and impersonal, comes online. Learning to discern between the personal at the level of Unique Self and the illusion of the personal at the level of ego is a crucial step toward your Unique Self enlightenment.

There are three intertwined experiences in which what you initially might mistake as personal and unique is actually impersonal.

Choice

We live under the illusion that we are making personal choices in virtually every area of our lives. But often we think we are choosing when we are not. In fact, an entire series of impersonal forces come together to create the conditions necessary for us to make the particular choices that we are making in this moment. For example, you are probably a person who is not tempted to steal baseball cards from a grocery store. However, this is usually not because you have chosen not to steal. Rather, the sum total of the cultural, parental, genetic, and religious influences on your life, none of which you chose, determined your course of action, in the very same way that genetic, cultural, and religious influences have much to do with whom you choose as your mate or what career you choose to enter.

But there are moments in life in which you do exercise personal choice. For instance, you might be powerfully pulled to choose something or someone that does not reflect your highest values or self. In that struggle, you will have to find the deepest divine point that will allow you to choose successfully. There is a very narrow window of choice that is ultimately and infinitely personal. This is what the mystics have called your personal point of choice. Every person has a different personal point of choice. *The spiritual evolution that wells from your learning to successfully navigate your points of choice is part of the very purpose of your life.* And in those choices you effect what the Unique Self mystics called a *tikkun,* a kosmic fixing or evolution. Through the personal evolution of your own Unique Soul, you effect a kosmic evolution of All-That-Is.

Your personal choice points are intensely private and not subject to scrutiny; they are vital expressions of your Unique Self. Virtually all other choices you make in your life are really the impersonal dressed up in the veneer of the personal.

Sex and Love

The second arena in which the personal and the impersonal get really confused is the realm of sex and love. Here again, everything seems so intimate and personal, but upon closer inspection it is not. The great Kabbalistic tradition of Hebrew wisdom explicitly describes the sexual as the evolutionary impulse that courses through all of creation. In Hindu and other ancient traditions, the sexual spark resulting from the union between the kosmic masculine and kosmic feminine principles ignites the initiating energy of the kosmos. It is for this reason that the sexual force is so powerful and can potentially overwhelm personal choice.

How many people have been overwhelmed by sexual desire and chosen against their larger interests? The archetypal version of this conflict is captured in *The Iliad*, by the Greek poet Homer. Paris and Hector, the sons of Priam, King of Troy, come to Sparta to seal a treaty. But during the negotiations, Paris begins an affair with Helen, wife of the Spartan king, and takes her home with him. There are many twists and turns, ultimately leading to the destruction of Troy, but the fact remains that, at least in one reading of the story, the overwhelming impersonal force of the sexual moves Paris to override his personal obligations and personal loves—to his mission, brother, father, sisters, family, homeland, and people. As a result of his impersonal lapse, all of his personal loves will ultimately be slaughtered.

As you contemplate the sexual, you realize that, while you thought it was always an expression of your personal freedom, in fact you have little freedom when you are in its throes. It rises up unbidden, demands attention, and then leaves—until the next visit. It may even undermine that which you deem essential to your values or life purpose. It virtually never delivers on its personal promise. It rarely brings liberation in its wake.

While this is far from the final word on sex, at some stage in your development you need to do a deep-reality consideration of the sexual. *The realization of the impersonal nature of so much of your sexing is a key stage in your awakening.*

Relationships

Relationships are a third area in which everything seems personal but isn't always. Here I am using the word "relationship" to refer to direct and intimate contact of an authentic, loving nature between two persons.

You are shocked when you awaken to the realization of how little contact you make with others is actually personal at all. You are sure you are relating with your teacher or your employer. Upon deeper reflection, you realize you have unfinished business with your father. You think you are talking with your teacher, but you are really talking to your father. You might, for example, feel a lack of intimacy or care from your teacher. This might be an accurate perception on your part. Or it might well be that you are not making contact with your teacher because in your unconscious mind you have confused your teacher with your father. Your inability to make genuine contact makes you unable to receive the teacher's care and love.

Freud pointed out a hundred years ago that the unconscious mind organizes itself in patterns. It places people in buckets or categories. It relates to people as part of larger, overarching patterns. Teachers and fathers, if there is even a slightly common dynamic, will tend to be confused.

You are a woman in deep, intimate, personal relationship with a man, or a man in deep, intimate, personal relationship with a woman—so you think. A deep-reality consideration yields that you have actually not made contact at all. Your mother or father is still in bed with you; they are still in the living room with you, sitting next to you in the kitchen and den. The dynamic at play between you and your lover, which you think is so intimate and personal, is really not personal at all. You may think you are talking to your lover, but you are really trying to complete unfinished business with your father. Authentic contact or intimacy has not been established. When the exasperated partner screams, "Why the hell do you take everything so personally?!" they are, paradoxically, right. It is truly nothing personal.

Sometime when you are suffering with your intimate partner, or in any personal relation in your life, stop for a second and take an inner elevator ride into your past. See if you can get off at the floor when this very dynamic or emotional situation was first being enacted, when these same words were first being said by you, one of your parents, early caretakers, or teachers. By identifying the source of the dynamic, the charge is released. Once that happens, whatever the actual issue at hand might be, it is virtually always gracefully resolved.

Shadows of the Personal and Impersonal

The light of the personal is its very personal nature. ***The personal affirms and recognizes the infinite value, dignity, and adequacy of every individual.*** In the personal, the rights of every individual and the rules of fairness, which govern those rights, are paramount. The full beauty and uniqueness of every story is affirmed and treasured. The personal creates intimacy and reveals the depth of the human heart. In this divine realm, you realize that God knows your name.

The light of the impersonal is its impersonal nature. Beyond the personal lives the infinitely larger principles and processes, which govern reality. They disclose themselves when you free yourself from the trance of the personal. The impersonal reveals the nature of All-That-Is. You are invited to trance-end the personal, and ecstatically bask in the infinite grandeur of reality, which literally takes your personal breath away. You are filled with radical amazement and wonder.

Shadows of both the personal and impersonal come not from their essence, but from their distortions.

Shadows of the Personal

The first shadow of the personal is narcissism and egoic self-inflation. Here, it is all about me. Any commitment to another's well-being or to evolutionary unfolding, any willingness to sacrifice—these take second place.

The second shadow of the personal is victimology. The hypersensitive self perceives every offense to its small self as abusive. It assumes a victim identity as its Ground of Being. The victim is filled with an inflated sense of rights, and a deflated sense of responsibility and obligations.

The third shadow of the personal is the diminished and distorted God. The human being makes God a reflection of their small, individual, or communal self. God is hijacked to serve the personal or communal ego, and all those outside the personal or communal group are denied spiritual dignity and redemption. Worse, they are all too often killed in the name of God.

Shadows of the Impersonal

In the first shadow manifestation of the impersonal, the dignity of the individual is devalued. Only the larger principle or process matters. The individual is no longer celebrated and honored for their own gorgeousness, value, and wonder, but becomes merely a means toward the greater end of the process or principle.

The second shadow of the impersonal, a natural by-product of the first, is oppression and persecution. It becomes legitimate to inflict wholly unjust pain and suffering on the individual for the sake of the larger cause or movement. Principle and process crush the rights of the personal.

The third shadow of the impersonal is the God who is process or principle, but neither knows your name nor cares about your existence. The tens of millions killed by Communism in the twentieth century in the name of the "principles of evolutionary process and progress" made this all too clear. In the spiritual realm, this shadow face is often seen in the teacher or group that treats all manifestations of individuality as negative manifestations of ego. So when teachers talk about aligning with an impersonal process or principle, but are not accessing and therefore not transmitting the personal face of the process or principle that affirms the infinite dignity and worth of the individual, there is reason for caution. Caution does not mean condemnation. It means that one must discern clearly the nature of the teacher or teaching, based not on hearsay or what people have written in blogs, but on direct personal experience.

The Unfolding Dance of Alignment

We can only begin to penetrate the mystery of existence when we align the personal and the impersonal. What is that alignment? It is the realization that personal and impersonal are two faces of one reality, and that there is no separation between them at all.

On the one hand, you realize that the personal God you experience is identical to those infinite principles that suffuse every iota of reality. You realize that the personal God is the same as the initiating energy of the kosmos, the same as the ecstatic evolutionary impulse that courses through the kosmos. You recognize that your own essence is not different from that awesome, infinite vastness.

Yet at the same time, you realize that *it is all completely personal.* The most important and oft-repeated phrase in the most ancient sacred text of Western civilization is "God spoke to Moses, saying . . ." The personal God is the voice that drives and seduces All-That-Is to higher emergence. The personal makes the impersonal intimate. The impersonal infinitely expands the personal to encompass All-That-Is.

To be fully awake is to incarnate both the ethical impulse of the personal and the utopian impulse of the impersonal. Any spiritual path that undermines the infinite adequacy and dignity of the personal in the end undermines all that is good, true, and beautiful. The infinite personal dignity and value of each and every Unique Self is the noble matrix of inter-personal ethics and obligation. It must therefore be affirmed with undying passion. At the same time to confuse level-one personal with level-two personal—separate self and Unique Self—is to reduce the personal to the mere grasping ego. For example, to not awaken to the impersonal, expressed as a profound consciousness of the larger evolutionary context, would under-mine the evolutionary ethos which moves us to act for the sake of the all. And then, beyond the impersonal, the higher personal comes back online with the deeper realization that the process is ultimately personal at its core. So unfolds the perpetual dance of personal and impersonal. Personal ethics and utopian ethics are held in grand dialectical tension, which is constantly moving toward higher integration and alignment. Failure to hold this dia-lectical tension results in either personal narcissism or various shades of impersonal alienation "for the sake of it all."

In the unfolding of the spiritual path, this dialectical dance between personal and impersonal is ever present. The core movements in this dance are the essential stages of your evolution. We revisit them here.

First, you begin your development as an infant at the pre-personal stage. Second, after a period of time, you ascend to the personal. For quite a long stretch, your individuality, agency, responsibility, and personhood deepen and evolve. Third, at some point, a mature observing ego, able to stand outside the drama of the personality, comes online. This opens as a space of insight. You see that much of what you thought was your natural personal-ity is actually a constructed false self. For example, let's say you are always telling jokes—being funny, you are sure, is a personal expression of your nature. When your observing ego comes online, you begin to realize that your comedian persona is actually a "winning formula," or mask, which you adopted early in life to win your parents' love, an impersonal reactive pat-tern that became the core of your false self. Your more authentic personal nature turns out to be very different from the funny person you have been imitating all these years. That which you thought was the personal in you is really not you at all. It is actually a mechanism of your false self. It is an impersonal reactive pattern of telling a joke to win the parental strokes, which your separate egoic self developed to survive the pain of alienation that would be caused by parental indifference or unlove.

Fourth, the more you can deconstruct your false self, the more you can allow for your essence or True Self to come online. The True Self is you as pure awareness, pure consciousness. Fifth, you realize that True Self also includes the Unique Self. The Unique Self is the essential personal prism through which unqualified consciousness, True Self, is refracted through you to the world. *The Unique Self is the refracted light of consciousness, shining as you.*

Personal and Impersonal Sex

As your observing ego sharpens its penetrating focus, you begin to recognize the dance of personal and impersonal manifesting as you. You begin by noticing how much of what you thought was intimate and personal is actually impersonal forces moving through you. For example, as I wrote earlier, you have taken it as a given that your sexuality is intimate and personal to you. At some point, however, you begin to recognize the impersonal nature of the sexual force of attraction that you feel coursing through you. Yet as you deepen, you find that you can deploy the impersonal force of the sexual in a highly personal way. *The more you evolve, the more the personal and the impersonal begin to melt into each other, ultimately revealing their complete identity.*

As you realize more and more of the impersonal nature of reality, you begin to align with the larger process and principles that live in you, as you, and through you. You align with the ecstatic evolutionary principle, which both drives and seduces you to your own personal evolution. You align with the urge to emerge. You incarnate the process of becoming in the becoming of you. You incarnate the principles of love, care, and compassion in the intimacy of your personal expression. You manifest the principles and process of creativity in the dynamic unfolding of your own self-creation.

It is in the full alignment between the personal and impersonal that the full glory of All-That-Is is fully revealed. This dance of the personal and the impersonal is modeled by the sexual. As you are called to ecstatic embrace with an other, your full personhood both merges and emerges. The essence of the sexual mystery is in this incarnation of the paradoxical identity of the personal and impersonal.

You lose yourself in other. You find yourself in other. You call the name of your lover when you climax in orgasm. In orgasm you see and are seen by another person in all of your personal vulnerability, beauty, and darkness. Your deepest, greatest sex is with the person who knows you most intimately. The sexual is ultimately intimate and personal.

At the same time, sex is ultimately kosmic and impersonal. You cry out, "Oh God, Oh God," when you climax in orgasm. Orgasm is a little death. John Donne, the English poet, wrote that to orgasm is "to die" into the beloved and God.[4] You die to your small self in orgasm. You are fucked open to God.[5] All that is personal dies and is reborn.

From this perspective, you can easily discern which sexual dynamics are more personal, and which are more impersonal. Making love is normally considered personal, while fucking is impersonal. But the way you engage impersonal sexing will depend on your larger frame of meaning, which depends on your level of evolution. When impersonal sexing forcibly violates the personal, it is rape. However, when your larger frame aligns the personal with the impersonal, an act of forceful but not forced sexuality can be evolutionary. It depends on your motive and your level of personal evolution. If the personal and impersonal are merged in you, then ravishing sexuality is both radically intimate and personal, even as it is radically kosmic and impersonal, participating in the larger evolutionary impulse that lives in you and as you.

It is evolutionary when you realize that the sexual models the spiritual in all facets of existence. That means that erotic merger is not limited to the sexual. *Erotic merger*[6] *occurs when you live the evolutionary and intimate fullness of any moment.* That means that you can not only fuck your partner open to God, but that you can fuck any moment of your life open to God. It also means *you* can be fucked open to God—by your partner or by the innate presence in any moment of your life to which you fully show up.

In the sexual, the personal and impersonal fully entwine. This is the source of the mystery and sublime grandeur of sex. It is also the source of the insane fear and hysteria that surrounds sex.

Personal and Impersonal Love

We are used to thinking of love as ultimately personal, and this is true. But it is not less true that the love principle is fully impersonal. It is the inner process of reality, which drives the evolutionary process and seduces us to our highest evolution. In a forthcoming book on world spirituality based on Integral principles, written with my dear friend and dialogue partner Ken Wilber, this is how we describe love:

> In every single moment, aware of it or not, you are drenched in the kosmic love that is alive in and as All-That-Is. Every single corner of you is loved and accepted. Every single part of you is absolutely loved and absolutely accepted, and it is that extraordinary love that is so utterly nourishing and utterly enlivening and utterly, profoundly awakening.
>
> When we get into spiritual practice, of course, one of the things we want to do is work on our own capacity to love. But the other thing that's just as important is our capacity to recognize and receive the love that's already raining down on us like a thunder-shower, and being able to open ourselves to that love. To just feel into the heart and just open the heart in gratitude and blessedness and feel that love entering us and nourishing us and breathing us and actually being us is an extraordinary phenomenon.
>
> We start to understand love as Dante put it—the love that moves the sun and other stars—as a kosmic force, a force that holds the Uni-verse together. Alfred North Whitehead said that evolution is really the gentle movement toward God by the gentle persuasion of love. We need to make sure we don't just reduce love to our own separate-self capacities. Looked at in the bigger picture, love is the fabric of the Uni-verse, the glue that holds the Uni-verse together.

So love is both impersonal and fully personal at the same time. To be loved is both to be held by the kosmos and to be personally addressed by the kosmos. You fall in love with a woman sitting next to you on a plane. It seems like a chance encounter in an impersonal Uni-verse. Until you open it up, and then you realize that countless strands needed to be woven in both of your lives for generations in order for you to come together in this exchanged glance on the plane. The personal and impersonal melt into one.

Intimate Communion

This idea that you need to get personal and make contact is called by some of the Unique Self mystics *devekut*. Literally translated from the Hebrew, *devekut* means "cleaving." It first appears in the ancient text in relation to sexing. A better translation, which captures the Hebrew sense of the word, would be "intimate communion."

Devekut is an intensification of the personal. It conjures up the image of a tight, skin-to-skin encounter, with nothing coming between you and your intimate partner. Of course, you can be naked, body close up against another body and not be making contact at all. The original Hebrew text from the biblical myth reads, "Therefore shall a man leave his father and mother and cleave to his wife." The intent of this several-thousand-year-old text is clear. You think you are getting down and personal, but you are not making contact—unless you throw Mom and Dad out of bed. As long as you are still locked in relationship with someone other than the person in front of you, it cannot be personal. This is the inner meaning of "forsaking" all others in the Christian marriage sacrament. ***Personal means you are relating to the person in front of you.*** It cannot be personal if you cannot see the other person. If you are unconsciously relating to some figure from your past, then no action is possible, only reaction. Reaction is a function of the ego. Action is a function of Unique Self. At the level of ego, you are always reacting to the original players in your script. You are blind to the actual person in front of you. To be a lover is to have eyes to see. But when you are reacting from an ego level, the other person becomes simply a screen on which you—unconsciously—project all of your old stuff.

To recapitulate: Until you realize your Unique Self, every encounter is a replay of some past scene, with the other in the encounter unknowingly playing their part in your old movie. This is how the ego operates. By definition, the replay in the present moment of an old scene, usually with different players masquerading, is not very personal at all. ***True love is always personal. Your Unique Self makes contact in a full, personal way.***

Teacher and Student

Unique Self teaching has two major implications in the spiritual context of teacher-student relationships. When teachers give their students only impersonal or kosmic love, even when it is genuine, the students cannot truly grow. Personal love releases the contraction of ego. When the teacher sees the student merely as a seeker whose ego longs for release, something of vital importance is lost in the teacher-student relationship. The student doesn't need to be coddled by the teacher, yet it is absolutely essential for the student to be seen and valued uniquely by the teacher. This is an essential human need. This is what it means to be loved. When this happens, a deep place in the student begins to stir. The student has been seen, and therefore their self-contraction begins to uncoil. Their ego relaxes its grasping grip. Their Unique Self begins to emerge though genuine contact from the Unique Self of the teacher, which elicits the Unique Self of the student, and vice versa.

The ability to make contact and be intimate or not is the essential distinction between Unique Self and ego. Unique Self can make contact; ego cannot. Many teachers trapped in ego fail to make contact, and therefore keep their students trapped in ego as well, even if their professed goal is to evolve the student beyond ego to True Self.

When the substance of one Unique Self touches the substance of another Unique Self, contact is made. Contact is a touching without ego boundaries and without the loss of the unique individuation of being. One is not "being in the past" but is totally "present in the now." Presence meets Presence. Both sides have personal history. Both sides of the contact are intensely personal, but neither side is attached to personal history.

When a teacher denies Unique Self by confusing it with egoic uniqueness, and thus views the goal of enlightenment as being the awakening of the impersonal, whether that be realization of oneness with the Ground of Being or alignment with the impersonal evolutionary process, the result is always apparent in the student. The students may be bright, articulate, and all-American. They may say all the right things and look the right way, but at some core level we cannot make contact with them. We get an uneasy feeling, and we aren't quite sure why. Images of the old movie *The Stepford Wives* come to mind. In this movie, the men of Stepford consider their wives to be nagging, troublesome, egoic, and generally underdeveloped, so the men kill their wives and replace them, in the same body, with wise, wonderful, devoted, mega-sexy, compliant Stepford Wives. The male teacher in the guise of husband often kills the Unique Self by mistaking it for the ego. The authentic divine feminine in both teacher and student has also been killed. What emerges is the student who is the perfect, appropriate, articulate, and clean-cut Stepford Wife—but there is something essentially effaced.[7]

It is because of this that the teacher is obligated to give their students radically personal love, which is the honoring and recognition of the Unique Self of the student. *The recognition of the student's Unique Self releases the student's contraction of ego.* Personal love always releases the contraction of ego. *Personal contact is the joyous essence of being. It can solve world conflicts and create the intimacy that makes life worth living.* When we feel like genuine contact has been made, we have the delightful experience of our Unique Self being received and witnessed. *Like in quantum physics, the process of being seen, in and of itself, evolves us; it invites us into our fullest majesty and reveals our inner splendor.* Unique Self offers a quality of presence that shows up when the ego is set aside, even if temporarily, and our deeper being and becoming emerges in all of its resplendent beauty.

The second implication of Unique Self in the teacher-student relationship is the natural limitation of the authority of the teacher, which is implied by Unique Self, particularly when it is contrasted with other more impersonal constructs of enlightenment. If one experiences that the awakening of self beyond ego is the awakening of an activated and engaged "impersonal" Authentic Self, then the teacher's authority is naturally greater than it might be, according to one who experiences the awakening beyond ego as True Self + perspective, which equals Unique Self. If the goal is impersonal enlightenment, then the teacher who is more realized than the students might naturally assume a powerfully authoritarian approach toward the students. The authority of the teacher is rooted in their having a profoundly higher degree of enlightenment than the student. If this authority is exercised with integrity, then this might be for the benefit of the student. If the authority is exercised in a corrupt or demonic manner, then clearly it would not be of benefit to the student. The potential shadow of the impersonal in the teacher-student context may therefore be stated as excessive authority exercised inappropriately.

If, however, the core teaching being used is that of Unique Self, then even if the teacher has natural authority based on a higher degree of realization than the student, the teacher's authority will nonetheless be limited. While the teacher may have a higher level of realization of True Self than the student, by definition the teacher cannot have a higher level of realization of the student's Unique Self for the very reason that the Unique Perspective of the student is not available to the teacher. It may well be the case that the realization of the teacher enables them to see and point to the student's Unique Self more clearly than the student themself. However, this pointing out of the student's Unique Self by the teacher must always be held with humility, because the teacher realizes that while their own experience of True Self fully exhausts and transcends that of the student, the same cannot be said for Unique Self. There is an intimate dimension of Unique Self that can never be penetrated by the teacher, hence the authority of the teacher is naturally limited. The ultimate authority of the student derives from their authorship of their own story, which can never be plagiarized by the teacher.

The potential shadow of the personal Unique Self teacher-student model might be excessive love or intimacy with the student, or insufficiently demarcated lines of authority between teacher and student. Naturally, the term "excessive" is profoundly subjective. The precise meaning needs to be defined in the space of integrity and love, jointly created by the student and teacher. This might well be a function of the sincere desire to radically embrace the student in a love that uncoils the ego and radically holds the student.[6] It might also be an appropriate beautiful dual relationship between teacher and student. Or it might be an exploitative relationship with the student exploiting the teacher, the teacher taking advantage of the student, or both. The potential shadow of the various impersonal self teacher-student models might be excessive authority assumed on the part of the teacher, while sincerely seeking to undermine the egoic structures.[8]

Unique Self Is a Quality of Presence

Uniqueness is not a concept! Unique Self is a quality of presence that shows up when the ego is set aside—even temporarily—and our deeper being and becoming emerges in all of its resplendent beauty. *When someone shows up in their Unique Self, you are aroused to love them and intensely desirous of being loved by them.* In Christianity this exercises itself as the personal relationship with Jesus Christ that so many sectors of Christendom understand so profoundly—and which is so derided by New Age teachers caught in the impersonality of so much misunderstood Eastern teaching.

In Hinduism the goddesses hold you in radical personal embrace. In classical Judaism the G-o-d loves you and knows your name, while in Sufism and Kabbalah she is your most intimate erotic partner. None of this is dogma. It is the first and second personal realization that the interior face of the kosmos is the infinity of intimacy. And it is the revelation of the infinite, who yearns to love you personally and uniquely.

PART TWO

Enlightenment is ego's ultimate disappointment.

—CHÖGYAM TRUNGPA RINPOCHE

Every man is more than just himself;
he also represents the unique, the very special
and always significant and remarkable point
at which the world's phenomena intersect,
only once in this way, and never again.

—HERMANN HESSE

CHAPTER EIGHT

UNIQUE SELF AND EVOLUTIONARY SPIRITUALITY

IN BUDDHISM THERE IS A BEAUTIFUL ARTICULATION of mystical realization called One Taste. One Taste means that underneath it all, there is a unified field of awareness. This One Taste is not only eternal, it is eternity itself. It is unchanging radical presence that is both the ground and substance of All-That-Is.

What does One Taste feel like? What does it taste like? Christian mystic Thomas Aquinas reminds us, citing King David in the Psalms: "Taste and see that God is good." What does this good taste feel like? It feels like peace, stillness, bliss, ease, sweetness, elixir of honey, unconditional love, detachment, profound depth of calm, richly textured silence of presence. In the depth of I Am awareness, all is exactly as it needs to be, and nothing could or should be any different than it is.

This is the good promised by most guides on the spiritual path. This is the intention of the Buddhist teaching that invites you to take refuge in the Buddha. These promises are real and true—however, they simply are not the whole story. To teach them as the whole story is spiritual ignorance. Ignorance is not knowing nothing. Ignorance is not clueless; it is insightful but only partially so. Ignorance is to take part of the story and make it into the whole.

Two Tastes

There is not One Taste but two, which are but two faces of the One. The Second Taste is not eternal and unchanging. Rather, it is dynamic and changing every moment. The Second Taste is not just peace, bliss, and quiet. It is wild, filled with cacophonies of sound, color, and texture, and makes the most beautiful, roaring, piercing music that you could ever imagine. It is not just silence; it is the eloquence and gorgeousness of great speech. It is not unconditional sweet loving, but passionate, stormy, and wild loving that makes uncompromising demands, even as it gives uncompromising gifts. A changeless reality that is absolute quiet and stillness—this is One Taste. Changing the world, the surge of emergence that begins with the big bang, makes loud and often raucous noise—this is the Second Taste that is grounded in, and moves beyond, the First Taste.

The First Taste

One accesses the First Taste through many of the classical forms of mystical meditation. One Taste is found through the realization of what early Buddhists called No-Self and later Buddhists called True Self. It is the taste of being. It is the place of Big Mind, the Ground, the unchanging Tao, and *atman*. Through meditation, we access the unconditional love principle of eternity. *However, in this place, love is not a quality of relationship but a quality of presence.*

In the great traditions, this has been one face of ecstasy, the ecstatic release as one uncoils the egoic contraction and rests in Being. There is urgency in the desire to release. This is the human hunger for the taste of Being. And there is ecstasy in the release itself. Many mystical paths are primarily focused on how to access and delight in the One Taste of Being.

All of this is good, true, beautiful—and it is also partial. It is fully half of the goal of the enlightenment path.

The Second Taste

The Second Taste is not that of Being but of *Becoming*.[1] The principle at work here is not the eternal impulse but the evolutionary impulse. It is found through the realization of what some Sufi mystics have called personal essence. Speaking from my own realization, grounded in some Christian and many kabbalistic lineages, I have called it Unique Self.

After the evolution beyond ego and the identification with the impersonal, a new personal essence arises out of the very ground of the impersonal. This is Unique Self. This Second Taste is dynamic, creative, and world transforming. There is urgency to the Second Taste. The God-impulse of Second Taste is no less surging, ecstatic, and powerful than was the urge to merge in One Taste. In Second Taste, however, the ecstatic urgency is to emerge. This Second Taste ecstatic urgency aligns not with the eternal transcendent face of God, but with the evolutionary impulse of All-That-Is. The spiritual path that this ecstatic urge invites you to is the way of Becoming. *Meditation is not only the path into pure Being; it is also a key path to access the surging life force that is the evolutionary dance of unfolding.* In particular, certain forms of tantric or kabbalistic meditation open the door to that ecstatic evolutionary impulse toward unfolding that lives uniquely in you, as you, and through you. It is the same impulse that utterly demands the creativity of the artist even as it moves the mother to ecstatically suffer the pain of childbirth.

The Evolutionary Context of Unique Self: Nothing to Something

At some mysterious moment fourteen or so billion years ago, Nothing gave birth to Something. In the language of the old mystics, *ayin,* "nothing," gave birth to *yesh,* "something." *Ayin* is not less real than *yesh. Ayin* is not less concrete than *yesh.* Rather, *ayin* is so infinitely real, so absolutely concrete beyond all that is relative, that the relative reality of *yesh* pales into virtual nonexistence beside it. *Ayin* is the infinite field of possibilities. It is no-thing. Infinite no-thing gave birth to some-thing. Infinity contracted into itself and became a limited, finite thing.

From the perspective of the world, before the big bang all was quiet and peaceful. Indeed, it was actually before there was quiet—for quiet only exists in relation to noise. Nothing had happened yet. From the perspective of the infinite, of course, everything was already true. Peace and tumult, bliss and agony, were all already present in potential.

The unfolding of the world of *yesh* from *ayin* takes place through the dynamic mechanism of evolution. The goal of the evolutionary process, of unfolding *ayin* to *yesh,* does not end with the birth of *yesh.* On the contrary, the big bang is but the beginning of the process. Schelling and the Hebrew mystics who influenced him taught that evolution seeks the awakening of all matter as spirit.[2] The goal is for *yesh* to realize that, beneath the surface, it is really an expression of *ayin.* This is the radical and wildly audacious endgame of the ecstatic evolutionary impulse that is God—to awaken even the hills to the spirit that has become them, and that they already are. *Yesh* sleeps as matter, body, and mind when it loses its connection to its true *ayin* nature.[3]

Ayin does not lose its nature in the big bang. That would be impossible. Rather, *ayin* disguises itself as *yesh,* wanting *yesh* to wake up and consciously choose to manifest and live its nature.

However, *ayin* before the big bang and *ayin* after the big bang expressed as *yesh* are not the same. *Ayin* before the big bang is pure unchanging Being. *Ayin* after the big bang, which has been evolved through the process of becoming while disguised as *yesh,* is of a qualitatively higher order of Being. This is the great teaching of Kabbalah called *tikkun,* the evolution of God.[4]

The Sexual Context

In all of the great traditions, the moment of creative explosion from nothing into something is characterized as a sexual moment. Sexing characterizes the divine energy of ecstatic evolutionary emergence.

To see a snapshot of this dynamic, simply note your own desire to emerge, to individuate into higher and higher levels of authenticity and accomplishment. When this evolutionary desire is aroused, it is often followed by your desire for ecstatic merger, be it through sex, food, music, or some other method. As your level of emergence evolves, so too does the level of consciousness that characterizes the merger. Each time the cycle takes place, it can potentially occur at a deeper level of consciousness. For example, the urge to merge will mean something very different at an egocentric level than it does at a worldcentric level of consciousness. In the former, you merge for your own comfort and pleasure. In the latter, you might merge for the sake of all sentient beings.

These are the two contradictory drives in sexing. You sex to merge and you sex to emerge. You sex because you seek to escape your separateness. Sexing is one expression of your urge to meld with contexts larger than your small self. You sex to become one with a reality outside of your separate and therefore lonely self. This is the urge to merge.

At the very same time, sex is a powerful means of being seen. In sexing, you let down all of your guises and masks, and if you are with an authentic partner, you can be seen, witnessed, and received in all your glorious uniqueness. In this sense, sex is an urge to emerge. Both are animated by an immense, pulsating power. Both are characterized by ecstatic urgency. *You emerge in order to be you, only in order to merge again, only to emerge more powerfully, ad infinitum. This is the glorious evolutionary spiral of existence.*

You are the first level of evolution that has a choice. *You have the choice of waking up and realizing your True Nature as a Unique expression of the infinite.* When you realize the fullness of your True Nature, you give birth to yourself, a human god, who lives as love, compassion, and integrity in the world. This goal is realized when, as Hindu mystic Muktananda once said, "You experience God residing in you as you." In mystical terms, we say that the *ani,* the contracted ego, realizes its True Nature as *ayin,* infinite divine consciousness and goodness. This realization of *ayin* then births a new *ani,* a new I. The new You!

This new You is Your Unique Self. In the realization of Your Unique Self, the goal of the entire evolutionary process is realized. In You.

The three stages of evolutionary realization are *ani-ayin-ani* in Hebrew mysticism or egoic *aham,* ego dissolution, and only then the authentic *aham,* in Hindu mysticism.[5] *Ani* means I. *Ani* is first-level personal of personality; *ayin* is impersonal realization of True Self; and then, *ani* comes back online as higher-level personal or Unique Self.

The move from *ani* back to *ayin,* when the coiled ego realizes the spaciousness of its True Nature, is achieved by meditation, chanting, and other spiritual practices. The movement from *ayin* back to the higher *ani,* the revelation of Unique Self, is achieved by prayer, chanting, meditation, analytic work, ethical mindfulness and activism, and full-bodied loving embrace of life in all of its manifestations.

Evolution Is the Mechanism of the Mystery

Spiritual living is about fully incarnating both of these impulses—the evolutionary impulse and the eternal impulse. In the highest expression of the eternal impulse, the part is absorbed by the whole. This is realized in the evolution from separate self to True Self. And in the highest expression of the evolutionary impulse, the part evolves the whole. This is the realization of Unique Self.

The Unique Self mystic Abraham Kook, truly one of the greatest realizers, scholars, and poets of the Kabbalah, and one of the two essential lineage sources from which I live and teach, offers two pivotal teachings on Being, Becoming, and the evolutionary nature of the divine.[6] These are radical teachings, expressing the evolutionary cast of Hebrew mysticism. It is worth noting that the word "evolution" is not my overlay on Kook's teaching. Rather, Kook used the modern Hebrew word for evolution, with all of its modern implications.

The First Teaching

We perceive there to be two types of Perfection in absolute divine Perfection: one type of Perfection is so great and complete that no additional evolution is relevant to it.

If, however, there were no possibility of additional evolving whatsoever, this in and of itself would be an imperfection. For Perfection that is constantly waxing greater has great advantage and is pleasurable, and is uplifting.

For we yearn for it exceedingly, proceeding from strength to strength. Divine Perfection can therefore not be lacking the dimension of perfecting, which is the evolving process of perfecting and unfolding power.

This is why divinity has the ability to be creative, to instigate limitless kosmic be-ing and Becoming, proceeding through all its levels and stages and growing.

It therefore follows that the essential divine soul of Being, that which gives it life, is its constant ascending. That is its divine foundation, which calls it to be and to evolve. . . .

The Second Teaching

The theory of evolution, which is presently conquering the world, is aligned with the most profound secrets of the Kabbalah, more than any other philosophical theories.

Evolution, which proceeds on an ascending trajectory, provides an optimistic base for the world, for how is it possible to despair when one sees that everything is evolving and ascending?

And when we penetrate the very center of the principle of ascending evolution, we discover that it is the divine principle that is enlightened with absolute clarity. For it is Infinity in realization that realized itself through bringing infinity from infinite potentiality to infinite actuality. . . .

Evolution enlightens all dimensions of reality, all of God's manifestations.

All of reality evolves and ascends, as is evident in its parts, and this ascension is general as well as particular.

It is self-evident that good and the whole are interrelated, and reality is prepared to attain this quality, in which the All absorbs all of the good in all its parts.[7]

For Kook, the evolution of the part is part of the evolution of the whole. The whole—the love intelligence that animates All-That-Is, God—is in a constant state of evolutionary development. Perfection itself is constantly perfecting. According to Unique Self mystic Abraham Kook, by consciously aligning yourself with the evolutionary principle, your "entire existence is divinely transformed and exalted."

We do not need to subscribe to the old biblical worldview of a God separate from reality, guiding it from without, in order to recognize the radical intelligence that animates reality. As Ken Wilber and many others have correctly pointed out, the idea that evolution is a random, chance unfolding, which is not internally animated by a living Eros and telos, is an absurdity. Statistically, it is billions of times less likely than a monkey typing out *War and Peace.* Those are not odds you would want to stake anything on, let alone the very meaning of your life. All of our faculties of perception, the eye of the flesh, the eye of the mind, and the eye of the spirit, make this obvious to us.

Each stage of evolution needs to receive the core gifts of the earlier levels and offer its own Unique Gift.

Human beings evolve through levels of consciousness until they become capable of reflecting on themselves and their True Nature. This reflection yields the awareness of evolution itself.

The awareness dawns that you are part of the divine whole evolving through you, and you begin to realize that you have a choice, one dramatic choice from which all else flows. *You can ignore your True Nature or you can realize your True Nature.* To realize your True Nature is to align yourself with God, who is revealed as none other than the evolutionary impulse of the kosmos itself, surging through you as you reflect, choose, and act in the world.

To align yourself with the evolutionary impulse coursing through you is to wake up as evolution. You experience yourself beyond your level-one personal, which is the separate-self ego. You experience yourself as a personal and potent incarnation of the process. You identify fully with the awakened evolutionary creativity, living consciously and uniquely in you. In you, evolution awakens to itself. This is the evolutionary context of Unique Self.

Being, Becoming, and Unique Self

Being is evoked by beauty. The wonder of a flower, a gorgeous woman or man, and the ocean all evoke the quality of Being. This is why we love them so much. All of these expressions of divine love-beauty are understood by the great traditions as being one face of the divine feminine. What is particularly wondrous about these manifestations of love-beauty is that you do not need to be especially evolved or perceptive to be moved by them. A baby is of the same ilk. The baby evokes Being. The value of a baby is wholly independent of any process of Becoming. This is why we are entranced by babies, beauty, and roses, for their own sake. We do not gaze at the ocean, a beautiful woman or man, a rose, or a baby in order to advance some noble goal. Rather, we delight in gazing at them purely for the sake of the pleasure we derive from looking. Indeed, not only are these experienced without the goal of gaining position in the world of Becoming, the very opposite is true—the reward offered by the world for success in Becoming is the delight of Being. Sensual beauty and delight, from the gorgeous partner to the oceanfront home, have long been the rewards of successful Becoming.

Becoming is evoked by the joy of achievement. It involves effort and it is directional—always moving toward a new goal. It delights in working hard, and views walks in the park with suspicion. *For those seeking the ecstasy of Becoming, it matters not so much what is achieved. The fact of becoming itself brings joy in its wake.*

The masculine is more drawn to Becoming, while the feminine is more drawn to the radiance of Being. The masculine gets together in order to do something. The feminine will more readily get together purely for the joy of being together.

Being requires Becoming. It is the quality of Becoming that moves us to build hospitals, make revolutions, and evolve our scientific knowledge of the kosmos. All medicine is a child of Becoming. Without Becoming, Being might become lethargic and comatose, and the evolution of consciousness and love might never take place.

Becoming requires Being. It is Being that allows the Unique Self to engage the world passionately, even as it is not attached to the fruits of its labor. It is connection between Being and Becoming that lies at the core of the *Upanishads*' prescription for living: *Action in inaction. Inaction in action.*

Both Being and Becoming are qualities of the Unique Self. In the evolutionary mysticism of the Hebrew sages, in radical departure from Aristotle, Being is infinitely inferior to Becoming. Even God, to be perfect—argued the mystics—must be Becoming. Which person do we think of as more evolved: one who is static, or one who is always growing and expanding? Clearly the latter, respond the mystics to their own question. A person who is not growing is in some sense flawed. Some would even say that the moment we stop growing, we start to die. Well then—why would you deny God the same perfection?

"Know yourself" is the Unique Self maxim of the Delphic Oracle. But we must not forget Oscar Wilde's remark: "Only the shallow know themselves." There is much more to you than you are presently aware of.

When you give up your commitment to the next moment's unfolding, you give up on God, on your divinely unfolding Unique Self. The essence of every moment, wrote philosopher Alfred North Whitehead, is "the creative advance into novelty." Every moment contains a new invitation for the evolutionary creativity of self becoming and personal transformation. God's gift to you is your life. Your unfolding and growth during that life is your gift back to God, for God expands in your growth.

Your Evolutionary Yes

Your divine spark manifests as your drive to attain something beyond the contracted self of ego. You do not simply want to *disappear* into the one. Rather, your internal drive is to *appear* as a unique *expression* of the One. It is the answer to the question you are constantly asking: "Who am I?"

In the daily practice of Kabbalah, the seeker goes back to the moment before the world was created, to when the divine spark initiated the evolutionary process. This moment is available right now. You were there at the very beginning. *Hitboddedut* is the name of one of many forms of meditation designed to get you there. You enter deeply into the center of your being until everything but that center falls away. It is the Ground of Being—*ayin* or absolute nothingness—that is paradoxically personal and knows your name. Holy paradox lives in this realization.

The God train to this face of being is certain kinds of meditation and certain forms of chant. You rest in the timeless time and placeless place. In the language of Solomon, "His left hand is under my head, his right hand embraces me." You feel the divine embrace. No matter where or how you fall, you fall into the hands of God. This is the ground. Even when everything falls away, you are still there. When you awaken in the morning, the first practice you do is to contact this ground and realize your presence in it and as it. It is about this ground that we speak when we speak of the One, the unified ground of reality that is always and already you. Even as it personally holds you.

Once you realize this identification, your relation with all of reality is transformed. You have left the narrow straits of Egypt and have started to walk in the wide places. You have accessed the truth of your wider self. You have discovered Big Mind, Big Heart, Original Face, All-That-Is, Essence—all names for what lies right beneath your personality. It is the *ayin* before the *yesh,* the unmanifest ground from which all that is manifest is born. In this place you taste, for the first time, your freedom. One Taste.

The moment when *ayin* reveals itself as *yesh,* when the peace-bliss of an unchanging God explodes with a big bang as dynamic and evolving divinity who is movement and direction itself, is called the Mystery of Creation. That which is perfect seeks an even higher perfection, as if such words could be spoken or understood. *The changeless, motivated by infinite ecstatic love, suffers the exquisite pain of change and evolutionary revelation in order to give gifts of love that would otherwise remain un-given. And un-given love is not love.* The Second Taste.

All reality emerges from what is called by the kabbalists *nekudah achat,* a single point. In that single point, you are there. At that moment, from the depth of that point, you decided to unfurl a world. You, God, created the Uni-verse. It was not your ego, but your unique divine essence that made the mysterious choice to create a world. It was your Unique Self that initiated the big bang. The purpose was simple and clear—for the higher good of all sentient beings.

At the moment of the big bang, the original light of infinite goodness is shattered. It is shattered in the way that the heart of the lover is shattered: by opening in love to the beloved. It is shattered by an infinite desire to move from Being to Becoming; to merge with the beloved, and through that merger, to emerge into greater Being. To be more glorious, more beautiful, more awake, and more in love than was ever possible before.

Infinity and unity explode into finite, disconnected shards of the original divine unity. The process of evolution begins. Slowly the light hidden in the dark shards of the broken vessels is re-gathered. Divinity is rebuilt through first-, second-, and third-person reconstructive projects. Buddha is the first-person project of meditation and introspection. *Sangha* is the second-person project of social artistry and transformation coupled with prayer, chant, and devotion to the beloved. *Sangha* is always with thou and with the thou of God. Dharma is the third-person project of developing discernment and right understanding, and therefore right action in the world.

This whole impersonal process of evolution is all very personal. It speaks directly to you. You feel it inside of you right now as the powerful desire to awaken and be more. That desire is God desiring to be more through and as you. *When you enter into your deepest self, you begin to clarify your desire.* You realize with absolute shock, joy, and delight that God not only desires but needs your Becoming. It is this realization that we call the New Enlightenment of Unique Self.

Evolution: Personal and Impersonal

Unique Self demands that you see your entire life, everything that you live, breathe, feel, think, or desire, on all levels of your Being, within the larger framework of your direct participation in the evolution of God. It is this larger context that is the key to your liberation. The Unique Self mystics have taught for over a thousand years that every human action should be preceded by an affirmative statement of meaning: "I do this act for the sake of unifying and evolving divinity."[8] When every significant action you take is for the sake of the all, infused with a profound awareness of your evolutionary context, you stop reacting from ego and begin acting from the place of a powerful evolutionary integrity.

Renaissance kabbalist Isaac Luria developed a highly elaborate series of *kavvanot,* intentions. Each was a formal affirmation said at a different moment during the day, in order to awaken and align the intention of the individual with the evolutionary divine context in which they lived and breathed. For Isaac Luria, arguably the most significant kabbalist of the last thousand years, the ecstatic human obligation to awaken to Unique Self is the primary source of joy. It is the giving of your Unique Gift that fills your life with direction, meaning, and delight.

The split between the personal and the impersonal disappears as you awaken to your unique *tikkun* (fixing) in the larger context of the field of all life that ever was, is, and will be. It is for this reason that there is little talk in the Kabbalah about individual enlightenment. The danger of excessive emphasis on the individual is that you become a spiritual narcissist, totally focused on your experience of freedom and spaciousness. You then confuse that with Liberation, which it is not. *Enlightenment is an embodied-activist relation to reality infused with evolutionary integrity, which is far beyond the awakening of True Self.*

In the kabbalistic teaching, everything takes place in the larger context of community and for the sake of the larger whole. And yet the whole is never quite reduced to a process. Somehow in both the liberation teaching and the lived communities of the kabbalists, the sacred and paradoxical tension between the individual and the process was held in fine attunement.

Liberation always requires that you make yourself transparent to Self. But it also demands that you realize your place in the larger historical evolutionary context. These are two distinct forms of awakening.[9] Your life is never limited by your go-around in this incarnation, at this particular time and place, with these particular people. That realization allows you to relax the usual obsessions with all the relational details of your life. And yet you must never so identify with the process that you lose your felt sense of the infinite value, dignity, and adequacy of yourself as individual—and of every single individual that you encounter in your life. You must engage people personally and not merely hold them as cogs in the kosmic process of evolution. The dialectical dance of the personal and impersonal must never stop.

When you fail to hold the personal, you may begin to engage in manipulation or possibly even psychological abuse. When you begin to see yourself as aligned with the process, which was the great teaching of Hegel, you may inadvertently give birth to the worst evils of Fascism, Communism, and Nazism, all of which were very heavily influenced by Hegel's teaching that demanded that the individual must awaken and identify with the great evolutionary process of divine unfolding in absolute Spirit. In Hegel's powerful clarion call to align with the ecstatic impulse of historically unfolding evolutionary God, the holiness of the individual was somehow crushed in all the grand rhetoric, with devastating results for God and humans. The process must always remain personal.

For me it was always the Hasidic master Levi Isaac of Berdichev who radically reminded me of the primacy of the personal even when in the throes of evolutionary ecstasy. Levi Isaac was once leading the prayers at the close of Yom Kippur services. Yom Kippur is a fast day and the holiest day in the Hebrew calendar. The twilight hours at the end of the fast are filled with potency. According to the evolutionary mystics of Kabbalah, the enlightened prayer leader, during that time may potentially enter the virtual source code of reality and effect a *tikkun;* that is, effect a momentous leap in the evolution of consciousness for the sake of all sentient beings, in all generations. This is precisely what Levi Isaac—greatest of all enlightened evolutionary prayer leaders—was doing on that Yom Kippur. Night had already fallen, the fast was officially over, but the ecstasy of Levi Isaac was rippling through all the upper worlds. All beings held their breath in awe of the evolutionary power of Levi Isaac's consciousness. All of reality was pulsating with him towards an ecstatic evolutionary crescendo. And just as the great breakthrough was about to happen at the leading edge, Levi Isaac spotted out of the corner of his eye an old man who was thirsty. The fast had been very long and the old man needed to drink. And so in the midst of his ecstasy, Levi Isaac brought the whole evolutionary process to a halt. He immediately ended the fast and personally brought the old man a drink of water.

CHAPTER NINE

EVOLUTIONARY SPIRITUALITY RELOADED

LET'S TAKE A DEEPER LOOK AT EVOLUTIONARY spirituality and Unique Self, this time from the fundamental perspective of parts and wholes. Right relationship between parts and wholes are the Source's code of reality. *In evolutionary mysticism, knowing the right relationship between parts and wholes is the secret key that gives you the mastery and wisdom necessary to make your life a triumph.*

Arthur Koestler, the Hungarian writer and philosopher, has correctly adduced the claim that the basic monad of reality is not quarks or atoms or whatever other smaller sub-unit you might dream up. The basic monad of reality is parts and wholes. All reality is made up of parts and wholes. Atoms are both whole and part of molecules. Molecules are both whole and part of cells. Cells are both whole and part of organelles. Organelles are both whole and part of larger organisms.

Jumping to the human level, you have the individual, who is both a whole and part of a larger whole, the family. The family is both a whole and part of a larger whole, the clan or community. The community is both a whole and part of a larger community. Until we get to the nation, which is both a whole and part of a larger whole, the world. The world is both a whole and part of a larger whole, the galaxy.[1]

When a part pretends to be a whole, or tries to railroad the whole, we have trouble. Imagine what happens when an organ in the body starts acting not as part of a larger whole, but independently of the whole system. When the whole tries to absorb or dominate the part, we have trouble. Imagine what happens when one nation, a part, refuses to be part of the League of Nations, but remains *apart,* attempting to conquer all the other parts. Conversely, imagine the loneliness of a person, biological cell, a sentence, an idea, or even a musical note that is not in right relationship with other parts.

It is in right relationship between parts and wholes that balance and harmony are created—which in turn create depth, productivity, and success.

Right relationship between parts and whole is utterly essential to reality. In this chapter, we will look at the compelling relevance of part-whole harmony in uncovering the significance and meaning of your unique life.

The Whole Is in the Part

God incarnates as the initiating and sustaining energy of the evolutionary process and of All-That-Is. *This face of God lives and courses through you when you realize your Unique Self.*

Of course, merely part of God cannot exist in you. Physicist David Bohm reminded us a few years back that divine reality, All-That-Is, God, is holographic. Or in mathematical terms, all of reality is composed of fractals.

Simply put, that means that in every part is the whole. The all lives in all of its parts and particularized expressions. *The mystery is that the more the part emphasizes its part nature, the more highly particularized the part is in its authenticity, the more freely the whole can express itself in the part.* The more you move beyond your ego, which seems to be personal but is really impersonal, the more your full, personal, particular gorgeousness can emerge as your Unique Self.

That Which Is Above Depends on You: The Whole Needs the Part

God's need is your deed. Without your deeds, God dies. This core realization of evolutionary mysticism lives in the consciousness of the Unique Self mystics. The following story is a twentieth-century expression of this living tradition:[2]

It is the turn of the last century, on the Lower East Side of Manhattan. A family of four live in a single-room flat on Ludlow Street. All day and into the night, mother and father work hard in a sweatshop. Every Friday, however, their table is set for a Sabbath meal. Their daughter, Sarah, and their son go to services with their father, and every Sabbath Papa brings home a guest to share in the Sabbath meal.

Now, Sarah knows that they do not have much to eat and that the presence of the guest means less food for everyone. "Why, Papa?" she asks.

"It is written—charity saves from death," her father answers.

One day, Papa comes back from the sweatshop alone. "Mama is sick," he says. For several long days, Papa goes every night to the two flats that serve as the makeshift hospital for the families of Ludlow Street. When Sabbath eve comes, Sarah takes her brother to services. She doesn't know it, but at dusk, her mother breathes her last.

Sarah dutifully brings home a guest for the Sabbath meal she has prepared. Long after the guest has left, and after Sarah and her brother have gone to sleep, Sarah awakens to see her father weeping, sitting in a corner of the room. She comes and sits on his lap. "Don't worry, Papa," she says. "Mama will get better."

He stares at her blankly. "What do you mean?"

"Mama will get well," Sarah says. "I went to services, Papa, and I brought home a guest for the Sabbath meal, and you always told me charity saves from death."

Papa smiles sadly. "My little one, you misunderstood. Charity does not save Mama from death. Charity saves God from death."[3]

What does it mean, "charity saves from death"? And it is not merely a phrase from a story. Its source is the sacred text of the Talmud. But what could it possibly mean? The divine Uni-verse is not a kosmic vending machine in which you insert some coins and pull the lever for the elixir for long life. There is an evolutionary mystical explanation of the phrase.

Giving is not charity; it is obligation. The original Hebrew word used in the epigram is *tzedaka*. Often mistranslated as "charity," it really means "justice." The difference is enormous. Charity means that the money is mine, and if I feel magnanimous, then I can give some to you. Justice, on the other hand, is understood by the masters to mean that your money is not owned by you at all. In Hebrew law, a portion of your money is in reality *owned* by the poor in the community. According to one legal school, the Tosafists, the only right you have to the money is to determine which poor person will receive it.

Wow! What this law reminds us of is the great truth of philosophy. You are not separate from everyone else. And as part of the whole, you have a Unique Gift. Your Unique Gift can only be given by God through you. The accumulation of property and possessions in this lifetime is overwhelmingly due to sets of circumstances entirely beyond your control. You may have worked hard, but there are a million people who worked just as hard, and the Uni-verse did not allow them to accumulate your level of wealth. Those possessions are not essentially yours. And so, a portion of your possessions, according to Hebrew mystical doctrine codified in law, belongs to those less fortunate than you, not because the government legislated taxes, but because nonseparateness is the essential metaphysical truth of reality.

Not to experience the entire interconnectivity of being is to live a non-erotic, dead existence. Not to experience your Unique Obligation within the tapestry of wholeness is to wither and die. Charity saves from death. A piece of God dies in the coiled contraction of the separate self.

God Needs Your Service

"God needs your service"* means that God in an act of radical love receives your service. To say "I need you" is to open myself to receive an offering. The greatest gift you can give to a significant other is to receive their unique offerings of love.

Once I stumbled across a couple lost in the erotic. It was one of the most passionate and stunning acts of Unique Self giving and receiving I have ever seen. It occurred in a moment on a darkened side street of Jerusalem. This man and woman were walking arm in arm. They did not see me, but I saw

*kabbalist Meir ibn Gabbai, sixteenth century.

them. I should not have looked, but I did. She must have been 163 years old, and he seemed around 173. Apparently—and I caught this all in a fleeting moment—her shoe was untied.

Seeing this, he stopped. They made eye contact for the briefest of seconds, and then he bent down, very slowly. I hardly knew a person could move that slowly. Gently, and somewhat painfully with his arthritic hands, he tied her shoe. It must have taken a full five minutes. All the while I watched, paralyzed by awe, in the shadows.

Her acceptance of that act of loving was an ultimate erotic expression. She was being received by him, and he by her. His offering was fully accepted by her. Had I, for example, noticed her untied shoelace and bent down to tie it, she probably would have pounded my back with her umbrella. I was not to be received in that way.

In their one act of receiving were the Unique Selves of a lifetime. Infinite moments of joy, laughter, pain, perhaps separation and tears, all merged together in that eternity of a moment. That was the mystic, the living Kabbalah, the esoterica of receiving.

"Charity saves from death" means that God allows us to tie her shoe.

"God needs our service" means that God accepts our gift and thereby gives us the gift of affirming our human adequacy, worth, and dignity.

But it is even more than that. "Charity saves from death" means that God *needs* us to tie her shoe. God in the moment that the creative process is initiated makes itself dependent on us. "Charity saves God from death" means that God needs the gift of your Unique Self.

But it is even more than that!

I understood the Kabbalah's teaching on God needing our service in a whole different way after I had kids. Two of my children, Eytan and Yair, are boys close in age. Like brothers, they love each other deeply, yet fought with each other vociferously growing up.

One day, while we were visiting Florida, after a particularly bruising fight, they each came to make up with me—for I was angry at them for fighting. "Do you know what makes Abba"—the Hebrew word for "Dad"—"feel the happiest, the most loved?" I asked them.

"No, what?" Eytan and Yair asked, in their best make-up-with-Abba voices.

"When you love each other," I answered.

The boys grew quiet, thinking deeply about what they had heard. Then Yair turned and gazed up at me. "Abba, I think that's what it means when we say God is our mother and father. It means that God is happiest and feels most loved when we love each other."

Wow! This was one of those moments of strange and beautiful sense. My sons and I realized that a great truth had just been spoken through us.

That night I was giving a guest lecture on theology to a local church group. You can guess what I talked about. Everyone was appropriately blown away—that is, except for one person. He stood up, clearly agitated. "God needs us? What a crazy idea! Didn't they teach us that God was perfect? Lacking nothing!"

Of course, it doesn't take an advanced degree in physics to figure out that need implies lack. If you need something, then you're lacking something. How could God have needs? Isn't the whole point of God to be all-powerful? Doesn't God's needing us imply that we wield power over God?

Yet deep inside of us, we know that a person who doesn't need anyone else is actually less developed, less perfect, and less powerful than a person who has needs, and who can acknowledge those needs. This is the radical ground realization of Hebrew mysticism. This is the teaching of the Unique Self mystics.

When I answered the agitated man at the Florida church group and realizing that dialectical theology probably would not help, I enlisted the aid of *Rocky*. In Sylvester Stallone's famous movie about the underdog boxer, the underlying cultural message—and all movies that touch the global heart have a spiritual message of some kind—was that talent isn't the only variable in life. Rocky is clearly not a better boxer than his opponent Apollo Creed. Rocky has two qualities that are enormously powerful: grace and grit. Even those admirable characteristics, however, are not enough for him to win. Indeed, the famous, triumphant *Rocky* music doesn't even start until after a pivotal scene, one that revolves around the parallel drama in the movie.

There is, if you remember, a second battle being waged by Rocky—for the heart of Adrian. Adrian, who loves Rocky, has decided to leave the relationship. Rocky is wonderful and powerful, but he refuses to be vulnerable. At the movie's great turning point, Rocky cries out from the depths of his being, "Aaaadddrrriiiaann! I need you!"

At that moment, a new sort of power and perfection surges through him. Immediately following, we see a transformed Rocky—running triumphant up the court house steps in Philadelphia—and we hear his special music. He has acknowledged need, and he has become more whole. That is the God moment in *Rocky*.

The medieval philosophers, had they seen the movie, would have called that a moment of *imitatio dei*—the imitation of God. Rocky, in theological parlance, has become like God. Just as the all-powerful God, in opening up to need, becomes paradoxically even more powerful and more complete, so too does Rocky, who is powerful, open to need, and becomes more powerful and more complete.

CHAPTER TEN

TRUE SELF AND UNIQUE SELF, PARTS AND WHOLES RELOADED

THE PART IS HELD IN AND EVEN ABSORBED by the whole.

This refers to the realization of True Self. This holding is the source of your peace and ecstasy. Peace and ecstasy come from the realization that your fractured and partial ego is not your essential identity; rather, you are your True Self, which is an inextricable part of the whole.

The part evolves the whole. This refers to the realization of your Unique Self, which realizes itself as personally implicated in the evolutionary process. Unique Self intends through right action to transform the very fabric of the kosmos. Once the part knows that it is part of the whole, it can then deploy its part nature to transform the whole. Since Unique Self is only realized after a glimpse of True Self, which is precisely the knowing that the self is—in truth—indivisible from the larger whole, the Unique Self is naturally able to affect the larger whole of which it is a conscious part.

Right Relationship between Part and Whole

The divine unity would not exist without you. You are both identical to and an extension of that unity. *God individuates in your individuality.* In this sense, you truly are a son or daughter of God. In Christian language, you

135

realize that you are Christ as you live your Unique Self. In the Kabbalistic language of some Hasidic masters, you are "a truly substantial *part* of God." It is in this sense, and as was mentioned earlier, that Hindu mystic Muktananda used to teach that "God lives in you, as you." Shifting to Buddhist language, what we are describing as the movement toward Unique Self awakening has two distinct steps. The first step is the liberation into spaciousness that results from evolution beyond ego, which has often been called *sunyatta*. This is sometimes called the realization of your Buddha nature. The second step is the emergence of your unique *bodhichitta* quality, the aspect of your Buddha nature that might be understood as your Unique Self. This refers to the expression of your Buddha nature, where according to one Buddhist text, "the unique texture and pattern of the grain of wood which is you" becomes readily apparent and beautiful. In Hebrew wisdom, this might be referred to as the *ani-ayin-ani*.

We have already pointed out earlier in the book that *ani* literally means "I" in Hebrew. In the context of parts and wholes, the true relationship between *ani* and *ayin* becomes clear. The first *ani* is the egoic personality. This is the part that thinks itself a whole. The second stage, *ayin*, is the spaciousness of liberation achieved when the conditioned mind is recognized for what it is. It is here that the human being tastes the sweetness of evolution beyond ego. The part realizes that it is not separate but part of a larger whole. The third *ani* is the Unique Self that emerges directly from the ground of the *ayin* realization. At this stage the distinct nature of the part—within the whole—is realized and celebrated, so there is a level-one *ani* and a level-three *ani*. The first is the I of ego. The second is the I of Unique Self. The difference between them is *ayin*, contact with the spacious, transcendent ground of all being, of which you are a part. *Ayin* is recognized as your True Nature through the overthrowing of the ego's domination. This is accomplished through different forms of spiritual awareness and expansion practice.

The deep entwinement of these three stages of your evolution is captured in Hebrew by the fact that both *ayin* and *ani* are made of the same Hebrew letters. The purified *ani*, small I, reveals its True Nature as *ayin*, Big Mind. Expanded Consciousness, *sunyatta*, is then the ground that gives rise to *ani*, the Buddha nature of your Unique Self. We just noted that ego and Unique Self are both termed in the original Hebrew, *ani*. The same three letters spell "ego" and "Unique Self." The difference is the melting of the ego through contact with the transcendent, which purifies the elements of personal pettiness, false self, and neurotic personality, allowing for your core personal qualities of essence to emerge as Unique Self. The core of this personal evolutionary process is the evolution of the right relationship between the part and the whole.

Love, Fear, and the Evolution of God: The Whole Is Evolved by the Part

Letting go of the self for the Self is the only way to achieve enlightened self-actualization. It is the actualization of the Unique Self that supports and evolves God. The root of evolutionary commitment to the evolution of God is what the old esoteric traditions mean by "love." Love of God, self, and the stranger—the three forms of love instructed by Hebrew mysticism—are all acts of perception, which change the nature of reality. Quantum physics hints at the old mystical truth: perception changes reality. ***God is changed, evolved, by our loving God.*** The stranger is changed and evolved through our love. You are changed and transformed through self-love. Love is not an emotion but a perception of the True Nature of what is, through which emotion is awakened. We become lovers through the profound perception of the True Nature of reality as it appears in first, second, and third person. This perception of love is the realization that you and other are part of the same fabric of All-That-Is. You are part of the whole.

This realization changes the nature of both you and other because you realize your ultimate indivisibility from the other. It is this realization that leads to compassion and then to compassionate action. The evolutionary mysticism of Unique Self teaches that it is this realization, and the compassion and action that it births into reality, that catalyzes the evolution of God. The whole is evolved by the part. This is the very purpose of existence.

Fear is a result of seeing separate otherness. Love is a result of seeing unique oneness. Fear is self-contraction. We always need to remember that fear is the contraction of the self into ego. In ego, the part withdraws from the whole to assert and protect its part nature. Yet we always need to remember that the core intuition of ego is always at its root a glimmering of something necessary and sacred. Healthy self-contraction is the divine self-contraction that allows the world to come into being. God, the whole, steps back in love to allow room for other—the part. Other—the part—is God in disguise from itself. The disguise makes other seem a-part from God rather than a part of God. The disguise, in other words, is the illusion that other is unique and special in a way that separates from God rather than in a way that manifests God. The goal of existence is to pierce the veil of the disguise and reveal the underlying love unity of All-That-Is. Right relationship needs to be established between the part and the whole. Ever-higher integration of parts and wholes is the basic dynamic of evolution.

Healthy human self-contraction motivated by love allows for the world of an other to exist alongside your world. ***Love allows me to step back to make room for you.*** You and I recognize each other as unique and special, even as we know that we are together part of the larger divine whole, the seamless coat of the Uni-verse.

Unhealthy self-contraction is rooted in fear, not love. Fear causes the human being to contract in a distorted fashion. The divine self-contraction into ego is a stage in the kosmic process of manifestation. The divine contracts into the pre-personal human, who then evolves to the personal. The personal human then evolves to the transpersonal, and the possible human is born. This is the birth of the enlightened being. Fear interrupts this process. Fear causes the ego to usurp its proper role as servant and claim to be king. So the ego self-preserves, self-glorifies, and claims to be a separate self. This naturally creates a competitive and punishing impulse toward other. With that, the whole cycle of unlove, which gives birth to hatred, ever more fear and brutality is born. Fear is self-contraction is unlove. The part pretends to be the whole.

The teaching of parts and wholes opens up a wide and deep space of love-intelligence in the journey toward realizing your Unique Self. The history of the evolution of consciousness, as well as the story of your particular life, are both gorgeously illuminated through a deep understanding of the relationship between part and whole. The whole is the larger context in which the part lives, but to which the part is sometimes blind. A classic example, to which we referred at the outset of our conversation, would be a human cell. A cell is both independent and a part of a larger context. A liver cell is autonomous and part of the liver. The liver is both an independent organism and part of the digestive system. The digestive system is both independent and part of the body. Each part in the internal body is both a-part unto itself and part of the larger whole.

Like the organisms of the body, the separate self only survives for a short time—the span of individual life—when it disassociates from the larger whole.

From the human perspective, the part is the personal. The part is the individual. The whole is transpersonal, the larger context in which the individual lives and breathes but of which they are often unaware. The whole trance-ends the part, which is the personal. The experience of the whole breaks the trance of the personal's thinking that it is alone and separate from All-That-Is. The whole includes the principles and processes that underlie and animate reality. But the whole also trance-ends and includes the personal. Principle and process do not efface the personal. The personal is the intimate and loving face of the principles and processes of the Uni-verse. The part that is the personal is *part of* the larger context. The whole is the larger context. The personal is one with All-That-Is, but does not *disappear* into that oneness. Rather, the part *appears* as part of the oneness.

Part, whole, and the personal: Modern psychology and any mother can tell you that when the baby is born, the baby experiences itself as part of a larger whole. The baby is *part of* the mother. The mother is for the baby the *whole* world. This is a very particular "part-whole" relationship in which the part has no separate consciousness. The baby is merged with mother. Then the baby emerges. The part has separated from the whole. We call this process separation-individuation, meaning the baby's conscious emergence from the whole as a distinct part.

The natural part-whole balance between mother and baby tells you worlds about the evolutionary maturity of both the baby and the mother. In one scenario, the part might so disassociate from the whole that there is total alienation between child and parent. "Dis-associate" sounds like a fancy word, but really it is very simple. The part no longer associates with the whole. In a very different scenario, the child becomes a momma's boy. He never separates, never marries, and never fully individuates. In this case, the larger whole—in this scenario, incarnated as the mother—overwhelms and even s/mothers the part.

Love itself is but a shift in perception in which the part recognizes that it is part of a larger whole. The evolution of love is then precisely the evolutionary expanding of care and concern from the egocentric to the ethnocentric to the worldcentric to the kosmocentric embrace. Love as an ever-deepening and expanding shift in perception is the source code of evolution.

The part recognizing and locating itself in ever-larger wholes is the core of language itself. A letter becomes part of a word, the word part of a sentence, the sentence part of a paragraph, the paragraph part of a chapter, the chapter part of a book. Arthur Koestler has referred to this as *holons*. "Holon" simply means a whole/part. Whole/parts behave in accordance with a number of kosmic laws:

* The part is never expendable.
* The part can never be destroyed by the whole. The word does not destroy the letter. Rather, the part is transcended and included by the whole.
* The part can never destroy the whole. However, the part can either weaken or strengthen the whole. The part can either evolve the whole toward greater consciousness and compassion, or exile the whole into unconsciousness.
* When the whole tries to usurp the place of the part, you have domination and tyranny. When the family suppresses the individual or the empire oppresses its constituent nations, you have tyranny.
* The part cannot disassociate from the whole without losing value, meaning, and depth. To dis-associate from your family or tribe is to lose much of your depth and richness. Take the letter away from the word or the word away from the sentence, and each letter loses value, meaning, and depth. Take the cell away from the larger organism, and it loses its life force and may eventually die.

This is not some abstract conversation. It is the basic nature of all reality. ***Parts and wholes live together in a dance of Eros.*** In sane reality, each one—part and whole—defines, influences, and evolves the other. In insane or pathological reality, one tries to dominate or disconnect from the other.

How do these laws of part and whole manifest in your life?

Conflict

All conflict happens when one or both sides claim that their partial truth is the whole truth. Each side has a perspective on the situation. Usually, the perspective of each side has some legitimacy and value. Each side, however, fixates on its perspective so dramatically that it is blinded to the partial truth in the other perspective. The usual result is war, violent death, and horrific suffering. The magic of language aids us here. In the original Hebrew, the word for "conflict," *machloket,* derives directly from the root word, *chelek,* meaning "part." **All conflict derives from the part pretending to be a whole.**

Ethics, Values, and Extremism

This relationship between part and whole is the soul and source of ethical integrity. Ethics are based on the values we hold. That which stands against ethical action is generally not evil people, but extremists who distort ethics and produce results that are evil. Extremists are not, as is commonly held, people with bad values. Rather, they are people who have taken a partial truth and disassociated it from the larger whole. Extremism takes a part and makes it into a whole. A partial value becomes a whole value. Ethical integrity comes from *integrating* a whole constellation of often-competing values. Each value is a part. When the part pretends to be a whole unto itself, then the value produces pain and suffering instead of love and compassion. An extremist picks one value as their own. The value is a good value. But they turn their partial value into a whole. For them, the part has usurped and replaced the whole. The part is masquerading as the whole. The goal of the extremist is to fool everyone, especially themselves, into believing they are whole. They use their value to create their own internal sense of wholeness.

To really get a hold of the part-whole pathology that lies at the heart of all extremism, I will now outline for you the six core characteristics of extremism:

1. First, an extremist is not a person with bad values. Extremists almost always hold a value that everyone agrees with.
2. Second, extremists can never have too much of their value.
3. Third, extremists think that their partial value should not have to compete with the larger whole. They oppose values that may limit or even oppose their value.

4. Fourth, what extremists most detest is compromise. They refuse to admit that their value is only a part and not a whole.

5. Fifth, what the extremists most fear is uncertainty. Uncertainty derives from the recognition of competing values—each one of which is only a part of a larger whole.

6. Sixth, a least on the surface, extremists feel better when they wake up in the morning. The reason is simple: They feel more pure than the rest of us. They hold one idea to be an absolute truth uncontaminated by any opposing ideas or values.

Here is a simple example. There is a famous argument raging in the United States that is often referred to as the pro-life versus pro-choice controversy over abortion. If you think about it, however, you realize that the extremists on both sides in the conflict are actually engaged in demagogic behavior that distorts instead of clarifies, even as it often produces unnecessary harm and suffering.

How many of you, dear readers, believe in the value of life? Virtually everyone. An extremist position would say that the value of life trumps any and all other values. Say, for example, that a woman is brutally raped by her father. The baby that would be born has been tested and will be born severely retarded. It is very, very early in the pregnancy. You would think it obvious to state what an utter horror it would be to force the woman to carry the baby to term, and then to have to raise a child who is a constant reminder of her trauma. Yet for the pro-life extremist, the woman must carry the baby to term and raise the child. The value of life trumps all other values. Life, which is a partial value, has become the whole. As a result, life is freed from the obligation to compete with other values like choice or compassion for the emotional suffering of the mother. The part has trumped the whole. The result is cruelty and suffering.

Lest my liberal readers are feeling too vindicated, I gently remind you that the same analysis holds true on the other side of the aisle. How many of you, dear readers, believe in the value of choice? Virtually everyone. An extremist position would say that the value of choice trumps all other values. An example: An aspiring actress tries out for a part in a movie to play a schoolteacher. She does not get that part, but instead is awarded the part of a high school girl. The problem is that, although she is not showing, she is five months pregnant. But the part just seems so good she decides not to pass it up. It is her choice. In this scenario, the partial value of choice has been transformed into a whole. As a result, the partial value of choice is freed from the obligation to compete with its opposing values. In this scenario, the opposing values might be the value of life and the rights of the father.

There is a law operating here. Whenever a part pretends to be a whole, a larger and deeper truth is missed, and great pain and suffering result.

This truth shows up gorgeously in the original Hebrew. In Hebrew the word for "value" and the word for "context" are precisely the same word. The word is *erekh*. The reason is simple. The specific value is only part of what determines how we act or move in a particular situation. The second factor that needs to determine our actions is the larger whole, the larger context in which that value is playing. Life and choice are guiding values in and of themselves. They are also both profoundly influenced by the larger context in which they are at play. Thus in Hebrew, "context" and "value" are the same root word.

Individual or Community, Autonomy or Communion

In the larger context, the relationship between part and whole and the great teaching of the New Enlightenment of Unique Self becomes ever-more clear. From time immemorial, there has been a great debate in the world. What is the basic structure of reality, which must guide our lives? Part or whole? Said differently, individual or community? Is the part that is individual and personal the basic monad of reality? Autonomy or communion? Or are the impersonal principles and processes the basic monads of reality?

Is the basic structure of reality the individual? If this is so, then the rights of the individual are what count, and the community exists largely to serve the individual. Or is the basic structure of reality the process and principles that underlie the larger whole? If this is so, then does the individual find their place only when they align with the underlying principle or process? This critical question about the nature of reality shows up in the two key usages of the very word "enlightenment."

One usage takes the first position. The part, manifesting as the separate individual, is the basic monad of reality. Everything revolves around the individual. This first use of the word "enlightenment" dominates the social-political discourse of the entire democratic Western world. The part experiences itself as ultimately separate from the whole. The individual is a separate, isolated self. This is the lonely hard truth of reality according to this understanding. It is also the source of human dignity and rights. The key human endeavor becomes protecting the individual from encroachment by larger dominating wholes. Wholes might show up as the state, ideology, or religion that threaten either the existence or the dignity of the individual.

The second use of the word "enlightenment," common in the East, regards our attachment to our separate individuality as the root of all evil and suffering. One of the great insights of classical enlightenment teaching is its recognition that if a person thinks that they are only an isolated part, they are deluded. In this second understanding of enlightenment, which dominates most of the spiritual discourse in the progressive Western world, the larger wholeness of All-That-Is is the core truth of reality. Individuals practice in order to absorb themselves into that larger context. Absorption is a key mystical goal. It then naturally follows in this teaching that the unique demarcating characteristic that makes you separate from the larger context needs to be swallowed or absorbed by the whole. A person living with the sense of being a separate self is living a constant delusion. They are in some sense insane, because they do not know the nature of reality. So enlightenment teachers, seeking to share the True Nature of reality, make the claim that there are really no *parts* at all. Only the whole truly exists. The part or separate self is an illusion. The only true reality is the larger whole.

In the teaching of Unique Self, the whole/part, autonomy/communion paradox is finally clarified. The Unique Self teaching allows us to create right relationship between whole and part, autonomy and communion. This right relationship is the absolute key to joy, creativity, meaning, and peace.

The separate self is an illusion. Every separate self is really part of a larger whole. *To realize oneself as part of a larger whole is to be sane. This is the ultimate communion. At the same time, the part is not absorbed in the larger whole, but is a distinct, unique part with reality and dignity.*

The unique part has its own Eros and eternity, which is precisely the Unique Self. This is the ultimate autonomy.

Being part of the larger whole does not efface the gorgeousness of being a personalized expression of the mind and heart of the divine love-intelligence. That is expressed by the Unique Self. The individual retains their Uniqueness even as the ego is clarified, and they realize their True Nature as part of the larger whole.

The first great evolutionary emergence of consciousness is about the part being able to distinguish itself from the whole. This is true on two precisely parallel levels, that of the collective and that of the individual. This emergence of part from whole is essential both in the life of the individual and in the history of humanity. The baby separates from the mother. The individual separates from nature. On a collective level this means that each person exists within, yet is also distinct from, their community or racial group. Each part has its own separate dignity and value.

When this is not the case, we have superstition, voodoo, and racism. Racism is the idea that every part that has similar characteristics is inseparable from the larger whole. So for a racist, every black person or Jew is viewed not as a separate individual, but as an indivisible part of the Jewish or black aggregate. When the Jewish or black whole is despised by the racist, the racist makes two distinct moves, both of which are wrong and both of which are necessary to justify the cruelty of their actions. First, the whole is viewed with hatred, and second, the part is viewed as having no individual reality apart from the whole. Racism could not exist in practice without denying the dignity of the individual part.

The emergence of separate self is a huge evolutionary leap. The individual separates from tribe, nationality, mother church, the cult, or any other totalizing or dominating whole.

Spiritual teaching in every tradition insists that to end suffering, the separate self of the ego must be made transparent to God. This is true. Yet the ego is not an accident, an unintended and unfortunate consequence of the emergence of the separate self. Rather, as we have shown, the ego points us toward the Unique Self. *The reason the ego is so strong is to provide an evolutionary bulwark in human psychology against various forms of dictatorship by the whole, be they spiritual or political. Dictatorships or group-think crush human spirit and dignity.* They come in all sorts of subtle disguises. It is not a coincidence that their first move is often to wage war on the individual human ego.

A second expression of the dictatorship of the whole over the part is found in versions of what is termed evolutionary teaching, including evolutionary spirituality, that give the individual dignity only to the extent that they are aligned with the evolutionary process. In this teaching, the personal, which is the part, derives its value and dignity from the process, which is the whole.

In the evolutionary mysticism of the Unique Self, the impersonal-process element—which lies at the very core of Lurianic Kabbalah—is sharply balanced by the radical affirmation of the personal that is inherent in biblical and Talmudic sources. Contemporary mystical teachers often take the impersonal-process teaching out of its dialectical relationship with the personal. When this happens, the great teaching of evolutionary spirituality runs the risk of slipping from the sacred impersonal to an aggressive de-*facing* of the personal—in the name of process and enlightenment.

Which side of this great argument is right? Personal or impersonal? Part or whole? Autonomy or communion? Why, both, of course. The goal is not to sacrifice your individual identity, as so many spiritual systems imply and political systems have demanded. *The goal is the death of your exclusive identity with the separate ego self, your lack of transparency to the divine.* In the great paradoxical truth of spirit, it is the death of the separate ego self that gives birth to the Unique Self. Autonomy and communion are integrated in the higher embrace of unique self.

The Part Needs the Whole

The part needs the whole. No one said it better than physicist Albert Einstein:

> A human being is part of a whole, called by us the Universe, a part limited in time and space. He experiences himself, his thoughts and feelings, as something separated from the rest—a kind of optical delusion of his consciousness. This delusion is a kind of prison for us, restricting us to our personal desires and to affection for a few persons nearest us. Our

task must be to free ourselves from this prison by widening our circles of compassion to embrace all living creatures and the whole of nature in its beauty. The true value of a human being is determined by the measure and the sense in which they have obtained liberation from the self. *We shall require a substantially new manner of thinking if humanity is to survive.*[1] [Emphasis added.]

This "new manner of thinking" described by Einstein is in fact the classical enlightenment teaching of the great masters. In 1954, when these words were penned, the old classical enlightenment teaching was in desperate need of renewal. It had been all but forgotten in the Western world.

The part needs the whole to feel safe and sane. The dignity of your individuality, or romantic love in all its glory between separate selves—these do not sate you. You have loved enough to survive but not enough to feel whole, and this lack of feeling whole creates suffering and conflict. Your self-experience as a skin-encapsulated ego leaves you feeling ill at ease, depressed, and not a little bit crazy. You do not understand why life feels so drab and pale. There seems to be a larger wholeness lurking just over the horizon, but you cannot see it. The part needs the whole to put down its burden.

Imagine that you are on a journey. You board a train. But you continue carrying your suitcase, refusing to put it down. You do not realize that the train will carry your suitcase for you. You are now part of a larger whole that you take, along with all of your baggage, to your destination.

This felt realization of being part of the whole is the core of the authentic journey of enlightenment.

The Puzzle-Piece Teachings

Unique Self is your free, indeterminate core of irreducible uniqueness. To be unique means to be irreplaceably singular, a constitutive exception to the universal, an unobjectifiable secret that resists full articulation or appropriation in any system of meaning-making. In this sense the Unique Self is nontotalizable, and infinitely exceeds all such systemizing approaches. Unique Self is an expression of irreducible singularity.[2] But that is only part of the story. It is precisely the singularity that merges and integrates one into the Single One, which is the ultimate universal, the whole in which every part participates. It is precisely this paradoxical insight that is the essence of the nondual realization of the self as Self. Paradoxically, the source of your oneness with All-That-Is is your Unique Self. Unique Self might be described as the puzzle-piece nature of one's essence and emptiness. Like a puzzle piece, Unique Self is both utterly unique and distinct, and yet paradoxically it is that very uniqueness and distinction that merges one with the larger context of All-That-Is. Uniqueness the currency of connection. While separateness separates one from the larger context, uniqueness integrates one into the larger context. As we have already seen, the distinction between separateness and uniqueness is a pivot point in the Unique Self-realization.[3]

The puzzle-piece teachings are core to the Unique Self dharma. The core of the teaching is simply this: the part itself is the way to the whole. In the original Hebrew used by the Unique Self mystics, the same word, *yichud,* is used for "unique" and "unification." The reason is simple: It is through your singularity that you find your way to the Single Oneness. It is your very nature as a unique part that connects you to the whole.

We are seekers of unity. The part seeks to find its place in the whole. We seek to trance-end our separate selves and locate ourselves in the greater oneness of All-That-Is. In classical teaching, the way to accomplish this is through the spiritual practices of meditation, self-inquiry, and chant. These inner practices move you from a place of identity with your small self to a place of witness. You are no longer identified with your body—you witness your body. You are no longer one with your emotions—you witness your emotions. You are no longer identified with your thoughts—you witness your thoughts. In the words of the psalmist, alluding to meditative practice, "Many are the thoughts in the mind of man, but the divine center, it alone will stand."[4] In the way of meditation, you locate your deeper center as conscious awareness itself. You realize that your essence is part of the larger field of awareness. You realize that your essence is consciousness itself, in which thoughts, feelings, and perceptions arise moment to moment. This is one important step in trance-ending your narrow identification with your limited body-heart-mind.

But it is only one step.

The second step beyond your limited body-heart-mind into identification with the great oneness takes you—paradoxically—in almost the opposite direction as the first.

In the first step, you move beyond your particular manifestation as a body-heart-mind. In the second step, you move back into your unique personal essence, carrying with you the realization that you are beyond it. You discover that in order to become one with the divine—that is to say, to live as the divine—you need to accept and even accentuate the particular curves, outline, and texture of your uniqueness. You understand that because the seamless coat of the Uni-verse is seamless but not featureless, you must realize your Unique Self in order to truly achieve the highest stage of nondual unity with All-That-Is.

This is what I call the puzzle-piece teaching. The divine field of essence is properly imagined in your mind as an infinite puzzle. You are a puzzle piece. If you try to round out the unique curves of your puzzle piece through meditation or any other spiritual oneness practice, the puzzle piece that is you will simply not fit into the divine oneness. The part fits into the whole through its unique part nature. You are not interchangeable with any other part. Only the puzzle piece that is your authentic Unique Self can seamlessly connect you to the divine one. Similarly, Unique Self is not absorbed in the whole. *Unique Self is integrated into the whole, meaning that the part does not lose its integrity as it merges.*

Merging into oneness, and unique emerging, become—paradoxically—the same movement. The puzzle piece becomes part of the whole only through its unique puzzle-piece nature. Any attempt, through wrongly deployed meditation or practice, to round out the edges of the puzzle piece will make integration into the larger divine whole impossible.

Meditation, chant, and inquiry can also be skillfully deployed to identify, realize, and live your Unique Self. First, if you are identified exclusively with your ego-separate self, then you think that your puzzle piece is the whole puzzle. Second, if you experience yourself only as True Self, then you think that the puzzle is an illusion and that reality at its core is really an undifferentiated whole. Third, only as Unique Self do you know that your puzzle piece is part of a larger puzzle. Then you experience yourself as fully fitting into the whole.

Once the puzzle-piece teaching becomes clear in your consciousness, you will feel the need to identify your Unique Self for two very different reasons. One reason is in order to save the world. Your Unique Self makes you what Nikos Kazantzakis called "the savior of God." In this sense, the Unique Self is the source of your gifts to the world and God. *But your Unique Self is not only the spiritual technology necessary to save our world; it is the only way you can belong in the world. You do not enter God by being the best, but by being your best.* You cannot access the one by imitating anyone, only by being yourself. In any event, you might as well be yourself, because all other selves are already taken.

CHAPTER ELEVEN

EROS AND UNIQUE SELF

The Eros of Living Your Story

EROS IS THE INITIATING ENERGY of the kosmos. Eros is the evolutionary impulse that surges through the kosmos, lighting the stars in the sky, creating molecules out of atoms, cells out of molecules, and entire organisms out of cells.[1] Eros is the inner face of the fifth force of the Uni-verse, which is the tendency of matter to self-organize, to rise beyond chaos to ever-increasing orders of complexity, consciousness, and love. While the outer face of evolution is the drive toward increased complexity, the inner face of evolution is the drive toward increased consciousness. This increase in consciousness yields ever-increasing circles of love and compassion.

The evolution of consciousness is identical with the evolution of love, within both the life of the individual and the life of the polis. The more conscious a person or society, the greater the level of inclusion of other. This increase in consciousness directly causes an increase in love, expressed in an ever-deepening ability to hold the perspective of other without abandoning the depth or integrity of one's own convictions.

Eros seduces man toward evolution, toward greater consciousness. Love seduces man to love. Eros is the inner animating quality of the ecstatic evolutionary impulse of the Ground of Being, evolving toward the most aware and noble expression of itself. It is love persuading us to ever-deeper levels of love.

Eros animates All-That-Is, reaching down from the cellular reality to the greatest displays of natural and human grandeur. At the cellular level, a primary expression of Eros is manifested as the cell expresses its particular specialized function. *The more unique and specialized a cell becomes, the more it is able to evolve. An essential moment in cellular evolution is the move from single-celled to multicelled organisms. This takes place as a direct result of the cells assuming unique and specialized character in their structure and function.* Cells whose inner quality is Eros or love increase in consciousness. By doing so, the cell is able to evolve and live in absolute harmony with other cells in a larger organism.

Writ large, as biologist Bruce Lipton has already implied, cellular reality models the essence of a realized human being. Although we look at human beings from a superficial perspective as discrete, separate individuals, this is not the case. The individual human being is a community of fifty trillion highly specialized unique cells that operate in magnificent concert with each other; fifty trillion cells each fulfilling highly specialized functions in radical, complementary integration with all the other cells. *The human body at a cellular level models the great love story of Eros.*

The specialized function of each cell is the "story" of the cell. When a cell stops living its special story, it becomes what Lipton calls a "homeless and jobless cell." It ceases to be a beneficial presence in the body, and instead becomes a cancer. *Imagine if we sent cells to a "No-Self" meditation teaching or to the Course in Miracles to teach them, "You are not special." The result would be the destruction of the foundations of life. Instead, the Uni-verse invests each cell with the primal directive, "You are special. Live your Unique Cell story."*

Of course, cells don't function with ego, so they are able to fulfill their unique free-functioning form without egoic clinging, fear, or striving. Human beings need to first realize their identity as a separate-self ego, then trance-end separate-self ego and realize their deeper reality as True Self—as an indivisible part of the one. True Self then naturally births Unique Self. The individual human being as a greater organism is no less uniquely special than their individual cells. When the human being realizes Unique Self, by living their story and incarnating their specialized function in the world, then they are in harmony with all of Being and Becoming. When that happens, Eros dances and the kosmos smiles.

There is nothing that arouses our love more than witnessing a person living the fullness of their story. You fall in love with that person. This is the interface of Eros and Unique Self—you explode into the larger field of Eros. Life becomes larger than life; meaning melts into mystery.

To get a sense of the erotic nature of your story, you must first touch deeply the essential meaning and quality of Eros in your own life. You must move toward a higher intimacy and union with the purpose of your own existence.

Listen to a story of Eros about a modern master with whom I have been delighted to talk deeply about the teachings on Unique Self shared in this book. This is a story from his imaginings when he was a boy:[2]

Reports reached the 14th Dalai Lama, Tenzin Gyatso, that a certain Master of Kung Fu was roaming the countryside converting young men to the study of violence. . . . Against all Buddhist laws, there had been unnecessary slaughter of yaks in order to provide the many husky monks, who had abandoned their lamaseries and robes, with black-leather outfits like the one the Master of Kung Fu wore from neck to ankle, his huge muscles making the costume tight as his own flesh.

These leather-sheathed disciples followed their master everywhere, challenging each other to duels, many of which ended in death or crippling. The Regent and other advisors to the Dalai Lama were concerned, especially after blasphemous rumors began circulating that the Master of Kung Fu was an incarnation of Shiva Nataraj, Hindu god of destruction.

The Dalai Lama decided to invite the master for a visit.

Pleased with the invitation, the Master of Kung Fu strode into the Dalai Lama's ceremonial hall. The Master of Kung Fu was indeed a handsome, dashing fellow, with thick blue-black hair falling down over the shoulders of his leather suit.

He assured the Dalai Lama that he wanted to do no harm.

"Well, when you do want to harm," asked the Dalai Lama, "what kind of harm can you do?"

The Kung Fu Master explained that he was a lover of beauty, and that his only enemy was ugliness. He offered to demonstrate.

"Royal Highness, the best way to show you would be for you to stand here in front of me while I do a little dance it took me fifteen years to perfect. Though I can kill a dozen men instantly with this dance, have no fear. This will only be a demonstration of ugliness destruction . . . "

The Dalai Lama stood up, and immediately felt as if a wind had blown flower petals across his body. He looked down but saw nothing. "You may proceed," he told the Master of Kung Fu.

"Proceed?" said the other, grinning jovially. "I've already finished. What you felt were my hands flicking across your body. If it pleases your Highness, this was a demonstration in slow motion, extremely slow motion, of the way I could have destroyed the organs of your body one by one . . . "

"Impressive, but I know a master greater than you," said the Dalai Lama.

"Without wishing to offend Your Highness, I doubt that very much."

"Yes, I have a champion who can best you," insisted the boy-king.

"Let him challenge me then, and if he bests me I shall leave Tibet forever."

"If he bests you, you shall have no need to leave Tibet."

The Dalai Lama asked for tea to be served and told the Regent to summon the Dancing Master. Soon the Regent returned with the Dancing Master, a small, wiry fellow who seemed to be well past his prime.

His legs were entwined with varicose veins and he was swollen at the elbows from arthritis. Nevertheless, his eyes were glittering merrily and he seemed eager for the challenge.

The Master of Kung Fu did not mock his opponent. "My own guru," he said, "was even smaller and older than you, yet I was unable to best him until last year . . . "

The two opponents faced off. The Master of Kung Fu was taking a jaunty, indifferent stance, tempting the other to attack.

The old Dancing Master began to swirl very slowly, his robes wafting around his body. His arms stretched out and his hands fluttered like butterflies toward the eyes of his opponent. His fingers settled gently for a moment upon the bushy eyebrows. The Master of Kung Fu drew back in astonishment. He looked around the great hall. Everything was suddenly vibrant with rich hues of singing color. The faces of the monks were radiantly beautiful. It was as if his eyes had been washed clean for the first time.

The fingers of the Dancing Master stroked the nose of the Master of Kung Fu, and suddenly he could smell the pungent barley from a granary in the city far below. He could smell butter melting in the most fragrant of teas, as the Dalai Lama, incomparably beautiful, sipped tea and watched him calmly.

The Dancing Master flicked a foot at the Kung Fu Master's genitals, and he began throbbing with desire. The sound of a woman's voice in the distance filled him with yearning. The Dancing Master was now assaulting him with joy at every touch, and he found himself removing his leather garments. His whole body began to hum like a finely tuned instrument. He seemed to have many arms and legs, all of them wishing only to nurture the blossoming of life.

The Master of Kung Fu began the most beautiful dance that had ever been seen in the great ceremonial hall of the Grand Potala. It lasted for three days and nights, during which time everyone in Tibet feasted, and visitors crowded the doorways and galleries to watch.

Only when the Kung Fu warrior finally collapsed at the throne of the Dalai Lama did he realize that another body was lying beside him. The old Dancing Master had died of exertion while performing his final and most marvelous dance. But he had died happily, for he had found his successor. The new Dancing Master of Tibet took the frail body of the old master in his arms and, weeping with love, drew the last of its energy into his body. Never had he felt so strong.

What a holy tale of Eros and Unique Self. The darts and lunges of emptiness and violence become the erotic soaring of fullness and love. Initially, the Kung Fu Master is estranged from his own story. Those who remind him how far he has strayed, he moves to destroy. The Dancing Master—fully immersed in his story—calls the dark lord of Kung Fu back home. In their meeting, both of their unique stories are fulfilled. It is only the Unique Self of the Dancing Master that can call the Kung Fu Master back to himself. *When you encounter someone fully living their Unique Self, all that is false in you melts away, and you are called back to your own Unique Self.* It is only the Kung Fu Master who can complete the last chapter in the Dancing Master's story, by becoming his successor. Their meeting is a Unique Self encounter. The Eros of the encounter is that each holds a piece of the other's story.

The Four Faces of Eros

The great mystery tradition of Unique Self enlightenment is about becoming just such a dancing master. It is about the dance with aliveness, the Goddess divine. In Kabbalah she is called the Shekhinah, in Hinduism the Shakti, in contemporary organizational theory she has been called flow.[3] This is the dance of Eros.[4]

Eros has many expressions. To gain a fleeting glance of Eros revealed, we will explore the four faces of Eros. These faces, taken together, form the essence of the Unique Self experience.

The First Face of Eros: On the Inside

Eros means being on the inside. Eros is aroused whenever you move deeply into what you do, who you are with, or where you are at. In the temple tradition of Solomon, the innermost sanctum is called by two names: the holy of the holies and the inside of the inside. For the Unique Self mystics, the holiest place to live is on the inside of the inside with another human being. It is from this place where time falls away, where the radical sensual and practical intimacy of lives entwined is the very fabric of existence, that the question of the meaning of life becomes irrelevant and even absurd. Every moment of existence, from the most ordinary to the most exalted, explodes with self-validating meaning.

The interiority of Eros stirs our heart and imagination.

Ralph Waldo Emerson once said, "What lies behind us and what lies before us are small matters compared to what lies within us."[5]

Being on the inside is, of course, not about location in space-time, but about soul terrain—a place inside yourself. Socrates writes at the end of the *Phaedrus*, "Beloved Pan and all ye other Gods that haunt this place, give me beauty in the inward soul, and may the inward and outward man be at one."[6]

In one of its most evocative mantras, the Zohar says that Eros is to be in the flow of "the River of Light that Flows from Eden."

For the Temple mystics, when your inside and outside realities are not connected in the daily routines of your life, you are in exile. Or to put it another way, exile is synonymous with non-erotic living.

When you are not living from the inside, your choices, reactions, and responses do not emerge spontaneously from what Teresa of Avila called your interior castle. You are not in the flow of your own life. You are not living from your Unique Self.

The opposite of Eros is alienation, exile from your inner castle, the betrayal and pain that come with making bad choices. When you are not "in the flow," you wind up always having to watch your back.

The Hebrew word for inside, *panim*, also means "face." Your face is the place where your unique interior is revealed. There are forty-five muscles in the face, most of them unnecessary for our biological functioning. Their major purpose seems to involve expressions of emotional depth and nuance. When we say, "We need to speak face-to-face," we are in erotic need of an infinitely unique inside-conversation. *Without uniqueness, there is no interiority.*

Face is the most direct and clear expression of Unique Self, the truest reflection of the erotic. To lose face is to become de-eroticized.

There is a third meaning to the Hebrew root *panim*, along with "inside" and "face." In a slightly modified form, *panim* also means "before," in the sense of appearing *before God*. The essence of the Day of At-one-ment is that it is the day on which the temple priest is summoned to appear "before" God. Usually the word "before" in this sense is taken to imply a sense of appearing before the court of judgment. This is the "outside" meaning of the word. On the "inside," the meaning is of an entirely different nature. Remember that all three English words, "face," "inside," and "before," share the same Hebrew root, *panim*. So for the Hebrew mystics, rooted as they are in the profound linguistic magic of the original Hebrew, the commandment is not a summons to appear "before God" in the judicial sense.[7] Rather, it is an invitation *to live on the inside of God's face.* **Once our journey to God is completed, the infinite journey in God can begin.** To be before God is to live your Unique Self.

The experience of Shekhinah—the sensual divine force that rests between the cherubs in the Holy of Holies, in the *lefnie u'lefnim* (literally "on the inside of the inside") is the erotic experience itself. In fact, the mystics often use the word "Shekhinah" as a synonym for Eros.

Now let's add another dramatic piece of the puzzle: the Hebrew word for "temple" is *mikdash*, literally translated as "sacred" or "holiness." Put it all together, and the picture that emerges is radical, revolutionary, and overwhelmingly relevant to our lives: the erotic and the holy are the same thing.

Eros = Shekhinah = Inside = Sacred = Unique Self

Finally, we have a definition of the sacred. *To be holy is to be on the inside of God's face.* Your face, which is a fractal of God's face, is utterly and absolutely Unique. Face is an expression of Unique Self. **It is through your Unique Self that you enter the inside of God.** This is the inner meaning of "holiness."

The opposite of holiness, therefore, is not impurity or demonic possession. *The opposite of the holy is the superficial.*

Holiness is Eros. Sin is superficiality. To be superficial is to fail to live the full Uniqueness of your story.

The Second Face of Eros: Full Presence

The second face of Eros is the fullness of presence. We can experience full presence even when we have not yet merged with the moment or crossed over to the inside of God's face. Full presence is about showing up—you can be fully present in a conversation, and full presence at work can mean that you derive joy, satisfaction, and self-worth from your vocation.

Presence is always Unique. Sit silently with two different friends, and each time you will have a different experience of presence. The fullness of presence that is Shekhinah, that is Eros, refers specifically to the fullness of your Unique Presence.

At retreats that I lead, we often do a face-to-face prayer, which we refer to as intersubjective meditation. People sit in pairs and read psalms to one another, singing praises to the God-point in the other. Before we begin chanting, I ask each person to look deeply into the other's face: "Begin by being wordlessly present for each other. Experience the full presence of another waiting for you."

How many people have come up to me after those uncommon (and often uncomfortable!) sessions of looking into another's face! They come in tears, in joy, in awe, each with a different story. But they all share a common theme:

> At first I felt awkward. I kept shifting my gaze, looking at her necklace, her earlobes, her hair, but it was so hard to look at her face. Finally, our eyes fell into sync. It was uncomfortable, but we kept at it. Eyes brown with freckles of color; a funny and imperfect face. And then suddenly, something gave. A rush of emotion, a moment of release into the other person's gaze.

Have you ever looked—really *looked* into another person's face? Have you ever witnessed that moment when the soul comes rushing up from its inner chambers through the windows of the eyes, seeing you seeing the other? Greeting your gaze like the first rays of morning light? This is the mystery of love, the spellbinding Eros of the eyes. ***Presence emerges when you gift an other with the experience of the full uniqueness of your being.*** Or when you receive such a gift from an other.

I ask the participants to feel the Unique Face of their partner as a sculptor would their clay: "Run your hands erotically—not sexually—over the skin; feel the bone structure, and then look again deeply into the eyes. In the Eros of a face touched and felt, the God-point of the other emerges, and we are moved with full heart to sing praise." ***Presence is always unique.***

The divine is a presence that waits for us to be present. She is Eros, standing outside of our window, simply waiting. Waiting for us to be overwhelmed by her love. Waiting for us to behold the wondrous vibrancy and vitality of her face.

The Third Face of Eros: Longing and Desire

When you are on the inside, when you are fully present, you are able to access the third face of the erotic experience: your unique longing. Longing and desire are two essential expressions of love and Eros. As long as you are on the outside, you can chase false desires not your own, and respond to superficial longing that does not well up from your uniqueness.

But your utterly unique longing and desire are vital strands in the textured fabric of Eros. We are filled with desires. Desire is holy.

The mystics lovingly counsel us to be fully present to our desires and gently watch them as they come and go—not to eradicate them, not to get off the wheel of suffering that they are said to create, but to simply remain present to them. We are invited to engage in what the old Unique Self mystics called *berur teshuka*, the clarification of desire. For Unique Self mystic Isaac Luria, this means to determine whether your desire wells up from your Unique Self or whether it is desire that is foreign to your authentic story. Spiritual practice is not to eradicate desire. It is to replace your small desires with your great ones.

True desire is attained through deep meditation, when you access the internal Witness. This is a place of radical nonattachment, where we can survey with penetrating but loving eyes all of our desires. This place of effortless witness allows you to move beyond an addictive attachment to any particular desire. At that point, the person engaged in *berur* does not abandon desire—rather, they move to connect to those desires that are truest to their most authentic Unique Self.

Detachment for the biblical mystic is a strategy, not a goal. *In the end, you must not remain a spectator in the drama of your own existence. Rather, you need to become the lead actor on your stage, fully merged with the part the Uni-verse has invited you to play.* Longing and desire are holy not because you believe that all of your yearning will be fulfilled or realized, but because the yearning itself guides and fills you, and leads you back to your Unique Self. For true longing is the longing to come home to your story. The desire itself fills the emptiness. When you yearn to grow, when you are alive with your desire, you touch fulfillment.

Your deepest desire and greatest pleasure as a human being is to become transparent to the interior face of the kosmos seeking to evolve through you. The yearning of the kosmos to evolve shows up as the evolutionary impulse living in you. You do this only by living fully the unique invitation that is the story of your life. Your Unique Self story. This is the great longing of every awake human life. ***When you awaken to your Unique Self, you allow the yearning of the kosmos to singularly fulfill itself through your eyes, your heart, and the Unique Perspective of your life.*** Your greatest yearning is to give the Unique Gift to All-That-Is, which can be given only by you and you alone. ***The yearning that lives in you is not less than the personal voice of the evolutionary impulse living in you, as you, and through you.***

The Fourth Face of Eros: Wholeness and Unique Self

Longing and desire remind us of the fourth strand in the erotic weave. They whisper to us that we are all interconnected, that there is an essential wholeness to reality. No human stands alone, and all the world's yearning exists in the spaces between us.

The word "religion" traces its source to the Latin root *ligare* (think "ligament"), which is about connectivity. Religion's goal, then, is to re-*ligare*—to reconnect us. It was the original intention of all the world's religions to take us to that inside place where we could experience all of existence as one great quilt of Being, and ourselves as patches in its magnificent, multifaceted pattern. The fourth face of Eros is revealed when you realize in your very being that you are part of a larger whole. But not only you. ***Eros reveals that every part is part of a larger whole.***

Now here is the key: drumroll please! It is through your very uniqueness that, like a puzzle piece, you fit into and complete the larger whole. All parts are Unique. All parts fit into larger wholes. Uniqueness is the core connector. It is the very uniqueness of the part that integrates it into the whole. Separation creates alienation. Uniqueness creates integration. Lack of uniqueness creates heaps, but never wholes. Uniqueness is the bond that connects, transforming heaps into wholes. Again, uniqueness is the currency of connection.

Eros allows you to move past the feeling of isolation and separation. Ignorance is to sunder your connection to Eros. Not only do you lose the source of so much pleasure, you also undermine the building blocks of connection—without which the world would ultimately collapse.

In the Kabbalistic myth, the great sin that caused what is called "the shattering of the vessels" was the sin of separation. Each divine force—*sefira*—held itself apart, autonomous and independent, free of any dependency on the other *Sefirot*. The result was that each was unable to hold its light, ultimately shattering and causing great kosmic disarray. The *tikkun*—the fixing of the shattering—involves experiencing every point of existence in full connectivity, as part of the quilt of Being.[8]

It is in this sense that the early mystics were often also magicians. *Ecstasy and magic are, in the end, inextricably bound together. Both seek to access the myriad lines of connection that underlie this wondrous web of existence.* It is this magic that a child intuitively understands. Psychology dismissively refers to this childlike intuition as magical thinking, and sees maturity as the triumph of the rational mind. The mystic knows that the child is partially right. There is a good reason why the Harry Potter books swept the world with such ferocity. The children were saying, "Finally you give me something that is true to my spirit." One child of a close friend said recently to her mother, "Mama, I am magic. Did you know that?" Children who had never read with pleasure before were suddenly consuming hundreds of pages at a time, volume after volume. *The sacred child in us understands that the world is filled with magic, with invisible lines of connection.*

The psychology and mysticism of a child is, of course, immature, as it has only reached the very first station of the Unique Self process, the pre-personal. But tens of thousands of years ago, almost all of humanity lived in this childlike pre-personal stage. This was also the time that our very first languages were being formed. These languages were themselves magical, each word carrying massive symbolic and energetic meaning in relation to every other word. As the rational mind evolved and became predominant, our languages were modified, refined, reformatted.

But if you look closely enough, you can see the magic at the root of language, organizing our perceptions and reminding us of the unbreakable wholeness that exists behind and between our words. The real secret of magic is that the world is made of words, and that if you know the words that the world is made of, you can make of it whatever you wish.[9] The magical formula "abracadabra" is a corruption of the original Aramaic phrase *avra kedabra,* which means something like, "I create by speaking the words."

"Eros" is another word for magic and enchantment, the knowledge that everything is alive, interrelated, interwoven, and filled with meaning. Eros is the evolutionary drive to wholeness—to healing and to health.

This enmeshment in a web of connection is the essential erotic experience of all mystics throughout all ages. But we catch glimpses of it as well in our normal daily lives. We have all known those moments of seemingly inexplicable coincidences—a mother feeling a piercing pain in her chest precisely when her daughter has been in a car accident two thousand miles away, or that time you were thinking of an old friend you hadn't spoken with in years, only to come home to a message from her on your answering machine. These subtle synchronicities are all part of our daily reality. They are the faint yet persistent whisperings of the Uni-verse, saying to us, "You are not alone. Love knows no distance. Everything is connected to everything else."

Connection never occurs by erasing Uniqueness, but by accentuating it. Through your own authentically lived Unique Self, you are able to create relationship and intimacy with your beloved. Through your Unique Perspective, you offer your gifts to the larger whole. *Your Unique Self is your deepest erotic nature through which you connect and complete All-That-Is.*

Love is the interpenetration of all living things, the Eros of connection—the great ether of Eros in which we all live. Again, uniqueness is the bond that connects transforming heaps into wholes.

The evolutionary impulse to wholeness demands that you live the "puzzle-piece" nature of your story, thereby filling the hole in the wholeness of God that can only be filled by you. It is only when you respond to this evolutionary invitation—which is in fact your evolutionary obligation of love—that you can feel a personal sense of wholeness in your individual life. For as we said earlier, mature individuality is only in the context of union—union with the larger whole of which you are a unique part, but from which you are never apart.

Eros, Death, and Unique Self

Eros is radical aliveness. The opposite of Eros is death.

You intuit that death is wrong. To you, death means "nonexistence," and fear of death unconsciously drives almost everything you do. Poignantly, you try to give yourself a sense of existence, meaning, and purpose. *You wake up in the morning and scream, "I exist!" And then you spend the rest of the day trying desperately to prove to others and to yourself that you are real, that your existence is valuable, worthy, and significant.*

But it is hopeless, because the tool you use to prove your existence is your ego—your identity as a separate self. You do everything you can to reify your sense of small, separate self. Every day, your separate self enters a race it can never win—the race against death. You know that this is so, but you hide this knowledge from yourself.

Something within reminds you that some piece of you is immortal. And your intuition is right. You are wrong only in applying your intuition of immortality to your finite and mortal separate self.

You see potency and life as your eternal birthright. Here you are telling the truth. You seek to fulfill your potency and life in the immortality of your separate self and your ego's accomplishment. This is the lie of your life.

Your separate self is not immortal. Your ego will inevitably die along with your body. But there is indeed something in you that survives death, outliving the brutality of time, precisely because it exists outside of time and is thus immune to the maddening forces of entropy. *Atman*, the eternal soul, Buddha nature—the Sufis call it your heart *lataif*—all of these point toward the evolutionary emergent of Unique Self. *All of your ego's accomplishments in the realm of money, relationships, power, and sensual gratification become forms of the denial of death. If, however, you were to wake up and realize your True Nature, these same forms would become stunning natural expressions of your infinite Unique Self.*

Eros and Pseudo-Eros

Eros is both a constructive and destructive force.

She appears both as the "terrible mother" or "destroying goddess," as well as the "nurturing mother" and "radiant lover."

Shekhinah in Kabbalah and Kali in Hinduism are two synonyms for Eros. Shekhinah in Kabbalistic text appears as both a constructive and destructive force, and Eros always has these two faces of destroyer and mother. The constructive face reaches toward prior union. But sometimes Eros appears as tough love. This is the Eros of de-struction, which is really de-construction. The destructive face tears down old structures, obsolete preconceptions, and the illusions of the separate self. This de-constructive expression has often been termed Thanatos.

There is, however, a second more terrifying form of Thanatos that is not animated by Eros. It is rather suffused with the desperation and brutality of the ego's mad craving for eternal power and existence. This is the face of pseudo-Eros.

Let me explain.

The refusal to die to the separate self, the ego's insistence that it exists a-part from the whole, is the cancer that eats away at all of existence. For what else is cancer but cells that ignore their own part-ness, and claim to be the whole? They multiply uncontrollably, forgetting that they are parts of a larger organism.

When Eros is not realized, pseudo-Eros always comes in its place. When Eros is denied, pseudo-Eros demands its pound of flesh.

If the separate self will not die, there remains a deep knowing that some sort of death is still required. No longer will the death be that of our own ego, but the death of the other. And so we bear witness to some of the world's most horrible atrocities, all in the name of a higher power to which we refuse to surrender our own lives.

The problem begins only when the ego usurps its role and refuses to die at the appropriate time. In the language of the Sufi mystics, "The servant refuses to serve and pretends to be king." The part pretends to be a whole.

But here is the critical distinction that is all too often lost in both old and contemporary enlightenment teachings: The wholeness of Eros does not require the death of your experience as a separate self. Eros requires only the death of your exclusive identification with your separate self. You are not less than your separate self. You are more than your separate self. The separate-self ego's fear of death stems only from the ego's belief that its death leads to nonexistence. The ego correctly senses the infinite dignity of its unique divine expression. But it identifies the eternal nature of its unique God-spark with the separate egoic self. It does not realize that it can die to separate self, and yet be fully alive as a uniquely gorgeous strand in the seamless coat of the Uni-verse. *The separate self dies only to reveal True Self, which having fully realized its uniqueness, turns out to be Unique Self.*

In ego death you move from being isolated and a-part to being part of a larger whole, part of the infinitely loving spaciousness of God rising through and as every moment. You enter the orgasmic process of divine penetration and purification. This is the stage of dis-illusionment, in which the shadowy specter of being merely a separate self dies into the love and bliss of participating in the original evolving wholeness.

In virtually all the great traditions, the circle is a symbol of Eros. In pseudo-Eros, you create the illusion of being in the circle by placing someone else outside of it. The realization that ego death is required is not understood. So death becomes displaced—the death of the other guy. Since he is outside the circle of Eros, which is life, he deserves to die. True Eros means the deep knowing that everyone is inside the circle, that everyone holds a unique and irreplaceable place in the great wholeness of All-That-Is.

The first part of the Great Story of the evolution of consciousness requires the emergence of the separate self from the prior embeddedness in the all-absorbing womb of the Great Mother, in all of her guises, from mother nature to prerational magic to mother church.[10] This is the movement from the pre-personal to the first stage of the personal—the separate-self ego with all of the rights, responsibilities, and self-worth that being a separate self implies. It is this trajectory of the evolution of consciousness that culminates in the Western enlightenment conception, with its affirmation of the human rights and dignity of the separate individual. Without the birth of ego, the evolution of human consciousness beyond the pre-personal indignity cannot take place. The second part of the great evolution of consciousness requires dying to the separate self in the realization of True Self, which when refracted through the Unique Perspective of the individual, is revealed to be Unique Self. *Without ego death, the evolution of human consciousness beyond brutality and terror cannot take place.* Consider: For the first time in human history, with the emergence of the separate-self ego, murder and large-scale warfare purely for the sake of conquest was born. The skull grins, but the skull now belongs to the other guy.

Ernest Becker, Norman O. Brown, and others have documented the precise connection between the emergence of the separate self and murder. Murder expresses itself in both religious ritual and the political ritual of war. Kings begin to list their conquests with special emphasis on the number of victims brutally butchered on the other side. One ruler recorded this through his scribe: "As we wound and kill our enemies in the field, our love for each other deepens."[11] This is the classic horrifying distortion of pseudo-Eros. Pseudo-Eros is only necessary when true Eros cannot be found. Pseudo-Eros is the desperate grasping of the separate self for immortality.[12] Eros is the graceful, wondrous infinity of Unique Self.

So many of the great teachers of spirit demand that humans give up their sense of being a unique part in order to realize the Eros of union and even absorption into the whole. But despite their best attempts, most of the world refuses to heed this perennial teaching. This is not because we are bad or weak. Rather, it is because there is something in the teaching, or the way it is taught, that seems to contradict our basic intuition. The result is that many seekers end up feeling that they are fundamentally failures. And this in turn causes the horrific pain of inadequacy. People who feel inadequate may become vengeful, capable of inflicting untold suffering on themselves and those around them.

Here we find the double bind of every human being, and of humanity as a whole: You want pure existence, value, and transcendence. You want Eros. You are taught that full Eros is achieved by dying to your separate self—and that to die to your separate self you must reject your Uniqueness. Uniqueness is explicitly and implicitly conflated—wrongly—with separateness. Yet your most profound intuition tells you that this is wrong, a violation of a higher truth. So you are left stuck in your egoic separate self with only pseudo-Eros to comfort you.

Here is the key point: Once you realize that by giving up your separate self you do not give up your Uniqueness—both the source and substance of your existence—the contraction of your ego is released, and the door to the next stage of the evolution of consciousness is opened. *You can realize the fullness of your Eros through the realization of your Uniqueness, which is the puzzle-piece nature of your partness, through which you merge with the larger whole.*

PART THREE

The pearl is the oyster's autobiography.

—FELLINI

At bottom every man knows well enough
that he is a unique being, only once on this earth;
and by no extraordinary chance will such
a marvelously picturesque piece of diversity in unity
as he is, ever be put together a second time.

—FRIEDRICH NIETZSCHE

CHAPTER TWELVE

THE STORY OF STORY

Only Half the Story

TEACHERS OF ENLIGHTENMENT HAVE TOLD YOU that you must give up your story to be free, that you must leave behind your personal history to be liberated. Story limits you to your skin-encapsulated ego.

This is a deep and true teaching. But it is only half the truth.

Classical Western psychology has told you that the road to health requires you to focus on the drama of your personal story. It has created a container called therapy—which is exclusively focused on your story.

This is a deep and true teaching. But it is only half the truth.

Here is the other half of the story. There *is* a story you need to leave behind to achieve liberation. ***However, there is also a story you must radically embrace and live, and without which you can never realize your enlightenment.***

The His-story of Story

Prehistoric humans, embedded in nature, understanding neither the full dignity nor the full terror of their separate self, told only primitive stories. This is because they did not yet need the artifice of narrative to cover up their terror. Death terror is born from a larger sense of time, which emerged together with the experience of being a separate self—apart and against nature. The development of farming created the ability to store food for *tomorrow,* because the hunger and challenge of today had been met. This was a novel evolutionary emergence that was substantively different from the experience of the hunter-gatherers, who were embedded in the cycles of nature, almost completely absorbed in warding off the threats that faced them *today.* With separate self and an expanded sense of time, a new form of anxiety and terror was born; at the same time, the stories of culture were born to cover up the fear.

There is, however, a second reason why story is directly related to the emergence of the self. This second reason is absolutely essential to understand for your enlightenment.

With the emergence of self, the full dignity of the individual slowly began to dawn on humans. Human beings joyfully realized that they had infinite value, adequacy, and dignity, that they are an end unto themselves. There was a new knowing that personal story matters.

The ego was born out of this movement into individuation. Emerging out of the pre-personal subconscious, the ego was the assertion of the dignity of the personal (personal = personal story). With the emergence of self came the first glimmering recognition of Uniqueness. Remember: *the separate self prefigures the Unique Self.* As Kashmir Shaivism teacher Sally Kempton pointed out to me, in the Hindu tantric tradition, the same Sanskrit word—*aham*—is used to designate both the individual-ego self and Spirit in the first person, the One Self whose I-ness encompasses All-That-Is. The same is true, as we have already pointed out, in the original Hebrew: I (*ani*)-No-thing (*ayin*)-I (*ani*). In tantric philosophical texts, the Great I, or pure, absolute Awareness, is called *purno-aham vimarsha,* the "full or complete I-experience." These are early glimmerings of the Unique Self teaching in which the ego prefigures Unique Self. The great lie of ego, which must be dismantled, is its belief in a separate, isolated self, disconnected and alienated from the larger whole of other, God, and Ground.

When we talk of the ultimate dignity of the story, we refer not to the egoic story of the separate self, but rather to the magnificent, courageous, and poignant love story of the Unique Self.

The violation of human dignity through slavery, violence, bearing false witness, or any other form of subtle or brutal manipulation is a violation of story and hence a defacing of God.

"Form" is another word for story. *To paraphrase the* **Heart Sutra,** *there is no awareness without story and no story without awareness. Form* *and emptiness, story and nonstory, are one.* When we say that God is One or that reality is nondual, we mean that form and awareness, story and nonstory, are but different expressions of the One.

Expand Your Story

I have referred before in this book to a painful period in my life during which my world as I knew it came crashing down. Had I only tried to understand what had happened within the narrow framework of my individual life with its personal betrayals and tragedy, I would have had no hope of emerging from the story. It was only by expanding my personal story to its mythic dimensions that I was able to emerge not only unbroken, but paradoxically gifted a kind of love and wholeness that was previously only available to me in ecstatic states. It was only the larger mythic understanding that allowed me to hold the betrayal and searing pain in the larger context of love and transformation.

I called my dear friend Jean Houston several weeks after the tragedy. We had just met at a wonderful public dialogue that we had done together in front of a large audience in Ashland, Oregon. Jean's advice to me was unambiguous and direct: "Mythologize, don't pathologize." She asked me, "What is the greater myth that calls you to a new and deeper destiny that was not available to you before?"

And then without waiting for my response, she answered her own question. "Marc," she said, "you would have never left Israel and never stopped teaching primarily in your narrow Jewish context. God needed you to teach a world, teaching on the world stage. You were unavailable. You received many hints, but you did not listen, lost as you were in your laudable loyalty to your people and tradition. So God arranged a trial by fire that would exile you—perhaps forever—from all you called home. This trial of exile and humiliation is your hero's journey, your mythic tale meant to purify you so that you will be able to meet the next call of your destiny."

In that moment, Jean's larger, mythic story utterly shifted my perspective on everything that had happened. It took several years and a few other attempts to leave the world stage and find my way back to what I thought was my obligation and my home, until I finally surrendered to Jean's grand mythic reading. At that point, somehow—almost in a manner that was beyond my control—I coined the term "World Spirituality." And now I find myself midwifing (with Ken Wilber and other cultural leaders) an international movement in consciousness, aimed at articulating and enacting an evolutionary World Spirituality that has the depth and power to meet the immense and unique global challenges of our time.

Sometimes in the wake of a crisis your story seems to crash to a sudden ending, and all meaning seems to evaporate. You break down. Tragedy and disaster in small or large portions can undermine the narrative coherence of your life. You lose the thread of your story.

When you lose the thread of the story and get lost in your loneliness, you sometimes go to therapists to regain your way. Your therapist may at times have a vital role to play in helping you find your way in your small story. But all too often, your story is diminished in the process.

Psychology, suggests contemporary philosopher Ernest Becker, tends to reduce human experience. It can disenchant human beings, estranging them from a sense of ultimate value. You want to focus your love on the absolute measure of power and value, and the therapist tells you that your urge is based upon your early conditioning and is therefore relative. You want to find and experience the marvelous, and the therapist tells you how matter-of-fact everything is, how clinically explainable are all of your deepest motives and guilt. You are thereby deprived of the absolute mystery your Unique Self requires. The only omnipotent power that remains is the psychologist who explained it away. And so patients cling to the analyst with all of their might, and dread the termination of therapy.

Psychological myth reduces your deepest yearnings and needs to a set of uninspiring, pitiful human drives that are beyond your control and ignoble at their core. Unique Self consciousness tells you that while the human condition might at times be tragic, it is never pitiful, and it is always full of hope.

Do not lose hold of your undiminished self.

The Grace of the Story

If you can continue to remember to value story, the grace of the story will rise again. The story will gift you with a deeper narrative, and you will begin to see the patterns that connect. The Great Story takes you out of the narrow pettiness of tired details and into the rich texture of the wider evolutionary context. This is precisely what happened to me and what can happen to you if you but re-vision your story in the heroic and mythic terms that address the deepest longing of your unfinished dream.

Larger patterns of meaning emerge. *You need to call forth the wonder of your story.*

When you call forth the wonder of your story, you align yourself with the evolutionary impulse that loves you so much that it personalized itself as you. That is what the Unique Self mystics mean when they say that God loves stories. Great Story is like a force field, clearing away the many unrelated and seemingly minor plots of your life with overarching meaning and significance.

The Loss of Memory

We all are inheritors of memories and stories larger than our individual lives. You carry the collective experiences that make you old and wise beyond your age or your local knowing.

You are a deeper well than your life history allows. The local stories of your life are entwined in the larger evolutionary story breaking out the world over. And so you must also tell mythic stories. Myth holds a memory larger than your individual story. That is why passionate engagement in a religion or spiritual tradition is so vital to the impoverished modern soul. Joseph Campbell is reported to have said, "A myth is something that never was, but is always happening." It is for this precise reason that myth allows you to regain access to the deep codings of Source that live in your story. Myth breaks your self-contraction.

Not all myths are the same. Some are rooted in lower consciousness, others in higher consciousness. An egocentric myth is not the same as a worldcentric myth. A racist myth is not expressive of truth in the same way as an evolutionary myth. You must deploy the necessary discernment. The miracle of the story is that it allows a different interpretation at every level of consciousness.

But without myths, without the larger stories, you remain stuck in the self-absorption of your narcissistic ego.

Myths demand that you mythologize. When you mythologize, you are freed from the obsessive need to pathologize, demonize, or anesthetize. A big failure takes on a different perspective when you mythologize it.

Recognize that failure is part of the hero's journey; transform it into a space of insight that catalyzes your next, greater evolutionary leap. That which seemed like a tragic detour of fate is revealed to be a fractal wave of your destiny and destination. ***When you mythologize, you regain voice.*** With your reclaimed voice, you may once again read aloud what my friend Jean Houston has called the unread vision of your higher dream.[1]

The Great Story of Evolution and the Democratization of Enlightenment

We live in the time of the annunciation of a new myth, the Great Story of Evolution. This Myth of Evolution is both a passion play, a morality tale, and a three-way romantic drama between the human being, kosmos, and God.

In the language of Unique Self mystic Abraham Kook, this myth raises "the public center of gravity to moral heights and ecstatic joy" in a way that was virtually unattainable in previous eras. Kook and de Chardin, inspired by evolutionary philosophers like Sri Aurobindo and Luria, embrace evolution as the highest and most noble expression of the ethical meaning of our lives on Earth.

Kook writes, "The deep understanding of the evolutionary context in forming our vision of the future exalts man to a moral pinnacle of spirit, radically raising the bar of his ethical responsibility."[2]

Aligning with the evolutionary impulse and taking responsibility for the entire process was, for the last several hundred years, limited to a very small circle of elite mystics. They functioned as an *axis mundi*. (*Axis mundi*, literally "cosmic axis," is an essential proto-evolutionary teaching that lives in all the great traditions.) It was their task to steady the world with the unbroken clarity and purity of their intention. The World Tree, the Pole in Sufism, the world mountain (Meru) in Hinduism, the pillar of light in Mayan and Kabbalistic lore, the rod connecting heaven and earth, Jacob's Ladder—these are different names for the *axis mundi*. The kosmic axis, according to the perennial wisdom traditions, incarnates in a human being, who is a vital point of connection embracing heaven and earth. The *tzadik hador,* the thirty-six just men upon whom the world rests, and the *jagadguru* or "world teacher" are names for this figure or group of figures. It is to this that Jesus referred when he said, "I am the Light," and when he said, "I and my father are one. When you see me, you see the one who sent me."

In the esoteric teaching of Unique Self evolutionary mysticism, the *axis mundi* is absolutely aligned with the ecstatic evolutionary impulse that courses through the kosmos.[3] In Hebrew mysticism, *axis mundi* = Unique Self = Goddess. But it is even more than that. She is not only aligned. She incarnates and expresses in her very being the God-impulse. The evolutionary impulse lives, breathes, and yearns in her. Her very being becomes ecstatic, and experiences heartbroken, joyful responsibility for the evolution of All-That-Is.

The Shift

The shift is that she is no longer one, or even one hundred. This is the movement towards democratization of enlightenment.

The shift is that God turns at this moment in time and says to each of us, soft eyes pleading and passionate, "Won't you be my *axis mundi?* I need you . . ."

We are now entering the time of the Shift. The Shift is from private to public, from the realm of the elite to the democratization of the New Enlightenment.

"You are the true Light, which enlightens every man that cometh into the world."[4] You means *You.*

Kook says it well:

> *Every person needs to know*
> *that he is called to serve*
> *based on the model of perception and feeling*
> *which is absolutely unique to him,*
> *based on the core root of his soul. . . .*
> *A person needs to say:*
> Bi-shvili nivrah ha-olam
> *("Through my Unique path the world is created.")*[5]

The core ecstatic ethical meditation of the New Enlightenment is, "The world is created for and by my Unique Path." This is not a declaration of hubris but a statement of responsibility. ***To be connected to your Unique Self means to know that your story is sufficiently important, significant,*** *and wonderful, and that the entire world was created for its sake. The dignity of your story demands no less than that you get up every morning and know that your very next action has the power to shape the destiny of our collective future.* Thirteenth-century master Maimonides writes that the superior man experiences the whole world as precisely balanced on a scale, with his next action tipping the scale for good or for bad.[6] Fourteen billion years of evolution are flowing through you, awaiting your choice. Living this consciousness in joy, your choice becomes filled not only with your goodness but with a radical evolutionary integrity that—in the language of Kook—"enlightens and frees all worlds."

All worlds: matter, body, soul, and spirit. In the vision of evolutionary spirituality articulated by de Chardin and Kook, the goal of evolution is no less than the full awakening of all reality. All matter will wake up to its full potential. The present neutrality of the earth in regard to human suffering is startling. Visiting Poland and Germany a few years ago, I was disconcerted to see beautiful meadows around the concentration camps and massacre sites. Why had the meadows not risen up in protest against the gas chambers and the murders? Why did the earth silently receive the bodies of all those gunned down into mass graves? Something in me felt it should not be this way. The hills should be alive in protest and violent objection to moral evil. Volcanoes should have erupted under the death camps. It is this sense of evolutionary potential that moves us when we see the trees taking a heroic moral stand in Tolkien's *The Lord of the Rings*.

Not All Stories Are Equal

An enemy is one whose story we have not heard. This is a great and partial truth.

At a critical point in my life, a woman I loved betrayed me. Not in a private way—not the relatively common private betrayal of infidelity, serious as it is. This was rather in a way that affected directly the entire course of my life, contributing to levels of pain that are literally beyond description. I had gone through a wrenching tragedy that affected her directly. I had hurt her. I wanted to sit with her and tell her what happened. She was a spiritual adept influenced by teachings that taught her to "move beyond the story." She said to me, time and again, "I do not want to get lost in the story." So we never entered the story. She used a spiritual bypass position as a cover for her refusal to hear my perspective, and ultimately to run from the scene. Her standing with us at that critical juncture would have shifted the entire trajectory of events. The story remained untold, the injustice unchallenged and therefore unhealed.

We all have a thousand covers that allow us to close our hearts. *To stay open as love is the invitation of your life.* You cannot do so, however, by abandoning the integrity of the story. Your ego becomes so obsessed with your hurt or fear that you are sometimes seduced to close your heart, rather than do the work of story. Hearing your enemy's story—really hearing— may be just what is needed to make them no longer your enemy.

Yet it is also true that not all myths are the same. Not all stories have equal gravitas. You may hear your enemy's story, and they may remain your enemy. Not all interpretations of *Romeo and Juliet* have equal value. There are some readings of this play that so egregiously violate the sense and facts of the story that they are simply wrong. There is a hierarchy of stories. Some stories are more true than others.

False hierarchies most often manifest as what we refer to as dominator hierarchies. They are built by assigning to something or someone a value that it does not have—for example, "White people are more evolved than black people" is a false hierarchy. Or, "People born in Tibet are superior to people born in Kansas." These are false hierarchies, false stories, false myths. The truest story is able to take in the greatest number of perspectives and align them with the greatest number of facts in all the quadrants of reality, in the best way possible.

The simplest example is in the realm of justice. A judge must first hear both sides of the story. The judge must examine the hurt that is claimed. Is it true? What are the potential hidden motives of everyone concerned? What are the consequences of each possible course of action? At that point, the judge must sit carefully for some period of time to allow the fullness of the facts and perspectives from all sides to emerge.

When we speak of a judge, we do not refer to the formal position of the judicial officer in the court. Rather, by "judge" we mean anyone whose decision has power over the fate of another's life. The more power, the more responsibility and therefore the more care and love required. The judge must be a lover. Judgment is a process of radical love. And love is a perception.

The art of the lover is the perception of the True Nature, the Unique Self, of every moment, person, and situation in the larger context of All-That-Is. Only a Unique Self can judge fairly with love. If you are not in your Unique Self, then you *need something* from the judgment. You are partial, meaning you are locked in your part nature, disconnected from your larger self. Your small self is grasping to steal from the judgment what it can, for its own survival.

Your True Self plus your clarified personal perspective, which is your Unique Self, is the only possible source of right judgment.

You may go through the entire love process of judgment—hearing and evaluating all motives and stories—and someone may still remain an enemy. You may decide, as the Dalai Lama once said to me, that we need to "deploy violence against the enemy when there is no other choice. Even so, we never stop loving them." Do what you need to do, but never put the enemy out of your heart. Forgiveness and reconciliation will then remain an ever-present possibility.

Five Movements against Story

There are five major spiritual and cultural movements today that stand against the integrity of the story.[7]

The first, as we have already seen, is Theravada Buddhism, of the variety taught at many spiritual centers around the world, which emphasizes the realization of No-Self. This teaching moves a person past personality and ego into the space of the unifying awareness or consciousness in which we all participate. This important teaching is true but partial. This teaching rejects story. The first thing you are told is to "give up your story" and "detach from desire." The teaching fails to distinguish between the pettiness of your ego's pseudostory and the dignity of your authentic Unique Self story.[8]

The second movement against story is rooted in what has been called, in one version of developmental theory, Spiral Dynamics, the Green-level consciousness. This is an extreme version of pluralism and multiculturalism. Of course, these are both good and noble principles that express a genuine evolution in consciousness. They are based on the claim that distinctions are rooted in ego, and if we would move beyond ego and take the perspective of other, we would see that position as equally valid. However, in Green consciousness, there is a rejection of all hierarchy, motivated by an obsession to level all differences. All differences are thought to derive from ego, and none from True or Unique Self. So along with the appropriate rejection of hidden dominator hierarchies, which is characteristic of Green consciousness, is a loss of all discernment and authority. As Habermas has already pointed out, the blogosphere in its shadow forms is the ultimate instrument of what has been called the mean green meme. The voice of distinctions, integrity, fact-checking, narrative authority, dignity, and decency are lost in the din of mean-spirited and all-too-often false distortions of the story.

The third movement against story is a particular strain of Christian instant forgiveness. Forgiveness is based—in this teaching—on the ability to access one's divine self beyond ego. The assumption of this teaching is that the only place where there is no forgiveness is where people are stuck in ego. It does not recognize that forgiveness may also be withheld out of love, which derives from the True Self and Unique Self. When instant forgiveness is deployed cheaply, it undermines the value of moral hierarchy and the dignity of the story. For example, when there is a massacre of schoolchildren and there is instant forgiveness of the murderers, the basic structure of story and human dignity are undermined.[9]

The fourth movement against story is the academic dogma of postmodernism, which demands the deconstruction of all story lines. Story lines are said to be purely subjective and rooted in ego. Stories in this view are held to be without objective correlates with which they may be checked and validated. This position is an extreme and obviously absurd distortion of a correct and critical core insight—the realization that perspective and context have a significant impact on the stories we tell about our lives and the world. However, this does not mean that there is no objective way to establish a hierarchy of stories based on assessing their validity from the most perspectives possible. It does not mean that some perspectives are not clearer and more valid than others. The grand narrative claim of postmodernity is that there are no grand narratives. All narratives are deconstructed. The only story that remains, however, is that there is no story, and in this contradiction, extreme postmodernity is undermined.

The fifth contributing factor to the undermining of the story is plain old flatland relativism, described by Lewis Mumford as the "disqualification of the Universe."[10] This is the simple denial of any depth to reality. There is no moral depth. All acts are equally valid. All moral distinctions are held to be the construction of the human ego. There is no authentic moral texture that can guide us, no genuine moral distinctions that can be authentically made about the nature of our lives or the quality of our actions.

Each of these five movements levels an important and powerful critique of the ego's story. Each fails to distinguish the Unique Self story, which is based on the ability to make depth discernments about the nature of reality and truth that are not merely egoic survival strategies.

The Denial of the Story Is a Primary Source of Evil

The central characteristic of evil is not what the old books used to call sin. There is no righteous person in the land who does not sin. The character trait that creates evil is the refusal to tell the truth about the story. Evil claims a story without sin. The result is that the evil person almost always projects their darkness outward. This virtually always results in the demonization of other. The most sure sign of individual evil or communal corruption is demonization and scapegoating. Since the demonizers refuse to take ownership of their own darkness, they must always perceive others as bad.

Mother Teresa wrote, "If you are willing to bear serenely the trial of being displeasing to your self, then you will for Jesus be a pleasant place of shelter."[11]

Evil originates not in the absence of light but in the effort to deny the darkness. In the smile that hides the hatred. In the tears and apparent hurt that mask the malice and fury. It requires great effort and commitment to truth to identify the locus of the lie. Unique Self teacher Martin Buber reminds us that evil "plays an uncanny game of hide-and-seek in the obscurity of the soul, in which it, the single human soul, avoids itself and hides."[12] It hides both from itself and from others. The primary method and motive of evil is disguise, which happens through denial, deception, and demonization. All are different ways to distort the story.

The individual, when ego is clarified, becomes an organ of experience for the whole Uni-verse. *Every human being is an infinitely dignified and worthy story that needs to be lived and loved and deserves to be told.* Every human also has a unique story to tell. That is what it means to be a Unique Self. That is what it means to be a lover. That is what it means to love God.

To love God is to allow God to see with your eyes, to uniquely see what can be seen from your perspective, with your unique depth and unique qualities. This is what it means to love God. Self-love is to know your own nature, to perceive your Unique Self. Self-love is enlightenment. The nature of the Uni-verse is that it evolves. Life-forms differentiate from earlier life-forms, and evolve in an ever-increasing order of complexity and consciousness. We know that complexity and consciousness are intimately related. They are the inside and outside of the same evolutionary unfolding. The more complex the physical organism, the more evolved are the inner workings of consciousness of that same being. A rabbit is more materially complex and more conscious than a snail. A human being is more materially complex and conscious than a dog. While it may be true that a dog has Buddha nature, the dog will never know it. *Each original form provides original Being with a unique experience of itself.* An amoeba serves the divine with a particular experience of itself, a butterfly with another, a fish with yet another. A bird and a horse each provide yet another experience in which the divine experiences itself. The human being, however, is a quantum leap forward in consciousness. The human being is conscious and self-reflective. *In a complete human being, the Uni-verse experiences itself completely.*

To love is to see through God's eyes. This requires you to shift perspectives from that of your separate-self ego to your infinitely expansive Unique Self. To love God is to let God see through your eyes. The truth of love is that you can only love God or another through your eyes—which are the eyes of God. It is this very realization that obligates you to cleanse your doors of perception—the way God sees through your eyes—and open the gates of divine love. You see with and as the eyes of God only if you purify the pettiness of small self and uncoil the self-contraction of ego. It is only thus that God can see through the prism of your Unique Eyes. That is why you are obligated to clarify your perception. Any lack of wholeness on your part defaces the divine. Any blurriness in your Unique Perspective and perception obstructs the vision of God. If you cannot see clearly, you blind God:

If you are bland and blend,
Tyrannized by the trend,
The God mind
Goes blind.

Your job is to make yourself so transparent to the divine, so open to the love-intelligence coursing through you, in you, and as you, that God can see with your eyes. This is your gift to God.

CHAPTER THIRTEEN

SACRED AUTOBIOGRAPHY

IN GREAT POETRY, CLASSICAL LITERATURE, mysticism, and sappy love songs, the most often used metaphor for soul and spirit is light. That is for a simple reason: love and light are one.

"This little light of mine . . . "

Love is in Kabbalah a form of light. One kabbalist writes that the very word *ahava*—"love" in Hebrew—is no more than an acronym for *ohr hakadosh baruch hu:* the "Light of God."

Thus, much of Kabbalah discusses in esoteric terms the various configurations of lights—of love—that define different planes of reality. For the kabbalists, all light is shaped by an expression of consciousness. Thus, much of kabbalist practice is a complex series of *kavvanot* ("intentions") and *yichudim* ("unifications") whose goal is no less than the shaping of reality through love.

How is it that our consciousness in-forms the light? Because in our essence, we ourselves are each, on some level, particular frequencies of light. This is the inner intention of the kabbalistic idea that every human being has a particular letter in the Torah. A letter in the Torah is a particular frequency. *Every human being is a particular frequency of light, that is to say, of love-intelligence. A meeting of lovers is a meeting of lights.* The mystical master Israel Baal Shem Tov, master of the name, is reported to have said:

> From every human being, there rises a light that reaches straight to heaven. And when two souls that are destined to be together find each other, their streams of light flow together, and a single bright light goes forth from their united being.

It is for this reason that the image used most often in biblical myth to describe the Unique Self is also light. Your Unique Self is your light. When we sing "You light up my life" or "You are my sunshine," we don't mean "You support me financially" or "You help me to advance politically." We mean "your infinite specialness—your Unique Self—illuminates my existence."

To decipher the innate truth that tells us that the physical property of light is the model of the soul—besides the obvious reason that light is bright and we can see by it—we need to introduce a principle found throughout the Kabbalah, which is a basic element of Plato's thought: the physical and spiritual worlds are refractions, reflections, mirrors of each other.[1]

Given that understanding, let's explore how physical light "illuminates" the nature of your Unique Self.

Light, modern science teaches us, is paradoxically both particle and wave. Understood as a particle, light exists as a particular point. Understood as a wave, it possesses a flowing and more amorphous quality. Light is a twofold phenomenon not only in modern physics but also in ancient biblical myth. Light in Hebrew is referred to as *sapir*, from which the English word "sapphire" is derived. Sapphire—blue light—is also the visualized image of enlightened Unique Self expression in the mystical biography of leading Hindu mystics. For example, Hindu master Muktananda—who taught that "God dwells within you, as you"—visualized his Unique Self as a figure of sapphire-blue light.[2]

Two Hebrew words spring from this luminous root *saphir: mispar*, which means "number," and *sippur*, which means "story."

Mispar implies a discrete unit, a place-holding point, a way of identifying a unique and specific moment, place, thing, or person in the sea of infinity. It corresponds to the particle nature of light.

Mispar is the calling dimension of our Unique Selves. By "calling," I mean the human experience of being summoned to a particular mission or destiny. The person called is summoned as a One, a singular being with a discrete, defined destiny to fulfill. *You are called to a "point" of meaning, one that you alone are charged to fulfill.*

Does the prospect of being singled out sound daunting, even lonely? Only at first glance. Only by responding to your unique call do you open up the channels in your Unique Self that create connection, loving, and community. Your singularity is actually the most powerful access point to the greater One. Number is the call of the One through the one.

Sippur, story, corresponds to the wave quality of light, flowing and streaming, just like the tales of our lives. The wave function of our soul is thus our story, the wavelike rush of events and emotions we experience in a lifetime, the waves of our life-light that we are called to shine into the world. The incidents, details, images, and apparent coincidences of your life all weave a story unlike that of any other human being.

Light exists in every instant as both wave and particle. So there will be natural overlap between the two spiritual equivalents as well. The two are not divisible. Indeed, living your Unique Self Story and responding to your Unique Self calling are complementary and sometimes even identical endeavors.

The specific qualities of light, its dual nature, reflect the masculine and feminine poles of your Unique Story—masculine and feminine as distinct qualities and textures that appear in both men and women. The particle quality of light is pointed and particular. It reflects your particular calling and mission. Its nature is directional. This is its masculine pole. The wave quality of light is flowing and radiant. It points to the unique quality of your presence, the unique radiance with which you light up your ordinary life, to the uncommon expression of your common story. This is the feminine pole.

The masculine and the feminine live in you, as in everyone, as distinct faces of the indivisible one. One expression of Unique Self is your unique balance and integration of your masculine and feminine poles. Every human being is a hermaphrodite—a combination of masculine and feminine qualities. And no two hermaphrodites are the same.[3]

Mispar—Our Clarion Call

A third-century biblical-myth text describes how the census of the children of Israel was taken in the desert. "Moses entered the tent of the person being counted in the census . . . At the moment of the counting, the Cloud of Glory [the Presence of God] left the Tent of Meeting [the traveling temple of the desert] and dwelled lovingly atop the tent of the person." The numbering of each individual person was an affirmation of the unique dignity, absolute adequacy, and value of that person.

Of course, when we reduce "counting" to a gathering of technical data—forgetting that number is the window to unique calling—then we make room for a dark shadow. Every great idea has its own unique and dangerous shadow side. The shadow side of numbering is the reduction of a person to an "it," an entity numbered like cattle merely for reasons of bookkeeping. This occurred centuries later when the biblical monarch David takes a census of the people to affirm his power and control. Bad karmic fortune befalls him when he counts—so much so that there grew a mystical tradition never to enumerate people aloud, as when one might count the number of people around a table.

The full shadow of the idea of a personal number became horrifically apparent in Hitler's Germany. In a demonic attempt to undermine the beauty of the number's personal call, the Nazis tattooed every person in the concentration camps with a number. Rather than evoking uniqueness, calling, dignity, or value, the intent of the Nazis' reckoning was to identify each person so that their execution—by gas, torture, shooting, or starvation—could be duly recorded. This image of the arm branded with a number haunts humanity's imagination, the numerical tattoo becoming a symbol for the most grotesque debasement of humanity's Unique Self.

Hitler's explicitly stated goal was to destroy the core ideas that biblical myth gave to the world and replace them with Teutonic myths of blood barbarism and what Hitler saw as Aryan grandeur. "I stand against the Bible and its life-denying Ten Commandments," said Hitler to his advisor Hermann Rauschning. "I set the Aryan and the Jew against each other, and if I call one of them a human being I must call the other something else. The two are as widely separated as man and beast." Since most of my family was killed by this very Teutonic myth, I count the fact that I am traveling all over the world helping reweave the Unique Self fabric of our civilization as no small victory over darkness.

Every person who embraces the singular gorgeousness of their Unique Self is one more proof that the light of *mispar*—of a person called—will triumph over the darkness that reduces human beings to statistics for filing or extermination.

Unique Self Story

We now re-turn our attention to story, to the wave function of our light. Our Unique Self story. This term refers not to one specific mission or moment—it is, rather, the uninterrupted flow of your entire life story. Life story is made up of the common moments that we all share—eating, sleeping, loving, arguing, studying, taking care of the details, and all the rest.

Poet Charles Reznikoff refers to these details as the "common table," that which is normal, routine, unextraordinary—life's daily fare of food. But "common" also means "communal," that which we all share, there where we all sit. Your story is in large part how you live uniquely at the common table. Each of us sleeps, eats, loves, rages, works, and speaks. Not one of us, however, does those things in quite the same way. ***Living your story is about expressing the originality of your commonness.*** It is about making the ordinary extra-ordinary.

Of course, that is not all. Your story is also the revealer of your unique destiny. *Unlike a call, which is focused and specific, your story is the unique weave, the blonding and the melding of all the moments and encounters of a lifetime. All of these are bound together into the book of your life.*

Appreciating Each Other's Purple Trees

There is a tale that educators love about the girl who paints a purple tree. The teacher, who has drawn a tree on the board and asked the children to copy it, is disapproving. "You didn't copy my tree."

"I know," says the girl. "I drew my tree."

"But I've never seen a purple tree."

"Isn't that a shame," says the girl.

In a similar vein, Hebrew mystic myth master Kook laments educators who efface the "Essential I," his term for Unique Self:

> Along come the learned teachers,
> and focus their gaze on all that is outside,

>they too distract us from the "I,"
>they add fuel to the fire,
>giving the thirsty vinegar to drink . . .
>stuffing the minds with all that is external to them . . .
>and the Essential I is more and more forgotten.[4]

Sometimes our educators, our leaders, and our parents haven't the eyes to read our insides. And so we write our own stories to fit their skewed sight, even if it means a betrayal of our own tales. Children are all unique until they "try to be." They try to be in order to get us to notice them—we, who weren't paying attention when they were painting purple trees. The job of an educator—and we are all educating each other—is to impart basic skills to the student *and* to honor their purple trees.

The purple tree is rooted in the part of us that cannot be fully expressed, cannot be narrowed into words, and cannot be subjected to laws. ***Ultimately, every person is completely free and has their own special salvation. No form of instruction exists; no savior exists to open up the road. No road exists to be opened. The road is you.***

In the teachings of Unique Self mysticism, there is a special prayer in which we ask to be written into what is called the Book of Life. Really, though, explains the kabbalistic master of Slonim, it is not us asking God to be inscribed, but God asking us. "Please, this year, write yourself in the Book of Life!" God entreats us.

Now, what could God, the force, the kosmos, possibly mean by such a plea? The beautiful teaching is hidden in the mysteries of ancient Hebrew. Remember that our core Unique Self word is *sapir*, light. The word for "book," as in the "Book of Life," is *sefer*—deriving from the identical three-letter root as *sapir* and its derivatives *mispar* and *sippur* (number and story). *Sefer*, your Book of Life, is made up of the chapters of your *sippur*, your story. "Answer your call. Write yourself in the Book of Life," God says, as he turns to every human being and says, "Live your story!"

God has placed a pen in our hands, inviting us—some would even say commanding us—to become both the authors and the heroes of our own tale. Every incident, relationship, residence, and experience is part of the plot. As Dickens wrote in *David Copperfield*, "Whether I shall turn out to be the hero of my own life, or whether that station will be held by anybody else, these pages must show."

The greatness of a piece of literature is not determined by whether or not its protagonist has succeeded or failed. The main concern is rather: Has the writer succeeded or failed? Have they deeply expressed the passion of the story? Have they deepened their hero? Do they lose the narrative's direction through all the plots and subplots? Are they comprehending and guiding the course of action from some deep, intuitive place, or do they aimlessly write, spurting and stopping, hoping that it will somehow become a flow?

Unique Self's radical affirmation of the value of your distinct and singular life story is a fundamentally different outlook from that of many contemporary, popular spiritual understandings. To cite but one example, Carlos Casteneda's Don Juan in *Journey to Ixtlan* says, "I had a terribly strong attachment to my personal history. . . . I honestly felt that without [it] my life had no continuity or purpose. . . . I don't have personal history anymore . . . I dropped it one day when I felt it was no longer necessary."

This notion of moving beyond personal history is particularly powerful in Theravada Buddhism, which is so popular in spiritual circles these days. In Unique Self-realization, you understand that personal history, the cycle of your life, or the cycle of your successive lives, is something you want to heal and evolve, but not escape. There is a *tikkun*—a fixing, in kabbalistic language—that is the plotline of your story, and of every story.

Our goal is never to escape our stories but to make them sacred. That is why the core book of biblical myth, called the Torah, is written neither as a series of Zen koans nor as a sutra, nor even as a Western philosophical essay. The Torah is, pure and simple, a story. Because as the masters said, "God loves stories."

Your story is the personal face of your essence. To move beyond it would be to lose yourself.

Don Juan Meets Dovid of Lilov

Hasidic Master Dovid of Lilov was asked by his students, "What section of the Talmud will you study in heaven?"

"In heaven," he said, "I will spend all my time studying Tractate Dovid Lilov."

Dovid of Lilov did not fall into obsessive narcissism late in his life. Instead, he realized that his very own life was sacred ground. Laura Riding, one of the most exciting yet unsung American poets of the twentieth century, captured Dovid of Lilov's idea in one elegant sentence: *"Until the story of your life is told, nothing besides told can suffice us: you shall go on quietly craving it."*

Recovering Your Story

It is in the telling of our stories that we realize the Unique Self upon which our very lives depend. Indeed, this was literally the case for Scheherazade, the queen who is narrator of the stories that make up *The Arabian Nights*. The sultan of Persia had issued a decree that any woman he married should be executed the morning after the wedding. Nonetheless, this heroine volunteered to marry this murderous monarch. But on their wedding night, Scheherazade began telling the sultan a story of great enchantment—and great length. When it came time for her execution, the sultan, thoroughly seduced by her tale, agreed to stay the execution in order to hear the story's end. When Scheherazade finished, she started another one, and then another, and so it went for 1,001 nights and 1,001 stories. By this time, the sultan, transformed by the stories and smitten with his wife, agreed to nullify his barbaric edict.

Scheherazade's story not only saved her own life and the lives of the sultan's brides, she also saved the life of the sultan himself. She returned him to his story.

The Lost Thread

When we lose the thread of our own stories, we lose our very lives. Remember Theseus, who travels through the underground labyrinth to slay the Minotaur? His challenge is more than slaying the beast; he must also find his way back out of the maze after his success. *Often we get lost in our own accomplishments. We slay the beast, but stay stuck in the maze.* Ariadne, the king's daughter, a symbol of the feminine energy, gave Theseus a length of thread to help him retrace his steps. The thread in our personal myth is what keeps us connected to the light as we wander in the labyrinth of darkness. The thread is the thread of the story. When we lose that thread (no matter how many beasts we slay), we are lost.

This is precisely what Franz Kafka had in mind in his masterpiece, *The Trial*. The plot of the novel is an intentionally impossible path to follow. Reading the novel, one becomes increasingly confused. The plot unravels, the thread of meaning slackens like spaghetti, ending up as a mess of words in the reader's confounded hands. At many points, the story line seems in reach, only to slip out of grasp again, like a lure drawing the reader along. Frustration, anger, and a radical hopelessness gradually build in the reader— as Kafka subjects us to the very feelings that his protagonist K. undergoes as he is arrested, for what and by whom he doesn't know. Every time he detects a glimmer of sense in the proceedings, it vanishes into nonsense. K. is over-whelmed, incapable of making sense of his story, tortured by a nonsensical system of bureaucracy and human inanity. In an all-too-apt passage, Kafka captures how we all feel on occasion about our lives: "He was too tired to survey all the conclusions arising from the story. . . . The simple story had lost its clear outline, he wanted to put it out of his mind."

What Kafka is describing is the unique torture of modernity and post-modernity, the sense of being disassociated, de-storied, displaced. K. is just an initial—essentially nameless, devoid of context, history, or Unique Self. The goal of the invisible torturer is to rob the victim of his story. The inflic-tion of pain is a method and not the goal. Through pain, the torturer aims to force the victim to betray and abandon his story.

To lose hope in life is to lose the thread of your story. ***To recover hope is to reweave the fabric of your story.*** A single thread can be enough to lead us back to reweave the full tapestry of our tale.

The Nobel Prize laureate for literature, S. Y. Agnon, who drew much of his inspiration from biblical myth and the Kabbalah, loved to tell the fol-lowing anecdote:

> When the Baal Shem was faced with a particularly difficult challenge, he would go to a certain place in the woods, light a sacred fire, meditate in prayer, and the challenge would be met.
>
> When his successor, the master from Mezerich, was faced with a similar challenge, he would go to the same place in the forest. There he would say, "We no longer know how to light the fire, but we have the prayer and that will be enough." And the challenge would be met.

When his successor, the master from Sassov, was faced with a similar situation, he would say, "We no longer know how to light the fire, and we have forgotten the prayer, but we know the place in the woods." He would go to the sacred spot and the challenge would be met.

Finally, however, in the fourth generation, a great challenge arose, and the master from Rishin, successor of the earlier generations, was called to action. "We do not know how to light the fire," he said. "We have forgotten the prayer. We do not remember the place in the forest. What shall we do?"

He put his head down in defeat, only to lift it a moment later.

"We shall tell the story of what they did!" he exclaimed.

So he sat in his chair and told this story. And the challenge was met.

A story can have the strength of a thousand incantations, the incense of the most sacred of spaces, the heat and light of the most brilliant of flames. Never lose your story, for the lines of your Unique Self are the lines of your story. Live it; tell it loud.

The postmodern context in which we all live has destroyed our existence. All stories, called "grand narratives," have been deconstructed. To recover from the disease implicit in our time, we must recover memory. First, memory of your Unique Self stories, and then on to the collective memory of the Uni-verse story, for this is the memory not only of the past but of the future.[5]

Wrong Turns and Leaking Buckets

One of the things that often prevents us from changing course is the sunken cost that we feel we have invested in the wrong path. It seems like changing course would be to acknowledge that we have wasted five, ten, or even twenty-five years of our lives. This seems too painful to bear. What do we do with our wrong turns, with our years of imitation?

You must understand that all of your detours are part of your destination. There is no way you could have realized your Unique Self other than the way you traveled. Once you have integrated that affirmation, you can look back over your path, in all its tangled briars and dead ends, and reach a new and sympathetic understanding of where you've been and why. *Every place you have been you needed to be. This is true even if it takes many years to understand why this might be so.*

> Every morning, the water carrier of Stanislov would walk from the well at the edge of town through the same *shtetl* streets, toting his two buckets of water to his customers. Day in and day out, he performed his routine with a simple joy.
>
> One day he was particularly joyous and burst out in song along the way. But his song was interrupted by the sound of weeping from one of his buckets. The bucket called up to him, "How can you sing so joyously? Are you blind? Don't you realize what a bum bucket you've got in your hand? Don't you realize that for years now I've been leaking? Look at your other bucket—he doesn't leak. I don't know why you didn't use me for kindling a long time ago. What good is a bucket that leaks?!"
>
> The water carrier gently responded to his bucket, "No, my bucket, you are the one who is blind. What good is a bucket that leaks, you ask. Well, look and see."
>
> With these words, the water carrier made a grand motion toward the ground beneath the bucket, pointing out the same path they had walked for years. "Look, my leaking bucket, look at your side of the path—the yellow daisies, the wild red strawberries, the luscious greens. Now look at the other side of the path, the ground beneath my sturdy, leakless bucket— it is nothing but gravel and dirt. All of this beauty is precisely because of your leak. For years now you have watered this side of the path, making it the most beautiful thoroughfare of Stanislav. Your leak is what makes me sing!"

In my own life, my mistakes brought me to places I might otherwise never have visited. They delivered me to ideas I might otherwise never have taken seriously. I regret my mistakes, yet I love them dearly, and understand that every path I walked was significant for me and was nourished by my being there. When I began my journey, I thought my calling was to be the king's irrigation system—watering the grand gardens around the palace with precisely distributed quantities of water. Today, I sometimes suspect that I am the king's bucket, or the king's gardener's bucket, or the assistant to the king's gardener's bucket—trying my best to hold my water. Leaking as I go, I am at least hopeful that I may leave behind a string of daisies to decorate the road.

For in the end, are we not all imperfect vessels for the light—leaking illumination along the way?

Deeper still, you realize that the detours on the way to your destination were really not choices at all. When you deeply embrace your Unique Self enlightenment philosophy, you understand that *every place you have been is where you needed to be.* The only path you could've possibly walked is the path of your pathos.

From the perspective of nondual realization, the physical world is but a reflection of the spiritual world. This does not mean that the physics in any way "proves" spirit. If the entire physical world disappeared, spirit would still be ever-present, radically full and alive. Rather, this means that every great idea of the spirit has an exterior physical paradigm. *The idea that every place I have been I needed to be—even if my life does not appear to be the proverbial shortest distance formed by a straight line between two points—is in fact a central and elegant postulate in physics.*

I learned this principle from scientist Victor Mizrahi, in response to a wonderful conversation we shared many years back about Unique Self.

One of the persistent ideas about this Uni-verse is that it has order. There are fundamental rules that govern the behavior of the Uni-verse. Physics is about discovering and stating these rules. It is said that physics does not answer the question "why," but only the "what." However, human nature being what it is, one cannot help but ask "why." It may be said that there is a sense in which physics addresses "why," and that is by restating a "what" in other, simpler terms that are more "self-evident."

Among the many basic and powerful rules that have been discovered and put to good use over the years, one can include Newton's laws of motion, Einstein's theory of relativity, and so on. But here I would like to give as a specific example a much simpler rule that shows some of the great beauty in the Uni-verse. I wish to discuss the path that a ray of light takes as it traverses from one medium (such as water) to another (such as air).

So, for example, sunlight traveling from beneath the surface of a still pond to the human eye in the air above the pond will generally bend as it crosses the surface of the pond. And so a fish below the surface will generally not be where it appears to the eye to be. (Just as the fish will not appear absolutely straight, but more blurry and bent.)

Now there are mathematical equations that can be used to precisely describe the path that this ray of light will take even if the medium is far more complex than air or water, but instead has a continuous variation in its optical properties. (One example would be a glass whose composition varies in a complex manner.) Yet all of these cases can be just as accurately described by stating a stunningly simple principle. The path that the light ray will take is the quickest path that it could have taken, of all the infinite possible paths in the vicinity of the true path!

Stated another way, all other paths in the vicinity of the path actually taken by the ray of light would have taken longer to reach the final destination. Note that other paths may be shorter (indeed, a straight line is the shortest), but they are slower, because light travels faster in air than in water. And so the quickest path will have the light traveling a greater distance in the air so as to reduce the distance traveled in the water. This is known as Fermat's principle, discovered by French mathematician Pierre de Fermat in the sixteenth century.

This simply stated truth, that light will take the quickest path, is an example of the order found within our Uni-verse. This rule is elegant and pretty, precisely because it is so simple, and yet it is by no means obvious that the Uni-verse should have been so constructed. And so to the question, "Why did the light follow the path that it did?" one might plausibly answer, "Because it is the quickest." Unfortunately this does not answer the question, "Why does the Uni-verse work this way?" and it doesn't even answer the slightly more obvious question, "How does the light know which path is the quickest, and therefore which one to take?" It is true that this result can be proven by appealing to some basic equations of physics. But this is just another way of saying that it is a consequence of the way the Uni-verse works.

Interestingly, there is a formalism of advanced physics developed by the great twentieth-century physicist Richard Feynman that suggests that the light actually tries every possible path, but that all but the quickest paths cancel each other out.

Now, you may remember that Unique Self-realization, the light of your story, finds its exterior expression in the nature and patterns of physical light. We identified the biblical-myth word *sapir* as referring to what we called Unique Self light. We further pointed out that Unique Self, like every unique frequency of light, has both a wave and a particle dimension. We identified wave with *sippur*, the story function of Unique Self, and particle with *mispar*, the calling dimension of Unique Self. What we have just done is added an important dimension to the structural parallel between Unique Self and light.

Just as light always takes the most efficient path to arrive at its destination, so too does our Unique Self always take the most efficient path to arrive at its destination. The destination of Unique Self, of course, is no less than the full flowering of the human being as a unique emanation of All-That-Is.

CHAPTER FOURTEEN

UNIQUE SELF
AND LONELINESS

LONELINESS IS THE INABILITY to share your story, your Unique Self story. For most people, the move beyond loneliness requires us to share our story with a significant other. For the spiritual elite, the receiving of our own story—and the knowing that it is an integral part of the larger story of All-That-Is—is enough. But for most human beings, loneliness is transcended through contact with another person.

When you cannot share your Unique Self with an other, you are virtually destroyed by loneliness. "To feel completely alone and isolated leads to mental disintegration just as physical starvation leads to Death," writes Erich Fromm in *Escape from Freedom*.

My teacher once wrote, "To be is to be singular, unique, and consequently lonely."[1] But it is more than that: To be is to be received, to communicate your story, your Unique Self, to an other. To make contact. To move from loneliness to loving. *To give your Unique Self, and know you have been received, liberates you from loneliness. It is a joy beyond imagination.*

Some years ago I found myself in a hotel in Denver, Colorado. I was lonely. Everyone deals with loneliness in their own way. For me (and I would not recommend this for everyone), second-century Aramaic texts seem to take the edge off. But on this day, during a book tour for a previous book, *Soul Prints*, my suitcase with my books had missed its connecting flight; I was tired, without loved ones or books around me, and I was feeling lonely.

A hotel room far from home can be the loneliest place in the world. So I opened the only book in the room, the Gideon Bible in the drawer by the bed.

At the front, I was surprised to see a detailed index. If you're depressed, read Psalm 19, it said. If you're drunk, read Psalm 38. If you're feeling lonely, read Psalm 23. So I read Psalm 23: "The Lord is my shepherd, I shall not want," the famous psalm begins. "Yea, though I walk in the shadow of the valley of death I fear no evil . . . " I read slowly, carefully, yet I have to admit I still felt lonely when I finished. Just as I was about to close the book, I saw a note scrawled at the bottom of the page: "If you're still lonely, call Lola."

When I recovered from laughing, I remembered again the simple truth: what drives me, and all of us, is a desire to move from separation to connection, from loneliness to loving. If you're still lonely, call Lola. Love, as we will see more deeply later, is a Unique Self perception. Loneliness is Unique Self alienation!

After all is said and done, after all of our grand self-actualization and accomplishments, our self-esteem and degrees, our meaning-making and financial success—we still feel lonely. Our Unique Selves crave contact, to recognize and receive, and to be recognized and received by other Unique Selves. We yearn to be seen and recognized for all that we are. At my core, I have heard the call of the lonely, and I know of no greater force than its low and penetrating hum. *The desire to move out of loneliness, to transcend alienation, sits at the center of our Uni-verse, enthroned as a fundamental human drive.* Virtually nothing is more important to us than the need to share our story, not the ego story but the Unique Self story, with one another—to imprint and be imprinted upon.

Exile

We are all familiar with the philosophical conundrum, "If a tree falls in a forest and there's no one there to hear it, does it make a sound?" Let's rephrase that: "If you are unable to tell the tale of your Unique Self, because there's no one to share it with, if you are left mute of meaning for lack of listening, then in the language of the mystics, you are in exile. In the exact words of the Hebrew myth, God says, 'It is not good for the human being to be lonely.'"

It was to these words that the epic poet John Milton was referring when he wrote that to be alone is "the first thing which God's eye nam'd not good."

Overcoming loneliness and moving to connection, to loving, to union, is not merely an exercise in pop-psychology fulfillment or personal gratification. It is, from one perspective, the very purpose of existence, of Being and of Becoming. It is the opposite of the "not good" and the very goal of the "good."

Levado

The original Hebrew word for "lonely" is *levado*. Evolutionary mystic Isaac Luria reads the text "It is not good for man to be lonely" as referring not only to humans but to God as well. For God to achieve the good, God has to move out of divine *levado*—God's own loneliness—and create a world to be in relationship with. Human evolution and divine evolution happen only in the arms of a beloved other.

In simple human terms, this means that God is the force in the Uni-verse for the healing and transformation of loneliness. ***God is the force that tells you that you need not be alone forever.*** The Uni-verse is friendly. God knows your name; God yearns and actively militates for your joy.

When we are alone, God is somehow more alone. Or put another way, our divine life-force ebbs when we are disconnected. A host of studies bear this out in the most powerful and concrete way.

Researcher H. M. Skeels did a long-term study of twenty-four children in an orphanage. Half went daily to be cared for and loved by mentally handicapped adolescent girls at a nearby institution. In a twenty-year track-ing study, Skeels found that the twelve orphans who had not experienced the afternoon visits were either dead or in institutions for the mentally retarded. The group who had received loving attention were self-sufficient. Most were in relationship, and almost all had successfully completed edu-cational degrees.[2]

We know as well that an infant who receives perfect care but no regular human contact will often simply die.

A fundamental drive of the human being is to move beyond the "not good" of loneliness to the "good" of connection, of loving, of union.

A Family Myth I Share with My Son

The beginning of a definition of loneliness came to me in the form of a mythic family story that my son Eytan and I hold dearly.

I woke up the morning of my departure for a lecture tour of Scandinavia, and almost immediately I was running late. I had some semblance of breakfast, said some form of brief morning prayers, and grabbed my suitcase to go. Just as I was running out the door to the airport for my all-important and very precious tour, my son Eytan, then five years old, said to me, "Dad, can you take this box with you?" He held up a little blue shoebox balanced in his hands.

He looked quite serious, and so I took the box, stuffed it in my suitcase—the one with the old Aramaic texts—gave him a kiss, got into the car, and sped off into the whirlwind of the tour.

A long ten days later, I returned home close to midnight. Eytan, usually in bed by eight, was wide awake, waiting patiently in the kitchen with a look of enormous gravitas on his face. "Eytan, honey, why are you up?" I asked him. He looked at me silently with a tear running down his cheek.

"What do you mean, Dad?" he asked. "I stayed up to hear what you think of my box. Abba, didn't you look at the box?" I didn't even have time to lie. The trip had been intense and exhausting, and Eytan's box had remained at the bottom of my bag of books.

I felt far worse than terrible. I ran back out to the car and found Eytan's box. I came into the kitchen. I sat down and gently said, "I'm sorry, Eytan. I had a crazy trip and I didn't get to look at your box. Your box is wildly important to me. Can I have another chance? Come, show me. What's in it?"

Inside was a seashell, a faded picture of me, a marble, the doorknob of an old apartment in Jerusalem, the silver Cross pen I used to write with, and a picture of Lisa, Eytan's wondrous mother. I was a little baffled. "What is all this?" I asked.

"Dad, these are my things," Eytan said to me as another tear ran down his cheek. "I gave them to you, and you didn't even see them."

At that moment, I understood what loneliness truly means. We all have boxes, and in those boxes are our things, our authentic stuff. Not your jobs or titles, not your salaries or public-status trophies, not your separate-self personality and ego stuff. Rather, your stuff. The unique patterns and swirls of the soul. Your Story. Your Unique Self.

Your life is made up of your unique dreams and destiny, both lived and unlived, conscious and not yet conscious. It is made up of your past—all of your yesterdays, into the earliest crevices of childhood, and perhaps even before. It includes your successes, and especially your failures. It is the partner you married and the partner you didn't. It is your fears, fragility, and vulnerability, as well as your grandiosity and larger-than-life yearnings. The core dynamics of that story hold your essence. Your essence is your Unique Self.

Loneliness is the inability to share your essence, your story, your Unique Self, with another. Loneliness is being systematically mis-categorized. Loneliness is when your Unique Self is not seen or received. To be liberated from loneliness is for your Unique Self to be truly seen and therefore loved.

PART FOUR

You are a divine elephant with amnesia
Trying to live in an ant hole
I love you. This is our oath of allegiance
to a higher order of Being.

—HAFIZ

CHAPTER FIFTEEN

LOVE AND UNIQUE SELF

THE TRUE NATURE OF YOUR VALUES is always revealed in death. At your funeral, you will hear in the eulogies, both in what is spoken and unspoken, something of the essential nature of your life and loyalties. Sometimes, however, before you die, you are strangely privileged with a final invitation to declare where your ultimate loyalty lies. The moments before your death might be joyous or tragic.

It was September 11, 2001. The planes had just crashed into the Twin Towers in Manhattan. People had very short moments to use their cell phones. No one called asking for revenge. No one offered philosophical explanations or profound insights into the nature of reality. People did one thing and one thing only: they called the people close to their heart to say, "I love you." "I love you" is our declaration of faith. Implicit in those words is everything holy.

And yet we no longer really know what we mean when we say, "I love you." It used to mean, "I am committed to you. I will live with you forever." Or it might have meant, "You are the most important person in my life." But it no longer seems to mean that. The old Greek, Thucydides, wrote in his great work *The Peloponnesian War* something like, "When words lose their meaning, culture collapses." When you no longer understand your own deepest declarations of love, you are lost. The very foundation of meaning upon which your world rests is undermined. You lose your way. You become alienated from love, which is your home. Despair, addiction, and numbness become your constant companions.

For so many of us, love has lost its luminosity as the organizing principle of our lives. Love seems to have diminished power to locate us and to guide us home. "I love you" has become banal, casual, and desiccated.

One day you feel the love; the next day you do not. One day love holds you in the place of your belonging, and the very next day you are cast out, exiled, and lost. For so many of us, "I love you" has ceased to be a place where we can find our home.

What do you really mean when your highest self says to another, "I love you"?

And if I might audaciously add to the question: why do all the great traditions, in one way or another, talk about the obligation to love God and love your neighbor? In the tradition of Kabbalah, this obligation to love God and one another is called a *mitzvah temidit,* a "constant obligation of consciousness." But does this truly resonate with our experience? Actually, if we admit it to ourselves, this injunction makes little sense. How does a human being love God? Is God lovable? Can you touch God, cuddle with God, or actually feel rushing love for God without entering into an altered state?

What emotional affect is there to the love of God? And does not that emotional affect, if it is even an authentic possibility for the common person, seem dangerously close to a kind of blind fundamentalist emotional faith?

How does one love God? And how can one be obligated to love another? How can you obligate an emotion? And can we truly feel love toward all of our neighbors? Isn't love reserved for the very few special people in our lives?

Said differently and more directly, what is love?

To know the way of Unique Self, you must know the way of love.

To find your destination in love, you must consider the reason for all of your detours. You must wonder about all of your wrong turns in love.

Where did you go wrong? Is there something you did not understand about the nature of love?

You are not alone in your questions. There is hardly a person alive who is conscious who has not asked these questions—this writer included. So I will speak to myself through you.

Love Is a Verb

If you are like most highly intelligent and sincere modern seekers, you are making two core mistakes about love. First, you think that love is an emotion.

When the emotion is gone, you feel like you are no longer in love and thus can no longer stay in the relationship.

Second, you automatically identify love with a particular emotion. The emotion with which you identify love is usually the emotion of infatuation. Both of these mistaken beliefs are significant obstacles on your path to spiritual liberation. Both of these mistakes obscure love's innate ability to take you home.

Love at its core is not an emotion. Love is a perception. Love is the ultimate verb. Love is a faculty of perception that allows you to see the inner nature of All-That-Is.

To love another human being is to perceive their True Nature. To love is to perceive the infinite specialness and divine beauty of the beloved.

To be a lover is to see beyond the limited and distorting vision of your separate-self contraction.

To be a lover is to see with God's eyes. Your beloved is both your lover and All-That-Is.

To be loved by another human being is to have your True Nature seen. Your True Nature is your Unique Self.

To love God is to let God see with your eyes, to empower God with the vision of your Unique Perspective. You are living out of a passion for God. You are being asked to live with God's eyes.

To act with God's eyes, to react with God's eyes, to write your Book of Life with God's eyes as God would see from your perspective. If you are successful, then your perspective becomes available to God. It finds God and feeds God. It gives God strength and joy. *You must consider that being a devotee is nothing but actually being God from a distinct perspective.*

This is the only truth about individuality. Mature individuality is not about being separate. It is about having a distinct perspective within the context of Union.

To be responsible for this perspective is to declare the truth from this vantage point, but without making it the only perspective, and without any degree of attachment to the vantage point we have clung to from the past—from our previous conditioning. This is what it means to be a lover.

This is the great paradox again and again. *To be a lover is to see with God's eyes. To love God is to let God see with your eyes.*

Once, I shared this understanding of love with the Dalai Lama. "Beautiful!" he exclaimed with sheer and utter delight.

Beautiful was the Dalai Lama in the direct and delicious expression of his delight. Particularly, he was excited to shift the understanding of love from an emotion to a perception.

It is this precise shift that clears up one of the great mysteries of love. Many great thinkers have been puzzled by the Hebrew wisdom commandment to love. How can you command an emotion? And yet in the evolutionary mysticism of Unique Self teaching, love is the ultimate commandment. Reading the old Hebrew text, "Love your neighbor as yourself—I AM GOD," the answer to the puzzle is now clear.

Step one: Love is not an emotion. Love is a perception.

"Love your neighbor as yourself" is the seemingly impossible demand of the Hebrew book of Leviticus, echoed in the New Testament in the book of Matthew. At least this is how the text is usually cited. But the quote, as it is usually cited, is actually missing three words. It's too short. What all too often gets left out of the passage are the three last, and perhaps most crucial, words. The complete verse is, "Love your neighbor as yourself—I AM GOD." To love your neighbor is to know that the "I" is God. *To love your neighbor is to perceive God's divine beauty in others and let it fill you with wonder and radical amazement.* To love your neighbor is to behold with wonder God's infinite specialness. Love is what the Hindus called *bhakti,* to truly see the other bathed in their own divine radiance.

Love is not an emotion. Love is not infatuation.

Emotions are involuntary reactions that come from the nervous system. The emotion of infatuation is usually a preprogrammed reaction that takes place when you meet someone that you recognize. You re-cognize them because you remember them. They evoke in you a sense of familiarity and intimacy. They unconsciously re-mind you of your parents or early caretakers.

The person with whom you are infatuated holds out to you the possibility of completing the unfinished emotional business you have with your mother, father, or early caretakers. Or you fall in love with them as an expression of your unconscious rebellion or alienation from your parents or caretakers, whom you experience as painful or dangerous.

Only when you fall out of infatuation do you see—sometimes for the first time. Before then, your perception is blurred. Infatuation is blind. Love is a magnifying glass. Initially the perception yields a more complex and less rosy picture then the blind adulation of infatuation, but if you stay with it, remain focused, and invest your self with full passion and heart, the perception begins to clarify. You begin to genuinely see the full splendor and beauty of the one you love. The delight of love is a natural result of your perceptions.

Love is perception's gift. Love is a faculty of perception, which allows you to see the inner nature of All-That-Is. Love is a realization. *Love is a verb. Love is the true inner nature of All-That-Is. Love is.*

Love Is a Perception-Identification Complex

When we say that love is perception, we do not mean it is merely perception. It is, as we have implicitly seen in our discussion till now, a perception-identification complex. And this is not a complex in the Oedipal sense, but rather in the simplest sense of a two-part structure. Love is a two-part formula.

The beloved not only perceives the divine, the Unique Self of her lover; she identifies him with that divinity. *She understands his divinity as his essence. She sees and identifies her beloved with his infinite specialness.*

This notion of perception identification is most clear in reference to parents and children. You love your kids. The neighbor's kids, however—well, they are just so incredibly rambunctious, annoying, and immature.

In fact, we all recognize that there may be no appreciable difference between your kids and the neighbor's kids. Why then do you love your children and not the neighbor's? Not merely because they're your children, but rather, because they are *your* children, you are invested in them. This investment causes you to focus your vision on them more intensely than on other kids. The result: you are able to perceive them in ways other people are simply unable to do. You perceive your child's beauty in a way that no one quite grasps.

But perception is not enough. If you are a good parent, you know your child also has faults, and those shortcomings are real. They need to be addressed forthrightly and never swept under the rug. Remember, love is not blind; infatuation is blind. Love is a microscope. Parents should be madly in love with their kids—they should never be infatuated with them.

How is it then that you love your children even after you know their long laundry list of faults? The answer lies in the second step of the love formula, identification. You perceive both your child's goodness and their flaws—but you identify their goodness as the true core of who they are. All the rest you will deal with in whatever way necessary—but you know that at core the "trailing clouds of glory" are the essence of your child. And you love them for it. With kids not our own, what we often (wrongly) tend to do is identify the child with their failing or acting out instead of with their infinite specialness and grandeur.

Have any of your friends every gotten engaged, and the response of your circle was something like, "I can't believe it! SHE is going to marry . . . HIM? Candice . . . is going to marry . . . Tom??!!" We do not understand what she sees in him. But see in him she does. She perceives him, sees him, discloses him in a way that we are unable to access. How did Emily Dickinson say it? "Not 'revelation'—tis—that waits, but our unfurnished eyes." Our eyes are too "furnished" to see the miraculous, infinitely unique gorgeousness that is Tom. *To love is to see with unfurnished eyes.* But let there be no mistake about it—Tom is stunningly gorgeous. To Candice, the man is a miracle. The word "miracle" comes from the Latin *mirari*, meaning "to behold with rapt attention." Candice has beheld the glory of Tom and found him to be divine. She has seen his infinite uniqueness, the snowflake essence of his soul that most miraculously never melts. To love is to witness the miracle of your beloved. Love is a Unique Self Perception.

Love, Being, and Becoming

To say that love is a perception of the True Nature of things is to recognize that love is subversive. The emperor struts around in his clothes. But it is not really the emperor. It is the servant disguised as the emperor. The separate self in the form of a skin-encapsulated ego rules the roost. The servant has displaced the king. Along comes love, and pierces the heart of all illusions. The true heart opens, and reality re-appears in its full and undivided majesty and splendor. The lover is the great hero who ushers in—through the penetrating power of their perception—a new world order.

Sometimes perception is a result of intense and sustained effort. This is called in the old sacred texts "arousal from below." At other times, it is a free gift of the Uni-verse. This is called "arousal from above."

There are moments when your eyes just open with delight. You have been gifted by the Uni-verse with a direct perception of essence. Your heart opens, your breath draws in, and you fall in love for a moment. It might be the ocean, a radiant sunset, the erotic curve of the feminine, or the lean, angular throbbing of the masculine. It might be a thirteen-petaled rose, a baby, precious stones, or a person fully in their gift.

All of these give you a direct, unearned gift of essence. A gift of love.

The first few examples are images of being. The last example, a person fully in their gift, is an image of manifested becoming. It is the revelation of Unique Self.

Love is a Unique Self Perception.

The old Hindu Upanishads teach, "Where there is other, there is fear." This describes your consciousness at the level of ego. If, however, you have upleveled your consciousness and are living as Source—from the place of your Unique Self—the teaching changes: "Where there is other, there is love."

The Perception of Love Creates a New Reality

Marriage in the old world served many ends. It created personal security and a stable context for parenting, and it ensured that order, and not chaos, reigned in society. Marriage in the new world is a Unique Self encounter.

As is often the case, an old text contains seeds of the new paradigm. An old Aramaic text reads, "The bride and groom reveal the Shekhinah." What might that mean? Do you know that moment in a wedding when it really happens? It has nothing to do with the music, catering, hall, or any of the other fanfare. It is that fraction of a second when they walk down the aisle or are standing at the altar or under the canopy. You feel the revelation that always waits for our unfurnished eyes. The bride and the groom look at each other. It is a glorious moment of Unique Self perception. They see each other in all of their depth and wonder. At that moment, the marriage is consummated.

But it is even more than that.

We become more—the more we are seen and recognized. The level of love after thirty years of life together is vastly and incomparably deeper than the love available at the wedding altar.

But it is even more than that.

Physics reminds us that perception not only observes but creates reality. See your beloved at their highest, and you will deepen and empower their highest. You then live with their highest. When you see your beloved at their lowest, you empower and deepen the lowest. You then live with their lowest.

Liquid Love—To See the Future in the Now

Part of perception identification requires the lover to be a visionary. To touch in the now what might be in the future. The lover's perception intuits unfolding and growth long before it actually manifests. If in any moment you are so enamored that you say, like Goethe's Dr. Faustus, "Linger, Thou Art Fair," you forfeit your soul. For what you have done is to freeze the moment and stop growing. Unique Selves are always unfolding. Unique Self is both a point of origin and a destination. We grow, but we were really always there to begin with—the fully developed lover senses the destination in the point of origin.

The Seer of Lublin, a nineteenth-century biblical mystic, said this:

> There are three kinds of friends in the world.
> An ordinary friend sees you as you appear to be.
> An extra-ordinary friend sees you for what you can be.
> But in the presence of the highest friend—you already are.

To love a person is both to perceive a person and to identify them with the best, not just of who they are, but who they could become. We are not simply human beings; we are human becomings. In fact, in the original Hebrew the words "I am" do not exist. "I am" in Hebrew is rather "I will become." Likewise, in the old Hebrew story, when Moses asks God his name, God answers, *ekyeh asher ekyeh.* Usually this strange and potent phrase gets translated as "I am what I am." But the actual translation is "I will be what I will be." God is "will be." God is Becoming.

To love is to see in an other what they cannot yet see themselves. "I love them for the person they want to be. I love them for the person they almost are." And somehow, through being loved, we begin to be who we want to be, who we really are. To love is to embrace another, not only as a human being but as a human becoming.

Words are a freezing of reality. Before I put the chapter down on paper it is infinite, liquid-like, and emerging. The second I pick one of the infinite possible turns of phrase, it becomes frozen. For every word I choose, a thousand others are rejected. How much more of a human violation it is when I freeze another person into what they are at a particular moment. *Worse yet to freeze people into their moments of fall and failure. That is a great failure of love.*

"Love is a Unique Self Perception" has four words too many. The truth is, quite simply, love is. For love has really been here all the time. *Love is the infinite, pulsating erotic energy of life and goodness that is the fabric of Being.* When we realize that love is, then we understand ever more deeply that love is but a shift in perception.

The Secret Is in the Eyes

An emotion cannot be commanded; perception can. The emotion of love is neither flickering nor fickle. It is directly dependent on the energy and effort of your perception.

There is an old mystical tradition that the world rests on thirty-six hidden saints. They are the polished gemstones of God's evolutionary creation. Israel, Master of the Good Name, was the leader of this group in his generation. He indulged his disciples with the stories and teachings he would hear from these sacred saints.

"But we want to see them also," begged his students. Day after day they pressed him to reveal the hidden men to them as well.

"So be it," said Israel.

At the close of the following week, he said to his disciples. "So . . . were you not impressed by them greatly?"

"But what do you mean?" replied the astonished disciples, "Impressed by who? We didn't see a single saintly soul."

"Ahh," said the master. "So you did not see them. That doesn't mean they were not there. Remember the beggar who came for a loaf of bread? A saint!

And the young widow crying that she had lost her husband? She too was one of them. And the juggler in the circus on Thursday? He too was of their number."

"Holy disciples," said the master to his beloved students. "The secret is in the eyes. The secret is in the eyes."

I bless you, dear friend and reader, with eyes to see. To see the saint hidden in each passing face. Who knows, perhaps you too are one of their number, so well hidden that even you have yet to perceive your hidden light.

Self-Love

Israel, Master of the Good Name, has a wonderful teaching on the Hebraic mandate "Love your neighbor as you love yourself." First, it is a statement of fact—you love your neighbor precisely as much as you love yourself. *You can only perceive another's greatness if you have glimpsed and believe in your own.*

Self-love is self-perception.

If this is so, then a powerful question arises! How do you love your self when you know all of your foibles, pathologies, and blemishes? If self-love is self-perception, does not honest perception yield all the reasons that we are not lovable? And yet most of us manage, at least to some degree, to love ourselves. Is it just self-deception? No, not at all. Love, as we have unpacked it together, is not merely perception. It is a perception-identification complex. Self-perception means that, although I am aware of the full complexity of my personae—the good, the bad, and the ugly—I identify the essence of who I am with my good. With my good, loving, giving, creative, and generous self.

That does not mean I deny my beast. It is, of course, critical to integrate all of me into my self-picture.

But the essence, the core of who I am, remains my goodness, virtue, and beauty. To love your self is to identify your self as part of the Shekhinah. Writes Master Israel, "To love yourself is to love the Shekhinah." Not to love yourself is to send the Shekhinah into exile. So proclaim the Kabbalists.

To which Rumi adds:

> By God, when you see your beauty
> you will be the idol of yourself.

In your deepest nature you must know that you are the hero of your story. In your deepest nature you are love, grace, strength, and splendor. Now you must decide to identify with your deepest nature. Do you focus on your innocence or your guilt? Do you focus on your inevitably dirty hands, or on your eternally pure spirit? To love yourself or anyone else, you need to know that your innocence is your essence. That your innocence is never lost. That you remain always worthy of love, even as you muster all of your energy and commitment to the evolution of your essence.

Self-love is a shift in perception in which you embrace—maybe for the first time—the full wonder of who and what you are. That is what it means to accept God. Perception always begins with knowledge—self-knowledge. Self-knowledge does not mean long-term intensive psychotherapy that explores every nook and cranny of your psyche.

Self-love means the perception and identification of your deepest self. Which raises the essential human question, "Who am I? Am I the public me that goes to work and office parties, or the private me, the sum total of all those deep and dark secrets I keep so carefully hidden?"

Evolutionary mysticism points to a different figure to stand forward when their name is called: the third me. The Unique Self.

The Three Faces

You have three faces. The first face, the social you, is called in the Zohar the "revealed world." Much of capitalist, accomplishment-driven, middle-class bourgeois society believes that this first face is the real you. The second face, the primal raging of the subconscious, is called by the Zohar the "hidden world." Freud believed that the real you is the second you, while the outside persona is just the thin veneer of culture. Evolutionary mysticism, however, teaches that your deepest face is your third face—Unique Self—what the Aramaic texts call *umka de umka,* the "deepest of the deep"! In the language of Abraham Kook, "The truth of your essence reveals itself in the moment of your greatness."

It is those moments of greatness that set the standard that defines you, that are you. Who you really are is you at your best.

During my first year as a rabbi in Palm Beach, Florida, there was one bar mitzvah boy I will never forget. Louis was his name, and he was the first child to be bar mitzvahed during my tenure. He and his parents came to my office just a few weeks after I arrived, in what turned out to be quite a disturbing meeting. You see, Louis was not a happy camper. He was overweight, awkward, and socially ill at ease, none of these traits easy for a twelve-year-old trapped in the superficiality of a culture that idolized fitness, grace, and cool.

But to add to the taunts of his peers, his parents seemed to be doing their fair share of damage to Louis's self-esteem. The parents informed me, with him in the room, that Louis was not the brightest kid, and that he probably would not be able to read the usual portion from Prophets that were usually read by other bar mitzvah boys. They figured that it would be enough for him to recite the blessings and be done with it. When they left my office I was bewildered, angry, and near tears. Perhaps it was his parents' insensitivity, or perhaps his awkwardness reminded me of myself at his age. I resolved to do something.

In the ensuing six months, I met with Louis approximately three times as much as I would have met with another bar mitzvah boy. To my extreme delight, I found that Louis had a beautiful singing voice and could do the normal reading from Prophets, but I believed that he could do more. Thus, we trained not only for the Prophets, but the entire biblical reading for the week, no mean feat for a thirteen-year-old by any standard. We practiced and practiced and practiced.

Come the morning of the bar mitzvah, Louis got up, and I tell you that angels carried his every word. He shined! He glowed! The room and the heavens stood still in awe and wonder at the beauty and grace that was Louis. I got up to give the speech that I had prepared, but only one thought filled my mind. I had to speak directly to Louis. I had to make sure he realized the full magnificence—and significance—of that moment. The whole congregation seemed to disappear as I turned to Louis and let the words flow from my mouth: "Louis, this morning you met your real self. You are unique, gorgeous, and beautiful. You are your best. This is who you really are. In this moment, your Unique Self shines with laser-like brilliance. It is who you are. You are good, graceful, talented, and smart. Whatever people told you yesterday, and Louis, whatever happens tomorrow, promise me one thing, remember . . . this is you. Remember, and don't ever lose it."

Several months after his bar mitzvah, Louis's family moved away, and I lost track of him. But a few years back I received a letter from Louis. He had just graduated from an Ivy League university, was beginning medical school in the fall, and was engaged to be married. The letter was short. It read, "High school was a nightmare. Sometimes I didn't think I would make it through. But I kept my promise—I always remembered my bar mitzvah morning when you said that this feeling of being absolutely special and beautiful is who I really am. Thank you."

The truth of who you are is you at your best.

Self-Love Is Not Narcissism

The master Menachem Mendel of Kotzk said, "A decent person never deceives others, and a special person never deceives himself."

To say that you are anything less than you at your best, at your most wondrous and beautiful, is to deceive yourself, deceive others, and to deceive God. In the end, though, the greatest deception is to think that you are separate and ordinary.

Whenever I talk to people about self-love—which is, after all, according to most authorities, the most important injunction and the goal of all life—there is always a group that gets upset. It sounds narcissistic, they claim, or it will lead to selfishness.

So let's take a moment to make two clear distinctions. Narcissism is to be in love with your separate self—your mask. This is not a good idea, because sooner or later masks fall off, and then you are left loveless. Self-love is to love your unique interior—your Holy of Holies.

Selfishness is to narrow your circle of caring until it includes only yourself and perhaps those that directly affect your well-being. *Selfishness is a narrowing of your identity. That is definitive non-erotic thinking. Self-love, by contrast, is not self-centered at all; it is ultimately expansive.*

Self-love is radically erotic in that it is the experience of being interwoven within the great One Taste fabric of being. It is the deep intuition that the world is a unified, loving consciousness in which you participate and which lives in you even as you are an indivisible part of it. To think you are not lovable is the ultimate arrogance, because it says that you are separate from God.

CHAPTER SIXTEEN

JOY AND UNIQUE SELF

HERE IS THE SIMPLE TRUTH ABOUT JOY: You won't find it in the ways you have learned to search for it all your life. When you pursue joy, it runs away from you.

A student came to his master and said, "Teacher, you taught me that if I run from honor, then honor will pursue me. Well, I have been running from honor for many years now, and honor is still not pursuing me."

"The problem," replied the master, nodding sagaciously, "is clearly apparent. When you run from honor, you are always looking over your shoulder to see if honor is pursuing you—so honor is confused, not quite sure which way you are going."

Joy, like honor and serenity and so much else we ache and sweat for, is only available to us when we actively seek something else instead.

The Babylonian Talmud discusses several wisdom texts that seem to hold contradictory views on joy. One set of passages denies the possibility of achieving true joy, while the second set is far more encouraging.[1]

A resolution is achieved by explaining that the two texts are in fact talking about two different sorts of joy. The first is joy as a detached value—a towering ideal, a castle that rests on an ever-retreating horizon. The second is happiness as a by-product—the ever-present companion that walks with life's meaningful goals. The Talmudic conclusion in a nutshell: Joy as a detached value is not achievable; joy pursued as an ideal, for its own sake, will never be attained. Happiness can only be realized as the by-product of the pursuit of some other goal.

What is the primary goal that you must pursue in order to achieve joy as a by-product? ***Joy is the by-product of your Unique Self-realization.*** In the normal course of living, you are happy when you are living your Unique Self and unhappy when you are not.

The joy that is a by-product of Unique Self living is called by the myth masters "the joy of *mitzvah.*" Although the word *mitzvah* is usually translated from the Hebrew as "commandment," the kabbalists, ever sensitive to the nuances of Hebrew language, understand *mitzvah* to derive from a root word meaning "intimacy." For us Unique Self seekers, that is a very valuable translation of the word, connecting joy with intimacy. Intimacy is both personal and interpersonal. Intimacy happens when you realize your Unique Self and intertwine it with that of another.

The imperative of biblical consciousness is not "be joyful." Rather, it is "choose life"—which in the biblical myth means choose *your* life. Live your Unique Self in the world.

"Joyous is the believer," proclaim the biblical-myth masters. The kabbalists would interpret this declaration to mean, "Joyous is one who believes that they have a unique destiny," a Unique Self. ***To believe is not to believe that "it" is true, but that "I" am true. When you live your Unique Self, you experience your truth of your existence and are thus freed from the need to affirm it by believing in an external set of dogmas.***

"He who is prosperous," teaches the Babylonian wisdom master Ben Zoma, "is he who is joyous in his unique part."[2] Usually we understand Ben Zoma to mean, "Happiness is to appreciate what you have—unhappiness is to appreciate what you don't have." That is generally sound advice. However, while appreciation is an absolute prerequisite for happiness, it is insufficient by itself to make a person happy.

We can learn from that sort of appreciation, and as we will see, we can move past it into a more sustaining "mere joy." However, appreciation is a very good place to start.

Your Unique Self fits you more perfectly than any tailored suit of clothes. To get up in the morning knowing that you are already clothed in your own uniqueness, that you are doing something in the world totally distinctive to you and you alone, which no one else in the world can do quite like you do—that is mere joy.

The Joy of Depth

If you're essentially on the wrong track, wearing someone else's shoes, leaving someone else's marks, living someone else's print—then there is a level of depth you can never achieve. And what you do achieve will give you far less satisfaction than if you walk a mile, or a lifetime of miles, in your own shoes.

When a person feels their own depth, they are granted a dimension of inner peace, which is the essential prerequisite to authentic joy, and they bring that depth to the surface. We've all heard people say, "Her face was radiant!" or "You're shining!" *When inner joy pervades, it emanates from the light of the face.*

Ultimately, however, the face is not about hope or despair. It is the primary expression of singularity. The Talmudic myth masters write, "Just as their faces are different, so is their essence."[3]

Indeed, if we do not respond to the call of our destiny—to the *mispar* of our soul's light—if we do not soar as high as we can soar, then we will endanger our fundamental joy.

We have uncovered the evolutionary mystical idea that joy cannot be pursued, that it is only achievable as a by-product of the pursuit of important goals—goals other than happiness itself. What are those goals? Some very good thinkers have suggested that those goals would be something general and admirable, like goodness, depth, values, and meaning. Will following those abstract goals make us happy?

Let's take one of those four goals—values—and see how it plays out. For all of us, there is a gap between the values we profess and the values we practice. By actively pursuing our values, we narrow the yawning gap between our professed and our practiced values, between us and our happiness. Thus, the more we pursue our values, the happier we can be—or so it seems.

For you can be good, be deep, possess impeccable values, live a meaningful life, and still be miserable. For there is still one essential element you are lacking. That is a profound connection with your Unique Self.

You can buy the best clothes in the world made from the finest fabrics by the most elegant of tailors. If the clothes don't quite fit—and even if you are the only one who notices—they will not give you that joyous feeling that comes from putting on great clothes that fall perfectly on your body. So, too, regarding what the Kabbalah calls the "garments of the soul." These are garments made of your unique goodness, meaning, depth, and values. Garments of that nature are transformative and joy inducing. Happy is the person who wears them.

From Daimon Comes *Eudaimonia*

The novelist Honoré de Balzac wrote, "Vocations that we wanted to pursue, but didn't, bleed, like colors, on the whole of our existence." *If we do not pursue our particular call, then the ghost of that call will pursue us, like a haunting that stains our days.*

For when you respond to cues that are not yours, when you're a police officer instead of a painter, ultimately you can't be happy. *Happiness comes from being yourself in the most profound way possible.* The ancient Greeks referred to happiness as *eudaimonia.* "Daimon" is the word for calling. You are happy only when you are responding to your daimon. Your daimon calls you to realize your Unique Self. Your happiness lies in your hands, if you would but take it.

To be happy, then, is to be responsive to the call of your deepest self. To be happy is to wake up in the morning and feel that you have a mission in the world that no one else can perform. To be happy is to know that among the billions of people on this planet, you are irreplaceable. This is true for every human being on the face of the globe, for *what we share in common is our uniqueness.*

The Western notion of the sacredness of every human life bursts from the bedrock of the Hebrew myth realization that brings forth the idea of the Unique Self. The prospect of happiness exists for us only because the call of Unique Self animates the Uni-verse.

A Paradigm Shift in Understanding Joy

Joy, teach the kabbalists, is both a source and a conduit of energy. The word most often associated in Kabbalah with joy is *chiyut,* roughly translated as "life energy," somewhat like the Chinese notion of chi. To be happy is to be plugged into the *chiyut* of the Uni-verse. The portal to that energy is the self, the vital Unique Self. At the same time, once you are plugged in, the joy itself is not only an energy source but also serves as a medium to channel ever-more divine energy.

Joy is more than an attitude; it is a potent and powerful source of energy. The idea of joy as divine energy is expressed by the kabbalists in many different codes. Let me share one of them with you. A favorite epigram of the kabbalists is *simcha poretz geder:* "Joy breaks through all fences." One kabbalist, the master Simcha Bunim (whose first name actually means "happiness"), used this epigram to give a novel explanation of a famous mystical passage, "All the gates are locked, the gates of tears are never locked." Traditionally, this verse has been taken to extol the power of a broken heart to break through all barriers when all other avenues have proven ineffective. When nothing else works, tears can still open all the gates.

In a subtle twist, Simcha Bunim turns the passage on its head: If you are sad, he says, then you can enter only if the gate is unlocked, already wide open. Thus, God has no choice but to leave the gates of tears unlocked. If you are joyous, however, then you can get through even the gates that are locked. After all, *simcha poretz geder,* "Joy breaks through all fences."

Choosing Joy

The kabbalists instruct us that happiness is a decision. In the original mystical language, this idea is expressed in the maxim, "The source of joy is *binah* [right understanding]." The simple interpretation of that sentence tells us that happiness is accessed through contemplation. One reflects on life and death, sickness, and illness; what is permanent and real; and what is fleeting and illusory. An entire biblical-myth book—Ecclesiastes, or in Hebrew, *Kohelet*—is devoted to this meditation. "Illusion of Illusion, All is Illusion," says the king named Kohelet, as he begins his Buddha-like quest for meaning.[3] In the end, he reaches understanding/enlightenment as he finds the inner lining of reality to be made of joy.

The deeper interpretation, however, points to the nature of joy as a *decision.* "The source of joy is right understanding." If joy is a product of understanding, then it is no longer an option or an event or a feeling we await. Joy is a *decision.* It is a conscious choice. But it is even more than that. *Joy is an obligation.*

CHAPTER SEVENTEEN

SHADOW INTEGRATION AND UNIQUE SELF

"INTEGRATE YOUR SHADOW" has become the battle cry of spiritual growth. Shadow integration is now seen as essential to personal development, success, and fulfillment. The centrality of shadow integration in these areas is most certainly a welcome evolution of enormous significance.

The only problem is that people, teachers included, often throw around highly charged words like "darkness" and "shadow" without actually explaining them or having a genuine understanding of what the words actually mean.

The reason the shadow conversation works at all, even without clear understanding, is that people have some natural idea of what "shadow" means. The word "shadow" automatically associates certain images, feelings, and ideas. When Shakespeare talks about "This thing of darkness I acknowledge mine," you understand he is talking about shadow, even if you can't fully articulate it.

Shadow is usually understood to refer to the darker sides of human consciousness. Pettiness, jealousy, betrayal, rage, violence, malice—these are all considered to be shadow material. Sexual misdeeds are also often associated with the use of the term "shadow."

In this line of spiritual and psychological teaching, "shadow" is explained to mean those qualities that live in you but that you are unable to hold in your first-person consciousness. Your refusal to own these qualities pushes them into shadow, where they exert enormous unconscious influence over your life choices. Some of the shadow teachers add that there is powerful energy in shadow that is—they say—liberated when you make your shadow conscious. Whether or not energy is liberated, and control over your life direction reclaimed by making shadow conscious, is at best not clear. From all my years of teaching, studying, and doing shadow work, I simply do not think it is true. Nonetheless, the explanations for shadow work offered by these teachers are helpful as far as they go. But they do not go nearly far enough. For the *raison d'être* of shadow work is said to be *shadow integration*.

Why would you want to integrate your darkest impulses? Perhaps those impulses need to be transmuted and evolved. At the very least, it would appear that they need to be disciplined and controlled. Is shadow integration merely a sophisticated license for ethical libertines, as some spiritual moralists have wanted to claim? And if it is not, if shadow integration points to some profound and important intuition about our wholeness and enlightenment, as others have loudly claimed, but not explained, then what is it?

A once-popular spiritual book called *The Book of Qualities* says, "The spiritual practice of shadow encourages us to make peace with those parts of ourselves we find despicable, unworthy, and embarrassing, our anger, jealousy, pride, selfishness, violence, and other evil deeds." The purpose of shadow work is said to be "a way of achieving wholeness by unifying the dark and the light," taking responsibility, and "embracing your full humanity."[1]

What exactly does it mean to unify light and darkness? Did the writer miss Aristotle's law of the excluded middle, which says that opposites do not unify? How do we unify that which is good and that which the writer calls "despicable"? And what does it mean to "embrace" your impulse toward murder, rape, and mayhem as part of your "full humanity"?

Perhaps a little bit of holy war is in order. Is it not possible that making peace with your shadow is just a saccharine way to let you off the hook of the full, powerful, and sacred obligation to evolve out of your darkness and into your light?

This confused understanding of shadow is the rule rather than the exception. For example, a similar approach to shadow is shot through poet Robert Bly's well-known and oft-cited *A Little Book on the Human Shadow*.

Though I am a fan of his poetry, his explanation of shadow does not offer us anything near an in-depth understanding of what shadow integration might mean. For Bly, shadow is composed of what you had to suppress as a child to please the grown-ups around you:

> When we were one or two years old we had what we might visualize as a 360-degree personality. Energy radiated out from all parts of our body and all parts of our psyche. A child running is a living globe of energy. We had a ball of energy, all right; but one day we noticed that our parents didn't like certain parts of that ball. They said things like: "Can't you be still?" Or "It isn't nice to try and kill your brother." Behind us we have an invisible bad, and the part of us our parents don't like, we, to keep our parents' love, put in the bag. By the time we go to school our bag is quite large. Then our teachers have their say: "Good children don't get angry over such little things." So we take our anger and put it in the bag. By the time my brother and I were twelve in Madison, Minnesota, we were known as "the nice Bly boys." Our bags were already a mile long.

With great respect to Bly, this paradigmatic passage is confusing. What is so bad about going through the ethical socialization required to become a "nice Bly boy"? Is it so heinous to leave behind your attempts to suffocate your brother with a pillow? Isn't growing beyond the murderous rage that spawned the first fratricide a good and noble goal of human evolution? Shouldn't authentic teachers help us discern between legitimate and inappropriate anger? Finally, Bly's implicit idea is regressive in the extreme: the one- or two-year-old with an energy-radiating 360-degree personality.[2]

Naturally, the understanding of shadow integration that I have outlined until this point is not without wisdom. It is true but partial. This teaching assumes that shadow means jealousy, rage, pettiness, violence, and all the other negative ethical expressions. Shadow integration simply means to own the fact that you are jealous, angry, filled with rage, insanely promiscuous, addicted to all forms of comfort, and much more. ***Bring your disowned*** *shadow into first person.* Shadow integration comes to mean something like, "Get out of denial and admit that you are an asshole." And free up the energy you have used to cover up being an asshole.

Now, this is not a bad idea. Indeed, it is absolutely critical for any form of spiritual or psychological growth. Someone who *owns* their dark side is generally more tolerable than someone who does not. When you are in denial, you are more dangerous, because it is impossible to engage in authentic conversation around any genuine issue. A good rule of life might be: self-acknowledged assholes are easier and more fun to hang out with than assholes in denial.

This understanding of "owning your shadow," however, might be called more accurately something like shadow confession. So where does the integration piece come in? How do you integrate your night virtues, and why would you want to?

Some psychological teachers explain shadow integration as making a place within your own psyche for your rage, envy, greed, dishonesty, and pettiness, so that you do not project them onto everyone else.

This good and important teaching is generally attributed to Carl Jung. Shadow is understood by Jung to be your "dark side," that part of yourself that you hide away—afraid to expose it to the light of day. Shadow is anything that you cannot hold as "I" in your self-definition—your less-than-noble qualities, including fear, rage, uncontrolled sexing, envy, greed, egoic pettiness, violence, frustration, depression, and more. It is in this context that Jung wrote "the most terrifying thing is to accept oneself completely."

Taking back shadow projection is a huge evolutionary leap forward and needs to be taught, practiced, and applauded. It allows for a more honest picture of reality, which always opens the heart up for deeper and more stable loving. But taking back projection still does not explain the core teaching of shadow integration.

Greater Is the Light That Comes from the Darkness

Jung himself offered a more profound direction in understanding shadow. His core teaching, drawn from many sources, is that we cannot be whole human beings without recognizing and incorporating our shadow energy. Jung has an expression that he uses constantly to express this idea: "In the Shadow is the Gold." By this, he means to say that most of what is valuable in the human personality—the gold—can be mined only from the shadow. But what does that mean, and why should it be so? It is to this all-important question that we now turn our attention. We will seek to fundamentally evolve what shadow means and how shadow work is done! At this point, I am going to unpack directly from the original tantric sources a radical new teaching on shadow integration.

So let us begin. In the book of Genesis, one of the oldest texts of Unique Self teachings, the creation myth is expressed in the words, "God said, Let there be Light. And there was light."

Light, with its unique frequency for every person, is—as we have already noted—one of the primary mystical symbols for Unique Self.

In the third-century mystical esoteric texts on Genesis, it is taught that this original light that initiated the creative process was too much for the world to bear, so "God hid the original light. The light will be revealed to the righteous in the world of becoming." In a similar way, contemporary neuroscience suggests that we deploy only a fraction of our mind's potential for consciousness.

Some centuries later, the Zohar picks up the thread of the earlier teaching. "Where was the original light of creation hidden?" ask the masters. To which the masters respond, "The original light was hidden in the darkness!" "Where does the original light still appear in the world?" ask the masters once more. "In the person of the enlightened ones," responds the text. And who are the enlightened ones? The enlightened ones, the righteous ones, according to the masters of Tantric Kabbalah, are the ones who have incarnated their Unique Self. The implication of the text is this: to realize your Unique Self, you must follow the path of the light hidden in the darkness.

Lost in the Darkness

One night, the Sufi trickster figure, Mullah Nasruddin, comes across a man intensely searching the ground under a torch that served as a streetlight. "Did you lose something?" inquires the master.

"Yes, my keys," responds the man frantically. So the master bends down to help the man search.

After much time, Nasruddin finally asks, "Well, where exactly did you lose them?"

"In there," said the man, pointing to a trail leading into a dark forest.

"Then why are you looking for them over here?" the master asks.

The man responds, slightly exasperated, as if it is obvious, "I can't look there—it's too dark!"

The key to your Unique Self enlightenment was lost in the dark. That is where you must search.

There are times when one must fight the darkness, both in the world and in our selves. You must discipline your own and the world's darkness so it does not harm yourself or others. Mahatma Gandhi wrote two letters in 1938 advising the English and the Jews in Israel not to fight Hitler:

> I would like you to lay down the arms you have as being use-
> less to save you or humanity. You will invite Herr Hitler and
> Signor Mussolini to take what they want of the countries you
> call your possessions. Let them take possession of your beauti-
> ful island, with your many beautiful buildings. You will give
> them all these but neither your souls nor your minds.[3]

This spiritual letter was correctly met with outrage. Spirit in this case incarnated more accurately in the brave fighters of England and Israel who knew that the force of evil needed to be met with the greater force of the good. Sometimes light and darkness stand in opposition. At these times it is essential for the mythic motif to be played out with the forces of the light vanquishing the forces of darkness.

But the dance of light and darkness is ultimately more subtle than the important but limited dualisms of good and evil, right and wrong.

The masters of Tantric Kabbalah pointed to three levels of consciousness. The first level is called submission—in Hebrew, *hakna'ah*. At this level, one either submits to the law that divides between the right and the wrong, or alternatively submits to one's default nature, which fails to make any such distinctions.

The second is called individuation, distinction, or discernment, from the Hebrew, *havdalah*. At this level of consciousness, one does not merely submit to the law but deploys one's own mind and heart in creating the ethical dharma. This is done by drawing proper and appropriate distinctions between light and darkness, good and evil, and constructive and destructive.

The third level of consciousness is called sweetness, in Hebrew, *hamtaka*. This is the level of nondual realization, where mystical tantric masters from all the great traditions lived. In the words of the masters, "The contraction of shadow is only sweetened in its root." *At this deeper level of consciousness, the relationship between your own light and darkness, as well as those of the world, is much more of an elegant dance than a vicious battle.* Picture a Möbius strip. To make a Möbius strip, you simply take a piece of paper and, before connecting the two ends, you twist one of them to its opposite side. If you pick up the strip and start drawing a line, you will end up with a line on both sides, without ever removing the pencil from the paper. The two sides are geometrically actually one. The image suggests something of the tantric understanding of good and evil. At the level of nondual awareness, good and evil are not opposites, but rather dance in an enclosed Uni-verse of curved time and space. And if you follow shadow to its root, you will always find the hidden light.

Greater Is Wisdom Than Folly

For the Tantric Kabbalists, this nondual understanding forms the core of one of the great sources of World Spirituality, known as the Wisdom of Solomon.

The Unique Self master King Solomon says, "Greater is Wisdom *than* folly; greater is light *than* darkness."

Simply read, this is a text about duality. Wisdom opposes and overcomes folly, even as light opposes and overcomes darkness.

The ancient Unique Self teachers, however, reread this text in a radically different way. The original Hebrew word *min* can be read not only as "than" but as "from." The reread text declares: "Greater is the wisdom that comes *from* folly; greater is the light that comes *from* darkness." The poet William Blake, intuiting the tantric principles, writes, "If the fool would but follow his folly he would become wise." The same may be said of light and darkness. *If you but follow your darkness, you will come to your light.*

You can now begin to feel into a core principle of Unique Self enlightenment. The source of highest light is the darkness itself. The *tzadik*, one who has incarnated their Unique Self, does this by accessing and transforming the light hidden in their darkness, and *as* their darkness.

The Shattering of the Vessels

It is this principle that informs the primary reality myth of these old masters—the myth known as *shevirat hacaylim*—the shattering of the vessels. In the Kabbalistic creation myth, this light streamed into vessels. Over time, the light became too intense to hold, and the vessels shattered. (For the Kabbalists, the big bang is virtually identical with this big crash.)

Some of the light folded back into its source. However, many sparks of light remained trapped in the shards of the shattered vessels—scattered across the kosmos. These dark shards, with their hidden sparks of light, are the source of the highest potential light for our world. The core of your life work is, in the language of Kabbalah, to raise up the sparks and return them to their source—that is, to free the sparks from their darkened prisons and let them shine again.

In this graphic image, the world is understood to be a place of broken vessels. Broken hearts, broken promises, and broken lives are all expressions of the primal shattered vessels. *In revealing the light hidden in your brokeness, you are involved in an essential and primordial fixing.* This, as we saw earlier, is what the Kabbalists called *tikkun*. Kabbalistic scholar Avraham Leader has correctly translated the Hebrew Aramaic deployment of the word *tikkun* in the Zohar as "evolve."[4] *Tikkun* is the obligation and privilege of every Unique Self. *Tikkun* is the evolution of consciousness, which is no less than the evolution of God. Every person's *tikkun* is Unique. Every person's *tikkun* is needed.

Befriend Your Darkness

Holding this image in your mind, we can now illuminate two almost shocking, koan-like assertions of Hasidic master Dov Ber Mezritch.

The first: "Higher is the divine source of *ra* [evil] than the source of *tov* [good]."

The second: "All-That-Is, in its original source on a higher plane, finds expression in this world on a lower plane."

Now, I translated *tov* and *ra* in the first koan as "good" and "evil." "Evil," however, doesn't quite capture *ra*, because "evil" associates in our imagination with an either/or dualistic way of thinking. We were educated on binary pairs—up and down, sure and unsure, order and chaos, right and wrong, good and evil. Many times we need to act based on these appropriately dualistic understandings. We need to put on our cape and fight for good against evil. And yet there are momentous leaps of meaning that leave these ideas behind.

Quantum physics, for example, shatters the old binary vessels: chaos and order are mixed up; motion and stillness, certainty and uncertainty are in a perpetual dance. Similarly, teaches Lurianic Kabbalah, *ra* is enmeshed in *tov*.

Indeed, the binary illusion is further collapsed in an astounding play of words. In the original Hebrew, the root word *ra* has a second meaning: "friend." Tantric Master King Solomon explains this to mean, "You must make friends with your *ra* in order to reveal your light."

The Tantric Kabbalists hid this teaching in their radical rereading of what might be the most famous verse in the Bible, "Love your friend as your self." The Hebrew word for "friend" is *ra*. Remember that the word *ra* means not only "friend" but also "evil" or "shadow." In this reading, the text is saying, "Love your shadow, befriend your shadow, for it is the key to reclaiming yourself." This secret mystical teaching is the hidden kernel in many seemingly innocent and charming stories of great spiritual masters:

> The great Unique Self master, the Baal Shem Tov, Master of Good Name, arrives at a town in which he is supposed to deliver a homily the next morning. He is informed that there is a very sick baby, on the verge of death. Would he organize a prayer service for the baby? The normal custom would have been for the master to invite the ten most pious men in the city to pray with him for the baby's healing. The Baal Shem Tov, upon hearing the request, meditates for a few minutes. He then issues an order to gather the ten most flagrant thieves in the city. He wants to pray with them for the welfare of the baby. The people are aghast, but he insists.
>
> By morning, color is miraculously returning to the baby's cheeks, and his raspy breaths are becoming more gentle and

even. The people know they have witnessed a great healing. "But why ten thieves?" they ask him.

Responds the Baal Shem Tov, "Because in my meditation I saw that the gates of heaven were locked, closed to our prayers. But a thief—a true thief—knows how to pick the locks even of the gates of heaven."

There is a secret in the darkness that allows for an evolutionary movement toward realization that is simply not available in the more conventional light. Sometimes it is only through accessing the Thief that lives inside you that you can open the gates of heaven. It is in this sense that the Baal Shem Tov proclaimed that he was the Rebbe of Thieves. And it was in this sense that Persian mystic poet Hafiz staked his place with the "rogues and thieves" rather than among the pious. Here we sense the first glimmering of a teaching in which the integration of shadow might lead toward wholeness.

The Teachings of the Blood

There is not just a thief that lives inside of you. There is a Unique Thief. The utter Uniqueness of your shadow, as the path to your Unique Self and as the source of your vitality, is the essential mystery of tantra. It has sometimes been referred to as the "teachings of the blood." "Blood" in this context means "body." The teaching of Unique Shadow and Unique Self are held in your very body.

Hermann Hesse, in the prologue to *Demian,* said it like this: "I have ceased to question stars and books; I have begun to listen to the teachings my blood whispers to me."

I am going to refer to shadow with a new word, a body word—"pathology." I introduce this word because of its immediate physical association. When something goes wrong in the normal functioning of the organism, it causes pathology. Mystics constantly draw analogies between psycho-spiritual sickness and physical illness—that is to say, pathology. In one mystical text it is said, "Through my body I vision God."[5] The teachings of the blood.

Shadow, or what we will now refer to as our (spiritual) pathologies, follows a similar pattern to physical pathology. Our physical organism is absolutely unique—each human being has a fully distinctive physical signature.

Shadow, as we will see, is well understood as a violation or distortion of Unique Self. This same dynamic shows up at the cellular level. In cancer, for example, "the diseased tissue emits its own unique energy signature which differs from the energy signature of the surrounding healthy cells."[6] The immune system of the body, the blood itself, the cells and cell markers, are all part of the absolutely unique signature of the human body. Our immune system immediately recognizes and destroys any foreign substances—microbes, tumors, and bacteria—that violate the signature uniqueness of our body. If one vial of the wrong blood is injected into a person's system, that person usually dies. The foreign blood has violated their specific and unique immune pattern. Pathology means the violation of your body's unique system.

The uniqueness of every human being is actually a core truth of biology. The violation of the body's unique signature causes shadow—that is to say, sickness in the body.* As Dr. Mark Kirschbaum has written, "One could argue that, in a sense, cancer is in part a breakdown of the individual's unique structure at the molecular level."[7]

In the metaphor of the body, we might say that cancer is to healthy cells what the ego is to Unique Self. Because of the signature singularity of the body, its pathological responses are also unique. No two tumors are the same. *The unique signature of the healthy body is the physical signifier of Unique Self. The distortion of the unique signature is the body's pathological responses and the physical signifier of Unique Shadow.*

---

*Many of the important questions facing modern molecular medicine and science are in some way related to this issue. The body is constantly recognizing and repulsing "invaders"—for example, the millions of hostile microorganisms we encounter with every breath. How? Through a complicated friend-or-foe recognition system based on unique identifying proteins found in most cells of your particular body. If the foreign cell does not have that marker—the unique ID card for entry—then the immune system is launched into attack mode, and the violator of the body's signature uniqueness is repelled.

An important recent understanding is that tumors are frequently related to a breakdown of this "defender" system. That is to say, tumors distort or otherwise violate the complex unique cellular signature of the body.

Tumors use many different mechanisms to blur the markers from their surface, thus allowing them to elude being destroyed by the immune system. Furthermore, one of the ways the immune system keeps itself from attacking normal tissue (failure in this regard is called autoimmune disorder) is by triggering self-reactive immune cells to self-destruct. This process, which is being intensely studied, is known as apoptosis. It has recently been reported that a number of serious cancers, such as melanoma and breast cancer, actually exploit this trigger in a destructive way, causing the good immune cells to commit suicide!

The old hermetic teachers rooted in Plato and the Hebrew mysteries always taught, "As above, so below." They meant to remind us that the internal structures of spirit and matter parallel each other. In regard to shadow, this means spiritual pathology parallels physical pathology. *Spiritual pathology is an expression of the violation of the unique patterns of the spirit.* When the psyche's signature is forged—if I am living a story not my own—then pathological symptoms are not long in appearing.

Furthermore, just as no two tumors are alike, specific shadow symptoms like anger, fear, phobia, jealousy, and obsession reflect the specific nature of the Unique Self that has been violated. Not which symptoms show up, but how the symptoms show up, and in what particular intensity, texture, and frequency, tells us about what is not being expressed.

This idea of not just shadow but personalized shadow lies at the heart of the thinking of Unique Self mystic Mordechai Lainer of Izbica. Listen directly to his teaching on Unique Shadow, woven from his writings and from the pen of his student, Tzadok the Priest:

> Everyone knows the place of his particular vulnerability to his darkness—to the attacks of his primal drives. . . . Every person has a unique *chisaron* [pathology or shadow] which inhered in them from the day of their birth. . . . Every person has a unique soul *tikkun* [fixing] to do in this world . . . and this fixing is connected to his unique *chisaron* shadow with which he was born.
>
> And it is this place that is the vessel of his potential blessing.
>
> It is with this place that the person must establish *kesher* . . . an intimate relationship.

The first key word in the passage is *chisaron,* which I have translated in the parentheses as "pathology" or "shadow." The literal translation of *chisaron,* however, is some combination of the English words "wound," "lack," "absence," and "emptiness." We all are empty and wounded in different ways. We are all pathological in wholly individual and unique ways.

This is true, according to Unique Self dharma, for the simplest of reasons. Shadow pathology at its ultimate source is rooted in *your* unlived life, which fosters the feeling that you do not really exist in any meaningful way. We all have different unlived stories. For Lainer, pathology is a foundational Unique Self quality. More specifically, pathology is the unique response of the spirit to a Unique Self distortion.

Chisaron as a signature characteristic actually reveals the unique work—the calling, or contribution—that the soul is called to do in this world. Stated in our terms, unique pathology is a vital path to Unique Self. Moreover, it is critical to note that this Unique Shadow pathology is, according to Lainer, not a function of childhood. On the contrary, he states clearly that every person is born with a unique *chisaron.*

Lainer's *chisaron* is your unique inferior function. It is your unique core wound. It is the place of your unique pathology. Your Unique Shadow has the same DNA print as your Unique Self. The great paradox of spirit is that your inferior function itself is also your greatest gateway to the numinous. So, for example, if your inferior function is a particular dynamic in the way that you love, it will also be the place of your greatest gift and Unique Self calling.

Walking in the Dark—From Demon to Daemon

Biblical-myth reader St. John of the Cross in the sixteenth century said, "If one wants to be sure of the road he is on, he must close his eyes and walk in the dark." This is the darkened path of following your shadow to the light. Lainer adds to John's thought that you walk not just in the darkness, but in your unique darkness.

Along this path, your demons become your daemons, those personal angels whom the ancient Greeks believed call you to your destiny. This idea appears in a subtly disguised but beautiful form in biblical myth. God appears in so many guises and forms that biblical myth has many names for the one God. One of them is *shad-ai. Shad-ai* is a combination of the word *shad*—meaning "demon"—and the letter *yud,* which in mysticism represents the divine point. The *yud* is your divine spark, a letter shaped like a flame, a point of light. It takes but a single candle to probe the darkness. *At the place of meeting between the darkness and the point of light, the deepest transformations occur.* The divine name *shad-ai* is that meeting between *shad,* the demon, the darkness, and *yud,* the daemon, the point of light. It is the evolutionary God-impulse in you that invites your demons to be your daemons.

Ralph Waldo Emerson writes that there is a crack in everything God has made. Meister Eckhart understood, six hundred years earlier, that the major crack is built *into* you not as punishment or even as a test, but rather as a directional signal, a hint in your search for your Unique Self. Eckhart liked to say, "To get at the core of God at his greatest, one must first get into the core of himself at his least."

Remember the story of the king who has a particularly rare and beautiful set of fine silver serving dishes:

> The intricacy of the design was unmatched anywhere, and the king took great pride in serving his closest friends on these plates. One day, the king notices that somehow one of the pieces has gotten scratched up. No one knows how it happened. But even worse, no artist can promise to fix it without marring the design—that is, until one unknown artist appears and says he can do the job.
>
> Despite his hesitancy, the king has no one else to turn to, so he entrusts the man with the contract. Strangely enough, the artist requests that the entire set—even though they were not scratched—be sent to his studio. And so it was.
>
> A full month later, the artist returns. The king is shocked . . . the plates are beautiful! The artist had integrated the scratch into the plate—actually making the flaw the guiding principle of the new design. All the other plates were repainted accordingly—making an even more magnificent set than before.

Your unique scar needs to be your guiding principle in revealing to your self your unique beauty.

The image of the scratched vessel returns us to the Kabbalistic metaphor of the shattered vessels. The primordial vessels of reality shatter, and sparks of light are hidden in the shards of the broken vessels. The work of a lifetime is to raise the sparks that are uniquely matched to your signature, and return them to their source.

Initially, I suggested that the vessels shatter because they cannot hold the light. At this point, I can explain more deeply. The vessels shatter precisely in order to *hold* your unique light. For the paradox of the vessels in Kabbalah is that the reconstituted vessel is far more powerful than the vessel before it shattered. In the Unique Self-realization of the Kabbalists, the reconstituting of the vessels is from the light itself—particularly from the light that was hidden in the darkness. *Your full light can only be held after you have shattered and deployed the uniqueness of your own particular shattering—the scar—to fashion the vessel of your full beauty.*

The master of Slonim, writing from a small, nondescript house in the depths of Jerusalem, said: "The unique service of the generation is to serve through our point of resistance. Every human being has a unique resistance which reveals to us the unique reason for our being in the world . . . and that is the key to service."

Unique Self and Unique Shadow

At this point, we can evolve from the tantric teachings and take a quantum leap in our understanding of shadow. The full implications of these tantric teachings are gorgeously essential to what we have called the New Enlightenment of Unique Self. I will now state this clearly in several core teachings.

Your shadow is not impersonal. It is not generic; the core of your shadow is absolutely personal. Your Shadow is more accurately termed your Unique Shadow. *Your shadow is unique because it is your unlived life—your disowned Unique Self. The way to identify and reclaim this disowned part of you is by following your Unique Shadow back to your Unique Light.* This is what it means to follow your folly and become wise: follow your Unique Shadow back to your Unique Self.

When you take the unique light of your story, and place it into darkness, does it lose its unique quality? Of course not. The unique quality is distorted, it is hidden, it is unlived, but it remains present. If you take the DNA print of your Unique Perspective, and place it into darkness, does it lose its particular quality? Of course not. Your shadow is unique, because your shadow is your unlived life. For that very reason, your Unique Shadow is the yellow-brick road back to your Unique Self.

In many of the great systems of realization, a core teaching is that for the light to evolve to new levels of realization and manifestation, it must first enter the darkness. When the Absolute is about to manifest, it goes into hiding from itself. It is this same dynamic that causes the seed to emerge from the darkness of the ground. In Unique Self mystical teaching, light thickens into the darkness of vessels in order to eventually evolve into even higher levels of realization. In that very same sense, your Unique Self light appears as your Unique Shadow in order to demand your higher evolution and manifestation.

The Unique Self is the Eros, the life impulse that drives us forward. Shadow is Eros turned around against itself. By integrating your shadow, you are liberating the trapped life energy of your Unique Self. Your life energy is not generic. It is your life energy. The portal to your energy is none other than your Unique Self. Your most persistent shadow-structure is also your most abundant wellspring of energy and life. The reclaiming of life energy happens through shadow integration. Thus, the tantric masters of the left-handed path saw shadow integration as a process of revelation by which the previously hidden Unique Self—the secret mystery—manifests as inspiration and Eros.

Integrated shadow, however, is not merely life force in some general sort of way, but is drawn by each person through the channel of their Unique Self. The integration of your Unique Shadow allows you to show up in the world as the particularly potent articulation of infinity that is your Unique Self.

> When a woman in a certain African tribe knows she is pregnant, she goes out into the wilderness with a few friends. Together they pray and meditate until they hear the unique song belonging to the child.
>
> The women know that every soul has its own vibrational signature, expressing its own unique texture and quality. When the women attune to the song, they sing it aloud. Then they return to the tribe and teach it to everyone else.
>
> When the child is ready to be born, the community gathers. They sing the song as the child is delivered into the world. When the child reaches the age of education, the village gathers again and chants the child's song. When the child passes through the initiations to adulthood, the people come together and sing. At the time of marriage, the people sing. Finally, when the soul is about to depart from this world, the family and friends gather around the person's bed, just as they did at birth, and sing the person to the next life.

In this African tribe, there is one other occasion upon
which the person hears their unique song. It is when the child
commits a crime or a hurtful social act, when the child acts
from shadow. When this happens, the person is called to the
center of the village. The people in the community form a
circle around them and sing their unique song. In that way,
they are called back to the light.[8]

The tribe recognizes that the healing of shadow behavior is not arbitrary
punishment; it is the recovery of memory—to be sung back to your Unique
Self. Your shadow is but the distortion of your Unique Self. *When you remember and recognize your unique song, you lose the desire to hurt
anyone else.*

CHAPTER EIGHTEEN

THE TEN PRINCIPLES OF UNIQUE SELF SHADOW WORK

AT THIS POINT, WE ARE READY to unpack the raw outline of this evolutionary mystical teaching of Unique Self / Unique Shadow in the ten principles of shadow and, in the next chapter, the eight tenets of love.

1. Shadow is your Unique Self distortion.

Shadow is not your night virtues—your lust, fear, anger, jealousy, or envy. This is why the teaching of shadow integration that understands the night virtues as the core of shadow makes so little sense. Why would you want to integrate your rage and pettiness into your person? These night virtues are ethical violations, which, if unrectified, have profound implications for your life and karma. This is the teaching of all the great traditions in the perennial philosophy. The night virtues are obviously shadow qualities, but the night virtues are not the core of shadow. Shadow *qualities* are not the essence of your shadow but merely an *expression* of your shadow. Your shadow is the distortion of your Unique Self—the part of your story that is unlived or distorted, and is therefore in darkness. The Hebrew word for story, *sippur,* you may remember, has the same root as one of the great mystical words for light, *sapir.* Your light is your story. Your story is your Unique frequency of light. The part of your story that is not lived—that is not in the light—is in darkness. It is that very unlived story that is the core of your shadow. Naturally then, the disowning of your Unique Story creates your Unique Shadow.

2. Your story includes both your True Self and Unique Self.

Your True Self is your freedom, and your Unique Self is your fullness.

Your freedom is beyond all forms: it is your realization of your utter identity with the divine, with All-That-Is. This is your absolute emptiness. You are emptied of all superficial and limiting identities. In this precise sense, you are absolutely free. You realize that you are not a skin-encapsulated ego. You are not a-part, separate, and alone, but an indivisible part of the one, seamless coat of the Uni-verse. This is the realization of your classic enlightenment. This is the enlightenment of True Self.

Your fullness is the uniqueness of your play within form: it is the fullness of your Unique Story, the distinct expression of your divinity, of All-That-Is. Your story is all the Unique Gifts, pleasures, needs, and obligations that flow from your singular signature in the seamless coat of the Uni-verse. Your story is the evolutionary service that you offer the world, the service that can be done by you and you alone. All of this is the fullness and fulfillment of your Unique Self.

3. Any part of your story that you do not live, lives in darkness.

In your meeting with parents, teachers, culture, and peers, you were wounded. This is true of every human being. It is part of the evolutionary journey. As a result of your hurt, you put part of your story in shadow. You forgot who you were. To come home, you must recover and embrace the memory of your fullest self. It is in this embrace that you overcome the distorting mechanism of what I call your hug formula. Every person has their own hug formula. Your hug formula determines the part of your self that you are willing to dis-own in order to receive the approval, the hug, that makes you feel like you belong in the world. This part of you becomes unconscious. It lives in shadow. This is your repressed shadow.

There are also parts of you that are unconscious, not because you unknowingly pushed them into shadow, but because they have never seen the light of day. They are unconscious because they have never been conscious. You have not evolved to the full realization of your identity, so it remains in shadow. For example, you may still identify with your isolated separate-self ego. You have not realized your True Self, distinctly expressed as your Unique Self. Any part of your enlightened True or Unique Self that is not realized lives in shadow. This is your developmental or emergent shadow. It is the part of you that has not yet developed or emerged—that is still in shadow.

4. When unique light is trapped in shadow, it does not remain static.

The untold and unlived night stories that are hidden, even from you, always devolve. They fester and fume. They demand to be lived and heard.

Consciousness, energy, and light, like fresh water, are meant to flow. Their nature is dynamic and constantly evolving. For this is the nature of the divine. When light is trapped in shadow, it does not remain static. It becomes stagnant. There is either evolution or devolution. This is the same principle that causes the festering of unexpressed hurt or an untransformed wound.

That which remains unseen either grows or shrinks, but it always changes.

That which is unconsciously placed in shadow always devolves. Once it can be seen and talked of, it can breathe again, and the evolution of your light can resume its normal trajectory. Hidden in shadow does not mean held privately. There are sacred secrets that are appropriately never public, but always held hidden in the love-light of consciousness.

Some sacred secrets must be held privately in order to grow, like seeds under the ground. (One must not confuse sacred secrets with sordid secrets.) But to hide your light from yourself out of fear or shame will cause the light to become dense, distorted, and destructive. Shadow refers to those untold night stories trapped in your unconscious that fester and fume, demanding their day.

5. When unlived life stagnates and devolves, it re-emerges as shadow qualities.

Shadow qualities include addictions of every form—rage, betrayal, envy, jealousy, and more. *You do not want to integrate shadow qualities. You want to re-integrate shadow.*

Your unlived life is stuffed in the darkness. It stagnates and devolves, and re-emerges as shadow qualities. ***Until the story of your life is lived, you will go on desperately yearning for it.*** When your desperate yearning is not nourished by the Eros of your story, it devolves to desperate craving, which is filled by the pseudo-Eros of addiction. They are shadow qualities. Once you have realized and integrated your shadow, which is your unlived life, the shadow qualities lose their raison d'être and begin to drop away.

Say you are frustrated and angry. You have been wanting to build a toolshed in the backyard all weekend.[1] This is the life that you need to live on this weekend. It is Sunday evening. You have not built the shed. In your interior, this unlived life makes you feel terrible. You feel incompetent, not powerful, and unable to take care of yourself. You feel like you did not keep your word to yourself. All the other times that you let yourself or someone else down come to the fore of your consciousness. All of these times are part of your unlived life. You did not live the life of the reliable and trusted friend who you truly are. None of this, however, is fully conscious. These feelings are not in the light, because they do not mesh with your self-identity as a person living a life that is good, competent, powerful, and capable. This is shadow material.

Your wife has been away all weekend on a business trip. She returns after she has successfully completed her weekend mission. She walks in the house, gives you a hug, and asks, "Honey, how was your weekend? Did you get that shed built?" Her tone is innocent, but you do not hear it that way. You explode with rage at her. You get angry with her for daring to be so frustrated and upset with you.

Shadow in this example is a Unique Shadow, which emerged from the unlived life that you needed and wanted to live that weekend.

What happened? There are several distinct steps.

You are frustrated and angry with yourself for not having fulfilled your commitment. The life that was yours to live at that time was "to build the shed." But you do not consciously "own" your frustration and anger for failing to live your life. You especially want to distance yourself from your feeling of being inadequate, not enough, or bad.

Your partner's innocent question unleashes a swamp of hidden bad feelings in regard to your unlived life and brings them to the surface. You naturally do not want to direct these feelings against yourself, but they need to be directed somewhere. So you turn your anger against your partner. This is the first level of what is going on.

On an even deeper level, you are engaged in projection. You project all of your own frustration and anger with yourself onto your partner. For that very reason, you experience her as being angry and frustrated with you. You then proceed to get angry with her for daring to be so frustrated and upset with you.

Your unlived life—the project you wanted to finish—has been disowned and placed into shadow. There it devolved into rage, anxiety, and frustration. All of these shadow qualities were then projected onto your beloved partner.

Shadow in this example is not generic but rather a Unique Shadow, which emerges from the unlived life that you needed and wanted to live that weekend. If you would enter the inside of your anger, it would lead you back to your own desire to build the shed. Building the shed in a timely and effective manner was the expression of your Unique Self on that particular weekend. Actually building the shed would be the way to follow your Unique Shadow back to your Unique light.

Let me give you two more examples of the Unique Self–Unique Shadow complex.

Unlived Passion

About a decade ago I spent several years working with a woman named Amelia. Amelia was the dean and a teacher of comparative religion at a prestigious private school for girls in Europe. She was a cultured, ethical, compassionate woman of considerable depth and insight, with a balanced and delightful disposition. The explicit goal of our work was to facilitate Amelia's Unique Self enlightenment. Amelia had this quite unexpected habit of getting into very embroiled verbal fights with her colleagues over seemingly nonsensical issues. She would take a position on an apparently innocuous matter, and then fight for it with a passion and vehemence that was way out of proportion to the nature of the issue at hand. This made little sense to Amelia or to myself. It was troubling not only because it caused her no small amount of grief, but also because it was so completely out of character.

Our breakthrough moment in regard to this issue came from the realization, which was then growing in me, that Unique Shadow is always the road back to Unique Self. During our work together, one of our major focal points was Amelia as a teacher. In order to confirm an intuition that had been brewing in me, I asked her to "teach me" several classes, with me as the student. She did. The classes were lovely, nuanced, and insightful.

But something was wrong. The quality of her teaching was profoundly feminine, in that it held space for everyone, received everyone's feedback, and sought to validate the opinions of all the students. But it was not compelling. It lacked the passion needed to penetrate the heart. The quality of masculine insemination that plants a great idea forever in the heart and mind of a young person was strikingly absent. Now, this was not because Amelia lacked passionate beliefs or deeply held certainties. She did not lack these things. But as it emerged, she was enculturated in the progressive ethos of teaching that viewed masculine passion and insemination as a violation of the autonomy of the student. It confused ecstasy with frenzy, and transmission of a truth with intellectual domination. In this ethos, the role of the teacher was virtually always that of facilitator and virtually never that of passionate inseminator. As a result, Amelia was never able to convey the depth of her teaching and deeply held knowing to her students. Her Unique Self as a teacher remained both unlived and distorted.

What naturally happened then was that Amelia's distorted Unique Self appeared as Amelia's Unique Shadow. Her petty fights filled with passion and fervor over irrelevant issues were but the unlived vocation of the passionate, compelling teacher showing up in shadow form. Once this became clear to us, Amelia began to shift her teaching style significantly, and within six months, the nasty fights that had dogged her career and relationships disappeared almost entirely. She evolved from being the lovely, nice teacher to the compelling, provocative teacher. Much to her surprise and delight, her popularity soared. Amelia had followed her Unique Shadow back to her Unique Self.

Taking Anger into Account

A second story involves a student from southern Israel who came to me because he had a terrible problem with anger. He was angry with his kids, his wife, and himself most of the time. I tried every kind of anger-management technique I knew and more for a period of many months. Nothing worked.

By profession, he was an accountant. He was also a man who had, from the time he was very young, a deep passion for social justice. After several weeks of talking, I shocked him by telling him I thought he should leave accounting and run for mayor of his small town. His wife was particularly aghast at the prospect. He made a good, stable living as an accountant, and was often home and available (if angry) for her and the kids. Why give this up for the financial and social vagaries of political life?

I shared with both of them my intuition, which had come to me in a flash in the midst of a late-night prayer. I sensed that his anger was not based on old childhood issues or any kind of character disorder. Rather, it was the sublimated anger of protest, of a leader and revolutionary trapped in an office adding up numbers for other people.

Now, being an accountant is a wonderful, honorable, and vitally needed profession—but not if you are a revolutionary! A few years and many ups and downs later, he in fact became the mayor of his town. To his and his family's surprise, what had been his petty and unpredictable bouts of rage simply stopped. He became a different person. He stepped into his Unique Self, so his shadow—his distorted or unlived Unique Self—naturally disappeared. In this case, the anger itself was re-channeled and vitally transformed. It remained passionate, but lost its bitter and sometimes mean sense, and took on a cleaner and even compassionate quality.

The path of transformation of identity teaches that only through using your Unique Shadow as a guide to Unique Self can you ever find your way back to your story.

3-2-1-0 of Shadow

There is a well-known shadow process in Integral Theory called the 3-2-1 of shadow. It was borrowed from various traditions of shadow work and evolved within the Integral framework.

Here's how it works. Let's say that you are massively annoyed by a coworker who seems to behave in a consistently deceitful fashion. This is the 3 of shadow appearing as the third person. Then you move shadow to 2, which is shadow in second person. At this juncture you simply create a second-person dialogue with shadow. Finally, you move to level 1, where you own the previously disowned shadow in first person. You do so by finding the quality of deceitfulness as it lives in your first person. Once, however, you understand the Unique Self and Unique Shadow nexus, you realize that for genuine shadow integration to take place a 0 must be added, and it becomes a 3-2-1-0 process. In this process you realize that there is not only shadow but Unique Shadow. This is 1, and then you follow 1 to 0, which is Unique Shadow back to Unique light.

6. You feel the full depth of the goodness and aliveness of your life only when you are fully living *your* full story.

When you are not living your full story, you do not feel that you fully exist. You do not feel adequate, dignified, or valuable. Anything less than your unique and special story makes you feel unworthy. The feeling of emptiness that always accompanies the feeling of unworthiness is the source of every form of addiction and acting out. Stories, of course, have many layers, plots, and subplots. You may feel the fullness of your story in one dimension of your life, and you may feel drab and adrift in other parts of your life. This is how you know where your story, your Book of Life, needs editing or rewriting.

If you're not living your story, you create a pseudo-story. If you're not in your Eros, you are seduced by pseudo-Eros and false stories. You fill up your emptiness with snakes and scorpions—all the shadow qualities, all the night virtues, all the addictions. Once your unlived life is in darkness, it undergoes degradation. You feel numb and empty. You unconsciously reach out for something to cover the emptiness. You cast about for depth and fulfillment, which can only be truly found by reclaiming your unlived life.

Often anger supplies you with a hit of pseudo-fullness. But since your internal self-image is that of a contented and successful person, you cannot own your anger. Unwarranted anger is a shadow quality. Your disowned anger remains in your space, but since your anger is not in you, you project it onto others, who you then think are angry at you. You then become sad because you feel that people are angry at you. Over time this turns into a low-grade depression. And the cycle continues its downward degenerative spiral of unlove and alienation.

When you are miscast, you cast about. You act out when you are the leading actor in the wrong script. You can only receive an Oscar for playing a starring role in your own life. Being in the wrong story creates massive interior pain, which in turn gives birth to your shadow qualities.

7. Shadow is a lie about your Unique Self. Shadow is a lie about your essential identity.

When you lie about your life, you create shadow qualities. It takes enormous energy to support a lie. This is especially true when it is not a "detail lie" about this or that, but a lie about the very fabric of your identity. You deny ownership of essential voices in your self. You hide those parts of you that challenge the image of the man or woman you want and claim to be. You do not have an accurate picture of yourself. Because this is so, you cannot accurately judge how to interact with others.

Since you have edited out or plagiarized part of your story, you do not feel whole or authentic. On the contrary, you feel desiccated and fraudulent. You feel fragmented. You feel like an impostor waiting to be found out.

In order to reclaim your story, you must accept authorship and ownership of all of your narrative. *Authorship is the source of authority. Only the author of your life story has control over the destiny and destination of your narrative.* You must go back to your Book of Life, and see when you started either editing or plagiarizing your life script. Your shadow consists of the parts of your story that have been left on the cutting-room floor. They are screaming to get your attention, so that you will re-include them in the story of your life.

Let me give a startling illustration of this principle. Every human being is a precisely unique balance of masculine and feminine. The precise calibration of these two qualities is unique in every human being. No two hermaphrodites are the same. To the precise extent that these qualities are imbalanced or not expressed, the essential truth of your Unique Self is violated. You are living a lie. The part of your unique identity that is not lived is in shadow. Any part of your masculine or feminine that is unlived, imbalanced, or distanced will create shadow. The lie of your shadow will ultimately express itself in your acting out in shadow qualities.

8. Shadow integration does not mean to integrate shadow qualities. Shadow integration does mean to reclaim your unlived life that is in darkness.

The popular teaching on shadow that I cited at the beginning of the previous chapter suggests that by integrating your shadow, you will gain the advantage of the shadow energy. But as I have already pointed out, it is more than unclear what this means. How do you integrate the energy of murder? Murderous energy explodes, and then dissipates. This is energy without depth or stability.

The energy of murder, at its core, stems from your own disconnection with the fullness of your Unique Self. Shadow integration means to reclaim your unlived life and thereby reclaim your life force. The energy you reclaim with shadow integration is the full force, power, and vitality of your Unique Self, directed not toward destruction but toward creativity, compassion, and Eros.

9. Joy is your life energy. Joy is a by-product of Unique Self living.

Joy, as we have seen, is realized as the natural by-product of the passionate pursuit of something other than happiness.

What is that other thing that you pursue passionately that is not joy, that is a by-product of its pursuit? Of course, you must pursue virtue, goodness, integrity, depth, values—all necessary, but insufficient to give you joy. It's not just virtue, goodness, integrity, and depth that you need to pursue; you must pursue *your* virtue, goodness, integrity, and depth—that is to say, your story.

Joy is a by-product of living *your* story.

The Chinese taught us that joy is chi, joy is energy. In Hebrew mysticism, joy is called *chiyut,* which means "vital energy," or "life force." So both the Chinese tradition and the Hebrew mystical tradition use virtually the same root word to allude to joy.

Once you understand all of this clearly, the imperative to integrate shadow makes sense once again. When you reclaim your unlived life and weave it back into the fabric of your sacred autobiography, you bring joy—energy—back into your life. Your Unique Self is the portal to your joy. You move from being depleted to being energized. Where you once were listless, you are now full of vigor. Valium gives way to vitality.

When all the principles we have enumerated until this point are brought together, you realize that there are five progressive steps of life destruction that are the direct result of the Unique Self distortion, which creates Unique Shadow. Each one of these steps drains your life energy in its own particular way. Their successive and cumulative impact on your life is nothing less than devastating. The healing comes directly from the evolution of your identity to your original and unique wholeness. Wholeness is the integration of your unlived life, your True Self and Unique Self, which are acting out as shadow.

1. Your story is your light. Your unlived life-light is shadow. If you take part of your story, part of the Unique Self that you are here to live, which creates your joy, and you put it in shadow, what have you done? You have taken a huge part of your *chiyut* energy and put it in darkness. You have lost the core of your life energy, which remains trapped in your unlived life. This is the essence of the matter. The natural joy-energy of your life, which is a by-product of living your Unique Self, is not available when your core story is in shadow. Your energy and joy are a by-product of the lived fullness of your unique life. You are fully alive and aflame only in *your* story and *your* life.

2. Without this core energy, you feel empty. You are left depleted, exhausted, and horribly depressed. Depression further drains your energy.

3. That unlived life that you placed into darkness then devolves and becomes shadow qualities. It devolves into unbridled rage, damaging lust, malice, jealousy, embezzlement, and violence. This further drains your life force.

4. You lose your core alignment with the ecstatic evolutionary impulse of the kosmos that moves toward higher and higher levels of complexity, consciousness, and love. This further drains you of your joy, and hence of your energy and your life force.

5. When your story is in shadow, you must expend enormous energy to maintain the lie about it. To maintain a constant and unnatural lie demands an enormous reserve of energy. This is a further source of your energy loss.

10. The technology for shadow integration is love. Shadow integration effects a transformation of identity. Love is the evolutionary force that transmutes shadow to light.

The inner magic and mechanism of love makes it the ultimate technology of Unique Shadow transformation. The nature of that magic and mechanism is an essential understanding necessary for your Unique Self enlightenment.

In order to integrate your shadow, your unlived life acting out and demanding attention, a transformation of your identity must occur. The key Aramaic phrase used by the Unique Self masters to describe the nature of this transformative path is *be'chavivut talya milta,* "It depends on love." Why and how love is the primary technology of shadow transformation is the topic of the next chapter. But first, a story that will close this chapter and introduce the next one.

Heart of Darkness

When the holy Israel Baal Shem Tov was five years old, his father became very sick. All the cures did not work, and he approached the hour of his death. He asked for his son Israel to be brought to him.

To Israel he spoke these parting words of instruction and love: "My son, remember that the dark side will always be with you. But know also that your essence is whole and pure. The dark side cannot violate your wholeness. You are part of God. Fear no man. Do not fear the dark side, for God is always with you, in you, and beyond you." With those words Eliezer, father of Israel, died.

Israel's mother had died soon after his birth, so he became an orphan. The people of the village raised him. Although he loved and lived the sacred texts of Kabbalah, he spent little time in the classroom. In fact, no one ever saw him poring over a text. Instead, they saw him wandering the fields and forests of the Carpathian Mountains. Israel spent most of his time outdoors, often lost in wonder, rapture, and radical amazement. He followed the ants, slept in the moss, and learned the language of birds. He listened. He heard the whispers of the winds, felt the flow of water, and swooned at the rapturous beauty of the forest. He communed in love with every creature. The ants and beetles were his friends, the small and larger animals his dearest companions.

When Israel was ten, he was retained as an apprentice to the headmaster and only teacher in the small school in Horodenka. He gathered the children from their homes and took them to school in the morning, and returned them to their parents in the afternoon. The children loved him, as did the parents, for their children would always return home radiant.

It was only the children and Israel, however, who knew the true source of their radiance. Israel took them to school in a very unexpected way. Instead of walking down the dirt roads and making the necessary turns, Israel took them across the fields and through the thick forests surrounding Horodenka. They sang with the squirrels and called out to the birds.

They sang songs of heart and joy to God, songs that Israel had composed and taught them. The chants as well as Israel's pure intention opened their hearts and carried them to depths of ecstasy that cannot be described to one who has not experienced such joy.

Indeed, their songs were so filled with innocent love that they broke through boundaries that separate the realms of heaven from our earthly world. The songs attracted the attention of the angels, who began to sing with the children. Soon all the celestial palaces were filled with the pure songs of Israel and the children. Elijah, whose job it is to herald the coming of the messiah, was awakened by the song. Rumors swept through the heavens that the messianic era might soon be at hand.

Satan, lord of the dark side, was incensed by this unexpected turn of events. Satan demanded of God, as he had done in the days of Job, "Let me challenge this boy Israel!" God, for reasons we cannot know, agreed.

So Satan, who must always operate through agents, descended to Earth to search for some representative of the dark side who could do his work. Satan called all the insects, searching for one who would poison Israel. But all the insects were Israel's friends, and so none consented. Satan searched among all the animals large and small for one who would be willing to attack and dismember the boy in front of the children he led. He was sure that such a sight would put an end to their singing. But all the animals refused, for they too were Israel's beloved companions. Satan was unable to find a single living being who would consent to harming the boy.

Finally, Satan was able to locate an agent. He was a very old man who worked as a charcoal burner. In truth, he was not really an old man, although this is how he appeared. He was of that very rare kind who was born without a soul. His body functioned normally, but he was disconnected from all emotion and from any sense of right and wrong. He could not bear the company of human beings. When his mother bore him, she abandoned him in the woods, for he frightened her. She somehow knew that he was more animal than human, and would be better raised by the creatures of the forest. He was nursed by a she-bear. He survived by eating insects. But he had a human intelligence of sorts, and so in the fullness of time he learned to make fire and charcoal. People who needed charcoal would leave him food and drink, and he would make them charcoal. He never spoke to a human being, and when he was occasionally sighted, it sent tremors through the one who beheld him.

Even before this set of events with Israel and the children, Satan had set his eyes on the charcoal burner. He sent a demonic power to enter his body. On nights where the full moon was high in the sky, the charcoal burner would grow fur, and then, possessed by a demonic power living through him, he would stand on all fours spitting fire and screeching at the moon. People spoke of a strange monster prowling the woods, but they were always too filled with fear to truly investigate the truth.

After being refused by all living creatures, Satan turned to find the charcoal burner, knowing that his will was too weak to resist Satan's demand. Satan came upon the charcoal burner as he slept. He reached into his body and removed his heart. Satan then ripped out a piece of his own heart, the heart of darkness, and placed this blackest of all hearts within the empty chest cavity of the charcoal burner.

The very next morning, Israel was leading the children, as he always did, through the forest. They were singing with their hearts open and pure, and their faces radiant. The angels sang with them, as they had grown accustomed to doing.

As the children entered a meadow in a section between two expanses of forest, they heard a ghastly sound behind them. A huge, dark, and shadowy creature stepped out from the forest that they had just left. It was ugly beyond words, snarling and spitting flames and phlegm. Its eyes were an insane shade of red, and its nose billowed dark and menacing spits of fire and smoke. Standing on its hind feet, it must have been twenty feet tall, and its strange and ugly arms reeked of violence and rage, but most horrific of all was the sound it made. A sound so ugly and vile that all the children fainted dead away, or ran for dear life.

Israel was the only one to stand his ground face-to-face with the monster. He did not budge. Eventually the monster returned to the woods, and quiet was restored. Israel gathered and revived his fallen children, but could not quite comfort them. They all ran home and cried to their parents of their fright and fear.

The parents were very angry at Israel for taking their children through the forest, but of course they did not quite believe the children's tale of fright. They were sure that the children had exaggerated greatly, and Israel did not contradict them.

Israel, however, knew that it was important to enter the forest once again. He spoke to each of the parents and each of the children. Somehow, the parents consented to let the children continue going to school with Israel. He gave the parents his absolute promise that they would be safe. The children's love of Israel and the way he was with them helped them overcome their fear.

The next morning, they entered the forest once more. This time, however, Israel gave them precise instructions: "When the monstrous beast appears again, and it surely will, do not be afraid. Just drop to the ground and cover your eyes, and I will do what needs to be done."

Sure enough, at the same place as the day before, the monstrous beast stepped violently toward them. He spit fire and hate, and was consumed by a rage so malicious and violent that the earth all around him shuddered. The children all dropped to the ground. The man-beast was standing on all fours, radiating a viciousness that cannot be described in words.

Israel walked forward toward the beast. He placed himself directly between the beast and the children. As Israel got closer, the beast seemed to rise larger and larger, until he was enveloped in a dark black cloud. Fear raced through Israel, but he centered himself in his father's dying words: "Do not fear the darkness, for God is always with you, in you, and beyond you."

With those words as a mantra repeating itself in his heart, Israel walked forward. He kept walking. The beast did not move. Closer and closer. The dark cloud wrapped Israel in its blackness, and he found himself on the inside of the beast. In the thickness of the shadow, he was able to make out the outline of its smooth black heart—the heart of darkness—blackly pulsing inside it. Israel reached out, took the heart in his hands, and stepped backward. He found himself outside the creature's body and outside the cloud holding the beating black heart.

Israel knew that this was the moment for which so many had waited throughout the ages. He held the heart of darkness in his hands. He had but to crush it, and with that to destroy the heart of evil forever. Redemption was at hand. The heart writhed and pulsated in his hands. It was slippery and repulsive.

But Israel noticed a trickle of blood rolling down one side of the heart. And he realized that mixed in the blood was a tear. The tear pierced his soul to the depths. Israel realized that the heart of darkness was in torment. Then a second tiny trickle of blood rolled down the side of the heart. Tears. He realized even more deeply that the heart of darkness was wracked with pain. He knew that deeper than the darkness was the pain. It was writhing in agony. It suffered the pain of alienation from Source. It too contained the spark of the divine and longed to return home. He allowed his compassion to be opened wider and wider as he held the beating heart of darkness in his hands.

As his heart expanded and expanded, he came to the point beyond choice. He released the heart and set it on the ground. The earth immediately swallowed it up.

The next day, the villagers found the body of the charcoal burner. They say there was a peaceful look on his tormented face. The children continued to sing, but not quite as they had before. For the heart of darkness had left fear behind. Israel realized that to shift the world toward redemption, he could not destroy the heart of darkness, but must rather learn to hold it in his hands. The heart of darkness must not be destroyed but transformed by the love of Shekhinah, the divine feminine, and that became the core of his great teaching. He knew that every human being has their own individualized heart of darkness. Israel gave this teaching:

Hold your heart of darkness as I did, in the palm of your hand. Let your divine feminine be aroused. Let your love rise up. Let your heart expand. You will then see the spark of divinity that is seeking to express itself through your heart of darkness. Take that spark and integrate it into your Big Heart, and the heart of darkness will melt into the light.

CHAPTER NINETEEN

SHADOW AND UNIQUE SELF RELOADED

The Alchemy of Love

"IT DEPENDS ON LOVE." In this old Aramaic phrase, "it" refers to shadow. This phrase will guide you on the path of shadow integration that the old Unique Self masters called the "left-handed emanation" or the "way of the dragon." The left hand implies the power of transmutation, while the right hand symbolizes the power of force. The left-handed path is referred to by the Tantric kabbalists as *Derek Hataninim,* which I have often translated as "the way of the dragon." The way of the dragon invites not the slaying of the dragon, but rather its befriending and healing.

To follow this way is to serve and to grow through the light and energy that emanates from the darkness itself.

With the understanding of the New Enlightenment, the energy that emanates from the darkness is not foreign to us. It is none other than the displaced fullness of your Unique Self and the dis-owned freedom of your True Self. It is the energy of the radical breaking of all boundaries. You have shattered the limits of your skin-encapsulated ego, and stepped into the fullness of your distinct expression of All-That-Is. You have realized your full identity with the divine, and all false boundaries crumble before the audacious power of your penetrating love. This is the ultimate expression of

Eros. The energy of darkness is but the pseudo-Eros of breaking boundaries in the world of illusion. *When you follow the attraction to the boundary-breaking pseudo-Eros to its root, it is revealed to be the yearning for the full enlightenment of Unique Self manifestation. The coiled boundaries of separate self melt before the radiance of Unique Self.*

This is the hidden intention of the old kabbalistic koan, "The contraction of darkness is only sweetened in its root." The word for contraction, *din,* refers to your shadow. The word "sweetness" refers to the tantric level of consciousness in Kabbalah, where light that comes from the darkness is of a higher quality than light that bypasses the darkness.

In the way of the dragon, the energy of shadow is transmuted through love.

One of the people who intuited this truth of shadow energy, even though he did not have a larger Unique Self context within which to integrate his understanding, was the philosopher Nietzsche. He writes in his maddening and wonderful work, *Thus Spake Zarathustra:*

> "Of all the evil I deem you capable: therefore I want the good from you. Verily, I have often laughed at weaklings who thought themselves good because they had no claws."

Nietzsche believed that the good could never gain the upper hand unless it is infused with "the energy generated by murder."

Rainer Maria Rilke captured the kabbalistic consciousness of the way of the dragon in à few short lines in his *Letters to a Young Poet:*

> "Perhaps all the dragons of our lives are princesses who are only waiting to see us act, just once, beautiful and brave. Perhaps everything terrible is, in its deepest essence, something that needs our love."

Shadow and the Eight Tenets of Love

The technology for shadow integration is love. Shadow causes a transformation of identity. Love is the evolutionary force that transmutes shadow to light.

This tenth principle of shadow has its own tenets. These eight tenets of love explain how love's mysterious technology transforms Unique Shadow into Unique Self. They are the elegant and essential posts on the road toward your Unique Self enlightenment. This is the way of the dragon.

The Way of the Dragon

1. Love is a perception.

As discussed in Chapter 15, love between people, at its core, is not an emotion. Love between people, at its core, is a perception. ***Love is a Unique Self perception.*** The emotion is a direct result of the perception. To be a lover is to have eyes to see. Love perceives the True Nature of things. To love another is to perceive their True Nature. Love is the joy and pleasure you receive from your perception of someone's Unique Self.

Deeper still, love is a realization of the infinite gorgeousness and beauty of other, which is their True Nature. Love of you is my realization of you. If love of other is the perception of the other's Unique Self, then self-love is the perception, the realization, of your own Unique Self. Self-love is your realization of the grandeur of you.[1]

2. Love allows for shadow to be held in the larger context of your enlightened Unique Self.

Because love is a Unique Self perception, sustained self-love gradually reveals the uniquely styled contours and texture of your Unique Self. Through love, we bring to consciousness the image of our own or someone else's Unique Self. By holding the steady image of the Unique Self, you begin to reveal its contours. This revelation of self produces the realization that your shadow at its root is but the distortion or unlived nature of your Unique Self. You begin to see that it is not a generalized or generic shadow. It is not an impersonal shadow. Rather, it is highly personal and intimate to you. When you love yourself, you are able to look at your shadow and place it in the larger context of your Unique Self. At that point, you can begin to follow the darkness to the light: your Unique Shadow back to your Unique Self.

3. Being loved is being seen.

When you are loved, you feel seen.[2] When you are not seen, when you are mis-recognized, you act out. *Acting out means to act out of the integrity of your Unique Self.* The experience of feeling seen creates a precisely opposite experience. Being seen naturally invites you to trance-end and transmute your shadow. This is because the experience of being seen softens the contraction of ego. It is for this reason that being seen creates the space for you to see your self and reclaim your Unique Self. Love creates self-love. Being perceived by an other in love creates the space for your self-perception. Self-perception reveals your Unique Self, which then illuminates your shadow as not more than Unique Self distortion.

4. In the safety of being seen and held in love, you can engage your shadow without the need to hide, deny, or project it.

A particularly powerful and transformative part of the experience of being seen is the creation of a holding container. When you are seen, you feel held. Because you are held, you are safe. In that safety, you can engage your shadow without the need to hide it, deny it, or project it.

5. It is the divine feminine, in self or other, that holds you in the gaze of love and catalyzes your transformation.

Being loved by another in a holding container is precisely the experience described in wondrous rapture in all the traditions—of being held by the divine mother, or mother energy. The divine feminine manifests in the steady, loving gaze of both men and women. It is the divine feminine in other or in ourselves that looks at you with the eyes of love.[3] It is that very gaze of love that allows you to see yourself. *In the gaze of the divine feminine is the mechanism for shadow integration. The power of the love of the divine feminine gives you an experience of your own gorgeousness, goodness, and grandeur. This is precisely what allows you to bear the experience of being displeasing to yourself because of your shadow qualities. This allows you to stay in the transformative fire of deep self-scrutiny.*

The experience of being held in love by the gaze of the divine feminine can be accessed in three primary ways. First, the gaze of another's love can hold you in the gaze of the divine feminine. Second, in meditation, your own Big Heart/divine feminine can consciously hold your small self in the gaze of the divine feminine. Third, the gaze of the divine feminine is the experience of being held by the personal God who knows your name. This is what we referred to earlier as "God in the second person." This is what Solomon alluded to in the Song of Songs when he wrote of the divine embrace, "Your left hand is under my head and your right hand embraces me."[4] This is the experience that you are resting in the divine embrace, held in timeless time and placeless place. This is the deep knowing that wherever you fall, you fall into the hands of God. It is precisely the knowing that you are thus held in love that affirms your goodness. Chant and prayer are the two major spiritual practices for this realization.

The experience of being held by the divine feminine in meditation is accessed through what I call the "holding heart" meditative practices.[5] If you are practiced in meditation, your heart will immediately recognize this pointing-out instruction. If you are not practiced, this instruction will open your heart and bring you home.

Holding Heart Meditation

There are two simple steps in the holding heart meditation.

In your meditation, you fall into what the great traditions called "expanded mind and expanded heart." You move beyond your small self and identify with the heart of the Uni-verse.

From that place, you hold your small self. Your small self feels totally held. It is an experience of deep trust and acceptance.

You larger self is your own divine feminine.

You have merged with the Shakti, the feminine goddess divine. She feels through you, is in you, and breathes as you.

You hold you. Your larger self holds your smaller self. You are held in the heart-palm of existence. You are safe, beloved, with your goodness radically affirmed. You are held by the gaze of your larger self holding your small self. With your goodness felt and affirmed, you are able to face into your shadow. It is only the felt sense of personal love that releases the contraction of the ego, and allows you to bear the pain of being displeasing to your self, to face everything, and to avoid nothing.[6] You own your shadow; listen to its whispering, and follow it back to your unlived life and light.

The key to the practice is to be so rooted in your absolute goodness as to be able to bear anything that arises in your meditation.[7] You have no relationship to the content that arises. At the time of its arising, there is nothing to do, say, or even feel. The practice is to hold an immovable center.

Do not identify with anything that arises. When you are not identified with your experience as it arises in your meditation, you are aligning with the deepest part of yourself, which is the free heart-ground of all being.

A person who knows and feels that they are held in the great heart of the kosmos may experience pain, fear, frustration, confusion, or anxiety, and not lose their ground.

In this way you learn how to directly experience the brokenness, chaos, and pain of your own mind without being destroyed by them. If you can bear everything that arises without closing your heart, only then will you be able to take responsibility for it. If you can't bear it, others will inevitably suffer the consequences.

Held firmly by the very heart of existence, you are able to see that your shadow is a reaction to unlived or distorted Uniqueness. This is a key step toward your Unique Self liberation.

Unique Self mystics called this path the way of the dragon.

In this way, you can no longer ignore your shadow by pretending it does not exist, or by trying to crush any seemingly dark impulse that violates the rules. *You must serve and grow by unblocking and reclaiming the light that you have pushed into the shadows.* You can only do this when you are held in love by the goddess. That is the inner meaning of the divine feminine.

The key Aramaic phrase used to describe the way of the dragon is *be'chavivut talya milta,* "It depends on love."

Love is to perceive Unique Self in the footsteps of the dragon. Love is, as we discussed earlier, a perception-identification complex. Love is to perceive the infinite and unique specialness in an other, and to identify them with that specialness. This is the realization of love. This is the way of the dragon.

The spiritual relationship to the dragon here is very different from the one that informed the founding myths of Western culture. The goal of this path is no longer to slay the dragon, but to make friends with the dragon. Making friends with the dragon is the way of love. It is the way of the divine feminine. This is called by the kabbalists the left-handed path. The right hand of God slays the dragon. The left hand of God holds space for the dragon to transform into a prince.[8] The holding container is created by the evolutionary power of love.

If you peruse folktales, you will notice something very interesting about dragons, monsters, and all such motley creatures. Dragons are usually vanquished and killed by male heroes. Female heroines, on the other hand, make friends with the dragon. This is the hidden teaching in the saga of the beauty and the beast.

The beauty lives with and loves the beast. She sees him and holds him. In that seeing and holding, the spell is broken, and he is transformed into a prince. The same dynamic is at play in the story of the princess who kisses the frog back into a prince. Here, the kiss is the perception that is love. In her kiss, she sees him. In his being seen, he is held. This gives him the courage to confront his frog or beast, and to evolve into the prince that he already is.

The difference between the masculine and feminine approach here is quite clear. Each is true but partial. In the first approach, the shadow energy needs to be destroyed. Since it is uncomfortable to talk about our own darkness, we project it onto a dragon, but everyone understands that we're really talking about ourselves. Slaying the dragon stands for the discipline and control that are often necessary virtues. The princess, on the other hand, understands that there is another way to dispel the darkness, and that is by lighting a candle. A little bit of light dispels a lot of darkness. The candle is a kiss, an act of loving and holding. The beast is not slain, but turned into a prince. The darkness is transformed into light.

6. Without the loving gaze of the divine feminine, the pain of your shadow would be impossible to hold in your first person.

The holding embrace of the divine feminine frees the fear in you.

Without this freeing of fear, your internal mechanism for avoiding pain automatically and invisibly prompts you to displace your genuine experience into shadow. Whatever is too painful to hold about yourself in your first person, you place in shadow. Since you do not want to see yourself in a way that is displeasing to yourself, you place your true feelings, reactions, or beliefs in shadow. Your authenticity disappears. The divine feminine inhibits this reaction by opening the contraction of your heart. This is accomplished through your being seen and recognized by the penetrating and holding power of radical love. This love sees and holds your beauty and goodness, beyond and beneath the superficial reactions of your shadow self.

If you could not bear to be displeasing to yourself, you would project your shadow outward. You would project your shadow outward onto another person or group of people. The love of the divine feminine inhibits your automatic mechanism of reacting to shadow material by projecting it outward. By holding your shadow material in the light, it loses its potency and power. Much of the shadow naturally dissipates, and the rest can be consciously healed and transmuted. Once you see your shadow clearly, you can begin to decode the Unique Self hints that it is holding. Shadow directly seen moves you to re-embrace your Unique Self.

The divine feminine appears in many guises. It is important for you to have at least some knowledge of her disguises so that you might recognize her the next time she appears. With that intention in mind and heart, allow me to share with you two true stories of the divine feminine.

The first is told, albeit with a different intent, by Milton Erickson, one of the great psychologists of the twentieth century.

The Gentleman

Joe, at the age of twelve, a farmer's son and only child, had been expelled from school because of brutality, beating up other children, vandalism, and incorrigible behavior. He had stabbed his father's hogs, calves, cows, and horses with pitchforks. And several times he had tried to set the barn and the house on fire.

At the age of twelve, his parents took him to court and had him committed to the Industrial School for Boys. At the age of fifteen, the Industrial School paroled him. On the way home, Joe committed some burglaries. He was picked up by the police, and promptly returned to the Industrial School, where he had to stay until he was twenty-one years old.

By that time his parents were dead, and they had disposed of their property without leaving Joe an inheritance. When he was discharged at age twenty-one, he was given a suit and $10, and he headed for Milwaukee. Shortly after, he was arrested for burglary and sent to the Young Men's Reformatory in Green Bay. He served every day of that sentence—in other words, no time off for good behavior. He was released from the reformatory, went into the town of Green Bay, and committed some more burglaries. The police picked him up, and he was sent to state prison. When he completed every day of that sentence, he was released. He went into a village and committed some more burglaries, and was arrested by another police officer and given a second term in the state prison.

Now, during Joe's time in the Industrial School and Young Men's Reformatory, he had been kept in solitary confinement most of the time from the age of twelve to twenty-one. Joe displayed such combativeness that he served most of his two years at the state prison in what was called the dungeon. The dungeon, eight feet by eight feet, was totally dark and soundproof. Once a day, usually at one or two a.m., a tray of food would be pushed quietly through a slot in the door. When they did take Joe out of the dungeon, they locked him in a solitary cell.

It was after years of such experiences that Joe finally returned to the village near Erickson's childhood home. Erickson was about ten years old at the time, and this is how he continues the story:

> That day I arrived in the village, it was his fourth day in town. Each of the three previous days he had spent standing beside the cash register estimating the day's take of the merchants at three different stores. And all of them knew that Joe had broken into their stores and stolen a lot of things. A man who

owned a motorboat had found his motorboat was missing. And the morning I arrived, Joe was sitting on a bench under the store awning staring into the distance.

Now it happened that there was a farmer about three miles from the village. A farmer who had three hundred acres of company land. He was a very rich man and had a beautiful daughter. To work three hundred acres requires a hired hand. His daughter Susie had graduated from high school; she was about five feet ten, and she could work alongside any man in the community. She could pitch hay, plow fields, help with the butchering . . . any task, she could handle. The entire community felt bad about Susie. She was a good-looking girl, she was famous for her housekeeping, her dressmaking, and her cooking, and she was an old maid at twenty-three years. And that should not be. Everybody thought Susie was too choosy.

On that particular day when I went to the village on an errand, Susie's father's hired hand had quit because of a death in the family, and said he would not be back. And Susie's father sent her into the village on an errand. Susie arrived, tied up the horse and buggy, came walking down the street. And Joe stood up and blocked her pathway. And Joe looked her up and down very thoroughly, quietly . . . and Susie with equal poise looked him up and down very thoroughly. Finally, Joe said, "Can I take you to the dance next Friday?" Now the village always had a weekly dance on Friday nights for all the young people. And Susie was very much in demand at those dances and she regularly drove in and attended the dance. And when Joe said, "Can I take you to the dance next Friday?" Susie fixed him in her gaze for one long minute and said coolly, "You can if you're a gentleman." Joe stepped out of her way. She performed her errand, and went back home.

And the next morning, the merchants were very glad to find boxes full of stolen goods at their front doors. And the motorboat had returned. And Joe was seen walking down the highway toward Susie's father's farm. Word soon got around that he had asked Susie's father for the job of hired hand, and he was hired. And made a magnificent wage of $15 per month. He was allowed to have his meals in the kitchen with the family. And Susie's father said, "We'll fix a room for you in the barn." In Wisconsin when the temperatures are down to 35 degrees below zero, you really need a well-insulated room in the barn. Joe turned out to be the best hired hand that the community had ever seen. Joe worked from sunup to long past sundown, seven days a week.

Joe was six foot three, a very able-bodied man and, of course, Joe always walked to the village on Friday nights to attend the dance. Susie drove in to attend the dance. And much to the ire of the other young men, Susie usually danced with Joe every dance. And Joe's size made them wary of pointing out to Joe the error of his ways by appropriating Susie. In just about a year, the community was buzzing with gossip because Susie and Joe were seen going out Saturday evenings for a drive, or "sparking," as the term was used. And there was even more gossip the next day—on Sunday—when Susie and Joe went to church. And after some months of this, Susie and Joe were married. And Joe moved from the barn into the house. He was still the best hired man imaginable, and Joe and his father-in-law, with some aid from Susie, ran the farm. And Joe was such a good worker that when a neighbor got sick, Joe was the first one to show up to help with the chores. And they soon forgot all about Joe's history of being an ex-convict.[9]

Not only that, but Joe's reputation blossomed. He was elected the president of the school board repeatedly. He was *the* advocate for education in the community, and an especially strong voice urging students, Erickson included, to continue their education beyond the normal rural grade school. He made a point of going to the state reformatory to hire ex-convicts to work on his farm, and over the years rehabilitated quite a number of them. And this is in unbelievable contrast to his past—a past that painted the picture of someone beyond the reach of society.

Erickson concludes, "All the psychotherapy Joe received was: 'You can if you're a gentleman.' He didn't need psychoanalysis for several years . . . all he needed was a simple statement . . . 'You can if you're a gentleman.'"

There was no therapy. There was no process of complex intervention. It all happened in one moment. Susie fixed him in her gaze for one long minute and said coolly, "You can if you're a gentleman."

The steady gaze of love, to be seen and held by the divine feminine, is the subversive catalyst for your great transformation. Sometimes you will be Susie. Other times she will appear in your life. You must look for her and listen for her. When she speaks, drink her words into your heart, for they are the very heart of the kosmos itself.

If you did not recognize yourself in Joe, you may well see yourself in the exaggerated caricature of the drunkard who has been cast out of society. He is called back—in this second story—by the divine feminine holding him in love and opening space for the transforming of his shadow.

The Beadle's Wife

The Unique Self mystic Levi Isaac of Berdichev tells the story of the beadle's wife in the town of Berdichev. Every morning in the days preceding the high holy days, the beadle, whose job it was to awaken the community to prayer, would walk the streets in the last darkness before dawn. He would knock on the door of each house and cry out, "Arise, awaken for the service of your creator. Arise, awaken for the service of your creator." Upon hearing his clear and strong voice, people would struggle out from under the cover of deep sleep and find their way to the synagogue for the morning prayers of forgiveness and transformation.

One year, the beadle took sick in the week before the high holy days, and died very suddenly. There was no time to recruit a new beadle. Yet people needed to be awakened for prayer. The widow of the beadle volunteered to take upon herself the job of her deceased husband. While this was somewhat unusual, there were no other candidates, and so her suggestion was accepted.

The very next morning, everyone was shocked to see the town's ne'er-do-well, known to all as a drunkard and vagabond, sitting in synagogue, intently serious, adorned in his ritual garments, ready and even eager for morning prayers. After prayers were completed, Levi Isaac commanded that the ne'er-do-well be brought to him for questioning. "What caused you to come to prayer this morning after so many years of backsliding?" he asked.

The ne'er-do-well, who was by now on the path to transformation, responded with tears pouring down his cheeks: "Every year before the high holy days, I would hear the beadle making the rounds knocking at people's doors. I would hear his call: 'Arise, awaken for the service of your creator.' But he never knocked at my door. I was so far from the community that I am sure he assumed that I would never come.

"It was for this reason that this very morning I was shocked to hear a very deliberate knock on my door. I awoke, frozen with fear. And then I heard the most beautiful voice, a woman's voice, singing directly into my heart, 'Arise, awaken to the service of your creator.' I did not recognize the voice, but I remembered that my grandfather used to sing Sabbath songs to the Shekhinah, which he explained to me was the feminine goddess divine. I knew when I heard this voice that it must be the Shekhinah. I realized that if she knocked on my door, she must love me. She must see me for who I really am. And in that instant I saw myself as well. Not through the eyes of the community, but through her eyes. So how could I not come?"

The princess is to the frog, as the beauty is to the beast, as Susie, the wife of the beadle, is to the drunkard.

In biblical myth, the snake in the Garden of Eden plays the beast/dragon role. A mystical riddle: What did Adam say to the snake in the Garden? The answer: Absolutely nothing. Adam never speaks to the snake. Men kill snakes. Boys who are still innocent talk to snakes.[10] But men do not engage them in conversation. The only conversation—in fact, the first recorded biblical conversation—is between Eve and the snake. This is the first dialogue with the dragon. For more than two millennia, the snake was understood to be the villain. And Eve the associate villain for engaging him in conversation. The Bible is after all a document inspired primarily by the masculine face of the divine. The kabbalists, however, reread the story.

Isaac the Blind, a mystic writing in the thirteenth century, goes so far as to point out that in Hebrew numerology,[11] the numerical value of "snake" and "messiah" are identical. This is not a mere numbers game. What Isaac the Blind is suggesting is that the messiah comes through the transformation of snake energy into redemptive messiah energy. Shadow transformed

275

to divinity. It is Eve's willingness to hold the snake in love that, according to Isaac the Blind, creates the matrix from which transformation can occur.

Eight hundred years later, Unique Self mystic Abraham Kook writes, "*Ani* [which means "I," or in our terms, Unique Self] is the messiah in each one of us." Only if Eve talks to the snake can you find your way from shadow to Unique Self. In Kabbalah, therefore, the snake energy is first received and held by the feminine, and then ultimately transmuted into a higher form.

To Not Grow Up

Finally, let's look at one of the great archetypal stories produced by modern Western consciousness.

A nursery's open window. A girl in a blue nightgown. A fairy. A boy in search of something he's lost. These are the familiar ingredients of the delightful child's tale *Peter Pan*. But *Peter Pan* is more than delightful, and speaks to more than just children. Much of *Peter Pan's* power of enchantment comes from the ingredient of darkness, which is thrown into its mix of adventure and sing-along. It is a story of the young masculine, a story of the Greek god Pan, who incarnates as the wild Dionysian shadow.

The story opens with Peter Pan darting around Wendy's room in search of his shadow. Peter, in search of his depths, finds Wendy, the one who has the loving thread to sew his dark side back on. Wendy is the divine feminine to Pan, the one with the ability to kiss the beast into a beauty! While Peter's natural masculine dissociates from his shadow, Wendy is able to sew it back on—a process of integration—stitch by stitch.

It is the ultimate Unique Self receiving story—Wendy loves Peter. Through her love, she is able to see and hold Peter for who he is, his lights as well as his darks. It is the stability of that gaze of the divine feminine that invites Peter to integrate his shadow side—to become fully himself. This is what it might have meant for Peter to grow up. For Peter to grow up, he needs to grow down into his Unique Self.

The image of growing down is one of the central images of the Kabbalah. It is graphically expressed in the picture of the Tree of Life, the tree of the ten Sefirot. The word *sefira* derives from the biblical myth words we have seen before—*sippur,* meaning "story," and *mispar,* meaning "number," and *sapir,* meaning "light."

These words taken together constitute Unique Self. As we have pointed out, *mispar* represents your unique calling, and *sippur* represents the unique narrative of your life. Taken together, the ten Sefirot are a symbolic map of all the dimensions necessary to form what the mystics call *komat ha'adam*— literally translated as "the full stature of Man"—what we refer to as Unique Self. What is most interesting and ironic about this tree of the full stature of man is that it stands upside down. Its roots are grounded on high, while its fruits ripen in this earthly realm. It grows down instead of up!

For the kabbalist, the image conveys the essential idea that your Unique Self is formed from top down, not from bottom up. You are born with a Unique Self. This is the DNA of your spirit. Your life is the process of revealing and then bringing your Unique Self to fruition. This is most definitely not Freud's vision of the human personality, which is formed in the crucible of infancy and early childhood, building up into our lives.

Of course, there is some truth in Freud's picture. Clearly, early childhood has an impact to some real degree on our lives. But it does not determine your Unique Self. You are born with a full-blown seed of Unique Self, and then work your way down. As you evolve, you reveal more and more of its design. ***Your Unique Self is the higher Unique Perspective of your soul, which you're born to unfold.*** Growing up is all about growing down into your Unique Self.

This happens only when you are willing to embrace and integrate your shadow. This is what Peter Pan never wants to do. In the words of Peter's anti-growing-up song, you never want to wear a serious expression in the middle of July. You don't want to "get serious" about your dark side, which sometimes requires gravitas, even in the middle of a bright July day. It is easier to think of yourself as a fully pure, always right, noble being of light. However, insist the kabbalists, the light that comes from the darkness is more powerful than the light that comes from the light. If only Peter would own the Captain Hook inside himself, he could stop projecting him as an outside figure.

7. Shadow and shadow qualities are both personal.

Shadow in much of popular writing is understood as your impersonal lusts, desires, and primal drives breaking in on your civilized and orderly life.

There is some limited measure of truth in this portrayal. But the core of your shadow is personal. You have a very personal shadow, which is your Unique Self distortion. Unique Self distortion creates Unique Shadow. You have a Unique Shadow. Your shadow has the same quality of uniqueness as your fully expressed self, because it is of the same unique material. Your shadow qualities are also personal. You don't have anger; you have anger at unique moments in particular situations. Your anger expresses itself in a particular way. You don't have lust; you have lust in particular moments at particular times, often to cover over unique provocations, which arouse your feelings of hurt, envy, or emptiness. It is in the particulars of the provocation that the hints lie. You need to check the specific character of your emptiness. What is the texture and context of the emptiness that provokes not the fullness of your arousal, but rather a hollow lust that seeks to cover up the hurt you felt in that particular moment? In the particularity of the provocation lies the prize.

8. Love gives you hints that show you how to follow Unique Shadow back to Unique Self.

Shadow maintains the print of your Unique Self, meaning you can follow your shadow back to the light. Your shadow, the unique nature of your acting out, actually contains within it the glimmerings, the hints, the bread crumbs, that lead you on the yellow-brick road back home to your fullest self.

> Sasha finally decided to turn the tangle of his backyard into a flower garden. He cleared the land, bought the seeds, and diligently set about the task. And sure enough, come spring, the land sprouted an exquisite array of flowers. But mingled within the arrangement were the same old dandelions. "Weeds," he grumbled, passionately pulling out each one. No matter how many he pulled, another seemed to pop up in its place. He tried everything, consulted every book, but to no avail.
>
> Finally, he consulted the elderly gardener who lived down the street, a wise old woman with a rose garden you wouldn't believe. She slowly walked with him to see his garden, listening to his lament along the way. When they arrived at his gate, she took one look at the yard and said decisively, "I'll tell you

exactly what you need to do . . . " Sasha nodded eagerly, cupping his ear to capture the precious advice. The old woman looked straight into Sasha's eyes and said, "You need to learn to love your dandelions."

The dandelions are not generic. They are your dandelions. They come bearing gifts, Unique Self hints that, if you but pay attention to them, may well lead you back to your light.

One clear example of this mechanism at work is jealousy. Once your jealousy moves from shadow to light, you can discern what lack in your life might be causing the arousal of your envy. You can identify what is missing in the story of your Unique Self. You can then move to reclaim your unlived Unique Self, which naturally causes the healing and transmutation of your envy's poison.

On Envy's Poison

> *It is burdensome to envy. The terrible heartburn of envy. Envy catches you by the throat and squeezes your eyes from their sockets.*
>
> —FROM THE NOVEL *ENVY,*
> BY RUSSIAN WRITER YURI OLESHA

Envy is the classic shadow quality. Our usual response is to deny it or hide it. Now, when I refer to jealousy, I am clearly not talking about the passing kind of jealousy I feel when I see the neighbor's new car. Fleeting thoughts or even feelings of jealousy occur to everyone and are generally harmless. I refer rather to the envy that gnaws at your core, causes you to lose sleep, and sends sharp streaks of emotional pain through your system. This kind of jealousy is the classical expression of Unique Shadow that results from Unique Self distortion.

To understand how this works, first you need to understand the inner linchpins of envy.

When you are living your story, you will rarely be moved to jealousy. So if you find jealousy to be a significant factor in your life, then it is probably because you are—to some significant degree—in the wrong story (or not doing so well at living your own).

Success—especially if enjoyed by someone you know well—is often not enough to arouse jealousy. For example, if I have a friend who is a successful lawyer but calls me every night to tell me how he despises law, his success will probably not arouse my envy. Envy is usually aroused in us when we meet someone who exudes that sense that they are living their story. Seeds of jealousy are present whenever the apparently vital, successful existence of another person in their story evokes your visceral reaction and inhibits your spontaneous love. Paraphrasing the old Hasidic Unique Self masters, I would say it like this: "If I who am not I, meets *you* who are *you,* then I will probably not like you, because you remind me that I am not I."

Jealousy is aroused by your meeting another person who seems to be living their story. This is so simply because you are reminded by them that you are not living your story.

This kind of jealousy will have one of two effects on you if you do not transmute it. It will cause every success of the other person to eat away at you, or else it will move you to want to hijack, destroy, or control their story.

Jealousy, then, is a function of the meeting between someone who is living their story and someone who is not. Of course, one more key factor is necessary to arouse jealousy. A writer is not likely to be jealous of a ballerina. The person who evokes your jealousy will be living a story with some significant similarity to yours. It is for this reason that their realized Unique Self puts your own lack of realization into such bold relief that painful envy is aroused. What this means is that the specific person who makes you jealous is someone living a life that at least approximates a piece of your unlived story. In this sense, the Unique Shadow of jealousy becomes an indispensable path back to your Unique Self.

Personally, many years back, jealousy helped me make one of the significant decisions of my life. Almost two decades ago, I took off three years from teaching to work with a close friend who was buying and restructuring hi-tech companies in Israel. I had just finished—for the second time—a marriage that didn't work. The decision to go into business was mine, and it came from deep feelings of emptiness and loneliness. Although I loved teaching, I felt like I needed to spend several years in quiet contemplation trying to understand all the things I had run away from. For me, the best way to take a vacation was to work hard at something that was not really close to my heart. So for several years, hi-tech became my world, but a world I could leave at the end of the workday.

At the end of three years of working with my friend, a number of commercial routes opened up that were potentially highly lucrative. In the end, I turned them all down and went back to teaching. It involved a substantial cut in my pay and standard of living, but I was happy to do it. It was absolutely clear to me that I had made the right choice. My guide in making the choice was jealousy. Here is what happened.

I used to jog back from my office on the western edge of Jerusalem to my home on the eastern edge of the city several times a week. It was an intense run encompassing Jerusalem's hills and sunsets, and I loved it. At some point I found myself jogging a different route on Wednesdays than I did the rest of the week. It dawned on me that if I ran my regular path, I would pass by an auditorium where people were streaming in to hear a popular clergyman, whom I did not particularly like, give the largest public lecture in the city. At the same time that I realized this coincidence, I also realized that I had no particular reason not to like this man.

I reviewed the past several months, and realized that in private conversations with two close friends I had made critical remarks about him of an unusually sharp nature. All of a sudden, it became crystal clear, and I burst out laughing. I was jealous of him. I wanted to be giving those lectures. He was living my life. I realized as well that three of my friends, who had recently taken hi-tech companies public with significant financial rewards and acclaim, had not caused me to feel even a hint of jealousy. At that moment, all my wrestling with uncertainty was over. I knew I needed to turn down the lucrative hi-tech offers and return to public teaching. Jealousy reminded me of my story and my Unique Self.

Jealousy always emerges from your unlived life. Once you have projected your shadow onto other, you are already at odds with other. You cannot see them clearly. This begins the mutual rituals of rejection and the cycles of unlove.

The unwavering loving gaze of the divine feminine inhibits this natural cycle. Being held in the love of the divine feminine allows you to clearly see your own shadow instead of projecting it outward. *The love of the divine feminine arouses self-love.* Self-love allows you to hold all of yourself. Nothing then needs to be placed in shadow, and nothing needs to be projected outward.

Transformation of Identity

Unique Self mystics in the old Aramaic texts spoke of two paths, *itcafya* and *ithapcha*. They called them the lower and higher paths. *Itcafya* means "to bend," as in to bend to the rules and to return to the "right way." Swallow the pill and exercise your will. Yield to or align with your highest values. This is an important and necessary path. The higher path, however, is called *ithapcha*, which means "to transform." In the language of the mystics, it means to transform "the bitter to the sweet." The bitter is not erased or diluted, however. The bitter becomes the pointing-out instruction for the sweet.

Ithapcha is the way of the dragon. It is far more that just making peace with your "dark side." It is the transformation of identity, which is an act of memory. You remember that you have forgotten. You have forgotten that you are Source.

In the language of one Unique Self mystic, the master Abraham Kook:

> *The primary transformation*
> *Which reveals the light in the darkness*
> *Is that a person returns to himself*
> *To the root of his soul*
> *And that in itself*
> *Is to return to God*
> *Who is the soul of all souls.*[12]

The Only Possible Path

Authentic personal evolution is a genuine option for every person. The reason relatively few people make the journey is simple. Inner development is largely a process of confronting head-on unpleasant truths about yourself. Since you seek pleasure, you generally seek to avoid that which brings pain.

However, the deeper truth is that pain is not pleasure's opposite. The opposite of pain is comfort. To achieve pleasure you must be willing to bear the discomfort of being displeasing to yourself, of feeling worthless, inadequate, depressed. It is only by sitting in the pain that you can find the pleasure. It is only by staying in the emptiness long enough that you will feel it fill up with particular expressions of your Unique Self. The core of the hole is the inability of your personality to fill your yearning for the expression of your essential Unique Self. The paradox of the hole is that if you are willing to tolerate the unpleasant feeling of your emptiness, the hole will eventually fill up with precisely the unique quality needed to fill your unique lack.

Your fear of recognizing your shadow is that it will reveal that all those years were somehow wasted. For example, if you own that your hidden rage is actually a shadow quality, you then have to face the truth that all the decisions you made based on your anger might have been wrong. Your hidden rage at your mother may have caused you to marry the wrong woman. Your hidden rage at your father may have caused you to rebel in places you might have been better off toeing the line. It is easier not to recognize the shadow quality of your rage, because then you do not need to face the terror of the years wasted, based on what now seem to be wrong turns in the road. Dramatic and destructive detours on the road to what seemingly should have been your destination are excruciatingly painful to own.

The deeper truth, however, is when you realize that the detours on the way to your destination were really not choices at all. The only path you could have possibly walked is the path of your pathos. Every detour was part of your destination. Every place you have been, you needed to be.

PART FIVE

If I am I because I am I, and You are You because You are You, then I am I and You are You. But if I am I because You are You and You are You because I am I, then I am not I and you are not You.

—HASIDIC MASTER

CHAPTER TWENTY

SEX AND UNIQUE SELF

I WANT TO OFFER YOU A NEW ENLIGHTENMENT, Unique Self map of the sexual that cuts through much of the confusion about sexing. You will see that an understanding of what we will term "Unique Self sexing" can radically evolve your relationship to the sexual in your life, even as it profoundly deepens your experiences of Unique Self.

I want to talk about sexing as it directly relates to the four stages of your evolutionary development and awakening: (1) pre-personal, (2) separate self or personality, (3) True Self impersonal, and (4) Unique Self personal.

What I want to draw, with a deep bow to your highest man and woman, is a map of six different core modes of sexing, which fall into these four general forms. The six types of sexing are vital sexing, separate-self or personality sexing, pleasure sexing, True Self sexing, Unique Self sexing, and *tikkun* or *bodhisattva* sexing. While each of these are distinct forms of sexing, two of them are qualities of sexing that can appear at all four stages of consciousness: vital sexing and pleasure sexing can appear in pre-personal, separate-self, True Self, or Unique Self sexing. All of this will become completely clear as we outline these different modes.

This map of the sexual will move beyond the old dichotomies of fallen and sacred, and allow you to feel into the different modes of sexing, all of which, when engaged appropriately, deserve an honored place in your being. These different modes of sexing might well reflect qualities in your own sexual relationships over the years. You might engage in different modes of sexing with different partners or with your monogamous partner, at different times of the day, week, or month.

1. Vital Sexing

The first mode I call vital sexing. This mode of sexing is at its core pre-personal.

This quality of sexing is radically raw and primal, wild, gorgeous, and vital. Your desire is to penetrate and be taken. You want to thrust forward and be ravished. You want to hold and be held. You are clutched in your very depths by the urge to merge. This moment in sexing might be hard and fraught with vital passion, as in the Nine Inch Nails song lyrics, "I want to fuck you like an animal." Or this vital moment might have more to do with the radical desire to be held and stroked, as in Leonard Cohen's "Dance Me to the End of Love."

It should be honored and fulfilled—always in the right context. At best, I believe, the right context is a sacred, committed relationship, where you have full permission to bring all of yourself to the table, and to bed. You may want to sex in this way with your romantic love or life partner. Or you may want to engage this way with people who are not your life or even love partner. The particular partners in this form of sexing may be but are not necessarily the central concern. A sacred, committed relationship does not necessarily mean one with your romantic partner. At a bare minimum, you require a context that will not create hurt, damaging complexity, or reams of unintended dramatic consequences that the Hindus call karma. Without attention and care, sex—more than almost anything else we do—creates karma. So context matters. Be care-ful.

Vital sexing may be a core element in your personality sexing with your marriage partner of forty years. It is, however, also a potential quality of enlightened sexing at all levels of consciousness, including True Self, Unique Self, and *tikkun* sexing.

2. Separate-Self Sexing

The second major mode of sexing we will call separate-self sexing. It might also be referred to as ego or personality sexing. Separate-self sexing is born of anxiety. Its goal is to soothe through arousal.

Separate-self sexing is virtually always aroused by some version of the following dynamic: Your separate-self ego is tossed to and fro in a painful, competitive world. Something in the present triggers an old feeling of hurt or wound. You then respond to the present through the prism of the past. This prism deflates or deadens the moment's natural aliveness.

In the deflated deadness of the moment, when you simply feel bad, you consciously or unconsciously seek comfort. This is what I call the comfort cover-up. Comfort is very different from pleasure. Comfort seeks to a-void the pain of authentic living. ***Pleasure engages and transmutes pain. Comfort rises to dull the incessant, deadening throb of your emptiness.*** Pleasure celebrates the pulsating aliveness of your fullness.

You open the refrigerator. You make a sexual move. You pick up the phone to gossip about someone. You are not genuinely seeking either food, sex, or information. Rather, you want to paper over the emptiness that rises in you, which you cannot clearly identify, but which deflates or deadens you to your own natural and full aliveness. Sexing that is aroused by this dynamic is separate-self or personality sexing. Personality sexing, fooding, and gossiping are all evoked by the same dynamic.

Personality sexing is unconscious and uncurious. It is unconscious because you think you are acting when in fact you are but mindlessly reacting. It is uncurious, because you have no genuine curiosity about your partner, the food, or even the topic about which you are gossiping. It brings comfort but not pleasure.

John has an unsuccessful conversation with his boss related to his advancement in the company. This is confused in John's experience with very old experiences of his father's rejection. John confuses the present moment of his boss with the past moment of his father. As a result, John hangs up the phone and unconsciously begins to cruise porn sites, feeling a need to masturbate and ejaculate. John loses the fullness of presence that holds the Eros of the moment. Instead, he seeks to replace it with the pseudo-Eros of unconscious or addictive pornography.

Separate-self sexing is the opposite of enlightenment, which is based on moment-to-moment awareness. It often leaves a bad aftertaste. It emerges not from yearning but from craving. It might be a craving for control, for relaxation, or for mommy or daddy. Or it might be a craving to be shamed or degraded, or to get off or be turned on in order to avoid the pain of your life. Many agendas drive separate-self sexing. Whatever the nature of the craving that is being sated, it needs to be said that separate-self sexing is not true Eros. Personality sexing seeks to soothe emotional trauma born of injury. Its method of soothing just happens to be arousal. It is pseudo-Eros. It emerges not from your freedom or fullness, but from your desperate if unconscious attempt to cover up your emptiness and dependency.

In separate-self sexing, you can be fully penetrated but never open up. You shut down even as you are thrusted into because you cannot bear to be hurt again. You may have been hurt or you may have inherited injury from your mother and father, or from the pathologies of your society and its collective shadows. You can be fully taken in but never held. Even as you penetrate, you refuse to enter, because you do not trust that you will be received. Personality sexing is not bad, sinful, or evil. It is simply ego and personality. It leaves the great invitation, wonder, and glorious potential of sexing unrealized.

Personality sexing is not intimate. Since it is triggered by the repetition of a past experience, there is no authentic contact in the present. Without contact, there can be no intimacy. The interior quality of personality sexing is somewhat like hearing your partner cry out, "Mommy, mommy!" when they have an orgasm. Or you think you are having sex with someone, and you realize you are really nursing them. You can do it four times a week and perform well each time, and still wonder why you feel empty, and still desperately crave intimacy. Personality sexing is not even particularly sexual. It is interchangeable with fooding, gossiping, and a host of other cover-up activities.

Before we go on, it is worth saying just so it is perfectly clear: personality sexing is not Unique Self personal sexing. Personality is level-one personal. Unique Self is level-two personal, which is realized after at least some dimension of True Self has been glimpsed or realized. Later in this chapter, I will describe Unique Self personal sexing, and the difference between *personal* and *personality* will be dramatic. Any number of teachers of classical impersonal enlightenment have confused the two. This confusion is less than helpful, because it rejects or regards as second-best all forms of sexing that are personal.

Separate-Self Sexing: A Deeper Look

Addiction is, at its root, the inability to stay in the emptiness. If you are not living your Unique Self, you are an addict. Most people are addicts. Addiction is not just limited to its more obvious forms of gambling, hard drugs, sex, or excessive alcohol. Goethe once defined addiction as anything you cannot stop doing. Gossiping—talking about other people, usually with a kind of casual negative or hurtful critique—is one of the easiest ways to fill the emptiness. It is a form of pseudo-Eros, a shortcut to fullness. You will find—if you pay careful attention—that a millisecond before you are moved to casual slander, you touched a moment of emptiness in yourself.

One of the beauties of a spiritual system that invites an occasional fast day is that you can't just jump to devour. Instead, you have to sit there in the hunger and emptiness. From there, you can observe the moments when you crave, seek out the source of the craving, and then discern if this is wholesome or unwholesome hunger.

Sex follows the same formula. Every human being meets at some point in their life two very different faces of sexing. The first is sacred sex, and the second is fallen sex. Sacred and fallen are not an external imposition of religious systems seeking to control you. Rather, you have some sense of sacred and fallen sex within your very own experience. What is the primary mechanism that allows you to discern between the two? Aftertaste. Sacred sex leaves you with a wonderful aftertaste. Fallen sex leaves you with a minor or major spiritual hangover.

Just as a fast day sensitizes you to the difference between wholesome and desperate eating, regular intervals of voluntary sexual fasting can be ever-so enlightening. Such fasts are critical in helping you to distinguish between fallen and sacred sex, between the authentic sexual Eros and pseudo-Eros. It is a brilliant spiritual practice for the clarification of desire and the purification of sex—according to your own inner value system. It is also the best practice available for rekindling desire and reclaiming passion in your relationship. For anything that is always available—such as married sex—soon becomes banal and boring. That is why 75 percent of married couples, according to surveys, live in sexless marriages.

Empty Wisdom

Wisdom comes only when you are willing to stay in the emptiness long enough to hold your center and walk through. Enlightenment is in the gap. When you try to fill it too quickly, you always wind up shocked and deeply unsettled when the emptiness does not go away. Instead, it gets deeper, thicker, more palpable, and virtually suffocates you. Eventually it kills many of us with heart disease, cancer, and the like. It is in the gap that the grasping of ego becomes apparent. *If you stay in the gap, the fullness of your True Self and Unique Self will begin to emerge.*

All of this is not to say that you should not engage in personality sexing. Not in the slightest. There is absolutely nothing wrong with personality sexing, just as there is nothing wrong with personality fooding, if you do it as a conscious choice. Indeed, there is quite a lot to be said for this particular comfort. Just engage mindfully. Do not confuse an action for a reaction. Pay attention. Be the rider, not the horse.

That is the whole difference.

3. Pleasure Sexing

The third mode of sexing is pleasure sexing.

Beyond the urge to merge of vital sexing, and the cover-up strategies of personality sexing, sex is pure pleasure.

First, I want to share the very fundamental teaching of worldly sensual pleasure as a path to God. If this were not the case, there would be no oranges. Or millions of other pleasures that are God's gifts strewn like rose petals all over the world.

Look at an orange. It is not merely to provide you with the vitamin C necessary to be healthy. All of it—the entire orange—is there to sensually delight you. Smell its fragrance, and feel how it delights you. Breathe it in. Run your hand over the texture of its outer rind. Feel how it awakens you. Look at the dancing color of orange and notice how it makes you feel alive. Relish the succulent juice of the orange swooshing for a moment over your palate. Savor the utterly unique and delightful taste of the orange. All of this has nothing to do with its vitamin C value, for which you are of course appreciative.

Conscious pleasure is a portal to eternity and a gateway to God. But it is even more than that. Pleasure is the experience of personal kosmic love that drenches you in every moment, made directly manifest in your world. Love at its core is the radical desire to give pleasure.

Pleasure is a verb. For two human beings to love each other through the radical desire to pleasure is a gorgeous incarnation of the divine force.

Pleasure reminds us that the world is more than friendly to you. The kosmos is designed for, and desires, your good and your pleasure. Pleasure at the most horrific moments returns us to the knowing that the kosmos is sane. In the old traditions, pleasure was a sacred obligation. Not giving direct sexual pleasure to your partner in the way they desire is, according to the Aramaic texts of the fourth-century Hebrew law, sufficient grounds for divorce. The Hindu *Kama Sutra* honors the sacred pleasures of sexing. To know that the evolutionary design of our bodies is for pleasure is to know the goodness of All-That-Is.

Pleasure sexing can express itself in three ways. Pleasure sexing can express itself together or apart from vital sexing. Pleasure sexing can show up at the level of personality, True Self, or Unique Self sexing.

First, pleasure sexing is one of many ways for the separate self to derive pleasure. Pleasuring the separate self is not sufficient to create a meaningful existence, but it is a necessary, valid, and sacred activity that honors life.

Second, pleasure sexing may be but a disguised form of personality sexing. You grab pleasure to cover up your emptiness, and not to bask in the fullness of the pleasure. So this is not really pleasure sexing, but personality sexing in disguise. This is neither good nor bad as long as you recognize it for what it is. Any time you are conscious of what is, you are in your enlightenment. If, however, you think sexing will transform your marriage through the power of communion and love, if it is personality sexing, you will be sorely disappointed.

The third mode of pleasure sexing is its optimal and desired form. In this form of pleasure sexing, it is through your pleasure itself that you experience your goodness and worth affirmed and held by God. You realize correctly that you must be extraordinarily worthy to merit such profound and extensive gifts of pleasure. You understand in your body the infinite value and worth of your own intrinsic being, just as it is right now. You feel personally held and addressed by the personal face of God. You let your consciousness take in and integrate the goodness and kind intention of the Uni-verse that seeks your pleasure.

On the core level of body, the pleasure opens and expands you beyond your small self to your True and Unique Self. Pleasure invites you to be taught, remodeled, and remolded by the three great virtues: surrender, passion, and devotion. Pleasure gently coerces you into radical surrender. Pleasure opens in your heart the channels of enlightened passion interwoven with the delights of wildly ecstatic devotion. Every form of pleasure demands its own particular form of surrender, passion, and devotion.

It is in this spirit that one third-century Talmudic wisdom text states that at the end of a person's life, they are judged on whether they fulfilled four obligations. The first three are obvious: honesty in business, work on behalf of social justice, and creativity. The fourth is more surprising, almost shocking: "Have you derived pleasure from my world?" Clearly, it does not mean to question if you have ever derived pleasure from the world. For every human being has been pleasured at some point in their life. Rather, the intention is, have you made experiencing pleasure a lodestone, a central goal and practice of your existence in this world?

4. True Self Sexing: Impersonal

In the past few decades, there has been a lot of talk in the Western world about sexual tantra. Tantra at its core is a beautiful and rigorous Hindu and Buddhist path that guides the initiate beyond the personal. In its sexual expression, it is a sacred-practice technology designed to expand you beyond the separate self to True Self. The exclusive identification with personality is trance-ended through the expansion achieved in sexing. In this sense, the core of Eastern tantra can be said to be impersonal, in the sense of "beyond the personality."

In impersonal tantra, you engage sexing as a path to classical enlightenment. The goal is to open up as love into divine communion. It is for this reason that in the advanced esoteric paths, you have sex with a yogi or yogini whom you do not know at all. You have no relationship to that person outside of the tantric ritual. This is the sexual path of True Self tantra. Your partner is not there to share or receive your Unique Self. Your partner is there to love-sex you open to God.

In No-Self tantra, the high priest or priestess who facilitates your communion is impersonal, just as enlightenment is impersonal. In impersonal tantra, intimate communion serves divine communion.

There are different paths in this practice. The following is an account of one of my own experiences with True Self tantra. While generally I am reticent to share personal experiences of an intimate nature, it is my hope that in this case it will be of service to the reader in getting a taste of what True Self tantra might be. This experience arose directly after, and I believe as a result of, a profound Unique Self tantric communion. I wrote the description a few seconds after it happened. This is what I wrote in my journal that day:

> I was lying with my partner. It was in the afternoon . . . or was it at the crack of dawn early in the morning? We are starting to rise to the world. Embraced, entwined. After having made love personally and passionately for what seemed like forever.
>
> And without warning a radical truth enters me.
>
> It speaks through my mouth as we touch.
>
> Impersonally . . .
>
> I say, I feel, I say
>
> to her
>
> "The whole world—
>
> all of existence—
>
> all of being—
>
> yearns to, lusts for, pines for orgasm . . . for the climax in which we know God . . .
>
> It is the inner throb of joy in all of the existence."
>
> . . . and the words were like an incantation—
>
> a gift of grace descended—
>
> we merged
>
> I was one with my words—
>
> she with her words
>
> that without any warning—opened all the gates.
>
> And I was inside all of the worlds, and all of the worlds were inside me . . . and my body began to convulse . . . there is no stimulation, no sexual energy . . . sexual energy feels so small beside this . . . all of me begins to shudder and all of the fulfilled yearning . . . the pleasure . . . the throbbing pulsating heart of kosmos flows through me wracking me with pleasure carrying me forward to the climax of all of reality in God.

She holds me—

I hold her

she is transparent—

clear—

shimmering . . . my body, my heart is wracked with wave after wave of love . . .

But the word "love" does not fully express it . . . it is sensuous, deeply moral, and alive . . . it is all of me and I am all of it . . . I cannot surrender to it because I am in it . . . and it is in me . . .

She holds me . . . I am gone someplace else and so radically alive and awake . . . deeper than early experiences

deeper than the awakening of shattering is the awakening of love.

I have been awakened by shattering to deep alive painful throbbing breakthrough . . .

I have been awakened by lonely yearning and carried into the bosom of God . . . when I was sixteen seventeen eighteen nineteen twenty I would walk the streets of Riverdale, New York, late at night and sing Hebrew chants for hours at a time, feeling myself walking with God and singing my yearning as his praise . . . and the yearning was fulfilled . . . in the yearning itself

. . . but here I was not the same—I was awakened by total fulfilled yearning not only in the yearning but the fulfillment of the yearning—it is fulfilled yearning in which the yearning and fulfillment are both renewed each moment that is love— total love.

The being of all being penetrated me—

through her

I cried out—

almost screaming . . .

crying out and crying out with intense pleasure and joy and holy abandon.

God was taking me and I was giving myself to God and there was no I and there was no God . . .

too small a word is God for God—

I needed to talk—I said to her: *Zeh kol haemet.* This is the whole truth—I promise you I promise you—this is the whole truth.

She said the same to me.

This is the whole truth.

—and we knew that we were not talking, that the Shekhinah spoke through our lips . . .

All of reality coursed through me—all of existence—there was no time—It is not that I moved beyond time—rather that there was no time—I was not beyond I—rather I was totally and wholly entered—penetrated by other—by reality—by being—by fulfilled yearning . . .

She held me through wave after wave—as I held her

She was transparent invisible holy and fully present . . . there invisible in her presence and thus infinitely present . . .

My body became inert . . . my mind told me to come down . . . it felt like I would die if I did not come down . . . and that was good and wonderful . . . my body relaxed awaiting the possibility of death's kiss

I could talk to my arm as I lay outside my body

I asked her to move my hand and to put it in her hand on my chest . . . it was not time to die—there is much that remains to be done . . . my body did not feel like it was going to die . . . not in a way that was frightening.

I said to her I am happy to die now . . .

Yet . . . my mind told me to come back . . . that it was not time to die . . . that I needed to come back . . . I could not talk . . . speech was difficult but slowly coming back . . .

I asked . . . in an almost inaudible tone if she could help me to descend . . .

As I came down arose again and came down—up and down Jacob's Ladder a text flowed through me:

"Greater is receiving the guest than receiving the face of the Shekhinah."

This told me that I needed to return—that I needed to write—to eat . . . with my partner with her . . . the sacred meal of the Sabbath . . . to learn to teach Hebrew wisdom to a spiritual teacher who is my student who will come later this afternoon . . . you must return she said with infinite love.

I asked her to help me down . . . not to let me slip away . . . her head moved to directly above my head—her eyes sparkled like the most clear wave of divinity—she shone full with light and purity— and I asked her to not let my eyes shut—I looked into her eyes . . . they were so clear and pure that instead of grounding me it convulsed me again—she was Shekhinah shimmering in my arms . . .

Yet slowly she held me in her gaze and touch and I came down . . . came back

Nothing was the same and everything was exactly as it was . . .

I needed to write. I said to her: you are my eternal partner at this moment whatever the future will bring. Nothing will ever make that not true.

I had returned to the personal the infinite and gorgeous transpersonal that lies at the heart throbbing inside the person waiting desperately to be recognized and redeemed.

The erotic merger with the divine Shekhinah—that is exactly what it is—exactly—it is not a simile—it is not a literary symbol . . . it is *mamash*—literally exactly that . . .

Oh my god oh my god oh my god oh my god

That the experience of enlightenment could be so sweet

To know with absolute certainty the Uni-verse of being throbs with pleasure and beats with joy

Thank you thank you thank you God

I said at the end to her as I was coming down—if we forget— and we will forget—then let us at least commit—from this moment on—that we will always remember that we have forgotten

And that will be enough.

I am in a trance as I write. I feel my foot sleeping and most of my body sleeping—I just realize now that I have fallen inside—en-trance—at the entrance

Thank you thank you thank You.
She said to me at the end—thank you.
I said to her
Thank you.

Impersonal tantra is the natural sister of impersonal enlightenment. If your goal is to move beyond the separate self and reside in the space of unqualified consciousness, then your sexing will serve that goal. This is the sexual path of True Self tantra. We have seen that the classical, mystical Eastern spiritual impulse is to move beyond the personal and the separate self. It is therefore not at all surprising that their teaching on sexing is about using the sexual to transcend the personal into the spacious ground of impersonal being.

Caution: Now I want to share something that is hugely important in understanding these different forms of sexing. You can experience genuine True Self tantra at the time of the relationship, like that which is described above. But if either of the parties is not sufficiently evolved or for whatever reason recoils into an egoic contraction, then the gorgeous True Self tantra that was experienced by both sides will be interpreted through the lens of personality sexing. In the memory of either one of the partners, the beauty of the Holy of Holies may be lost or even radically distorted. The reason is very simple: sex is a state of consciousness. All states of consciousness are interpreted through the stage or level of consciousness of the person experiencing them. So if a person has a stunning state-experience of sexing, then during the actual experience their ego will disappear. But when the experience is over, it will usually be remembered through the prism of the untransformed wound of the contracted ego.

5. Unique Self Sexing: Personal
The impersonal tantra teachers suggest the path of No-Self tantra as the alternative to negative visions of sexing. The negative visions described by the impersonal tantra teachers and other teachers of enlightenment virtually always describe the mode of sexing that I have called separate-self or personality sexing. The key limitation of the No-Self tantra school is that it confuses separate-self or personality sexing with personal Unique Self tantra.

"Unique Self tantra" is the tantra of the New Enlightenment.

In impersonal tantra your partner is not the issue. You engage sexing as a path to God. The goal is not momentary release. Lovemaking is a spiritual practice whose goal is to open up as love into divine communion. This is why in the advanced esoteric paths you have sex with a yogi or yogini whom you do not know at all. You have no relationship to that person outside of the tantric ritual. *The entire goal of the tantric ritual is your expansion beyond your small self into your True Self.* Your partner is not there to share or to receive your Unique Self; instead, your partner is there to sex you open to God.

This is no less true in personal Unique Self tantra. The difference is the path. In impersonal tantra the path is not through the uniquely refracted heart-body-mind prism of yourself and your beloved. In Unique Self tantra, it is your personal beloved who serves as the high priest or priestess, who facilitates your divine communion. In True Self tantra the high priest or priestess who facilitates your communion is impersonal, just as the nature of the enlightenment is impersonal. In True Self impersonal tantra, intimate communion serves divine communion. In Unique Self personal tantra, intimate communion *is* divine communion. This is precisely the puzzle-piece image we have talked about so much. Through the radical accentuation of your Unique contours, you are able to penetrate and be received by the personal face of All-That-Is. The personal naturally explodes into the transpersonal.

To be in Unique Self sexing is to be on the inside of the inside. The words "face" and "inside" are the same in Hebrew. Face, symbol of Unique Self, is the way inside to the enlightened face of divine communion. Unique Self encounter is personal, face-to-face. In the intensified face of your beloved's rapture, you meet and incarnate the divine.

Unique Self sex is utterly personal and absolutely impersonal, or better yet, transpersonal. You find your Self by losing your self. This is the inner mystery of orgasm. This gorgeous yet simple truth is called by the Unique Self mystics the "secret of the name." "Name" is the symbol for Unique Self. It is the recognition of radical uniqueness implicit in a person's name that makes the human being a "thou" and not merely an "it."

This dialectical dance in Unique Self sexing between the personal and the transpersonal finds wondrous expression in the rapturous cry at the moment of orgasm. If you are like most people all over the world, you probably say one of two things at the moment of orgasm. You either cry out, "Oh, God," or you call out the name of your beloved. The name is personal; "Oh, God" is transpersonal. This is an expression of the paradoxically personal and transpersonal nature of the mini-enlightenment experience in the sexual.

At the deepest level of nondual consciousness, however, the paradox resolves itself. The resolution is in the ecstatic realization that ultimately the name of God and the name of the beloved are one and the same. *When you are lived by your name, your Unique Self, you incarnate the divine name. You are being lived by the personal expression of the divine name that lives as you.*

The original description of sexuality in biblical myth is that of Unique Self sexing. Adam and Eve are both lonely. Their loneliness is transcended through the sharing of their Unique Selves in the intense contact of Unique Self sexing. The word deployed to describe Unique Self sexing in Genesis is the same word deployed later in biblical myth to describe mystical cleaving with God. The word is *devekut*. The teaching is simply that intimate communion and divine communion are one and the same.

The goal is *echad*, "Oneness." Again, the same Hebrew word *echad* describes both sexual oneness and mystical union with God. There are different paths in same practice.

There are different technologies deployed in intimate divine communion. In some practices, you circulate the love-light through your body in a circular loop going up the spine and down the front of your chest as you expand into the spaciousness of divine communion. In other practices, the little death of orgasm is the death of the small self into the larger self. All that is closed, opens. The contracted heart is opened into God as love and light. Any vestige of the separate self is left behind. All loneliness is absorbed and transmuted in the heart of God.

In Unique Self personal tantra, who you are sexing with is your specific partner, your beloved partner with whom you share past and future, history and dreams. Sex is not a spiritual practice in and of itself. Rather, sex with your Unique Self partner is the spiritual practice. You meet and merge with the Unique Self of your lover. Through the unique erotic sexual encounter with your beloved—of giving and receiving collapsed into one—you are exploded open into God.

Unique Self sexing is the ultimate personal tantra, but it is not personality tantra. Rather, it is the most awesome and glorious expression of true transpersonal sexing. Remember, the transpersonal is that which trance-ends and includes the personal. Unique Self is not merely ego, separate self, or grasping personality. Rather, Unique Self is the manifestation of your most authentic Uniqueness, which appears in its most crystalline form only after you have clarified your limited identification with your separate self ego. It is from that place that you practice Unique Self tantra, in which you merge through sexing with the Unique Self of your partner. In that merger, you emerge as your Unique Selves meet in rapturous embrace, fucking each other open to God.

Unique Self always transcends and includes True Self. In the same way, Unique Self sexing transcends and includes True Self sexing. And just like the level of consciousness of separate self is clearly distinct from the personal level of Unique Self, separate-self sexing is profoundly different from Unique Self sexing.

Personal Unique Self tantra creates a gorgeous explosion of the erotic and the holy that resonates in all worlds. The explosion of ecstasy, tears, and inexpressible joy occurs when two Unique Selves merge in radical penetration and radiant openness. Unique Self sexing is not a cover-up for any form of emptiness. Quite the contrary. It bursts out of the passionate personal fullness that lives in and as the lovers.

It is not just that the grasping and desperate parts of the personality are left behind in Unique Self tantra. Personality is actually healed. In being touched, licked, sucked, caressed, penetrated, and received, a great and wondrous healing takes place. All the anal and oral fixations of early childhood that form the matrix of so much of what Freud called "neurosis" are healed when one is touched in love.

But it is not only about being touched; it is also about being witnessed. In being witnessed in your fullness, there is healing. Unique Self sexing is the mutual witnessing of the other's radical abandon and loss of control. In that witnessing, a great and paradoxical healing takes place. The personality relaxes its grasping, and the truly personal Unique Self comes online in its authentic fullness.

In Unique Self tantra, you are never fully lost in the oblivion of oneness. One teeters at the edge—with oneness and oblivion on one side, and mutual recognition and compassion on the other. In personal tantra, you dance to the end of love, where the personal catapults your whole body in the infinite heart of the transpersonal. Your Unique Self emerges from your realization of your distinct self being inseparable from the larger Self incarnate in the entwined body of your beloved.

Sexing calls you to your divinity even as it invites you to your death. The French description of orgasm as "little death" feels into this invitation. John Donne's call to his beloved in the moment of orgasm—come, my darling, that I may "die" with you—is compelled by this very invitation. Sexing is the place where you are most personally addressed, and it is the mystery through which you evolve to the transpersonal. Sex is the door to the twin mysteries of birth and death. In that sense, sex is both the gateway to the personal—personified by birth—and the move beyond the merely personal to the radically impersonal, which is personified by death. Enlightenment, and indeed all of life, is found in the right relationship between the personal and impersonal.

The divine kosmos, all of reality, is one great puzzle. We are all puzzle pieces. In order to fit in, to become part of the great puzzle, you must accentuate the precise contour of your puzzle piece, for it is through that very Uniqueness that you merge into the larger whole. That is the essence of the Unique Self orgasm. For orgasms are not in the least bit generic. They are rather a signature expression of the personal self. This is the essence of Unique Self personal tantra, where sex and story merge as one.

6. *Tikkun* Sexing or *Bodhisattva* Sexing

The sixth form of sexing we might call *tikkun* sexing, or *bodhisattva* sexing.

Bodhisattva is the Buddhist expression for the being who vows to work to end suffering for all sentient beings. *Tikkun* is the Kabbalistic path of practice in which all of life is intended toward healing the broken heart of the kosmos. In this teaching, which is not far from you but as close to you as your nose is to your mouth, your entire life is utterly dedicated to fixing that which is broken. In all quadrants of reality. In heart and mind. In your community of caring. In your body. In all the structural systems that define our world. You are a fixer, a healer of that which is broken.

In the language of the scholars, this has been called theurgy. Simply put, this means that your deed is God's need. Your deed has the power to fix, to heal, and to evolve all of reality.

This is expressed in four core ways. First, whenever it is possible, in direct interventions of healing and fixing in all areas of life. Second, in any act that is done with fullness of presence and clarified conscious intention. Third, in offering the clarity of your intention in spiritual practice, including ritual and prayer. (Prayer is not merely a supplication for world peace and blessings, although on some level it is also that. Prayer is an esoteric mystical practice that heals the shattered heart of the kosmos.) And fourth, in offering up your sexing for the sake of the healing of all sentient beings.

In the spiritual will of my original lineage master, the Baal Shem Tov, it is said that the traditional swaying motion of the supplicant that characterizes traditional prayer is because prayer is erotic merger with God.

Prayer as erotic merger with God is the revealed teaching; the hidden teaching is *tikkun* tantra. This teaching was esoterically passed down from King Solomon through the generations of Kabbalistic teachers. In this dharma, not only does

Prayer = Erotic merger with God—with All-That-Is,

but the converse is true as well:

Erotic merger = Prayer.

Sexing is a form of praying.

Prayer, as we just defined it, is an esoteric mystical practice that heals the shattered heart of the kosmos. Prayer in this teaching happens through you and your lover embodying the masculine and feminine faces of the kosmos. The full power of all man and all woman, the god and the goddess, flows through you. Your sexing is the sexing of all worlds that unites all the world. In that Kabbalah, this form of sexing is called the *sod ha-yichud,* the "secret of unification" or *"tikkun."* It is sexing to unite the god and the goddess, and at the same time it is the god and the goddess. The masculine and feminine principles personalize in you. At the same time, your sexing is intended to heal all the ruptures between man and woman, between the masculine and the feminine, between all lovers everywhere and through all time.

Below is a personal testimony of an initiate into *bodhisattva* sexing. Read it as a meditation.[1]

They really couldn't be called "orgasms" anymore, though. That term implies a sudden, forceful contraction and release centered on a focal point. But I was experiencing a multitude of repeating pulses, like a hundred beating hearts, unleashing ripples of pleasure over and over again.

"This is what God feels all the time," I whispered.

"Yes. This is what Goddess feels all the time," Celia answered.

"So we're imitating the Creators of the Uni-verse right now?" I said.

"Well," she said, "in a sense we are imitating them. In another sense, we *are* them."

"I'm having a million orgasms every second."

"Me too. Let's shoot for a billion."

"OK. How?"

"Turn the orgasms into prayers."

"What do we pray for?"

"We pray for what God and Goddess pray for. Which is different from what humans pray for."

"I seem to be having a divine memory lapse, Goddess. Remind me what we pray for?"

"Our prayers are the engine of creation. They're how we reanimate the Uni-verse fresh every nanosecond—orgasmic bursts of divine love that keep everything growing and changing forever."

"So if we want to imitate God and Goddess—I mean, if we want to *be* God and Goddess—we should act as if our orgasms are actually prayers with which we beget the Uni-verse anew over and over again." . . .

Images and emotions began streaming into my imagination. They had a life of their own; were independent of my will. They came in bursts, each of which bore the imprint of a person I knew and cared for. There was my friend Fred, the entomologist, with whom I traveled in Europe; Regina, the old girlfriend with whom I had three abortions; Maddy, the woman I sang with for five years; Sunyatta, the professional ballet dancer who taught me how to do a pirouette; Mr. Riley, my high school French teacher, the only older male who ever gave me a blessing.

In each case, the person's life seemed to pass in a flash before my eyes, downloading into my psyche all the memories of everything he or she had ever done and thought and felt, the pain mixed with the pleasure, the rot with the splendor. It was all happening impossibly fast: as if the old 2.5 GHz microprocessor in my brain had been replaced by a new model that ran at 2.5 million GHz. . . .

She playfully rolled over, pulling me with her so that now I was on top.

"Now fuck me with your prayers for all those souls who leaped into you," she commanded, "and I'll fuck you with mine."

I shoved a pillow under her ass to change the angle at which I entered her, and raised her legs a little by lifting from behind her knees.

"I visualize and pray that my old friend Fred will come to a new, supple accommodation with his ex-wife so that they create more harmony in the life of their daughter," I said, as I moved in Celia. "May this unfold in ways that send benevolent consequences out in all directions, diminishing the suffering and enhancing the joy of every sentient being."

"I declare and desire that my Aunt Ruth will find the key to supporting herself as an acupuncturist, so she can quit her gig as a grocery clerk," asserted Celia. "And I pray that in doing this she will become a more potent force for beauty and truth and goodness, lifting up everyone whose life she touches."

"I foresee and demand that Regina will summon the power to cut back on her work doing hospital murals so she can write that children's book she wants to do. May this in turn redound to the benefit of all creatures."

"I envision and confirm that John will get the help necessary to heal from the death of his wife. As he receives what he needs, I further envision and confirm that all of creation will gather inspiration from the changes he sets in motion."

Many other friends, acquaintances, and loved ones made appearances in our ritual. My heart broke open again and again, ripped sweetly apart by a yearning to help them thrive, to love them as they needed to be loved, to enhance them and enliven them and share with them the blessings Celia and I had conjured.

CHAPTER TWENTY-ONE

EVOLUTIONARY INTIMACY

The Seven Laws of Unique Self Encounters

SEEN FROM ONE PERSPECTIVE, life is a series of encounters with other human beings. Of these encounters, the ones that are most profound, pleasurable, and transformative are Unique Self encounters. The following are seven core rules that define a Unique Self encounter:

1. In every Unique Self encounter, each person holds a piece of the other's story, which must be returned to the other in order for both to be complete.

Every person you meet—in a significant meeting—possesses a piece of your story. Some people may have a sentence, others a missing word, while still others may hold a paragraph or even a whole chapter. Significant meetings involve Unique Self encounters.

The ultimate Unique Self encounter may well be with your significant other in life. The person you choose should be the person who can return to you a significant piece of your story, which you have either lost or never found. Conversely, you hold and need to return the missing and magnificent pieces of their story to them. The Unique Self relationship is the committed, caring, dynamic process of discovering just what these missing pieces might be, and puzzling them back together.

A Unique Self encounter, however, is in no sense limited to romantic partners or long-term connections. Others may have pieces of your story, and you of theirs. Nor are Unique Self encounters limited to your sphere of colleagues, friends, family, neighbors, employers, and employees. *A Unique Self encounter may last a minute or a lifetime.* You may be riding an elevator with a person you have never met and will never meet again, both of you inching up to the twenty-third floor, and somewhere in your casual conversation there will be an important message for each of you. Similarly, the person who returns your lost wallet may have more to give back to you than your credit cards.

There is a Unique Self ethos that cannot be externally enforced or legislated, yet it demands a far higher moral standard than passive public morality. When you have an encounter with another person, you are called on to ask yourself, "Have you brought your Unique Self to the table in the encounter?" And when a Unique Self encounter that should have taken place does not, then we have committed a Unique Self misdemeanor—sometimes even a felony. No one will ever know—except for you, God, and possibly the person with whom you failed to have an encounter.

A Unique Self encounter may be a wisdom encounter. Through your Unique Self convergence with someone, you gain a deeper insight into your own Unique pleasure, joy, obligation, need, or shadow. A Unique Self encounter can also be action oriented. You and the person you encounter may be agents of change for each other, each of you provoking the other to do something in the world you never otherwise could have done. Encounters take place between teachers and students, between lovers, among friends, in casual acquaintance, or in chance meetings.

2. To have a Unique Self encounter, you have to make authentic contact in the present.

The second law of Unique Self relationship is that to have a Unique Self encounter, you have to make authentic contact. Without contact with the Unique Self of the other, no encounter may happen. It is for this reason that Unique Self encounters can take place only in the present. *Contact is only possible in the present. The only place your story is ever happening is right now.*

Yesterday's and tomorrow's story help shape your identity today. This is as it should be. But presence—showing up as your God-self, your Unique

Self—is possible only in the present. ***When you think you are talking to me but you are really completing an unfinished conversation with your mother from years ago, contact cannot be made.***

Inter-action is the opposite of re-action. Re-action comes from an unconscious re-play, re-hash, and re-living of moments long dead and done. ***You cannot live a dead moment.*** Unconscious re-enactment is precisely what psychology calls transference. You are transferring your reactions from an old situation to the present situation, even though they do not apply.

You must enter the inside of the present moment, which is the Unique Self of time. The inter-action is in the inter-face between two people who are face-to-face.

Often, in a potentially intimate encounter, when an inner discomfort arises, that feeling of discomfort has many layers and often arises from our reactions to past events. The discomfort both blocks the process and offers a doorway into the Unique Self in that moment. So one way to deepen contact in an interpersonal encounter is to identify the discomfort present in a particular moment. ***Stay in the discomfort. Feel into it, and let it well up. Do nothing to dispel it.*** If you stay in it, even for fifteen minutes, you will feel something new, something deeper arising. As the energy of discomfort is released, a feeling of fullness and well-being can arise. This is the essence that lies just beneath your personality, ready to reveal itself.

A Unique Self encounter occurs when the essence of one personal being touches the essence of another personal being, without ego boundaries and without loss of the unique individuation of each unique partner.

A Unique Self encounter requires contact with the person in front of you in the Uniqueness of the present moment. One of the well-known teachings in biblical myth states this principle: "Therefore shall a man leave his father and mother and cleave intimately to his wife."

If you look at the text from a psychological viewpoint, you see that it is not just a formal recommendation of marriage. It points to a primal truth about relationship. You cannot create true intimacy without leaving behind, in a psychological sense, your parents. If you do not leave your parents behind, you marry them. You marry someone similar to, or the opposite of, your parents, in order to finish your unfinished business with them. Through that person who is similar to Dad, you seek to receive the love you didn't get from Dad. Or through that person who is the opposite of Mom, you seek to run away from Mom. In either case, you are in a relationship, not with your partner, but with your parents. There is no Unique Self encounter.

Contact only takes place in the present, in the Unique Self of the present moment in time. You think you are in the present relating to your partner. Really you are in the past, arguing or pleading with a parent. In this situation, the energy and wisdom that you need to be intimately present with your partner is unavailable.

The Pain Trance

Our inability to remain present—that is, in the present—is the source of most of our pain and dysfunction. We fail to meet the challenges of each moment not because we lack the resources, but because we allow encounters in the present to trigger past experiences of pain.

An example: Jonathan is up for review at work and the boss says to him, "I think you have potential, but your work is still sloppy. Get that together and you have a great future here." Rather than hearing the promise in his boss's words, Jonathan hears rejection. He gets angry at his boss and feels that the critique was unfair. This causes him to feel so depressed that he later gets into a vociferous argument with his partner about nothing. Or he may call an old romantic partner up for dinner, and inappropriately sleep with her in order to cover the emptiness opened up by his boss's critique. Or he may start a binge of excessive drinking, which in the end causes him to lose the job he held so dear.

What happened here? Essentially, his boss's words triggered old reactions. Jonathan slipped into a trance that took him out of the present moment and threw him into the past. His fastidious father used to shout at him when his room wasn't clean. Dad would go into a rage and call him "a worthless, sloppy mess." Jonathan remembers that phrase. It is indelibly imprinted on his soul. So when someone critiques him as being sloppy, even if it is in the context of great praise and even with a promise for the future, all Jonathan can hear in his subconscious is "worthless and sloppy."

He probably does not consciously associate his boss's critique with that ancient moment in his life. He may not even consciously remember his father's words. Yet whenever something or someone presses certain internal triggers, he regresses to those early childhood moments and responds as he did then. This is precisely the image of "pressing buttons." He is in a trance, acting not in the present but in response to old pain.

We all have trances. A trance means simply that you leave the present moment and enter another time or dimension. Daydreaming can be a pleasant version of such a trance. A second example is what psychological literature calls spontaneous age regression. This can also be pleasant, as when the taste of banana slices in Cheerios returns you to the feeling-state of a sweet Saturday morning in childhood.

Jonathan's experience, however, is a typical example of negative age regression—what I call a "pain trance." Because it is unconscious, it takes Jonathan out of the present. Because he is not aware that the past is coming up again, he also lacks the presence to heal the past.

Staying in the Present

The most important identifying characteristic of a trance is the distortion of time. You are taken out of the present and regressed to an earlier, more unconscious time in your life. Psychologist Stephen Wolinsky calls this kind of age-regressed unconscious experience a deep trance phenomenon. All such trances are triggered by a narrowing of focus. This is precisely what happens, for example, in most phobias or anxiety attacks. Our focus shrinks to the extent that the rest of the world feels completely cut off. We narrow our focus to a specific image, word, or sensation that effectively blocks out all other words, images, or emotions. In the story we began with, it was the word "sloppy" that became the involuntary mantra of the trance.

At such moments, we forget our larger selves. We don't see options or resources that are right in front of us. We become virtually paralyzed, and cannot change our course of action.

Essentially, the trance takes you out of the present moment. *In the mystical understanding of time, the present moment contains everything you need for healing and health, so by leaving it, you are bound to get sick and hurt. Therefore, the goal of spiritual therapeutic intervention should be to return the client to the presence of the present moment.*

Remember, a trance that takes you out of the present and prevents a Unique Self encounter is usually a return to the childlike reaction that we used to protect ourselves from trauma long ago. Any event that is too painful for the child to integrate is met by a childhood trance. Let's say, for example, that your mother was verbally abusive. If you responded defensively to her abuse, she would either hit you or scream in an even more frightening and insane way. Your protective trance response was a combination of two internal movements. First, you would watch—without noticing that you were watching—your mother very carefully. This allowed you to anticipate her moods and try to be out of the way when the trauma-spewing volcano erupted. In watching your mother, you would gather all of her misdeeds, much like a prosecuting attorney. Then when she started yelling, you would list off silently to yourself all of her faults. By the time she finished yelling, you had the mental satisfaction of having tried and indicted her in the courtroom of your mind.

Later on in life, when you would get into an argument with your partner, something about it might spontaneously and unconsciously regress you back to your encounters with your mom. This would then elicit in you a withering attack on your partner. You might now have a terrible knack of bringing up all sorts of details you had noticed, and using them to bash your spouse. When your outburst is over, you are ashamed, but the damage is done. The retaliation you used to do mentally to your mother, you now do out loud to your spouse. However, having cultivated the art of careful watching, your outbursts are profoundly more insightful, and therefore more devastating.

These outbursts have been a primary cause of your inability to create lasting, intimate relationships with either friends or a romantic partner. The root of this challenge, which has devastated so much of your life, is your tendency to go into the age-regressed trance state, which takes you out of the present. *One purpose of your spiritual practice is to help you remain in the present. In the present, you have all the resources you might need for healing and intimacy.* But before you can stay in the present, you first have to learn to catch yourself going into trance.

To Walk in the Wide Places

Stephen Wolinsky tells the story of a client named Clare. She was a binge drinker, and before one of these binge episodes, she would first slip into an invisible trance. She would get very tight, create distance between herself and the world, and would not fully see the people around her—they would seem to blur out of focus. Her normal level of unease in the world would quickly become more pronounced, and she could only think about having a drink.

This was the strategy Clare used to survive childhood abuse. She would shut out her external environment. The abuser would shift out of focus, and she would withdraw into her own world. Wolinsky writes, "In my break-through moment I realized that in order for her to create the distance she needed to survive as a child, she had to not see much of her immediate external environment." She would withdraw and enter—en-trance—her own world.

What provokes this reaction in us later in life is virtually always the meeting with something or someone that triggers our core unique wound. We are suddenly and unconsciously thrown back to that early place where we first met the emptiness and the wound.

Our sense of our goodness in early childhood depends on our caretakers serving as a conduit for the Uni-verse's loving embrace. When those love vessels are constricted and narrowed, our soul feels attacked. We then with-draw into our contracted-ego small-self for self-protection. This prevents the pain of the emptiness from drowning us. We only shut down when the pain overloads our circuits; instead of blowing our system, we turn off. We withdraw—no longer present in the present. When meeting with "empti-ness" in the present, it often evokes this old challenge to our self-worth. We slip into a "past" without ever noticing the slippage. Thinking we are in the past, the same set of survival strategies kick in. *We withdraw into what-ever our unique trance patterns are—and look for a way to navigate the emptiness without being swallowed up.*

In childhood, such an event is always interpersonal—that is, a reaction to another person or people outside of ourselves. But in adulthood, *when the reactive mechanism is triggered, it kicks in autonomously—that is, without it being a protective strategy against a real person.* Anything that sets off our emptiness barometer returns us to the place of original unhealed trauma where we encountered the wound originally. We then react—automatically and unconsciously—as we did then.

Staying in the Symptoms

What Wolinsky brilliantly noticed was that in telling the story of the symptom, the trance was re-induced. What that meant to him—in a simple yet elegant insight—was that if he could help his client short-circuit the trance in the telling of the story, then the client would be able to short-circuit the trance when it kicked in at other times. The key is to pay attention and notice when trance symptoms are kicking in. The critical assumption is that the negative behavior can kick in only after the trance and as a direct result of it. Short-circuit the trance, and nine times out of ten you have short-circuited the destructive behavior.

Wolinsky also tells of a young woman who comes to therapy with the real problem of not being able to have an orgasm. She knows that she was molested by her stepfather at age nine. One could engage a long and complex process of "working through" the abuse. Or, in a far more direct and effective approach, the trained therapist or guide might say something like, "Jill, when you are having sex, at that moment that you go numb, or freeze up, or space out, get a picture of that moment and describe it for me."

While re-creating her symptom trance, Jill might answer slowly, "My shoulders are tight . . . my jaw is tight . . . my stomach is tight . . . I'm holding my breath . . . I'm thinking to myself, 'Don't touch me, don't come near me, don't hurt me.'"

"All right, Jill," the therapist continues, "what I'd like you to do is to merge with the picture . . . continue to hold your muscles tightly while you breathe and look at me."

This is the pivoting point. The therapist says to Jill, "Stay with your trance symptoms but don't disappear. Stay here with me." A trance is almost always induced in part by a shift in normal breathing. In many sacred languages, the word for "breath" has the same root, or is even the same word, as the word for "soul." In biblical myth, God fashions the human being through an act of inspiration: "God breathed into man the breath of life." *This breath of life is the loving flow of divine life-energy in the Uni-verse. In trauma, this loving flow is cut off, reflected in a tightening in the chest, or other shifts in breathing. In reconnecting to the breath, you reconnect to the life force.*

In this case, establishing a loving and trusting relationship allows the client to move through the trance symptoms and reconnect with the loving breath of the Uni-verse. By doing so, the trance is short-circuited.

In light of all this, let's reread the spiritual principle of biblical myth with which we began: "Therefore shall a man leave his father and mother and cleave intimately to his wife."

There are two steps. Step one: You need to de-trance. Those meetings with emptiness that cause spontaneous age regression need to be short-circuited. You need to move beyond old conversations with father and mother. Here father and mother are, of course, only symbols of the formative relationships of our early years.

Step two: Having become de-tranced, you can now create intimacy with your partner. A Unique Self encounter is now possible. You are in the present, with the person in front of you—not a figure from the past. Contact can be made.

3. Labels obstruct contact.

Labels can be anything from "smart," "stupid," "beautiful," or "ugly," to words noting race or religious affiliation or role designation. A label is naturally illuminating when it describes or conveys important information about the object or subject being labeled, like properly labeled medicine. A label is blinding when it prevents your attention from actually settling directly on the object or subject that you are encountering. It is this kind of label that obstructs authentic contact between Unique Selves.

> Janis did her internship at Bellevue Hospital on the locked psychiatric ward. After her first session, she hurried to leave the ward to get to class at NYU. When she went up to the guard and asked to be let out, he looked at her with a slightly surprised smile and asked, "What do you mean? I'm not going to let you out!"
>
> Janis was a little bewildered by his answer, but tried to explain. "I'm a student at NYU and have to get to class. Can you please let me out?"
>
> He laughed at her again incredulously. "Yeah, right! And I'm the dean of Harvard Law School. I can't let you out!"
>
> Janis suddenly realized she was stuck in a locked ward, and that anything she said would not be believed. She was locked in the guard's conception of her as a patient!

Finally, after some panicked moments, she found a super-
visor on the ward and told him what had happened. He
looked at her, suppressing a smile, and asked, "But Janis, why
were you asking a patient to let you out?"

Positive or negative, every blinding label builds walls. When you hold on
to your labels and self-definitions ("I'm not good at this; I could never do
that"), you refuse to treat yourself as a full human being with infinite potential. When you give labels to other people or types of people ("She's bad with
numbers," "She's a narcissist and can never heal"), you estrange yourself from
other people's Unique Selves. You are no longer able to make contact.

The most often mentioned ethical guideline in biblical mysticism—
appearing no less than thirty-six times—is, "Deal kindly with the stranger."
***A stranger is anyone whose Unique Self is blocked from view by a limit-
ing label.*** This might be a label of their place of origin, family, nationality,
or religion. It might be a carelessly affixed label of their ability or potential.
Limiting labels often can refer to physical characteristics or psychological
typologies of virtually any kind.

It is not that third-person descriptions, definitions, and categorizations
are not helpful. They are. Accurate diagnosis in every field of endeavor is
essential to wise and compassionate interaction, whether that is with your
doctor, psychologist, romantic partner, or friend. There is a particular form
of spiritual consciousness that resists or rejects all labels with the argument
that you can do or be whatever you want, and labels simply serve to box
you in. This is a partial truth, but like all partial truths, it is also a partial lie. Labels illuminate, reveal, and guide. But as much as they disclose
and divulge, labels also obscure and obfuscate, and therefore stand against
Unique Self encounters.

You often label compulsively to feel a sense of control and comfort in a
situation. Naturally, these labels are often sloppy, inaccurate, or just plain
false. A false label will yield false conclusions, which will lead to wrong and
destructive action. The simplest example is the destructive, heartrending
result of labeling a child retarded or unteachable. At the same time, an accurate diagnosis of a learning disability might lead to wonderfully constructive
interventions that heal hearts and open minds.

In Unique Self enlightenment, the absolute demand is to never let external labels transform the other into a stranger.

Labeling happens all the time, even when we don't think we are doing it. We label ourselves, as well, in subtle and pernicious ways. "There is no possible way I could ever do that," someone might say about an ambition or desire. That kind of sentiment is a kind of label that estranges us from ourselves. Such comments are certainties that lie. We hold them because they allow us a comfort zone in which we do not need to challenge our self-perceptions or stretch to the fullness of our Unique Selves. Labels are the archenemy of Unique Selves. *Relying on labels is like trying to take someone's fingerprint when they are wearing a Band-Aid.*

4. You never know.

The goal of Unique Self consciousness is to fully receive and be received in deep understanding and empathy. Yet how often are we simply unable to understand one another? Receiving each other becomes next to impossible because of distance, strangeness, hurry, deafness, carelessness, or inevitable differences in the languages of our Unique Selves. Try as we might, the Unique Selves of so many people are ultimately unknowable to us—just like the Unique Self of God.

Are we to give up, or is there a path of receiving what is true even when you cannot fully grasp the Unique Self of other? And is there a way that an other can honor you in your Unique Self even if they cannot fully receive you in understanding and empathy? Is there a way to receive what seems so unreceivable, whether human or divine? This quandary inspires one of the more subtle ideas of St. Thomas Aquinas, the medieval writer who did so much to define Christianity, and of Moses Maimonides, perhaps the most important Jewish philosopher of the last thousand years.

For theologians like Aquinas and Maimonides and many others past and present, the very essence of God is God's incommunicability. According to these two medieval philosophers, God is unknowable. In the language of one scholar, "If I knew him, I would be him." And yet at the same time, they held that the *summum bonum* of human existence is to know God.

But how can you know the one who is not knowable? Aquinas and Maimonides proposed an ingenious solution, which they called *via negativa* or "the affirmation of not knowing"—that is, we know God in acknowledging that we do not know God. In the words of one of French writer Edmond Jabès's characters, "I know you, Lord, in the measure that I do not know you."

It is in the same way the Unique Self mystics teach that we receive another even if we do not know them; the Unique Self encounter takes place through the affirmation of not knowing.

For years, I thought the "affirmation of not knowing" was a classic example of irrelevant if clever medieval sophistry. Until on a rare stormy day in Jerusalem, I made my way through the rain to the small neighborhood grocer right next to my house to pick up some essentials for my bad-weather hibernation. A gust of smoke greeted me at the door. The source of the noxious fumes, I soon found out, was a swarthy-faced middle-aged man, loitering in my corner store! Shirt open to the chest, large gold necklace and all, he stood there smoking his 9 a.m. cigar.

Coughing and fanning my way through his smoke, I mumbled to the grocer my consternation at the torrential rains that had soaked me through and through, trying to hide my growing annoyance at this obviously uncouth and obnoxious loiterer.

And then, ever so slowly, the man with the gold necklace turned and looked at me—I promise—with the gentlest look you could possibly imagine. All his features suddenly appeared handsome and majestic. The gold necklace seemed regal, the smoke sweet as an incense offering. "Don't you know," he said, "it's raining today because a holy man has gone to his world."

I felt like some gate had swung open inside of me. Something in my heart just fell open—I just wanted to reach out and hug him for being so beautiful. It was an epiphany pure and simple.

Only later when I got home and read the paper did I see that one of Jerusalem's great mystics had in fact died that morning—the Rebbe of Gur, a Hasidic master and leader of a thriving community with origins in the Eastern European town of Gur, a community that had been virtually wiped out during the Holocaust. This master had slowly, painstakingly, and with endless love, passion, and daring, rebuilt his community in Israel over the past forty years. The world felt darker without him.

I had totally misjudged the man at the grocer's. I thought he was a boor—coarse and crass, involved only in his immediate needs. However, the shining beauty and the subtle and deep knowing on his face as he told me that a holy man had died let me know how superficial my vision had been. I had assumed I knew him, and I had not truly known him at all. I had not received him.

"You never know—you never know—you never know." *A Unique Self encounter is only possible in the felt humility of not knowing.* And realizing that at the end of all knowing is—not knowing.

The temptation to label, categorize, dismiss, or otherwise try to put another person in a box is the desire for conquest through knowing. People in boxes threaten us less. Instead, we must seek to receive an other's Unique Self, even as we are aware that the other remains mysterious to us, ultimately unknowable, just like God. We are called to honor the Unique Self by gently saying to ourselves, "You never know—you never know—you never know."

5. Unique Self encounters create evolutionary We Space.

Meaningful Unique Self encounters foster the experience of entering together into higher states of awareness and intelligence. The next evolutionary leap in consciousness involves a recognition that, together, we have access to a collective wisdom and intelligence that is much smarter than our individual intelligence.

This is, in a sense, something the mystics have always known: the whole is so much greater than the sum of its parts. What is "new" is that nowadays, in workshops and retreats, in corporate boardrooms and organizational development seminars, as well as in spiritual groups, so many people are experimenting with engaging the phenomenon of collective intelligence.

Here's how it works: a room full of people with clarity of intention come together with focused attention. They engage a challenge, seek a solution, or reach for deeper direction. They seek something precious that was previously unavailable to any of the individuals in the room. It was also unavailable through the classic collaborative methods of sharing information and comparing notes. They use certain group technologies to create a group consciousness within which a new space of insight is revealed. The insight that comes forward often has a visionary wisdom that exceeds the limitations of any of the individuals in the room. Something happens in the center of the room.

The "voice" that rises in the center of such a group, whether in an organizational setting or a spiritually oriented one, is the voice of an emergent higher intelligence. It is the voice of the "whole." All the distinct parts are held, heard, and honored, yet the whole transcends them into the larger love-intelligence that speaks in, as, and through each of us, even as it calls from beyond us. It is from this precise space that collective intelligence wells up.

The famed basketball coach Phil Jackson, who brought the LA Lakers and Chicago Bulls to multiple championships, was explicitly referring to this phenomenon when he talked about "the subtle interweaving of the players at full speed to the point where they are thinking and moving as one."

One participant in a collective consciousness exercise describes it as follows:

> When someone else spoke, it felt as if I were speaking. And when I did speak, it was almost egoless, like it wasn't really me. It was as if something larger was speaking through me. . . . And in that space we started to create. We started to say things that we had never thought before.

Ralph Waldo Emerson writes of this phenomenon: "All are conscious of attaining to a higher self-possession. It shines for all." In Jewish Mysticism, this is called the voice of the Shekhinah—the feminine face of the divine, which in the Hindu traditions is called *Shakti*. Jewish mystics who wrote in the third century taught, "Whenever ten people gather with clear holy intention, the Shekhinah speaks." Or as Matthew said, "When two or three gather in my name I am in the midst of them." Modern Hindu mystic Aurobindo called this "the evolution of truth consciousness in which [they] feel themselves to be the embodiment of a single self." Theosophist Rudolf Steiner said, "People awake through each other . . . then real communal spirituality descends on our workplace." Finally, the French Jesuit Teilhard de Chardin, one of the key founders of modern evolutionary spirituality, describes this collective spiritual awakening as "sustained, certainly, by the individual person, but at the same time embracing and shaping the successive multitude of individuals."[1]

The intelligence of wholeness cannot arise when people in the group are locked into their separate-self egos. Nor does it happen at the level of True Self. At the level of separate self, you remain separate from everyone in your community, so you cannot join to create a We Space that will yield a higher wisdom than that which emerges from the collaboration of separate selves. *If you are living in True Self, then you are absorbed in the one, and your Unique Voice merges in silence. Collective intelligence is rather a direct function of shared Unique Self experience.*

Through the unique contours of your puzzle piece, each member of the group merges with and completes both themselves and the larger whole. *The Unique Self experience is both the heart of the phenomenon of collective intelligence and the key to its emergence in any given situation.* Said simply, evolutionary We Space is only a genuine possibility if we deploy the awakened technology of Unique Self-realization. There are very few pleasures in life which compare to the awakened We Space of Unique Selves living together. It was toward this pleasure that Teilhard de Chardin pointed when he said, "There is almost a sensual longing for communion with others who have a large vision. The immense fulfillment of the friendship between those engaged in furthering the evolution of consciousness has a quality impossible to describe."

6. To engage in a Unique Self encounter, you must stay open as love through the pain.

To make contact in a Unique Self encounter, you must know how to avoid the ritual of rejection that so often arises from the ego's contraction. When you feel hurt, your small-self ego contracts. Unless you make an effort to counter the ego's inertia, you fall out of divine communion. You fall into UnLove. Unique Self encounter asks that you not fall out of divine communion and become degraded by UnLove. It demands that you not get stuck in the coiled contraction of the small self.

The ego will tend to take hurt and turn it into an insult, which offends your existence. Then to compensate, you set into motion the ritual of rejection. It goes something like this:

1. You experience the pain of hurt and/or rejection.
2. As a result, you feel small and insignificant. It even puts you in touch with your nonexistence.
3. To feel less small, you lash out and inflict hurt. In your ability to hurt the other, you experience power, which makes you feel like you exist again.

To enter a Unique Self encounter, you must resist the gravitational pull of UnLove. You must identify as part of the larger field of love. You experience yourself as part of the seamless coat of the Uni-verse. This is the source of your authentic power. This will allow you to receive hurt inflicted by others as a wound of love and not as an insult. You wear your hurt as a battle scar in your struggle for love. You bear it with pride and dignity. You are freed from the compulsive need to inflict pain on the one who hurt you in order to prove you exist. You know you exist because you are in divine communion, that is to say, identified with the larger whole beyond your particular part nature. The trance-ending of ego into Unique Self-realization is animated by the quality of love. Love motivates and manifests the spontaneous action of care and compassion. Egoic self-contraction is the quality of fear. Fear motivates and manifests the reactive rituals of egoity.

To live and act as love means to keep your heart open through the pain of heartache and hurt.

To live and act as fear means to allow the pain to close your heart.

You can practice love by practicing opening your heart even when you feel hurt. Rather than turning away, closing down, and striking out, you keep your heart open. This will help you act skillfully instead of reacting clumsily in these situations.

When you practice opening as love moment to moment in the face of the hurt, the power of the past weakens. Old wounds are in the past. If you open your heart in the present, time after time, the power of the past recedes.

You will probably always feel the pain when you meet UnLove in relationship. But you do not need to feel the closure, which deadens your heart and your life force. You can continually practice love rather than closing down into UnLove. You can feel your self-contraction and choose to change the way you react.

You are not a victim of your past. When you stop either ignoring or overdramatizing past events, you also stop unconsciously using life trauma from the past to avoid giving the depth of love that is yours to give in the present moment.

The pain of the past may have come to you through another. Your present reaction is yours. You are doing it. You must assume responsibility for your own complex of reactivity. Reactive emotion and reenactment do not need to be a fact of your nature. You can take your armor off. You can unguard your heart and trust yourself to live and love from an intense armorless vulnerability. This is the safest place from which to live.

For some people, especially those with fortunate childhood circumstances, opening through hurt is not so hard. For others, it may be the work of a lifetime. For all of us, it is perhaps the most important work we can do for our own love and freedom, and the love and freedom of the others in our lives.

To be weak in love is to exclusively identify with your separate self, which is always already insulted and empty with craving.

To love is to know that we are all lost and found in the same reality together. To love is to stay open in gratitude and joy even as you know that love breaks your heart.

In one of the great mystical moments of Western biblical myth, the patriarch Jacob sees Rachel, the love of his life, for the first time standing by the well. It is the original story of love at first sight. When you see another truly, your seeing plunges you into love. In their first meeting, the story goes, "Jacob kissed Rachel; he then raised his voice and cried."

Why the crying? Answer the Unique Self mystics, "Because he saw he would not be buried with her."

To love is to know that you will feel the pain of separation. This is the paradox of love: love is suffering, yet to live and not to love is madness. We do not liberate ourselves from the suffering of love by detaching ourselves from love itself. *Liberation in the path of love is to suffer the mortal circumstances of your love so completely that you are moved beyond your self.* You are moved beyond your small self to your True Self and then to your Unique Self, where you realize that you and your beloved will always meet again. Only then can you love fully from your unguarded heart. You are profoundly in relationship from the fullness of your unique personhood, even as you have evolved beyond the egoic self-contraction of your small self.

7. Unique Self encounters require not only integrity but evolutionary integrity.

Your Unique Self is also defined by your evolutionary context. In a Unique Self encounter, you seek not only romantic, pragmatic, or emotional connection. You seek evolutionary relationship. In evolutionary relationship, you seek to manifest the evolutionary potential in your meeting. You let go of the narrow narcissistic needs that initially brought you together.

In an evolutionary relationship, you are obligated by evolutionary integrity. You identify the Unique Gift that your meeting holds. You see how this gift supports and furthers the ecstatic, evolutionary God-impulse that motivates and moves all of existence. *Evolutionary integrity means that you bring all the people of the past, present, and future who might be affected by your decision into the room. You widen your sense of time from the immediate shallow time to deep evolutionary time.*

The ethics of your decisions are then determined not just by the interpersonal matrix between the two of you, but by your evolutionary obligation to all that might be born from your meeting.

PART SIX

The greatest tragedy of the family is the
unlived lives of the parents.

—CARL GUSTAV JUNG

Death is the mother of beauty.
Only the perishable can be beautiful,
which is why we are unmoved by artificial flowers.

—WALLACE STEVENS

People living deeply have no fear of death.

—ANAIS NIN

Let's purge this choler without letting blood:
This we prescribe, though no physician;
Deep malice makes too deep incision;
Forget, forgive; conclude and be agreed;
Our doctors say this is no month to bleed.

—SHAKESPEARE, *RICHARD II*

CHAPTER TWENTY-TWO

PARENTING AND UNIQUE SELF

IN UNIQUE SELF LIVING, events are understood not only by their push dimension but by their pull quality. Push theory explains our lives as determined by a complex web of previous causes. I am who I am today because of my upbringing, heredity, environment, parents, ancestors, and so on. Perhaps the most important factor, according to virtually all the push theorists, is parents.

Yet Unique Self theory argues that the teleological factor—the pull dimension—is ultimately more decisive. *Teleological* derives from the Latin word *telos,* meaning "purpose." My life is ever pulled and drawn forward by its unique purpose and direction. I am following my rainbow as much as I am being pushed by my history. Indeed, my case history cannot be analyzed by the classical cause-and-effect terms of causal history. Rather, I must summon to the table the methods of analysis of what one philosopher termed teleological history.

According to Freud, the impress of personality is made by parents and early childhood, in a fairly consistent manner in every human being. There are a finite and standard set of complexes and reactions that determine the functional capacity of the human machine. *Of course, since Freud was vitally concerned that psychology be recognized as a science, he needed to downplay or even ignore the fact of uniqueness.* Science, after all, is built on universal laws that apply equally to all, and can be demonstrated under laboratory conditions. *Freud is the ultimate push thinker. Parents are the ultimate push-cause from the past.*

A simple question captures much of the pull school's objection to Freud: how can you drive forward while only looking in the rearview mirror?

Freud left a legacy of looking into the past, particularly at parents, for the root of present problems. And indeed, many of our problems are rooted in our childhood. But many are not, and are instead pathologies that result from not living our Unique Self. From this essential perspective, it is critical to internalize the pull possibility that parents do not create children. Rather, in a psycho-mystical way, children create parents.

The biblical masters took this future orientation all the way back to the womb. According to Lurianic mysticism, before a child is conceived, their soul hovers above, inspecting the landscape of possible parents laid out for their preference. The child then chooses the pair who fit the fulfillment of their soul's future plan. *We choose our parents, and not the other way around.* We somehow know the task we must fulfill, the fixing of our soul, and with this knowledge we choose the couple who will best help us to realize the call of our Unique Self.

That help, of course, can come in many forms. It could be in the form of parents who recognize their child's unique call and help to further this in a million ways. Or conversely, the child may realize their soul print by rebelling against everything the parents stand for. Even more complex realities can also present themselves. It could be that the damage inflicted by the parent on the child is the precise soil required to nurture that Unique Self. Of course, that does not excuse the parent. Our issue, however, is not punishing parents but exploring the dynamics of Unique Self development.

The Job of Parents

What is the role of parents in the Unique Self development of the child? *The parent's ultimate mission is to ensure that the child knows—beyond a shadow of a doubt—that they are infinitely special, that their ray of light is unique and precious to the planet.* The parent needs to reflect the child's gorgeousness back to them in a loving gaze or quiet words of confirmation, to be a prism that refracts to the child the infinite love that God feels for them.

Parents and lovers can't and don't need to make us beautiful—but they can and must remind us that we already are. And being so reminded, we become even more beautiful than before. And in reminding us, they move us through the ultimately motivating power of love, to express our beauty in our every step.

God had partners in making God's myriad masterpieces—God's partners are parents. "Three partners are there in creation," read the wisdom texts, "mother, father, and God."

Our first lovers in this world are our parents. Parents are at center stage of our love lives for many crucial years. A parent's obligation to a child is, above all, love.

"What to do with a child who has fallen under negative influence?" the parents asked Master Israel of the Good Name. "Love them more," the master responded.

Ideally, the goal of the parent is to provide the child with the certainty of Being necessary to find their own Unique Self. To recognize the Unique Self of the child is often beyond the ken of the parent. A stable and loving environment is the parents' responsibility, but Unique Self Perception may be beyond even their loving scope.

This is what Kahlil Gibran was getting at in his oft-cited verse from *The Prophet:*

> *You may give them your love but not your thoughts,*
> *For they have their own thoughts.*
> *You may house their bodies but not their souls,*
> *For their souls dwell in the house of tomorrow,*
> *which you cannot visit, not even in your dreams.*

Letting Alone—Like Soil for the Soul

In what I regard as one of the most important psychological essays of the twentieth century, Donald Winnicott writes that ***the job of a parent is to make the child feel safe in their aloneness.*** I remember growing up with a great dread of bedtime, a horror of the dark, and the terror of being left alone. My mother tells me that when she tucked me in, I would beg her, "Talk! Talk!" Even after the exhaustion of every subject, I would think of ploy after ploy to get her to stay. Finally, we would agree that she would sit in the hallway outside of my door until I was sleeping.

Such scenes feature in hallways the world over. Slowly, lovingly, the parent must move away from the bedside, allowing the alone space into their child's life. "Love" is the critical word here. If the child feels loved by the parents independently of all the parents' agendas—*if the child feels loved and not used—then the child will feel safe in their alone space.*

If the parents cannot communicate a sense of loving safety to the child, then this alone space will be terrifying. The child will be in constant need of parental presence, and will learn to behave in a way that will ensure that attention. The child then begins to be motivated by the need to win the approval of Mom and Dad. This unleashes a dynamic that is one of the great underminers of Unique Self. Winning behavior, which keeps Mom and Dad close, is repeated time after time, until it becomes a second skin.

Eventually, the child—who is us not so long ago—develops a false self. The motivating goal of this false self is to be embraced by the parents in a special way, to know that the parents are proud of them and will keep them safe. This is the hope that if I am good enough, my parent won't leave my bedside—that the embrace will always be there. The false self is the polar opposite of a Unique Self. It is not the self of the child—it is the persona that the child sees reflected in the parents' eyes.

Being alone—beyond the reach of the parents' eyes yet not beyond the reach of their love—is seen by Winnicott as critical to the individuation of the child. It is only under these circumstances that authentic uniqueness can emerge. Winnicott intuitively understands Unique Self theory. Although he does not phrase it in this language, he implicitly understands that the role of the parent is to provide a safe context for the child to unfold their Unique Self.

Can I Make My Children Happy?

The weakness, however, in Winnicott's argument is the all-too-accepted premise that Unique Self is formed exclusively in the early years of life. Here, Unique Self pull theory takes issue, and suggests that just as every baby is born with a unique DNA code and fingerprints, every baby is also born with a Unique Self. The role of the parents therefore is neither to be a decisive factor in Unique Self formation nor even to bear the essential responsibility of Unique Self Perception. *The parents are superfluous in Unique Self formation, for the child is already born with a Unique Self.*

Moreover, the parents cannot be expected to hear the call of the child's muse. It is, after all, the child's muse and not the parents'. The sole and critical job of the parents is to provide a framework in which the child feels sufficiently powerful, adequate, and dignified to hear the call themselves. The call of the parent is not the call of the daemon.

Parents are not responsible or capable of ensuring their children's happiness. The idea that they are is simply not true. The empirical evidence for this is overwhelming. We all know kids from genuinely good families who are miserably unhappy, sometimes even tragically ending their own lives. We also know of many children raised in the most unhappy circumstances who are able to build productive, stable, and happy lives.

Happiness is a function of whether we are living our Unique Self, and not who our parents might be. I am happy if I am living my Unique Self. Remember our earlier discussion in the chapter on joy. Joy is a natural by-product of living your Unique Self. I am unhappy if I am living a false soul print, foisted on me by my parents or anyone else, for that matter. There is nothing more dangerous to children than the unlived lives of parents.

The poet Rilke writes this about parents' unlived personalities: "Since they have several faces, you might wonder what they do with the other ones. They keep them in storage. Their children will wear them."[1]

If we don't want our children to be saddled with our unexpressed faces, the most important present we can give them is the alone space to choose their path, seek their soul, and make their own faces.

Erich Fromm wrote on this subject that "the mother-child relationship is paradoxical and, in a sense, tragic. It requires the most intense love on the mother's side, yet this very love must help the child grow away from the mother, and to become fully independent."

The Kabbalists referred to this loving movement as *tzim tzum,* which means "contraction" or "withdrawal." To paraphrase the mystical tradition:

> Just as an all-powerful God stepped back to allow the world to choose, even if the world chose against God, so too must all-powerful parents step back to allow the child to choose, even if the child chooses against the parent.

Or as John Wolfenden said, "Parents exist to be grown out of."

The essence of biblical-myth thought on this aspect of the child/parent dynamic is captured in two short citations. The psalmist writes, "Mother and Father leave me, and God gathers me up." This refers not to the tragedy of abandonment and the comforting succor of God in tragic circumstances. It rather describes the necessary and healthy process of development. Mother and Father must leave me "alone"—in the Winnicott sense of the word—in order for me to respond to my call of divinity. And I must let them leave. I must begin that bedside conversation with the daemon that enters the room as soon as my parent steps into the hall.

Early Voices

To get to Unique Self, we have to free ourselves from the voices that are not ours.

This is true even if those voices are wise. Zen master Bashō gently admonishes us, "Do not seek to follow in the footsteps of the wise. Seek what the wise sought."

A healing of our world, however, cannot come exclusively as a result of each soul identifying its song. In sifting through the voices, we need to recognize not only which one is our own, but also to see and hear the other voices in all their richness and range. *You join the great symphony of Being and Becoming—first by mastering your own instrument, and second by listening deeply to all the other instruments.*

To say something in the name of another is to have "learned the lines" of another's Unique Self. *Peace will come to the world when each person can hear themselves for who they are, without needing to drown out all the other voices.*

It is, of course, parents' voices that are so hard to ignore, even when it is absolutely necessary for our growth. And for good reason. Our parents are the guides who kept us alive in the world during the physically vulnerable years of our formation. In that sense and more, we owe our parents an enormous debt of gratitude. And yet the persistent voice of parents is often a debilitating force in our lives as well. Living your Unique Self means to live with lifelong profound gratitude for all the gifts of parents and parenting, even as you leave the house of your mother and father to find your own voice, your own promised land.

Tradition? Tradition!

True growth is when I am able to distinguish my voice from all the other voices that would usurp the integrity of my Unique Self. I need to be able to find my voice among the crowd.

My grandfather used to say, in the name of his teacher, who received it from his teacher, who received it from Mendel the Master of Kotzk, *"Everything in the world can be imitated except truth. For truth that is imitated is not truth."*

And yet we need to receive from our parents. Without a tradition of values, ethics, and wisdom, each generation would have to reinvent itself. Our ability to stand on the shoulders of those who came before us sustains the core evolutionary trajectory of progress. So much of the pain and impoverishment we experience as people and as a society is the result of throwing out the baby of inherited wisdom along with the bathwater of outmoded family, culture, and religious dogmas.

Just like flowers, we need a connection to the soil of our inherited wisdom, or we wither and die. This is the core teaching of cut-flower ethics. Cut a rose from the bush. The first day, it looks grand in its new vase, standing tall on the living-room mantel. The second day it still stands tall, but if you look closely, you may detect a worried edge in its mood. By the third day, of course, the rose has started to wilt, the desperation is now obvious, and it is not long before the rose is dead. In the same way, our Unique Selves wither and die when uprooted from the soil of what has come before.

CHAPTER TWENTY-THREE

MALICE

The Denial of the Unique Self Encounter

THE OPPOSITE OF A UNIQUE SELF ENCOUNTER is an encounter motivated by malice. *Malice manifests as both the denial of, and the attempt to destroy, the Unique Self of the other.* The desperate attempt to destroy the Unique Self of an other is based, paradoxically, on a primal recognition of the other's Unique Self, and a feeling that somehow the other's self makes one less, or not enough.

Most of the literature of the human potential movement and its daughter, the New Age movement, ignores or even denies malice. But you cannot skip malice if you want to truly understand and practice love. *Love is a Unique Self perception that creates pleasure and joy in its wake. Malice is a Unique Self distortion that creates envy and hatred in its wake.*

Malice is a verb in the same way that love is a verb. However, it is essential to remind you that being aroused to malice does not mean that you let yourself be seduced by the arousal. You have every ability to clarify your arousal and transmute it into goodness and love. The kinds of people that might arouse you to malice are:

- People who remind you that you are not living your Unique Self.
- People who you think, by their very existence, are taking away your ability to let the radiance of your Unique Self shine in the world.

      • People you believe stand in the way of you fulfilling your
         Unique Self.

In these situations you will be sorely tempted—if you think you can get away
with it—to seek to destroy their Unique Self in order to cover up the inchoate
yet agonizing pain of your disconnection from your personal essence.

Know in advance that you will experience great resistance to this teaching. Your primal, desperate desire is to deny any connection between
yourself and malice. It may be that you have never acted it out. This is good.
Or you may be one of the people that M. Scott Peck describes in his book
People of the Lie. I have called them people of malice. People of malice are
people whose own early pain has made them evil in the way that they act
in the world. ***The core expression of people of malice is that they attack,
undermine, or demonize others, instead of facing their own failure.
The attack may be subtle or overt. However, it is always covered by the
sophisticated fig leaf of respectability, or even by noble motives.***
You may know someone like this; they seem respectable, even noble,
yet underneath the veneer, they have wreaked brutal destruction—often
on those who were or are in their closest circles of intimacy. This might
include parents driven by malice toward their children, an employer toward
an employee or the converse, friends and colleagues, a teacher toward a
student, or a student or group of students toward a powerful teacher. Their
malice is almost always covert. Echoing Milan Kundera, it would be correct
to say, ***"Since malice can never reveal its true motivation, it must plead
false ones."*** Leading British psychoanalyst Joseph Berke informs us that
malice is to moderns what sex was to Victorians.[1] It is to be repressed at any
price. It is an obsession, best denied, avoided, or forgotten. The perpetrators
of malice often claim to be "protecting" some imagined victim from harm.
If you even suggest they might have any other motivation that is less than
the pure mask they don in the world, they are outraged. There is nothing
the people of malice fear more than having the lie of their motivation or the
ugliness of their hidden machinations exposed. There is a ferocity to malice.
This makes it intuitively frightening for people to confront. So most people
withdraw into the shade of their own cowardice, covering their coward's
tracks with well-reasoned and plausible disclaimers.

Often the coward finds it easier to energetically join with the movement of malice than to oppose it. This is the worst and most deplorable form of laziness, albeit one of the most common, even if hidden from the public eye. It might take the form of blaming the victim or exaggerating their responsibility. If in some sense "he had it coming," it is easier to rationalize joining the executors of malice than it is to arouse the discernment and courage necessary to oppose them.

In the great spiritual traditions, much of the judgment after our death about who we were in this world, as well as the greatest creator of karma, is related to *how we behaved when confronted with malice that was disguised as a righteous cause. Did we speak truth to power? Or did we cleverly disguise our cowardice with a thousand rationalizations, even as the Unique Self of your friend, colleague, or teacher was thrown under a bus?*

Malice Is Painfully Private, Publicly Dangerous

Let's look more closely now at the phenomenon of malice, so you will be able to identify it clearly. It is absolutely necessary to liberate the world from malice. As you read, keep in your heart that malice is a poison that threatens the blooming of Unique Self more than anything.

Malice operates through a simple four-stage process: Malice (1) perceives genuine flaws, (2) exaggerates or distorts them, (3) minimizes the good in the attacked person's character, and (4) absurdly and insidiously identifies the person with their distorted caricatures, painted by the purveyors of malice themselves.

The internal perception of malice operating in you or your friend is the same as love, for malice is love's opposite. *Just as love is Unique Self perception, malice is Unique Self distortion.* The malice-motivated distortion happens in two ways. First, you might see the Unique Self of the other, but since that image provokes the pain of your own lack, you try to tear it down. Or second, distortion might mean that you cannot see—you see only distorted images of the other—you have lost the ability to see with God's eyes.

In malice you sense the awareness of something provoking you as either an unbearable feeling of intense pleasure or as a "grenvious" vexation. "Grenvy," a term coined by Joseph Berke, is the ill-fated brew of greed and envy that produces the potion of malice.

Malice elicits forceful attacking and even what psychologists in the field have called annihilating behavior. Malice is not connected with legitimate causes at its core—it always hides behind them. It is painfully private, yet when it bursts out of control, it is publicly dangerous in the extreme. It is fed by what Berke calls a distorted "inner world of fact and fantasy, brought about by the confused interplay of perception, memory, and imagination."

"There is bad intent that arises in the world; there is intent to hurt and do evil to other people—we have to confront that." This sadly correct truth was spoken by my beloved friend Ken Wilber several years back in a public dialogue we did on the topic of evil in the world. Ken was responding to a questioner who made the all-too-common argument that all the tragedy that befalls us is ultimately our own creation, and thus we must take 100 percent responsibility for everything that occurs. The New Age narcissists cannot bring themselves to bow before the mystery, so they claim all power to themselves.

Of course, more often than not, the hidden agenda is that the victim has no right to be outraged or demand justice. Since the victim is the creator of their own reality, the ones who have been hurt should be taking responsibility. This cleverly lets the inflictor of pain off the hook. The moral context of justice and injustice, right and wrong, and good and evil is undermined by a subtle relativism in which no ethical discernments are genuinely possible. Or, in a related scenario, the abuser themselves claim to have been abused, thus legitimizing the pain inflicted by them on the true victim. This type of claim is one of the most aggressive and insidious disguises of malice.

This New Age view has found a strange bedfellow in distorted American presentations of Theravada Buddhism. Since everything is the result of cause and effect, you must be the creator of everything in your reality. If you take total, 100 percent responsibility for everything, you will find your way to spiritual depth and maturity. So the popular dharma goes.

This view is not all wrong. It is in fact a powerful and desperately needed antidote to the victim culture that so pervades much of the American spiritual scene. We have been ushered into a new world where any hurt party claims victimhood and uses the claim to inflict all manner of abuse. This often comes together with an abdication of responsibility and often the filing of some sort of suit or complaint. The filing of a complaint gains the ostensible victim a long list of goods, far beyond finances. Attention, focus, community, love, and a feeling of power and aliveness are high on the list. Those who encourage and even instigate false complaints are often driven by hidden or disowned malice.

Often, the true predator is the victim who inflicts cruelty and pain on their alleged tormentor to a degree far greater than whatever imagined or even genuine hurt the victim themselves may have felt. Disguised as the victim, the true predator receives the communal love and support. The true victim, cast as the predator, is debased, dehumanized, and ostracized in a thousand cruel ways.

In this context, it needs to be said that while the Buddhist teaching, with its demand for self-responsibility, is a desperately needed and crucial counterweight to the abdication of responsibility through the *false* claim to victim status, it is only part of the story. At the same time, what is clear from the scenario of false complaints is that self-responsibility is no more than a partial truth. ***Whenever something happens, you must identify what part you played in creating the conditions that allowed for suffering to occur.*** You may have contributed 5 or 50 percent to the system. Even if you have only 5 percent responsibility, you must take 100 percent responsibility for your 5 percent. But not more. The other part of the story is often the malice of other players in the situation.

Taking total responsibility is actually a disguised form of hubris. It is a refusal to give up control. In this case, the control is maintained precisely through "taking responsibility." But your insistence on being the sole creator of your reality ignores the larger creative field of which you are but one small part. It ignores the greater evolutionary intelligence at work in and through your life. It ignores the mystery, and blithely dismisses all other people in the story as but supporting actors in your narcissistic control drama.

Total control of your life in the form of total responsibility is not an expression of spirit—quite the opposite. It is one of the more clever disguises of the narcissistic ego.

What is appropriate is for you to identify your contribution, if any, to creating the conditions that led to your suffering. You can and must take 100 percent responsibility for your part. This, however, is a more nuanced, sacred, and humble posture than 100 percent responsibility for everything.

This posture bows before the mystery, even as it recognizes the possibility of malice.

The Murder of Christ

Humans seek the death and destruction of others, even as we seek their happiness. Both drives and both voices exist in every person who lives in the separate self of the ego. We think that malice only appears "out there," that it does not show up in respectable or polite society. Sadly, this is completely untrue. Lynch mobs manifest in many and varied ways. The prime movers in lynch mobs are energetically attracted to each other. They find each other. They move in unison, almost always hiding their own malice, even from each other. They are drawn to the lynch party to partner in destroying the common energetic emotional threat.

Freud's brilliant student and colleague, Wilhelm Reich, called this not-uncommon phenomenon "the murder of Christ." *The murder of Christ is the attempt to murder life force.* All sorts of reasons justify the crucifixion. A thousand demonizations build the cross. The murderers support each other, often outdoing one another in their maligning of Christ. "See, he is calling himself Christ," they say, in order to give evidence of his narcissism.

Remember that malice is sourced in Unique Self distortion. This is the matrix of the endless cycle of demonizing by those disconnected from their daemon and incapable of owning their demon. They lack the spiritual courage to name what moves them in their breast, which is that "he," the always-flawed Christ they seek to destroy, has a light that threatens their light. He has an appeal, a draw, that is different from theirs. They cannot explain it. So they seek out his imperfections, magnify them a hundredfold, distort and add some major dose of lies for good measure, and the necessary mix for murder is set. Hidden envy, jealousy, and greed are the basic ingredients necessary to conjure the witches' brew.

This is the source of the "Foul whisp'rings . . . abroad" that Shakespeare saw as the source of villainy and even murder. As author Philip Roth describes it:

> The whispering campaign that cannot be stopped, rumors it's impossible to quash . . . slanderous stories to belittle your

professional qualifications, derisive reports of your business deceptions and your perverse aberrations, outraged polemics denouncing your moral failings, misdeeds, and faulty character traits—your shallowness, your vulgarity, your cowardice . . . your falseness, your selfishness, your treachery. Derogatory information. Defamatory statements. Insulting witticisms. Disparaging anecdotes. Idle mockery. Bitchy chatter. Galling wisecracks.

It is in this regard that Geoffrey Chaucer wrote, *"It is certain that envy is the worst sin that is: for all others sin against one virtue, whereas envy is against all virtue and all goodness."*

The Evil Eye

Envy, as we saw earlier, is often the envy of an other's Unique Self, which reminds you of your own unlived life. Envy that motivates malice is directly related to what has been called through history the evil eye. The evil eye is not a superstition, but an inner trait of black character. St. Thomas Aquinas wrote that "the evil eye is affected by strong imagination of the soul and corrupts and poisons the atmosphere so that tender bodies that come within its range may be injuriously affected." Envy then partners with greed, which is an "insatiable desire to take for him what another possesses." It is motivated by a ruthless acquisitiveness, which is publicly denied.

A greedy person is concerned with possessing. An envious person is obsessed with that which they do not possess. Often greed and envy come together in "grenvy." Berke's work remains the most insightful analysis of the inner dynamics that animate people of malice. According to Berke, for the envious person, the "goodness must not be preserved, only attacked, spoiled, and destroyed."

The first stage of envy is often idealization. The idealization, however, cannot last. It arouses too much anguish in the heart of the envier. Therefore, the reverse process sets in. Denigration, equally extreme and unrealistic, follows idealization. This is done to mitigate the anguish of the previous perception. So the elephant becomes a midge, the palm tree becomes a toadstool, and a cloth coat turns into a rag. A kind of hysteria sets in, and there is a refusal to see any goodness at all in the person attacked.

The distorting impact on awareness shows up not only in the envier, but also in the envied. The envied often engages in two forms of self-deception: the envied person idealizes their envier, which is not that hard because often they were once loved by their envier; or they shut down in order to avoid the pain engendered by the awareness of the envy.

One of the demarcating characteristics of malice is its intense cruelty. King David writes in Psalms, "Many have risen against me," and he goes on to describe in exquisitely accurate detail the dynamics of deception and self-deception that guide the ostensibly respectable lynch mob disguised by the fig leaf of the "noble cause." In Joseph Berke's incisive formulation, "The politics of envy culminates in the effective disguise of individual or collective enmity and its expression through political relationships or institutional decisions that are ostensibly virtuous."

When an individual in the mob is confronted, they refer to "all of us," or say, "There are many people throughout this life who say this," and the like, ignoring the fact that the righteous and disgruntled always attract each other.

The philosopher Socrates is perhaps the most notable victim of the "slander and envy of the many," including, of course, the political and religious establishment of his day. All of them nodded knowingly to each other, demonizing Socrates even as they—in their collective pathology—denied any suggestion of their own envy being a motivating force, discounting this as an absurd and malevolent suggestion that did not deserve serious rebuttal.

The envy of the "successful one" by students, teachers, and colleagues was much more forthrightly recognized in older cultures. Among the Khoikhoi people of South Africa, if a hunter has scored a great kill, he is sent to his hut until the village elder calls on him. He is then placed in the center of the circle surrounded by his fellow hunters, who literally piss on him. In this way, a legitimate outlet is created for the enviers to express their discontent and even rage.

If this seems culturally hard to grasp, just note the same custom in Western culture. On Yom Kippur, the holiest day of the year in the Jewish tradition, when the priest offers sacrifice to the divine in the temple, a sacrifice to the "other side" is offered as well. The psychological premise is that shadow must first be owned in the person of the individual and the community before it can be transmuted and atoned for.

Envy corrupts and corrodes love. It turns good into bad. In Shakespeare's *Othello,* Iago accomplishes this by a lethal mixture of slander and duplicity, a process of bad-mouthing and backstabbing. *Envious revenge is fueled by hidden arrogance, unyielding aggression, and pride.* It is based on distorted or exaggerated hurts rather than significant injury. The envier, in their internal self, considers only their accomplishments in comparison to the one envied. Envy, at its core, is grasping for Unique Self.

Envious destructiveness is deliberate. The envious person denies goodwill or love toward the object of their ire. What they want to do is remove the bilious anger and bitter vindictiveness that lurks just beneath their surface self. Their surface self appears more often than not as spiritual, and filled with ostensible good intention and light. It is also possible that the surface good intention and light are real. Envy is often a vicious streak in an otherwise decent and even good personality. This is precisely why the malice of seemingly good people is so persuasive. The envious person wants to get rid of the feelings that they vaguely know exist right beneath their surface personality. They violate their own sense of goodness and even righteousness. Since he (unconsciously) blames the one he envies for how he feels, he sets out to make him feel bad or appear bad. *It is no accident that "evil" is "live" spelled backward. Evil stands against life force. And life force is nowhere more powerful than in the full bloom of Unique Self.*

CHAPTER TWENTY-FOUR

DEATH AND UNIQUE SELF

LIVING YOUR UNIQUE SELF transforms not only your relationship to life, but to death as well.

There are classically three core human responses to the grim reaper: prepersonal, personal, and transpersonal.

The pre-personal response to death expresses itself as various forms of pathological regression, marked by a break with everyday reality, in order to avoid the confrontation with death.

The personal response to death is classically expressed at its best by exoteric religion. It involves accountability, responsibility, and judgment in their highest expressions.

The transpersonal response to death is classically expressed by mystical religion at its best. It involves transcending the personality and separate self into the transpersonal oneness of True Selves, the total number of which is one.

Most presentations of spirit show these latter two responses as mutually exclusive, with the mystical, or what is termed the transpersonal approach, being the advanced response, and that of exoteric religion being the more primitive response, based on its orientation and teaching.

Unique Self teaching critically uplevels this understanding, with its more evolved insight into the distinctions between personality and the realization of the personal beyond the impersonal.

In Unique Self teaching, these two responses to death and the two different maps of culture they represent not only complement each other in very profound ways, but are in fact two faces of the same movement of spirit toward eternity. This understanding fundamentally alters both how you prepare for death and how you choose to live life.

Response One: Pre-personal

The pre-personal response to death comes from the level of consciousness called "submission" (*hakna'ah*) in Hebrew mysticism. Overwhelmed before the reality of death, one submits and is unable to form a response that offers either comfort or transcendence.

The pre-personal response takes on many guises. One expression of the pre-personal response to death is pathological. It appears in its most severe form in various kinds of psychological regressions, psychotic breaks, and the like. The logic behind these all-too-common occurrences is actually relatively simple. The notion of one's personal realm being overwhelmed by death, one's Eros being suffocated by Thanatos, is so painful that the person breaks with the personal realm of reality and regresses to the pre-personal realm.

At the appropriate developmental phase, the pre-personal realm has great loveliness and even seductive charm. The baby who has not yet broken out of their identity with the mother radiates just such loveliness. It is the safety of just such a state, free of all the responsibilities of personhood, that for an adult is the siren call of insanity. We all somehow know the intuitive wisdom of the biblical tale that portrays a flaming sword guarding the entrance to the fabled garden after Adam has begun his evolutionary ascent up and away from Eden. The flaming sword guards against the seductive sirens of regression into the pseudo-eros of the pre-personal, be it a cult, narcissistic materialism, or any other form that affirms the abdication of personal responsibility.

The manifestation of the pre-personal response is moral breakdown. The realization of death causes a disintegration of the ethical boundaries of a life lived in integrity.

The pre-personal response to death produces pre-personal tears. They might be the tears of the depressive who has retreated from the integrity of the personal to the black-holed womb of the pre-personal. Or the desperate cries of emptiness from the one who has regressed to the sound and fury of pre-personal hell, because their life has lost all ethical mooring and meaningful anchorage.

The pre-personal might also express itself in an obsessive pursuit of goals such as money, power, or even knowledge. The obsession itself is but a disguise for the Great Mother in whom the individual loses their authentic personhood. The original Hebrew word for money, for example, is *kesef*, which literally translated means "yearning." The virtually universal obsessive pursuit of money and power is the pathetic and pathological translation of the sacred yearning to transcend death.

All these pre-personal responses are driven by a sacred spark, the essential human desire to survive and live a life that is whole, healthful, and sacred. It is either the thwarting of that desire or the yearning for that desire that is expressed by pre-personal tears.

Response Two: Personal

The second response to death is the response of the personal. The personal response has both an authentic and an inauthentic expression. It expresses itself both from the level of consciousness that we have called "separate self" and from the enlightened awareness of Unique Self. Both are levels of the personal, but they are separated by the True Self. Separate self is, as we have seen, level-one personal—the level of ego—and Unique Self is after at least a glimmering realization of True Self, level-two personal.

The separate-self response to death comes from the level of consciousness that Hebrew mysticism termed "individuation," or *havdalah*. It affirms the human being as standing before God in the realm of time, and in its authentic form insists on the possibility of human dignity and meaning even in the face of death. The personal drive that comes from light is motivated by the authentic need to have a narrative to justify our lives. This is the great Eros that derives from living our story. Even at the level of separate self.

Our natural desire is for Eros—interiority, fullness of presence, yearning, and wholeness. ***By its very nature, Eros is beyond the limitations of the separate self.*** To be in Eros is to uniquely live your story from the ground of the timeless time and the placeless place. Eros is eternity. The inevitable failure of the destroyed separate self to achieve genuine Eros thus creates in its wake an almost insatiable drive to pseudo-Eros, whose goal it is to construct a reality in which the overwhelming reality of Thanatos, of death, is pushed back to a safe distance.

Failure to achieve eternity or Eros produces all forms of what I have termed pseudo-Eros, and what Ken Wilber calls "Atman projects," in which we erect edifices of ego and culture to protect ourselves from the ravages of time and mortality. Some of these edifices are important and positive, many destructive and negative, but all are doomed to ultimate failure, for death always comes knocking at the door. The realization of life's limitation and eventual collapse is sometimes so painful that the individual acts out in a thousand ways to affirm their life force. Ernest Becker reminds us powerfully in his classic book *The Denial of Death* that the fear of death is the essential and overriding motivation for many, if not most, of the most sophisticated cultural, material, religious, and psychological edifices that humanity has erected.

I would put it slightly differently than Becker. It is not so much a fear of death but a love of life that drives humans. It is not merely a fleeing from Thanatos but a yearning for Eros that motivates the human Being and Becoming. ***Humans are afraid to die because they want to live.*** Therefore, if a person has tasted the essential goodness of life, then there is little to fear from death.

When a person transcends separate self and realizes that they are part of the greater one, which we have termed True Self, they are not yet at the end of the journey. They have not achieved realization. True Self is but the ground from which emerges Unique Self, personal Eros, and Essence. ***The personal Eros and Essence of Unique Self is the second response to death. It is the response of "authentic personhood," of a life well lived. A person who has lived well, responding to the call of ethics and Unique Self, has little or no fear of death on the most primal level.*** The fear of death at its depth is the fear of not having lived; it is the profound intuition that our lives are not merely our own, and therefore to waste them is a violation of some great kosmic principle. ***Unique Self's response to the fear of death is not just your life well lived, but your life fully lived.***

In this understanding, both the life of the individual and the history of humanity have a destination and therefore a purpose. Ontogeny mirrors phylogeny. It is this purpose that invests everything with meaning. Life is not just a poor player that struts and frets its hour upon the stage and then is heard no more. It is not a tale told by an idiot, full of sound and fury, signifying nothing. And tomorrow and tomorrow and tomorrow does not merely move in its petty pace day after day till the last syllable of recorded time. Rather, for biblical consciousness and all of its offshoots, it is tomorrow and tomorrow and tomorrow and judgment.

Judgment and mortality are the major themes of level-two consciousness, *havdalah,* or what we might term "personhood." *Havdalah,* which literally means "separation," can express itself either as separate-self consciousness, or in its higher form as Unique Self consciousness. Judgment is not about hell and fire and brimstone. Judgment for evolved biblical people is a source of great joy and ecstasy. ***Judgment means that your life matters.*** Mortality means that your choices make a difference, that they reflect what William James called "genuine options." Judgment affirms that everything you do matters before the divine, the ultimate source of joy, love, and truth in the kosmos, indeed before God who is the kosmos itself. ***Judgment means accountability, and you can only be accountable if you count.***

It is here that the Unique Self teaching parts with the old teaching of grace, which came to free a person of the obligation of law. In Unique Self teaching, grace and dignity are found precisely in a person's ability to be responsive to the law.

This is the great affirmation of law in Hebrew mysticism. Law affirms the intimate relation between joy and responsibility. Law affirms that the human being as a responsible and choosing agent has infinite adequacy, dignity, and worth before the divine. It is for this reason that the classical sources of Hebrew wisdom viewed the day of judgment as a day of great joy, "the time of our joy," *zeman simchatenu,* a prominent refrain in the liturgy of the day of judgment.

The negative view of judgment seems based on the idea that, since the human was bound to always fall and fail in one way or another, judgment was the bad news that needed to be replaced with the good news of Christian love. For classical biblical consciousness, however, law and love and joy were virtually identical. The parents who love their child teach that child to walk knowing full well that the child will fall, but always believing in the child's ability to get up and try again.

The core axiom of biblical thought is the dignity of personhood, which is rooted in the ontology of responsibility. ***Human actions matter.*** The basic breakthrough of consciousness that stands at the center of Hebrew wisdom and is the source of all human dignity is that *there is something that needs to be done.* Every human being is called to do something with their life. That something is infinitely unique in the life of every person. To respond to that call, both in one's private and public life, means having enjoyed a well-lived life.

A life well lived does not mean a life without mistakes. It means making mistakes in the right direction. A famous Talmudic passage, reread by my teacher Mordechai Lainer of Izbica, says roughly, *"One cannot follow the direction of one's life until one first fails in pursuing that very direction."* In another passage, the Talmud itself says, "The wicked man falls once and does not rise, the Master falls seven times and rises again each time." Our response-ability is a constant process of *teshuva*, "return." In the language of Rabbi Abraham Kook:

> Man has forgotten himself. When he remembers himself, he must gather the fragments of his soul from their exile, he must return to himself, to his essential I, and when he returns to himself, at that very moment, he will have returned to God.[1]

Every person has a story to live. If one lives that story with integrity—meaning that by the end of life, one integrates the successes and the failures and rises to a new level of authenticity—then one can stand before God and not fear death.

Response Three: Transpersonal

The third approach to death is quite different. It is usually called the transpersonal approach. However, we have seen that the second approach—that of the personal—when it appears in its Unique Self expression, is also a profoundly transpersonal moment. *Unique Self trance-ends separate self and lives in the eternity of human Being and Becoming.* The third approach to death might be more appropriately referred to as the True Self approach to mortality. It is rooted in human voices that seek to be freed from the fear of death, which is understood to be the tyranny of time. It is the terror of tomorrow and tomorrow and tomorrow, which ends not by standing before God at the end of time, but by entering the realm of the timeless. This level of consciousness is called nondual sweetness, *hamtaka* in Hebrew mysticism.

The great teaching of the Hasidic Kabbalists is that the "world to come"—usually understood as reality beyond our world—is in fact the ever-present spaciousness, the timeless time and placeless place, that is here right now. *Olam haba* is hidden in this world, in *olam hazeh*—beneath and within the illusion of the material and the temporal. In this reading, one transcends death by entering the realm that is beyond death, the realm of Eros that is the realm of eternity, the realm of the timeless.

In this vision, life is a journey, not toward judgment but toward super-consciousness. This is commonly referred to as the transpersonal, but as we have seen, it is more accurately termed True Self. This is the third level of Hebrew mystical consciousness, *hamtaka*.

It is to this level that the Baal Shem Tov refers when he says the crying on the day of judgment leads to *hamtakat hadin,* the "sweetening of judgment." Tears themselves are understood by Hebrew mystics both as the pathway to erotic union with the divine and as primary expressions of that very same union. Transpersonal True Self teardrops hold the very divine image that is the essence of humankind, which when realized invites humans to transcend time into the timeless, mortality into eternity. In the erotic merger with the divine of the Songs of Songs, you realize that there is no outer and no inner, there is neither yes nor no, there is neither here nor there. There is only the radical One that arises and resides from your own True Nature. You are Abraham even as you are Sarah; you walk in Canaan and Manhattan in the selfsame moment; the stars are your eyes even as the earth is your body. Your Unique Self rises spontaneously, and oceans of compassion flow from you to embrace all of Being in the One Taste of your Original Face that is the name of God. In that moment, your tears fall and purify all of existence.

These two complementary responses, that of Unique Self and True Self, are in the actual moment of death expressed in Hebrew wisdom by the two last actions of the human being in a death well died. The first action, or complex of actions, reflecting the *havdalah* consciousness of individuation both at the separate-self level and the Unique Self level of consciousness, is called *cheshbon hanefesh* and *viduy,* roughly translated as "taking account of one's life," a kind of life review and confession. The purpose is twofold: to die without any unfinished business in relation to either people or God, and to think deeply, to garner and gather the insights and wisdom of a lifetime, and to internalize them with joy as the soul evolves through the growth of consciousness achieved in this incarnation. This is the purpose of life review.

Related to this is a final confession and asking of sincere forgiveness, coupled with restitution to anyone whom the person may have harmed in any way, including God. In this understanding, the crying before death is personal crying. They may be tears of joy from the person's integration of insight, which brings a glimmer of understanding and acceptance. They might be tears of regret or yearning for deeds undone and songs unsung; they may be tears of joy at the memory of a life well lived, and even tears of relief as the burden and pain of this world are lifted from one's shoulders.

The second action at the moment of death, emerging from the matrix of nondual sweetness, *hamtaka* consciousness, is the recitation of the *shma mantra*. Why would a person, at the moment of death, waste precious time on a theological affirmation? Is this not at best very strange and insensitive? At this time of great fear, do we need to engage in theological affirmations of the unity of the Godhead? The answer, rooted soundly in the texts of Hebrew mysticism, is that *shma* is not the affirmation that there is one God and not many, but rather the realization that God is the ultimate unity, and that everything, including ourselves, is included in that oneness. No detail is ever separate from the wholeness.

Death, therefore, can vanquish only the separate self. It is death to the separate self that the *shma* meditation seeks. When this is achieved in the final *shma* meditation, the actual physical event can take place in tranquillity and even joy. It is in this sense that some of the great Hebrew mystics have understood the tears before death. They are not separate-self personal tears of grief or pain, but transpersonal tears of ecstasy. The paradox of the personal and the impersonal nature of enlightenment is captured best at the moment of orgasm, the "little death" of the sexual, the Holy of Holies; it is marked by a strong sense of vulnerability, intensity, authenticity, and pleasure. It is one of the many ways that the sexual models the holy.

These two responses to death do not conflict with each other in any way. Unique Self both emerges from True Self as well as being the door into

True Self. Spirit is not linear. True Self and Unique Self are inextricably linked. They are actually two different stages in a process, in which the first stage is the portal to the second stage. From a different perspective, Unique Self and the True Self are not two states but two faces of One, for there is no True Self without Unique Self. Every True Self sees through Unique Self eyes. For in Hebrew wisdom, it is not only that the personal is before the transpersonal (as it is, of course, in Buddhist and Western developmental psychologies), but rather that—and this is very different from both Western and Eastern systems—*the personal itself is both the gateway to and the inner fabric of the transpersonal.* One is invited by life to embrace one's most ultimate and most radical subjectivity, and at some point that subjectivity gives way, collapsing the walls of illusion that separate it from the ultimate subject.

CHAPTER TWENTY-FIVE

SAY YES

THE CHOICE TO LIVE FROM UNIQUE SELF instead of merely ego is the only true choice a human being ever makes. Every other choice flows from this pivotal point in a person's life. It is in this moment, which recurs again and again at deeper levels, that you choose to say Yes or No to life. You can choose to identify with your Unique Self instead of your ego. This is the miracle of meaning upon which the entire kosmos depends.

Emerson said, "Love is the universe shouting out a joyful *yes* when our names are called."

In Hebrew the word "yes"—*kein*—means "integrity." Yes is the ultimate affirmation of our integrity. *The question of your existence is whether you can say Yes to the unique destiny and adventure that is your life.* That is self-love! From the place of ego you remain perpetually unsatisfied. Located in Unique Self, everything fills you.

John Lennon tells about the first time he met Yoko Ono. He heard she was having an art show in London:

> So I went and there was a little white ladder that led up to the ceiling. There was a little hanging magnifying glass and something written on the ceiling. So I picked it up and looked through it at the writing. And what was written was "YES." If it had been something like, "rip-off" or something negative I would have left. . . . But it was positive and loving and so I stuck around.

Love is a perception of the infinite specialness, the full uniqueness of the beloved. *To love another is to say Yes to their Unique Presence, to their Unique Being and Unique Becoming. The greatest of love affairs begins with a simple imprint of Yes.*

Remember, we come into this world trailing clouds of glory with core knowledge of our omnipotence, beauty, infinite power, and infinite potential. And then we hear a chorus of voices for the first ten years of our lives, and the only word they seem to be saying is No, No, No. We gradually come to associate maturity with saying No. When an idea or new direction comes up, our first response is to posit why it won't work. We are brilliant at it. Even the most simpleminded person becomes a genius when it comes to saying No. We can think up twenty reasons why it will not work before we can think up two reasons why it could. *We have all become Dr. No with advanced degrees. But somewhere deep inside, the Yes remains, an eternal child of your Unique Self. We know on the inside of the inside that Yes is the answer.*

One of the great literary masterpieces of the twentieth century is James Joyce's *Ulysses*. Joyce spends reams of pages portraying the No reality encountered in the streets of Dublin by the main character, Leopold Bloom. Joyce masterfully maps the life of the archetypal human whose life is a series of unnecessary losses. The death of Bloom's son and father, his daughter's leaving, the passing of his youth, and finally the adultery of his wife.

Yet in the last scene of the book, Bloom returns home to his sleeping wife. Never mind it is a recently desecrated bed. Never mind he sleeps with his feet at her head. It is still home, the erotic haven of the inside. The book ends with a crescendo of Yes. As his wife feigns sleeping, we float along in her stream of consciousness, finally concluding with reminiscences of the early ecstatic hours of her and Leopold's love. It is a definitive return to Yes:

> And then I asked him with my eyes to ask again yes and then
> he asked me would I yes to say yes my mountain flower and
> first I put my arms around him yes and drew him down to me
> so he could feel my breasts all perfume yes and his heart was
> going like mad and yes I said yes I will Yes.

The Yes here is sexual. The sexual in this passage models the Eros of life. The overwhelming perfume of this sexual Yessing signifies hope, promise, and possibility in the most expanded erotic sense. For the sexual is the full ecstatic urgency of the urge to merge and the urge to emerge throbbing inside of us. This final Yes has magically transformed the seven-hundred-plus pages of modern existentialist Nos. It was James Joyce who reminded us that Yes is a feminine word that signifies the end of all resistance.

The high priests entering the Holy of Holies once a year say Yes with their every step. The cherubs murmur to each other, "Yes, yes." The Temples of God and Man are built with Yes stones. The Presence of God is a great green light that says, "Yes, you are gorgeous. Yes, I need you." The Uni-verse is an open entryway, crowned by a neon Yes sign. To be lived as love is to know that—as Wallace Stevens reminds us: "After the final No there comes a Yes."

In those heart-opening moments when truth suddenly bursts through your everyday routines, you know that the purpose of your life is to uniquely incarnate in the story of your life the love-intelligence that governs the Uni-verse. Are you willing to utter a sacred "Yes!" to your conscious participation in the evolution of consciousness?

To awaken and say Yes to the unique invitation, delight, and obligation of your life is the reason you were born. It is the only authentic source of joy and meaning in your life. *When you slumber and say No, your loneliness, fear, and contraction live in you, through you, and as you. When you awaken and say Yes, you are living as Source. When you awaken and say Yes, Source lives in you, through you, and as you.*

The choice is yours, and yours alone. Do you want to live as an isolated ego, deluded into thinking that all you are is your small separate self? Do you want to rely on the limited strength and power of that isolated self to lift you up and guide you?

Or do you want to open your heart as love, and feel
all the power,
all the glory,
all the love,
and all the goodness
that ever was, is, and will be—

pouring into you, through you, and as you,

raising you up and taking you home?

Everything that happens in your life flows from this choice. It is the choice between living disguised as your ego, or taking off the mask and shining as your Unique Self.

When you are merely in your ego, you *think* you are God's gift to humanity. As a result, you take without asking, and enter without being invited. When you are in Unique Self, you simply *are* God's gift to humanity.

When you are merely in ego, you pretend that you are God, but deep down you believe that you are not. The gap between your pretension and your belief is the source of all of your pain and pathology. When you are in Unique Self, you no longer have to pretend. You have closed the gap. You are joyfully living the mystery of your mythology.

Unique Self is realized by great masters and by simple people. There have always been great masters who were able to move beyond their limited personality desires and align themselves with the God-impulse itself. Sometimes they were hidden, and other times they were revealed. Sometimes they were hidden to themselves.

The evolution of God does not only, or even primarily, take place at the leading edge where people are educated and awake enough to articulate their conscious decision to align with the God-impulse. It takes place every place people say Yes to their highest selves. It is often a hidden Yes, with no audience to applaud. But the Yes is heard in the heaven above and the earth below. All reality claps in ecstatic approval and appreciation.

Some people say Yes because they are expressing their devotion to a God before whom they bow. Others say Yes because they feel God pulsating in their breasts as the desire to grow, to love, and to embrace in compassion All-That-Is. Still others, students of Kabbalah, Sufism, Kashmir Shaivism, or contemporary World Spirituality, say Yes because they hear God on hands and knees pleading with them to say Yes. They say Yes with the full consciousness that they are choosing to recognize, in that loving pleading, the evolutionary impulse surging through them as the true reality of their lives.

God accepts all offerings in love.

"Give power to God," writes King David in Psalms. The Kabbalists teach that God-power is in some insane, paradoxical, and wonderful sense dependent on us. There is a way that God is only as powerful as the power that we give God. We live to be *mosif coach le-maleh*—we "live to empower God," write the old teachers. How? Through realizing the God-spark within you that is your Unique Self, which is God wanting to emerge as you. Through the Unique Gifts that your God-spark obligates you to give.

Are you big enough to be the One?

Are you a big-enough lover to be the One?

Is your heart big enough to be the One?

Do you have enough guts, courage, and audacity to be the One?

All hangs in the balance, and the future of the world depends on your next act. It depends on you.

EPILOGUE
UNIQUE SELF, WORLD SPIRITUALITY, AND EVOLUTIONARY WE SPACE

YOUR UNIQUE SELF IS RADICALLY SINGULAR, gorgeous, and special in the world. But it is even more than that. Your Unique Self is a puzzle piece that is utterly necessary to complete a much larger puzzle that is vital to our planet today. The unique contours of your puzzle piece allow you to connect with and offer your gift to All-That-Is. Giving your puzzle piece unto the world adds an irreducible dimension to the completedness of the kosmos. Uniqueness is no less than the currency of connection. It is the portal to the larger evolutionary context that needs your service. But it is even more than that. Your Unique Self is evolution waking up as you. Your Unique Self is animated by its puzzle-piece nature. As such, it is naturally connected to a larger context that it uniquely completes. It is paradoxically through the inimitable contours of your Unique Self nature that the alienation of separation is overcome. Unique Self is the source code of all authentic relationships, and it is only through a fraternity and sisterhood of Unique Selves that we can begin to bring profound and loving transformation into the world.

As the great connector, Unique Self is the only technology that can create the evolutionary We Space necessary to affect the evolution of consciousness. Ego cannot form evolutionary We Space. At best, ego can cooperate in limited ways for the greater good. Conscious collaboration, while better than mindless competition, lacks the necessary Eros and imagination to change the world. Unique Self is drenched in Eros and imagination.

One might assume that in order to foster an authentic We Space, we must simply emerge into our True Selves. This is the teaching of the classical enlightenment traditions. Yet we know that True Selves cannot create a We Space, for the total number of True Selves is one. In the grand impersonal realm of True Self, there is only one and not two, and therefore, not relationship and certainly not evolutionary We Space. It is only our Unique Selves that have trance-ended separateness and entered the larger field of We as unique emanations of the All-That-Is. Enlightened We Space in which individuals and individual systems realize enlightened consciousness beyond ego is the essential technology of transformation for tomorrow.

Unique Self must be fully embodied today, because only through an enlightened consciousness will we find a way to heal suffering and ameliorate needless brutality and pain. Normal consciousness produces suffering. And if you think this is but a spiritual aphorism, then you have only to inquire from the hundred million people brutally tortured and murdered in the last century—all as a direct result of the mad delusions of the grasping ego. The ego of normal consciousness is insane. Enlightenment is simply sanity. In enlightened space, you realize that you are part of the one. You realize that you are not alone, so there is no reason for desperate grasping. You realize that you are not limited to the power, healing, or fulfillment available only to your separate self. Rather, you know that all of the healing, goodness, power, and depth of All-That-Is lives in you, as you, and through you. Not to know this is not to know who you are. It is to be essentially confused about your identity. The confusion between ego and Unique Self is far more substantive than a person simply thinking she is someone else. This is a minor confusion of identity and hence a minor insanity when compared with the sheer madness of mistaking your ego for your Unique Self as your essential identity.

Why is Enlightenment Rejected by Mainstream Society?

Given the power of enlightened consciousness, which I just described, how could it possibly be that mainstream culture, both East and West, has rejected the attainment of enlightenment as the essential human goal? Should not this transformation of consciousness—which can do more than any other force to heal our planet—not be the essential and even passionately yearned-for goal, of both every individual and every collective? Enlightenment is simply not part of the mainstream discourse. Enlightenment is often mocked and at best relegated to the sidelines, not treated as a genuine option for fully normal people. Why not?

The answer is simple, and it is woven into the essential teaching of Unique Self enlightenment. Classical enlightenment says that to attain realization, you must overcome your sense of being *special* and realize your true identity as part of the one. This instruction is resisted by virtually everyone, for no one wants to give up his specialness. When the price of enlightenment seems to demand that we relinquish our innate sense of being unique and special, enlightenment is rejected by the intelligent mainstream, because at his or her core, virtually everyone in the world feels special. The reigning assumption is that to be special, you must be a separate self, which is the core intuition of the Western enlightenment. So, it emerges that the core intuition of Western enlightenment—that you are separate and therefore special—contradicts the core intuition of the Eastern enlightenment—that you are not separate and therefore not special. As we saw in the main text of this work, for the West, the affirmation of the special separate self is seen as the key to healing suffering, while for the East, overcoming a false sense of separate self and specialness is the key to transcending suffering.

When a person takes their nagging sense of absolute specialness to their spiritual teacher, the usual instruction is to leave behind this feeling of being special, for the desire and experience of specialness is a function of the unenlightened ego. This instruction, while it speaks a great truth, is at its core not fully true. It is true but partial, for it fails to make two essential discernments. Those are the distinctions we have drawn in this work between separateness and uniqueness and between Unique Self and ego. At the level of ego, you are separate, and you are not special. This is the core and correct intuition of Eastern enlightenment. And for this reason, this tradition says you must get over your sense of being a special separate self. But, at the level of Unique Self—beyond your separateness, as a unique expression of the one—you are absolutely and ultimately special. This affirms the dignity of the special individual, which is the core intuition of Western enlightenment. It realizes that you are special, not at the level of separate self ego, but at a much higher level of consciousness, the level of Unique Self.

When you realize your enlightenment, you give up the small games of your ego seeking to reify its specialness, and you move far beyond the alienation of separate self to realize the tremendous joy of uniqueness. You give up the small self sense of being special as you begin playing an infinitely larger game in the widest context, the game of your Unique Perspective, which has singular gifts to give the world, which can and must be given only by your Unique Self.

The Democratization of Enlightenment

This evolution of the enlightenment teaching paves the way for the democratization of enlightenment. As long as enlightenment seems to demand abandoning the essential specialness of every human being and of every human collective of persons or system of knowing, it will intuitively be rejected by the masses. We all hold an intuition—even if inarticulate—of Unique Self. On a deep level we know that every human being is both part of the great collective consciousness, the creative force of evolutionary Eros that animates and drives All-That-Is, even as she is also a unique incarnation of evolutionary creativity and Eros. Each human being is an irreducible personal expression of the process incarnating infinite dignity and adequacy, as well as being a singular expression of creativity and Unique Gift. Since every human being is unique, every human being is an irreplaceable and ultimately necessary expression of the enlightened consciousness.

And, it is only through communities built on this We Space, which emerge from the democratization of enlightenment generated by the Unique Self teaching, that we can foster the genuine global commons that is the next necessary and glorious step in our evolution. Spirit awaits our unpacking. This is the evolutionary impulse, manifesting as Spirit in Action.

Each and every tradition functions as a sort of macro Unique Self, holding a particular medicine that is crucial to the health of the whole. And, that is one of the essential reasons that as we are being called to become our Unique Selves, we are also being called to a World Spirituality that speaks compellingly to the hundreds of millions of people who have moved beyond the religions or beyond exclusive identification with any one tradition. World Spirituality is nothing less than the grand and dynamic gathering of micro and macro Unique Selves who gift the world with their Unique Perspectives and their Unique Gifts, in a way that evolves the one and the whole. It is only through a communion of World Spirituality, in which all gifts from all traditions are taken into account and woven into a higher, integral, evolutionary embrace, that we have the ability to heal our world.

The Why of World Spirituality: Initial Thoughts by Marc Gafni and Ken Wilber

Below are a few preliminary thoughts we would like to share in regard to why evolving the movement we are calling World Spirituality is an urgent need and great adventure of our time. This is not a finished essay; it is rather a set of framing insights that have emerged through our own process of thought and in deep conversation with other leading partners in the movement. All of us are working together closely in catalyzing, articulating, and serving the emergence of an authentic World Spirituality, based on Integral principles, that has the potential to provide a context of meaning for hundreds of millions of people.

Let us begin with a bold and audacious statement on behalf of the incredible group of committed leaders from around the world who are coming together to catalyze and incarnate this new movement of spirit. We believe that a World Spirituality speaks compellingly to the hundreds of millions of people who have moved beyond the religions or beyond exclusive identification with any one tradition. And we believe that this may be one of the vital next moves in the evolution of consciousness. Before we go any further, let us state clearly and unequivocally that World Spirituality is emphatically not, in any sense or form, a world religion. World Spirituality is more like a symphony. In the symphony, there are many instruments. Each one is sacred. Each one has its unique music. Each contributes a particular texture and depth of sound to the symphony. But, all of the instruments are playing music. No single instrument can claim to be the music itself. Each one bows before the lord of music. Each instrument plays a unique and gorgeous sound.

World Spirituality engages all the instruments of knowing, including the ancient traditions of premodernity, as well as modern and postmodern wisdom streams. The term "ancient tradition," here, refers primarily to the great systems of religion and philosophy. "Modern tradition," refers, for example, to neuroscience or to the various schools of psychology. And "postmodern tradition" refers to the insights of deconstructionist writers, phenomenologists, ethnographers, and more. Each great tradition has insights that are gifts to the world. Each has a particular medicine that we need.

That said, each one overreaches in its claim that its particular insight is the whole story. When the part pretends to be a whole, it needs to be rightly critiqued for its overreach. World Spirituality seeks to be in dialogue with all of the great traditions and articulate a framework in which all of the traditions have an honored place at the table and can benefit from the insights of each other, woven together in a higher integral embrace. The job of World Spirituality is to try to cogently articulate a big picture in which a person might locate him or herself in a larger context of meaning and purpose.

The Who of World Spirituality

Many people at the leading edge of culture and creativity today, who are born in the postmodern world, unconsciously assimilate critiques of the great religious traditions. As a result, religion and sometimes spirit itself never become a genuine option in their lives. If citizens of the world today carry the wish to engage spirit, they often meander along, trying to find their way. They are confused and unable to orient themselves to a genuine worldview of meaning that compels, delights, and infuses their everyday life with meaning and direction.

World Spirituality speaks equally to the hundreds of millions of these leading-edge cultural creatives around the world who feel that they cannot locate themselves in a tradition at all, as well as to those firmly ensconced in a tradition who might feel that their identity and hunger is not exhausted by that tradition. They experience themselves as *dual citizens*—deeply involved in their tradition but at the same time part of the broader global community of spirit.

One of the key goals of a World Spirituality is to help seekers, all Unique Selves in the world, feel as though they have some direction and guidance on the way, which helps them to identify: What are the issues that need addressing? What are the general forms or types of practice that need to be engaged in order to live on the spiritual path of life? In a sense, the job of a World Spirituality framework is to help people cultivate discernment as they seek to find their way, grounded in spirit on a genuine path of obligation and freedom.

New Conditions that Catalyze the Evolution of World Spirituality

There are seven conditions that make World Spirituality both possible and necessary today in a way never seen before in history:

1. **Global challenges require a global response.** For the first time in history, the core challenges to survival that we face are not local to a particular religion, country, or region. They are global challenges, ranging from the very real threats to the ground we walk on and the air we breathe, to world hunger, to the danger of nuclear weapons falling into the hands of a rogue state, to the most pressing issues of social and economic justice. There is no place left to hide in the word, and the old spiritual truths of the essential oneness of everything, the interconnectivity of it all, is no longer a hidden teaching, but an obvious truth for all to see.

2. **Whenever new life conditions come to pass, an evolutionary leap in consciousness and culture is required to meet them.** The global challenges we face require the evolution of a new spiritual collective intelligence, which has the erotic imagination necessary to chart the paths that are essential for the next stage in our evolution. In a time when the threats are world threats, the spirituality must

be World Spirituality. The world is in turmoil on virtually every level of reality, even as it is pregnant with possibility and promise. The world faces world problems. Gone is the era when local kings, seers, and shamans dealt with their local issues. There are no more exclusively local issues. Everything affects everything else. Everything is interconnected and interdependent.

Of course, from a spiritual perspective, viewed through the eye of the heart and the eye of the spirit, this was always the case. However, the essential interconnectedness of all of reality was not apparent. The King of Burma had no felt sense or evidence that his actions and decision would affect the ancient Indians who populated the Americas. Now, however, the underlying wholeness of all of reality, the inextricable interpenetration of all of its parts, is becoming visible to the naked eye. One needs to look only at environmental and ecological issues to realize the essential wholeness, interconnectivity, and indivisibility of it all.

New world conditions are always precisely what necessitate the next evolutionary leap. As we realize that the challenges that confront us are world challenges, we realize that we must evolve World Spirituality to meet those challenges. But not only to meet those challenges.

3. **World Spirituality is not just a solution to problems**; it is also the delighted expression of the evolving Eros of consciousness, realizing its potential to dance in the dialectical tension between unity and diversity. We are unique and autonomous as people and faith systems. We are also One in communion and even union with each other. Both are true. Autonomy and communion, diversity and plurality, the One and the many dance in higher integration as World Spirituality begins to emerge.

4. **We desperately need to recover memory.** Not only the memory of the past, but the memory of the future. Without that, there is little hope for the healing and transformation that our individual and collective consciousness so urgently needs. And what is hope but a memory of the future? What exactly is it that we need to remember? Said simply, we need to re-member and recover the story. Postmodernity was built on the rejection of any grand narrative. Metaphysics of any kind were deemed the enemy. Any sense of a canon, a worldview, or big picture was reviled and rejected as a violation of postmodern integrity. Paradoxically, however, the grand narrative of postmodernity became that there is no grand narrative. All contexts of meaning that could in any sense guide or even obligate were undermined.

World Spirituality accepts in part the rejection of metaphysics and grand narratives. It recognizes and affirms that core intuition of postmodernity that contexts matter enormously and that no knowledge exists independently of its context. It is furthermore clear to all of us that the grand stories of metaphysics, each claiming to hold exclusive truth, which were virtually all hijacked by various religions of both the spiritual and secular variety as tools of domination, need to be re-constructed for the sake of the evolution of love. World Spirituality based on Integral principles is a reconstructive project. No longer can we allow dominating grand narratives to crush the subject, the personal, and the intimate.

And yet, all of that does not mean there is no story. All of the not knowing does not mean that we do not know. All of the metaphysical uncertainty does not mean that there is not post-metaphysical certainty. Nor can we allow for the deconstruction of spirit and what Lewis Mumford called "the disqualification of the universe" and its reduction to become an insipid flatland. Even as we bow before the mystery of unknowing and recognize the post-metaphysical evolving nature of our gnosis, we need to "story up" and reclaim our worldview. We need to once again begin to engage in meta-theory and big picture thinking. For, truth be told, there is much that we know in every discipline. We do have deep knowledge, which has been arrived at through carefully engaging double-blind experiments, enacted in the realms of both the physical and spiritual sciences. We do have shared depth structures of knowledge and meaning, which have been arrived at independently and virtually unanimously by the leading researchers of mind, heart, body, and spirit. We have—for the first time in history—been able to gather their data and reveal the profound shared depth structures of knowledge. These sturdy knowings form the basis of a powerfully effective and inspired human user manual. And when we string together these solid beads of knowledge, a truly stunning Integral worldview begins to emerge. This is the worldview of a World Spirituality.

But, in the mad rush to deconstruct all knowing, we have forgotten. We have forgotten that we know. What's more, we have forgotten that we have forgotten. To become whole we need to recover the memory of what we know.

It is precisely a prescient sense of this situation that moved W. B. Yeats to write these famous lines in his poem, "The Second Coming":

> Mere anarchy is loosed upon the world,
> The blood-dimmed tide is loosed, and everywhere
> The ceremony of innocence is drowned;
> The best lack all conviction, while the worst
> Are full of passionate intensity.
> Surely some revelation is at hand;
> Surely the Second Coming is at hand.

The deconstructions of meaning motivated initially by the desire to liberate the human spirit from the shackles of tyranny have run amok and cut the roots of the great universe story that is the Eros and ethos of the All-That-Is sacred and All-That-Is meaningful. So a World Spirituality must be bold, audacious, and rigorous as it weaves together the deepest structures of shared meaning upon which to base the story that we will pass on to our children. It is utterly necessary to re-story and re-enchant the universe in order to create a context for life that is the absolute birthright of billions of people around the globe who have been cut adrift by overzealous waves of deconstruction that sought to de-story the universe.

5. **For the first time in history, there is a critical mass of people who have reached world centric consciousness.** These people have expanded their circle of caring and concern beyond their ethnocentric affiliations. They are at home in the world and feel responsible for the world as a whole, not merely for their country or religion. They cannot be served by ethnocentric religion. For the first time in history, there are hundreds of millions of well-educated people who, although they cannot find their homes in the traditional religions, are searching for a compelling universal set of spiritual principles by which they can live their lives. This can only be addressed by a World Spirituality.

6. **For the first time in history, the notion of what we are calling a dual citizen of spirit is readily understood and available.** Not only can one be a dual citizen of two countries, but also, one can remain committed to one's native or chosen spiritual tradition, while at the same time being a citizen of World Spirituality.

7. **For the first time in history, the most profound teachings, as well as living teachers from all the great systems of spirit, are readily available in non-coercive and open-hearted forms.** These are available not only to people of that particular religion, but to all who would come to study and practice.

World Spirituality Transcends and Includes the Perennial Philosophy

The perennial philosophy fully revealed itself in the latter half of the twentieth century when great researchers of spirit realized that all the great traditions shared a common set of depth structures. This was not to suggest that there was not real and substantive divergence between the world views of the great traditions but rather to point out that beneath the diversity there is an underlying set of powerful shared truths. The great mistake of the perennial philosophy is that—influenced by the great traditions—it made a pre-modern move that undermined its own relevancy. The perennnialists by and large ignored or rejected evolution. They located themselves outside of the evolutionary context and consequently tried to reify a set of eternal truths. They did not realize that we have a shared set of evolving truths and in their overreaching claim they ignored some of the key advances of modernity and postmodernity and undermined the cogency and effectiveness of their own otherwise powerful insights.

World Spirituality = Perennial Philosophy in an Evolutionary Context, with all that this implies. But let us at least make some key points on this utterly essential issue.

It might be fairly stated as follows: to suggest that World Spirituality consists of the perennial philosophy, that is to say of the shared truths of the great traditions, is to be almost certain that World Spirituality will be rejected as an evolutionary emergent. And this is so for two very different reasons:

1. First, if this is what World Spirituality is, the traditions themselves will roundly reject it. If the prerequisite for an emergent World Spirituality is the abandonment of the traditions in the form of reducing their distinctions to a

set of common shared truths, then the traditions themselves will be the fiercest opponents of World Spirituality.
Again, for two reasons. First, no one likes to be put out
of business. Second and more profoundly, the greatness
of the traditions often lies in each religion's unique self
and perspective—which yields its unique insight and practice—and not in the common truths it shares with the
other great religions. Often, as I noted above, the peren-
nialist writers and the interfaith proponents of religious
perennialism posit as their essential distinction the difference between the depth structures and surface structures
of a religion. The argument goes somewhat as follows:
The religions differ only in their surface structures, which
are determined by the contextual factors of culture and
language. Surface structures might include rituals, laws,
and specific forms of worship. Underneath, however, are
said to be depth structures, which the religions share in
common. Depth structures might include the core worldview of the religion, as well as its ethical and mystical core.

This argument is absolutely true, but partial. There
are highly important depth structures that are shared in
common to some significant extent, both by the mystical
and ethical strains of virtually every great religion. This is
true. And the gathering of the shared depth structures of
the religions was one of the great spiritual projects of the
latter half of the twentieth century. Writers such as Fritz
Schuhon, and those influenced by him, including Aldous
Huxley, William Stoddard, Gerard Heard, and Huston
Smith, put forth the core shared tenets of the perennial
philosophy of religions. However, and this is a huge however, the differences between the religions are not only
rooted in the surface structures of the religions. It is more
accurate to say that the religions contain surface structures,
on the one hand, and two distinct forms of depth structures, on the other hand. There are, for sure, the depth

structures that are shared by all the religions to which the perennials correctly pointed. However, there are also the depth structures that are singular and distinctly rooted in the deepest strata of unique revelation and contemplative insight that nourish and sustain the tradition. The distinction between these insights might be termed the Unique Self of every religion. Unique Self = True Self, which is enlightened consciousness, + Perspective, which is the irreducibly unique perspective of every significant culture.

Buddhism, for example, made huge contributions in understanding and training mind states. Talmudic Judaism made a huge contribution to ethics and social activism in the form of *Tikkun Olam,* the responsibility to heal and repair the world, based on the infinite dignity of every Unique Self. Christianity made a huge contribution to the evolution and propagation of the biblical teachings on forgiveness.

While each of these traditions dealt with significant depth in all of these three areas, it is fair to say that each of these religions was also specialized, with a highly evolved and unique area of excellence. Each great tradition has its own radically unique worldview, its own distinct medicine, and its own radically wondrous particular contribution to the music of spirit. It would be precisely accurate to say that each tradition is an instrument in the symphony of spirit. It is not only true that all the instruments produce music—much like all the religions intuit and enact spirit— it is also true that each instrument produces utterly unique music—just as each religion enacts utterly distinct forms of spiritual expression. It would be not only ignorance of the most base kind, but tragic, to reduce all the traditions to their shared truths. And, the key opponents of this reductive dishonoring of the religions would be none other than the religions themselves. This cannot be the goal of an evolutionary World Spirituality.

2. To make the common truths of the great traditions the exclusive or even primary content of World Spirituality would be a monumental mistake for a second reason as well. It is absolutely true that the distinction between the surface structures of the religion and the shared depth structures of every tradition is a crucial insight in the evolution of consciousness and a key part of World Spirituality. This by itself, however, is woefully insufficient as the core of World Spirituality. For, essentially, what that would mean is that World Spirituality is the shared truths of the pre-modern traditions. In this reading, World Spirituality itself would be a regressive movement. It would be regressive because it would suggest that we be guided by a spirituality rooted in the common insights of the pre-modern traditions.

That would take us back before modernity and before premodernity, which is exactly where we do not want to go.

Now, do not misunderstand this point. The pre-modern traditions of Buddhism, Christianity, Judaism, Hinduism, and other great religions, are wildly deep on many levels. The pre-modern traditions are radically profound at a level of interior understanding, which is most likely beyond anything we know today in our interior reaches. The radical inner focus on spirit in the pre-modern age—some would say, the receptivity to the graces of revelation—yielded a depth of interior vision and knowing which is virtually beyond imagination. At the same time, the mainstream of all these traditions remained premodern in many essential ways. They were ethnocentric, marginalized the feminine in various ways, lacked historical consciousness, showed a profound disparity between the elite and the common person, had an underdeveloped sense of human rights, and much more. Each system at its core thought that its truth was primary, if not exclusive, and that in time history would validate its truth claim as the only authentic one. It is precisely that form of pre-modern religion that is once again spreading around the globe with disastrous results, as evidenced in the meteoric rise of fundamentalism the world over. So, to develop a World Spirituality which shares the best of the pre-modern traditions—while an evolutionary step in the right direction—is certainly not the final goal of an emergent and evolving World Spirituality.

Rather, as we have already insisted, we want a World Spirituality that shares the best of pre-modern, modern, and postmodern insights. *That* would be an enormous leap in the evolution of consciousness. Let's bring on board in World Spirituality the deepest insights of *all* the great traditions, including all of the great modern and postmodern traditions. This would include the best insights of psychology and psychoanalysis, not least of which would recognize and actively engage what Freud called the unconscious and Jung called the shadow. It would also include fantastic advances in family systems, economics, law, the healing arts, negotiation theory, and conflict resolution as well as the best insights of systems and chaos theory. It would naturally embrace all of the best insights of modern science. It would include critical advances in health care, forms of governance, and human rights. It would include the leading-edge understandings in the postmodern disciplines of hermeneutics, phenomenology, metrics, and developmental thought. This understanding of World Spirituality as embracing the best of pre-modern and postmodern traditions brings online the evolutionary emergent of Unique Self as a core element in a new World Spirituality.

The How of World Spirituality

At this point, it is essential to locate Unique Self in the larger global context in which it lives. Stated simply, Unique Self is the lodestone of an emergent World Spirituality. World Spirituality has five essential practices, all of which are fulfilled in the awakened realization of Unique Self enlightenment.[1]

Showing Up: Unique Self

The core practice of World Spirituality is the Unique Self awakening or enlightenment of every individual. This democratization of enlightenment, in turn, fosters the evolutionary We Space of collective intelligence and creativity, which is essential for the healing and transformation of our world. This is the next necessary step in the evolution of consciousness, which is the evolution of love, which is the evolution of God. This core practice, which animates all other forms of practice, in the terminology of World Spirituality is called showing up. To show up as your Unique Self and give your Unique Gifts is to awaken as evolution, as the personal face of the evolutionary process.

Waking Up: States of Consciousness and Unique Self

Waking up has three distinct levels.

1. To wake up means to move from separate self to True Self. To wake up is to awaken to your true nature, to know that you are not merely a skin-encapsulated ego, but that you are essence. Waking up is the continual movement from ego to essence. In waking up, you realize your true identity; you are an indivisible strand of the seamless coat of the Universe.

2. Yet full awakening does not end with True Self. In postmodernity, we realize that everything, including enlightenment, has a perspective. As the last vestiges of sleep are wiped from your eyes, you drop in to the realization that you are not only essence, but also the personal face of essence. You are part of the seamless coat of the universe, which is seamless but not featureless. In other words, you realize that True Self always sees through a unique set of eyes. You awaken to the knowing that enlightenment always has perspective. Your Perspective. To wake up therefore means to awaken to the full realization of your Unique True Self.

Waking up means waking up to your true nature—not as separate, but a part of All-That-Is. Moreover, you are an infinitely unique expression of All-That-Is. You wake up *as* the personal face of essence, whose heart is a unique expression of the infinity of intimacy that is the heart of the kosmos. This democratic realization transcends and includes all of the traditions. It is an essential shared practice of World Spirituality.

3. Finally, to wake up is to wake up to the process itself. To wake up means to wake up to the evolutionary context in which you live and to the evolutionary imperative that lives in you, as you, and through you.

In the old enlightenment, to wake up means to wake up to your eternal true nature. As consciousness evolved we realized that your true nature has perspective and it is always ascending and evolving. Therefore, in the New Enlightenment, to wake up means to wake up to your Evolutionary Unique Self. You are the Unique Perspective of evolution. When you wake up, then the process of evolution becomes for the first time aware of itself. And this is the momentous leap in consciousness that potentially changes everything.

Growing Up: Levels of Consciousness and Unique Self

To grow up means to up-level your consciousness. Your level of consciousness is the set of implicit organizing principles that create your worldview. These ascending levels or structures of consciousness have been mapped by extensive cross-cultural research done by leading ego developmental scientists over the past fifty years. For example, it has been shown that human beings in healthy development evolve from egocentric to ethnocentric to worldcentric to kosmocentric consciousness. Each level expands your felt sense of love and empathy to wider circles of caring. In the first level, your caring and concern is limited to you and your immediate circle. In the second level, ethnocentric, your identity expands to a felt sense of empathy and connection with your larger communal context. In the third level, worldcentric, your identity shifts to a felt empathy with all living humanity. In the fourth level, you move beyond merely identifying with humanity and experience a felt sense of responsibility and empathy for all sentient beings throughout time, backward and forward. You identify with the process itself and with the unique evolutionary imperative that incarnates as you. This last evolution of consciousness has also been described as the move from first-tier to second-tier consciousness. One of the key findings of developmental research is that as you up-level to ever-higher stages of second-tier consciousness, your Unique Perspective becomes readily available. Said simply, according to leading developmental theorists, the more you grow up, the more your Unique Self comes online.

Lighten Up: Shadow and Unique Self

Cleaning up is simply a catch phrase for shadow work, which is an essential component of any Integral World Spirituality. The full recognition of the necessity for formal and ongoing shadow work is a modern and postmodern realization, which is implicit but not fully developed in the great traditions. It was Freud and Jung and their respective students who first made shadow work an essential dimension of full human development and health. Unique Self teaching significantly evolves the meaning of shadow work. Shadow is finally realized to be a Unique Self distortion. Shadow is a function of gifts ungiven and life unlived. To clean up is to identify your Unique Shadow and follow it back to your Unique Self, to your unique frequency of light. It is only in light of this Unique Self understanding that it makes sense to actually integrate your shadow, for you are integrating your own displaced Unique Self. This is the essential World Spirituality process of cleaning up, which we call Shadow Integration.

Opening Up: Unique Self and Love

Opening up means opening up to and incarnating love. From the perspective of Unique Self teaching, love has three essential components. Love is at its base not an emotion, but a Unique Self perception. To love is to recognize other. The lover has eyes to see the personal essence of the beloved, so love is a Unique Self perception. More than that, love is a Unique Self perception-identification process. To love is not only to perceive the uniquely beautiful essence of the beloved, but to identify him or her with that essence. Second, to love is to stay open through the pain. To love is to open up to the full depth of life, despite hurt, which seduces us to close and contract. You can only stay open as your Unique Self. The ego can never stay open under attack. The third principle of opening up recognizes to love is to give. To love is to be committed to suspending your ego and giving deeply to another for the sake of their higher good, whatever that may be. Once again, you can only truly give to another and stop using him or her to support your existence after you have evolved beyond identification with your ego and realized your Unique Self.

Showing Up: Unique Self and Unique Gift

It is the matrix of *waking up, growing up, cleaning up,* and *opening up* that allows you to *show up* as your Unique Self. It is your Unique Self that gives birth to Unique Gift. As mentioned earlier in the book, your Unique Gifts are what enable you to address a Unique Need that needs to be filled. The core realization of a World Spirituality is that every human being is both part of the whole, and at the same time, a high priest or priestess in a religion of one. The core obligation, joy, and responsibility of your Unique Self is to give your Unique Gift, fulfilling a Unique Need in the kosmos that can be met by you and you alone.

Each one of these pillar principles has its own set of practices. In our book on World Spirituality (Marc Gafni and Ken Wilber), and in our World Spirituality Practice Book (Marc Gafni and Tom Goddard), we will outline a complete set of practice modules and guidelines.

World Spirituality is Not the Shared Truth of Pre-Modern Religions

As we have already alluded to, it is not only to the pre-modern religions that we turn to create World Spirituality. Each great system of knowing—pre-modern, modern, and postmodern—participates in the forging of World Spirituality. The emergence of modernity with science, the evolution of the social sphere expressed in the rise of democracy and human rights, and the ascension of the feminine are all key components in the formation of a World Spirituality. Can you imagine today a serious World Spirituality without taking into account the implications of Neuroscience, what I call

Neuro-dharma, on our understandings of ritual and spiritual practice? Can you imagine today a World Spirituality without the emergent insights of postmodernity, without its manifestation as multiculturalism and pluralism, without its profound understanding of the distinction between surface structures and depth structures and the role of interpretation and hermeneutics in creating all forms of spiritual and social culture?

Particularly, can you imagine World Spirituality without the evolutions that have taken place in our understanding of Evolution? More important than anything, can you imagine a World Spirituality without a profound embrace of the evolutionary context which depends on us and within which we live? The evolutionary context—the realization that consciousness is evolving and that every generation is responsible for giving its own Unique Gift to this process—is the animating Eros in our attempt to give voice and language to the emergence of a World Spirituality that is already happening worldwide.

World Spirituality is Not Interfaith

World Spirituality is not interfaith. It is a major step beyond interfaith that transcends and includes the evolutionary strides that have been made and are still being made by that great movement of spirit. If one were to map the stages of spirit's evolution from the pre-modern religions to the contemporary emergence of a World Spirituality in which we are participating, they might be something like the following:

1. **In the first stage, when the classical religions reigned supreme in the age before the Western Enlightenment, each religion believed that it was supreme, or at the very least superior, to all the other religions.** Much was beautiful and noble and civilizing in these great traditions. And yet their sense of ethnocentric superiority fostered significant shadow. This superiority created in its wake a sense of entitlement, the rationalization for massive oppression, and more often than not, a license to kill. This stage of religious development has been called mythic religion.

2. **The second stage emerged with the advent of modernity.**
Modernity came along and appropriately weakened the
authority of the mythic religions by demanding evidence.
Moreover, modernity pointed out that many of the prop-
ositions which religions had held to be dogmatic truths
were, in fact, factually wrong. These ranged from the view
of the universe which placed the earth at the center of all
things that the church held as dogma (and was later falsified by Galileo's telescope), to a dogmatically held belief
regarding the structure of the human body (which was
falsified by the dissections and autopsies of Renaissance science), to the belief in the divine right of kings (which was
undermined by the rise of the Western Enlightenment).
Mythic conceptions of religion substantively were weakened. Secularization began its creeping annexations of
the world mind. Within the old mythic religions, three
distinct progressive voices emerged. First there were those
voices often sought to remake the religions in the image of
modernity, and generally lost their authentic mooring in
the core lineage mind of the religion. Second, there were
those who both opened to modernity and maintained a
strong and authentic connection to their core religion
without formally working out the contradiction between
the two commitments. This stage in the development of
spirit has been called rational religion. Third, there was
in every tradition, a leading integral edge of "dual citizens" who remained deeply grounded in the authentic
lineage, even as they embraced an evolving set of modern
and postmodern ideas. They were able to discern between
the evolving depth structures of their religion, which were
good, true and beautiful and the surface structures, which
often invited reinterpretation. This hermeneutic process of
reinterpretation was seen, however, not as foreign to the
religion, but as integral expression of the spiritual impulse
itself.

3. **The third stage is perhaps characterized by the interfaith movement and has been called pluralistic religion.** The interfaith movement made a beautiful contribution to spirit's evolution by getting people talking to each other from the different faith traditions. This movement itself has four distinct expressions. In one expression, what I will call the humanistic expression, the implicit assumption is that the religions cannot be genuinely reconciled at a deep theological level, but if people could just get along at a human level beyond doctrinal difference, this itself would create a mutuality of respect and recognition which would serve to deepen love and lessen religious conflict of all forms. This version of interfaith has been called by contemporary activist and theologian, Charles Randall Paul, religious diplomacy. In this approach, serious "contestation" between religions is encouraged, even as each "contestant" opens his or her heart to "influence," which is a corollary of face-to-face dialogue.

In a second expression of interfaith, what I will call the shared truth or perennial expression, the core issues that separated the religions mattered less because the leaders of interfaith dialogues did not truly take the unique teachings of each of the great traditions, including their own, seriously. In this version of interfaith, the Unique Self of the traditions was often effaced and reduced to some very banal expressions of liberal spirit. Someone once said that the early interfaith dialogues were between Jews who did not believe in Judaism and Christians who did not believe in Christianity, who got together and discovered they had a lot in common. However, this search for shared understanding in the interfaith movement had a third and more profound expression as well. The crucial developmental insight in this third approach was that the shared truths in all the religions are their essential teaching. The shared truth in this version of interfaith both overrides and undercuts what are seen to be the far less important doctrinal, theological, and value distinctions between the religions. This understanding made a highly significant contribution to the realization that what we have in common is far greater than that which divides us.

The core matrices of this highly intelligent and profound interfaith work are the key insights of perennial philosophy. The perennialists, led by the like of Frithjof Schuon and his circle of students and championed effectively and eloquently by Huston Smith, pointed to the essential shared depth structures, which existed in all the traditions. They distinguished between the surface structures, which were held to be culturally and otherwise contextually determined and the depth structure, which was held to be the shared essence of all religions. And let it be said clearly, the perennnialist camp and its highly critical insights have made a pivotal contribution toward the evolution of consciousness. And let it be said clearly, the perennial insights are an important part of the emergent World Spirituality. However, let it be understood no less clearly that the shared perennial truths found in all or most of the great religions are only the first step in the emergence of World Spirituality. Perennial philosophy is a part, but in no way the whole, of World Spirituality.

The Evolutionary Emergence of Unique Self and World Spirituality.

Unique Self, as we have said, is an essential lodestone of World Spirituality. Like World Spirituality, Unique Self is an evolutionary emergent, which transcends and includes all that comes before it. If you have read this book carefully, you realize that Unique Self emerges from an integration of a number of distinct streams of knowing. Unique Self transcends any particular lineage tradition, even as it is uniquely anticipated in key lineage and cultural traditions that preceded it. Unique Self emerges from the deepest insights of pre-classical, pre-modern enlightenment teaching. Unique Self emerges from modern ideas of individuality, the rights of man and the democratization of power, and a growing awareness of the centrality of evolutionary ideas in all realms of thought. Unique Self emerges as well from the postmodern notions of context, evolutionary context, and Unique Perspective—all essential components in the post-metaphysical ontology of meaning-making.

The personal life project of Unique Self invites and obligates every individual in the name of spirit to live their Unique Story and give their Unique Gifts for the sake of the all. It is an ultimate expression of spirit, which cuts across lineage and cultural lines. Unique Self offers a simple yet profound shared spiritual language of World Spirituality that is both accessible and compelling. It addresses the deepest yearning of the human being: to live a life that matters. World Spirituality of this kind is urgently needed today to heal the fragmentation that lies at the very core of the world's heart. It is only this kind of leading-edge evolutionary emergent that will have a wide enough embrace to catalyze a shared world commons. It is only from the space of the shared world commons that we can write a new source code of human culture, rooted in ever-higher levels of mutuality, recognition, union, and embrace. It is only such a World Spirituality rooted in such a source code that will be powerful enough to catalyze this urgently vital evolution of love. It is only through the evolution of love, which is the evolution of consciousness, which is the evolution of God, that we will be able to inspire and write a new Cosmic Scroll. In writing this Scroll, we gather as Unique Selves to create an evolving great story that will provide a framework of meaning, obligation, and joy for hundreds of millions of people who are currently cast adrift on seas of relativism and deconstruction of all world views and big pictures. It is only a new Cosmic Scroll that will provide us a glimpse at the pattern that connects and makes meaning of our lives, inviting us to higher joy and responsibility. It is only in a new Cosmic Scroll that all the great religions and all the great systems of knowing and doing will have a place and will therefore no longer seek to usurp the place of an other. It is only in the context of such a Cosmic Scroll that every Unique Self will have a dignified, honored, and beloved place on Earth. And it is only the democratization of enlightenment as the core teaching of that new Scroll, written by a congregation of Unique Selves in an emergent World Spirituality, that will send ripples of healing presence and peace across the globe.

AFTERWORD BY
KEN WILBER

WE LIVE IN EXTRAORDINARY TIMES. In the history of all humanity, there
have been only five or six major world transformations: somewhere around
a half million years ago, humans began to emerge as a distinct species, with
an archaic worldview that separated us from the great apes. Around fifty
thousand years ago, the archaic worldview gave way to a magical worldview,
anchored in foraging, hunting, and gathering. Then, around ten thousand
years ago, farming was discovered—simple farming, with a handheld hoe,
called horticulture. Concurrently, the worldview of simple magic gave way to
mythic-magic—more complex, and more sophisticated.

Around 4,000 BCE, the animal-drawn plow was invented, and horticultural gave way to agrarian, while mythic-magic gave way to fully developed
mythic, with its traditional fundamentalistic values. The mythic world ruled
until right around the Renaissance in the West, when myth began to give
way to reason, which exploded during the Enlightenment. The rational
worldview, along with its scientific materialism, and with its modern values,
became in many ways the official worldview of the modern West. Until,
that is, the 1960s, which saw the last major world transformation—this
time from modern to postmodern, from monolithic reason to postmodern
pluralism and the "cultural creatives."

And so, there are the major transformations of humankind—archaic
to magic to mythic to rational to postmodern, correlative with techno-
economic modes going from foraging to horticultural to agrarian to

industrial to informational. And there the world stood, with its five major transformations—which are, in general outline, repeated today in the growth and development of every newborn individual. Born with an archaic worldview, each individual develops infantile magic from one to three years, mythic-magic from three to six, mythic from six to eleven, rational from eleven onward, with the possibility of post-rational beginning in late adolescence.

The thing about each of these levels of consciousness, which altogether are called first-tier, is that each of them believes that its view of the world and its values are the only ones that are true and real. The mythic fundamentalist view, the basis of most of the world's exoteric religions, believes its truth is eternal truth—the one and only. Rational science, on the other hand, finds myth to be just that—a myth—and replaces it with evidence-based truths, which religious myth maintains cannot capture the truly important questions of life (Who am I? What's the meaning of life? and so on), and is an approach for which religion condemns science. And then postmodern pluralism comes along and deconstructs both of them, maintaining they are both nothing but social fabrications with no more truth than poetry or fiction. But this postmodern truth, of course, is maintained to be really real. And so goes the battle between first-tier levels in these endless culture wars.

Sometime during the middle of the twentieth century, pioneering developmentalists began to detect hints of an entirely new and higher level of development—a new and higher level of consciousness. Called integral-aperspectival by Jean Gebser, and integrated by Jane Loevinger, it represented what Clare Graves called "a monumental leap in meaning." Abraham Maslow noticed that it was a move from deficiency motivation—needs driven by a lack of something—to being motivation—needs driven by a fullness, an abundance, an overflowing. Spiral Dynamics called this new Integral level "second-tier," in contrast to all the previous "first-tier" levels of development.

And the difference between first-tier and second-tier? Of course, first-tier levels are all driven by deficiency needs, and second-tier by being needs—but beyond that, where each first-tier level thinks its views and its values are the only real ones, the new integral level realized that all previous levels have some significance, some importance, and therefore are to be included in any truly integral, comprehensive worldview. Where first-tier levels spend their time trying to exclude each other, second-tier spends its time including all of them. As such, Integral is the first level historically to overcome partialness, fragmentation, and discord. This is the truly monumental leap spotted by these pioneering developmentalists.

The good news is that studies show this integral level is now, at the beginning of the third millennium AD, starting to emerge in a serious fashion. Right now, approximately 3–4 percent of the population is at second-tier, compared to around 25 percent at postmodern pluralistic, 40 percent at modern-scientific, and 30 percent at traditional fundamentalist. But this 3–4 percent is rapidly increasing, and might reach 10 percent within a decade. At 10 percent, an important tipping point is reached. And with the tipping point, the level's values have profound repercussions throughout the entire society.

In the meantime, those at integral second-tier are already starting to rewrite culture—turning medicine into integral medicine, education into integral education, politics into integral politics, and spirituality into Integral Spirituality.

Which brings us to the essence of this book, *Your Unique Self.* Before continuing, let me first give you some of the context for the evolution of these teachings within the Integral context. These teachings have been evolved primarily by Marc Gafni for over three decades, drawing from his own realization, insight, and the enlightenment lineage in which he stands. In Gafni's reading of this lineage, brilliantly articulated in his three-volume opus *Radical Kabbalah: The Enlightenment Teaching of Unique Self, Nondual Humanism and the Wisdom of Solomon,* which I read in several highly excited nights, Unique Self is a post-egoic nondual realization of Unique Perspective, which expresses itself both as the Unique Perspective on a text and as the Unique Perspective of the realized individual, what Gafni terms, in Lainer's thought, the Judah Archetype, whose perspective is a unique incarnation of unmediated divinity. In essence, the realized individual whose True Self has been disclosed expresses that True Self through their Unique Perspective, what Gafni calls Unique Self. Hence, one might say that the nondual humanism of Unique Self is rooted in the equation I present below:

True Self + Perspective = Unique Self

This teaching was further clarified and evolved in a series of pivotal conversations between Marc and myself in 2005.

These conversations were coupled with intensive dialogue with other leading Integral Spiritual teachers, including initially Diane Hamilton in a catalytic role, and later Swami Sally Kempton, as well as important input from Brother David Steindl-Rast, Father Thomas Keating, Patrick Sweeney, Genpo Roshi, and many, many others. All of this took place in a wonderful translineage context provided by the Integral Spiritual Center, which has now evolved into the Center for World Spirituality, where Marc and I are partnering with some seventy-five other teachers around the world in evolving a World Spirituality based on Integral principles.

The full crystallization of this New Enlightenment teaching in which Marc and I have partnered and this highly significant new chapter in Integral Theory appear in this radically exciting, groundbreaking book. So with that context in mind, let me continue the story.

Traditional contemplative spirituality—not traditional religion, which involves the mythic level and its literal-dogmatic beliefs, but direct spiritual experience—involves not the evolutionary levels of consciousness, but what are known as natural states of consciousness. Not archaic, magic, mythic, rational, pluralistic, and integral; but waking, dreaming, deep sleep, *turiya* (or the True Self), and *turiyatita* (or nondual oneness), which are the five natural states of consciousness found in all humans according to the world's great contemplative traditions. The aim of traditional meditation is to experience all five states in full awareness, moving wakefulness from gross waking to subtle dreaming, to causal deep sleep, to One Self *turiya,* to nondual oneness or *turiyatita.*

In Integral Spirituality all of those states are still important, and the aim is still to contact and resurrect all five—especially including an experience of One True Self and nondual Suchness. But these direct experiences are now experienced and interpreted not from first-tier partialness, but from second-tier fullness—from an integral level. And so all the traditional contemplative concepts and experiences are reinterpreted from an integral perspective. Not mythic, not rational, not pluralistic, but integral.

And this changes, to some degree, everything.

Take the One Self. Traditionally, the experience of the fourth state of consciousness is an experience of the One True Self, or One True Spirit, in all sentient beings. It's a state of pure, clear, timeless, ever-present witnessing—or unqualifiable, infinite Awareness. The Sanskrit term for this is *turiya,* which means literally "the fourth," as in the fourth major state of consciousness, after waking, dreaming, and deep sleep. In Zen, this is your "Original Face," the face you had before your parents were born; that is, your timeless, eternal, ever-present, ultimate Spirit self. In Christian mysticism, it is the state of I AMness—the pure I AMness that you are before you are anything else, the I AMness that you are aware of right now as the simple feeling of being.

The overall number of True Selves is but one. The same True Self in you is the True Self present in all sentient beings. But notice something. Let's say five of us are sitting around a table, and all five of us are 100 percent enlightened, 100 percent aware of the True Self. Each of us has transcended the ego—the small self, the finite self, the self-contraction—and is alive as the One True Infinite Spirit Self. But even though we are all equally the One Self, there is at least one thing that is very different for each of us: namely, the angle we are looking at the table from. Each of us has a Unique Perspective on the table—indeed, on the world itself. So the One True Self is actually taking on a different perspective in each of us. Each of us has a different view of the world, even though each of us is the One True Self. And that means each of us has not just a One True Self, but an infinitely Unique Self as well.

Paradoxically, we each experience not only a singular True Self, which is the same in all of us, but also a radically unique manifestation of that Self, special and unique to each of us. Each of us has different talents, different gifts, and different unique views—and enlightenment involves discovering and honoring our differences just as much as our sameness.

After the egoic self-contraction is removed, and after I discover that One Self, that One Spirit, that One Reality, how do I manifest it? What special and Unique perspectives do I bring to the picture? In other words, how do I discover that my One True Self is actually an infinite, all-pervading Unique Self? How do I honor my Unique Self, discover my Unique Self, manifest my Unique Self?

Well, those are just the questions this book is designed to answer.

The Unique Self gets its primary injunction from the emergence in recent times of the understanding of perspectives—the cruciality of perspectives as being ontologically prior (to reality). What the world is composed of is perspectives, before anything else. We say, for example, that the world is composed of holons—wholes that are parts of other wholes. And that's true, but that's already a third-person perspective of what the world is composed of. So it doesn't negate holons; it's just that even that view is a perspective—namely a third-person perspective. There are first- and second-person perspectives of what the world is composed of as well, and all three of those have validity. But that conception itself is something that has only recently been understood.

Prior to this, in both the East and the West, in premodern and up to modern times, the fundamental nature of perspective simply wasn't understood. Things were assumed to simply be seen, because that's the way they are. The world is pre-given, either in the relative way or as eternal ideas in the mind of God, and we are tapping into those and seeing those pure essences. So in the previous understanding, there's a metaphysical foundation to the world that doesn't change, that is true for all eternity, and the only thing that changes is our degree of understanding of these archetypes. The more we understand these eternal ideas, the closer we get to them, and the more enlightened we become. In that system, in the East and the West, the enlightened nature of human consciousness is understood to be tapping into a "True Self"—a real self, a higher self.

There are always two selves in a human being: a small, relative, finite "Old Adam" (the egoic self-contraction) and a true, infinite "New Adam" (the One True Self). And with these two selves, the small one is responsible for basically everything that's bad, uncomfortable, unpleasant, and painful, because it doesn't see its connection to these eternal ideas, or these eternal patterns in the Mind of God. Awakening to the True Self is the alleviation of that, and by definition, there is only one of those selves.

In all sentient beings, the overall number of True Selves is one.

Now, with the new Integral understanding, there is still a degree of truth to this. As Erwin Schrödinger, founder of modern quantum mechanics, put it: "Consciousness is a singular, the plural of which is unknown."

The overall number of I AMnesses is but one. So every single one of us in this world has direct and immediate access to that One Self—an infinite self that is ever present. Right now that One Self is in some sense hearing everything that's being said, seeing everything that's being seen, knowing everything that is arising. We all have access to that True Self, and our degree of enlightenment is measured by how close we feel to this One Self, how aware we are of this infinite openness, infinite radiance, infinite transparency, infinite unqualifiability.

But even though there's only one True Self in this world, even if every single one of us were to awaken to it, right now, even if everyone shared this absolutely identical sense of One Self, there would still be something that is irrefutably different in each of us. That is, every single one of us is looking at the world from a different angle.

There is only One True Self, but in each of us it has a different perspective on the world.

There is only One True Self, but it is manifesting in as many perspectives as there are sentient beings.

The formula is:

One True Self + Perspective = Unique Self

So my Unique Self is this One True Self, but as seen through the perspective that my body-mind alone inhabits, it is therefore radically unique. So say there is light shining right now, there will be what my gross body sees, what my subtle body sees, what my causal body sees—and even if we are all looking at the same object, we each have a completely different perspective.

And so understanding this formula—One True Self plus Perspective equals Unique Self—suddenly lights up all the individuality of the individual organism that had previously gotten wiped out on the way to discovering the One True Self.

In that journey, following the previous understanding of just One Self, everything is deconstructed and everything is dis-identified with: I am not this; I am not that. Thoughts are arising; I have thoughts; I am not those thoughts. Feelings are arising; I have feelings; I am not those feelings. Emotions are arising; I have emotions; I am not those emotions. *Neti, neti*—"not this, not that" in this pure emptiness, this pure unqualifiable awareness, this one absolute True Self.

All the multiple intelligences are deconstructed—those are not what I am either. So then in a traditional sense, you end up with your One True

Self liberated, but not much idea as to what to actually do with it. How is my awareness in any way different from the *bodhisattva* sitting next to me?

What we really see is that the *bodhisattva* next to me, and next to you, has the same True Self but a different Unique Self—and that Unique Self reinhabits the perspectives that were, in some sense, denied on the way to transcending the ego. That is, the True Self, once discovered and expressed as Unique Self, reinhabits those natural capacities of the human body-mind and all its multiple intelligences. It embraces its capacity for math, or for music, or for introspection, or for interpersonal connection—all the talents and capacities that are given to human beings. These are now reanimated—not from a separate-self sense, but from a True Self, from a radically One Self, One Spirit condition, expressed through your particular perspective.

And that's what makes it unique. That's what makes the activities you then engage in unique. And so this uniqueness is indeed a new version of the traditional union of emptiness and form, because it is one with the unqualifiable vast emptiness that is the Ground of All Being, and that is one with all form that is arising—but now there is an extra little factor added into that. And this is that the awareness of this form is unique in every sentient being. Every sentient being has a unique and special perception and perspective on what is arising.

So that becomes the basis of your particular, special, enlightened capacities. It is the way you can become a true *bodhisattva*—but a *bodhisattva* that is unique to your own perspectives. It is a way to enhance your own talents, and to find your own gifts. And these gifts and talents and capacities are the way that the One Spirit, the One Self, actually expresses itself in the world of form and makes itself known. It's still, in a classical sense, Spirit making itself known—but now it's making itself known through the specialness and uniqueness of each and every sentient being that comes to awaken to the One True Self.

So now there's a whole different way to look at not only what *bodhisattvas* are doing, but how they are doing it, and the capacities they can use, and also to see what really happens in the contemplative process when the Unique Perspective of an individual is realized, and the teaching stops interpreting that as egoic, and we finally end the confusion that Gafni has pointed out; the conflation of uniqueness and separateness.

So there becomes a point in contemplation, once you've deconstructed the ego over and over, and you've gone through causal and gone through *turiya* and gotten into *turiyatita,* when all of a sudden in this vast emptiness you are one with everything that's arising, and you feel that oneness and you will still feel a Unique Perspective on how this arises in your experience.

That feeling of uniqueness would traditionally be interpreted as an egoic holdover, which will prevent you from acting in the world on that uniqueness. All that really does is gum up action completely, because the actual number of things that are recommended without a particular perspective on reality are pretty small and pretty bland. These are often stated as common phrases that everyone is supposed to understand: "Love your neighbor," "Don't be selfish," "Don't get attached," "Act with selfless service," and so on, instead of:

> Now rest in these perspectives that are arising in yourself, and
> see how those are inhabited by the One True Self in a way that
> is unique to you, in a perspective that only you inhabit.

So now it's all about how to spit shine that Unique Perspective, instead of just deconstructing and deconstructing and deconstructing and trying to get rid of any sense of uniqueness—because that's what happens when you're driving toward a pure emptiness without an understanding of inherent perspectival differences. Uniqueness is confused with ego, and denied altogether, instead of being understood as the base through which infinite reality shines.

The capacity for this sort of perspectival understanding is not something that was for the most part completely obvious two thousand years ago, but was oppressed or repressed or not understood by the traditions. It was simply an understanding that evolution had not yet gotten rich enough to bring forth. It was understood that there was *turiya,* or the One True Self, the Pure Witness, and there was *turiyatita,* the Witness one with all form, in a true nondual Suchness. But the perspectival nature of all this was not a part of that equation. And as I said, the understanding of perspectives and how they are ontologically prior to anything that arises in the manifest world is itself a recent emergent of evolution. It's something relatively new, coming into existence with the integral level of development. It is One

Spirit's own evolutionary realization about itself, which is: not only do I as pure Spirit see the world, I see it through many, many, many different perspectives—all of which are I AMness seeing what is arising, but each being unique and special to the pair of eyes that is seeing the world. And yet I am rich enough to be all of it.

It's a bringing forth, an enactment, an evolutionary unfolding that is itself, in a sense, a harbinger of the integral age. It's an understanding on the spiritual plane or in the spiritual intelligence, concomitant with the type of integral understandings that are occurring in other disciplines as well. And all of these have to do with the emergence of integral second-tier, which is unique because, again, it involves perspectives—and understanding for the first time that all previous perspectives have some role to play in evolution. Whereas in all the thousands and tens of thousands of years that first-tier values dominated human behavior, all we did was try to deny each other's perspective. We could see these perspectives, but we couldn't see through them, and we couldn't take the role of these other perspectives. We couldn't inhabit them. Only by the time we reached the pluralistic level was there enough perspectival power required to make the momentous leap to second-tier.

All these previous perspectives are important, and we have to start including them all in order to really encompass reality. And when we add the infinite dimension to that (namely spirituality), it means that Spirit itself, the One True Self, is realizing for the first time that it can manifest and embody in all these different perspectives, and not just force all of them to be reduced to the perspective of the One True Self. There's still just One True Self, One Spirit, one I AMness—but now all of these involve perspectives that I am taking. And it's the same I AMness arising in all of these perspectives that makes them real. And when a sentient being awakens to who it really is, then they have awakened to their own True Self, which will then show up in them as their Unique Self—because it is their awareness of who I AM as seen through their particular perspective.

I AM is now the sum total of all these perspectives. These are all part of what I AM, even though I will act through my own Unique Self.

And so *turiyatita*—nondual Spirit—is itself evolving. It has evolved to a new level of emergence, which is not just One Self one with form, but

One Self seen through many selves, all one with the world of form. And so there's a type of reverse *e pluribus unum* arising: out of One, Many.

The great thing about Spirit's evolution is that it transcends and includes. So we see the essential truths of *turiyatita;* we see the essential truths of One Self, One World, and the union of emptiness and form. All of these are still true. It's just that every evolutionary unfolding adds a new truth—and this one adds the truth that all that previous stuff is still partially true, just seen through various perspectives now. So *turiyatita* is *ex uno, plures*—and that, in a sense, changes everything.

There's still the slow evolutionary unfolding and settling in of this new emergent, and so we're seeing the role of integral perspectives settling in across the board of humanity. Maybe 3–4 percent of humanity is itself actually at second-tier, as we noted, and in the same way we're seeing the switch from the old (but still foundational) form of *turiyatita* to the new perspectival form—evolutionary and unique. That's also a process just slowly taking its role and having its impact in many, many areas.

But the point with these emergents, including the Unique Self, is that they have emerged now in enough people, and in enough minds, and in enough hearts, that they are available to every human being out there. They've become a kosmic habit, a kosmic groove, that is now set. And so it is there, and that's why we can draw on it now, anytime we want. Any sentient being can draw upon their Unique Self, and not just go to the One Self and stay there. So that changes entirely the way that they can relate to their lives—to their spiritual lives, to their *bodhisattva* lives.

As a *bodhisattva,* you vow to go out and change the world. But what are you going to change it with, if not your unique talents and gifts? So even thinking about what you do now as a *bodhisattva* is radically changed by the fact that you're going to act on your Unique Enlightened Self. Your Unique Enlightened Self is going to be the doorway that is going to show you what to do—a new doorway from which you will act, and not just, "I will act on One Self, and my One Self will be the same as your One Self, and we will go out and do One Self things together." That's no way to change the world.

The One Self is still there, but as soon as you come into the realm of manifestation, as soon as you come out of the radical unmanifest, you hit perspectives—that is why there is, for example, an understanding of hitting first-person, second-person, and third-person perspectives of Spirit.

What are those? First person is the person speaking, so that's "I" or "me." Second person is the person being spoken to, "you" or "thou." Third person is the person or thing being spoken about, "him," "her," or "it." And Spirit can be, and has been, approached through all three of these perspectives, whether realized or not. For example, in third-person objective terms, Spirit is a great Web of Life, the sum total of the manifest world as a single, great, living, dynamically interwoven system. When you sit on the edge of the Grand Canyon and behold its splendor, you are perceiving Spirit in the third person. Spirit in second person is a great "Thou," a great "other," which is the source and ground of the entire world. Having conversations with God is approaching God in its second-person form. Virtually all the theistic traditions rest on this form. And Spirit in first person is your own True Self, your own I AMness, the One Self in and through all sentient beings.

All three of these forms are true—first person, second person, third person. Spirit manifests in all three of these perspectives, and an Integral view includes them all. And so the first-person degree of spirituality is no longer just I AMness, but unique I AMness, I AMness in its Unique Perspective. And then that infinite true Unique Self drenches and permeates the entire relative system, the entire relative self, and all of its multiple intelligences are drenched in, soaked in, and open to being part of the manifestation of their Unique Self. So that means that it is the combination of this One True Self, one radical Spirit, manifesting through the talents that happen to be awakened in every human being in the particular way that they show and experience their natural intelligences. For some people, the Unique Self will especially show up in emotional intelligence. For some people, it will show up in cognitive intelligence. Some people will be plugged into infinity in their physiological intelligence. Others will find their connection to infinity in other ways, through any of the patterns and capacities and intelligences that are there.

And then, of course, that's when spiritual practice becomes open—both on the way up to discovering the Unique Self, and on the way down to having it manifest—to a lot of practices that can be done to help clarify the Unique Self: for example, clearing up shadow elements that inhibit this realization. Wherever there is growth of any sort, there is a possible shadow connected with it. There is a functional and dysfunctional developmental scheme in everything, and the same thing goes for this new evolution of Unique Self. There's a shadow going with it, too. And so working with shadow takes on even more importance.

There are different forms of practice available now as well. In particular, certain errors are not compounded that previous schools would have made. The previous schools, one way or another, tried to deny any division at all, and let any uniqueness still be vilified as egoic. All that does is get you using contemplation to not only transcend the ego, but to continue denying your Unique Self. And so contemplation becomes a really sticky, messy thing of using your Unique Self to deny your Unique Self. If I wanted to think of a definition of a dysfunctional thing, that's it.

Now, when this existence of absolutely, inherently Unique Perspective is understood, then with that we can go back and still use many of the great practices of the traditions, because many of them are still dealing with parts of reality that have been transcended and included. But we're also looking for new practices. Just like in psychotherapy we're looking for integral psychotherapy, and in medicine we're looking for integral medicine, and in education we're looking for integral education, and in contemplative studies we're looking for integral contemplative studies. We're looking for an Integral Spirituality that combines a double fullness: the finite fullness of second-tier integral, with its superabundance motivation, and the infinite fullness of *turiyatita,* nondual oneness, now as Unique Self. Not a double lack, but a double fullness, abundance, overflowing.

And that's an entirely new lineage—a trans-path path. This includes all the good stuff of the previous paths, but adds this whole new level of emergence.

And that is something that is extraordinary, and historic, and not to be denied.

EVOLUTIONARY LOVE

One Love—
Kosmic and Impersonal,
Intimate and Personal[1]

IN MUCH OF CONTEMPORARY ENLIGHTENMENT teaching rooted in Eastern sources, the evolutionary impulse is assumed to be impersonal in its essential nature.[2] In this sense, it is viewed as being beyond and higher than the "merely personal." Sharp distinctions are made between absolute love, which is considered "real," and relative love, which is said to have nothing to do with absolute love at all, so much so that they should not be "called by the same term" or in any way compared.[3] This teaching, which has been referred to at times as impersonal enlightenment, reflects a powerful mystical teaching that views enlightenment as moving beyond the personal.[4]

As I have already implied in our earlier discussion of the personal and impersonal visions of enlightenment, in many explicit passages this teaching seems to mistakenly conflate the personal with the separate self's egoic personality.[5] The personal is therefore relegated to the realm of ego, and seen as an expression of the striving and grasping of separate self. It is taught that to evolve beyond ego (ego being understood as the personal egoic personality) is to align with the impersonal evolutionary process, or to awaken the impersonal creative impulse of evolution that lives in you. The higher Authentic Self, which Zen master Maezumi Roshi referred to as the "free functioning human being,"[6] is considered to be an awakened impersonal function. The assumption rooted in the great traditions is that the awakened self, and the evolutionary impulse or process with which the awakened self aligns and even incarnates, is profoundly impersonal, that it is utterly beyond the personal.[7] Evolutionary processes and impulses are assumed to be impersonal. All of this is a true and important teaching. But from the perspective of Unique Self enlightenment, it is only part of the story.

In the teaching of the Unique Self mystics and in the leading edge of Integral Theory, the inner nature of the evolutionary impulse is none other than love. That love is both intensely personal love and at the same time fully beyond the personal—an impersonal love. Deeper truth always lives in paradox. ***Holiness is not paradise but paradox.*** The impersonal evolutionary impulse, which beats in your personal heart, is the very heart of the kosmos. It is one love. Personal and impersonal are simply distinct faces of the One.

In a dialogue on love that I did with John Mackey, the founder of Whole Foods, John said, "Love is not weak. Love is strong."[8] He then talked about the strong force of love in the Whole Foods organizational culture that he developed. John was absolutely right. Love is not weak. Love is strong. It is the strongest force in the Uni-verse. John was intuitively pointing to the great teaching of one love.*

To really get the great esoteric teaching of one love, to know love as the strongest force in the Uni-verse, we first have to understand that love is not just a feeling. Rather, love is the motivating force driving and animating the entire Uni-verse.[9] ***Love is not merely a human emotion. Love is both the currency of connection between human beings and the essential Eros that drives the evolutionary process as a whole.*** Love is the Eros of all relationship even as it is the very Eros of evolution itself. Personal and impersonal love are one. One Love. Evolutionary Love.

At this point I want to share with you something of the Great Story of One Love. It is the deepest insight we have into the nature of all-that-is, an understanding shared by the great traditions and implicitly supported by leading-edge scientists. It is this story that is the narrative and mechanism of evolution itself.

---

*This essay emerged from the first dialogue in the Future of Love Series between Ken Wilber and Marc Gafni. It is a version of that core content which additional pieces integrated at a later date by Marc. This might be considered a first take on this material. A fuller essay on Evolutionary Love by Ken and Marc is forthcoming in a future publication.

There is one thing upon which virtually all the great traditions of knowing fully agree. The transcendent, unmanifest Thatness[10] decided to move from nothing to something. From infinite no-thingness to Uni-verses of infinite diversity, from the splendid eternal perfection of aloneness to dynamic evolutionary imperfection of relationship. The Unique Self mystics realized that this mysterious movement of manifestation within divinity is motivated by love.[11] The great traditions, supported today by the implications of quantum physics, taught that this process of manifestation takes place anew in every moment. The mystics were able to access something of the intention of mystery which motivates manifestation. They did so through the investigative methods of the eye of the spirit. It is through the eye of the spirit, sometimes called the eye of the heart, that we are able to catch the reverberatory waves of spirit's information available in the subtler fields of knowing that undergird and animate all-that-is. The mystic sees that, all-that-is, is motivated to manifestation by love.

Love, however, is not only the initiating energy of evolutionary manifestation. Once manifestation takes place—at the moment of the big bang—love continues to reveal itself as the animating Eros of evolution, from the cellular level all the way through to the highest levels of human evolution.

The movement of love at the human level is the Eros that motivates us to move beyond separation to higher and higher levels of mutuality, recognition, union, and embrace. It is the very same moment of love that motivates the very process of evolution itself from the subatomic to the cellular level, all the way up to the highest reaches of human consciousness.

One Love. Evolutionary Love. It is really very simple.

Let's start with the big bang. Here, separate subatomic units, which physicists have called quarks, are the only forms in existence. Some force then moves these separate quarks to transcend their merely separate existence and reach for a level of union with other quarks. They are attracted to each other, allured by each other. This implicit allurement is the face of mystery itself. It did not have to be this way. The mutually attracted and allured atoms recognize each other and embrace. Separate subatomic units are moved to form a single unit. A boundary drops around them. Whole atoms are formed. What moves them? The Eros of evolution, which is the Eros of love.

Then it happens again. Various groups of separate atoms are moved by a mysterious force to come together. Separate atoms recognize each other in union and embrace. This is Eros as allurement. Molecules are formed. What drives this process? There is a self property inherent in matter itself that moves toward higher and higher levels of mutuality, recognition, union, and embrace. It is this mysterious internal Eros that drives separate subatomic particles to form a new union, an atom, and which drives the separate atoms to form a new union, a molecule.

Then it happens again. Separate molecules, what are called complex molecules, are in proximity to each other. Against all statistical probability, these separate complex molecules come together, reaching for higher and deeper levels of mutuality, recognition, union, and embrace. A separate boundary falls around them. The first cell is formed. Life is born.

Shimon bar Yochai describing the Eros of existence, writes in the ancient Zohar, "It all depends on love." The Christian mystic Thomas Aquinas perceives the same truth, and Dante writes of the love that moves the sun and the stars. Rumi sings of the same. All of these great mystics see through the contemplative, ecstatic, or discursive methods of the eye of the spirit. But the modern person is able to nakedly see the motivating force of love at play in the very cellular roots of reality.

The Eros of evolution is love. Seen from the outside, it is what Erich Jantsch refers to as "self-organization through self-transcendence."[12] The individual "self" of an atom trance-ends itself. The trance of separation is broken, and the individual atom organizes itself as part of a larger molecule. A new identity as a molecule is formed even as the old identity as an atom is not lost. Rather, the core mechanism of self-organization through self-transcendence is "transcend and include." The atom transcends itself to a higher level of complexity, even as its core identity is not lost, but rather expanded and evolved. It is this internal drive within matter that, according to Jantsch and many other leading-edge theorists, moves evolution to ever-higher unions, through ever-higher levels of complexity. From quarks to atoms to cells to molecules, onward and upward. Teilhard de Chardin, Abraham Kook, and many other evolutionary mystics point out that complexity is but the outside view. The interior—not addressed by Jantsch or any of the chaos theorists—reveals that the higher the level of outer physical complexity, the more evolved the inner depth of consciousness. What emerges is that the movement of evolution is the movement to ever-higher levels of complexity and consciousness. At this point, the eye of the mind has reached its limits. Now, a new faculty of perception enters our conversation, what the Christian mystics called the "eye of the spirit," what the Sufi teacher Rumi called the "eye of the heart," and what Hebrew mystics called the "hidden eye." The eye of the spirit, deployed throughout recorded time by the great realizers in all the traditions, in a great double-blind experiment of spirit, always revealed the same inner picture. The eye of the spirit sees clearly that the inner fabric of consciousness is none other than love. It would therefore be entirely accurate to say that the Eros of evolution is none other than the force of love.

Then it happens again. Numerous perfectly tailored cells are all brought together into a single functioning unit with one boundary. Multicellular organisms are formed. The Eros of evolution dances up the evolutionary spiral to higher and higher levels of complexity, and deeper consciousness emerges from the evolutionary soup. It is a continual process of self-organization through self-transcendence, in which self transcends itself to recognize and join other in higher embrace. Love by any other name. The evolutionary ladder continues to spiral to ever-higher and deeper levels of complexity and consciousness. Each higher level is always defined by ever-higher levels of mutuality, recognition, union, and embrace between the evolving cells and organisms. Plants, amphibians, mammals, then higher mammals, until we get to the full bloom of human consciousness. This is the Great Story of One Love. Evolutionary Love.

As human beings emerge in the evolutionary unfoldment—their emergence motivated by the same love that moves the sun and the stars, the upward driving Eros of all reality—there is another momentous leap of development. At the higher levels of human development, manifest consciousness awakens to itself. Human consciousness becomes aware of itself. The evolutionary trajectory is to ever-higher levels of union and embrace driven by Eros. Now, at the human level, love continues its evolutionary unfolding to higher and higher levels of human consciousness. But in human beings, love sheds its disguises and reveals itself in all of its naked wonder.

It was the pioneers of developmental psychology, through cross-cultural empirical studies, who caught this movement of evolution.[13] Human beings at the first level of development are *egocentric.* At this level, our sense of mutuality, recognition, union, and embrace—at the level of our fundamental identity—is limited to ourselves and the close circle upon which we depend for survival.

Then it happens again. Love expands and deepens, and we move up the evolutionary ladder of human development. We transcend egocentric consciousness, and move into *ethnocentric* consciousness. Again, we see operating the same process of self-organization through self-transcendence. As we saw is the core mechanism of evolution from the very cellular level all the way through to the highest levels of human development. The individual transcends self into a higher level organization. The tribe emerges, which both honors and transcends the individual. The move from egocentric to ethnocentric is a move to expanding circles of mutuality, recognition, union, and embrace. This produces the sense of connection that was traditionally the inner fabric of tribes, clans, villages, cities, and even nations.[14]

At the ethnocentric level, love extends its recognition and union with larger contexts of identity. Your feeling of love extends to the whole tribe or group in which you include your self as a core part of your "I" identity.

Then it happens again. Eros continues its expansion. You develop from an ethnocentric level to the level that Lawrence Kohlberg defines as *"worldcentric,"* increasing dramatically your circle of mutuality, recognition, union, and embrace. At this level of consciousness you feel love—a sense of identity and empathy—with all human beings alive on the face of the planet. You are still at the level of separate self—but you are able to feel your connection to all the separate-self personalities living around the globe. You can feel empathy and essential connection with a Rwandan mother, a French truck driver, and an Algerian farmer.

Then it happens again. The movement of evolutionary love continues its upward dance of deepening. Human beings at the leading edge of consciousness move from worldcentric to what has been termed *Kosmocentric* consciousness. At the Kosmocentric level of consciousness, you initially experience a felt sense of identity with all sentient beings, with animals, and with the earth itself. Your circle of recognition, union, and embrace has extended still beyond even your narrow sense of egoic identity with all other separate selves. You identify now with all beings—with the natural world itself. And your consciousness continues to deepen until you transcend your limited identity with your separate self egoic personality, and realize your True Nature. You recognize your True Self as being an intrinsic part of the larger whole, and eventually as being the wholeness itself. You realize what the Sufis called your ultimate Supreme Identity with the Godhead, with all-that-is.

And then your consciousness deepens one last level. You realize that you are not only True Self, not only one with the Wholeness. You recognize yourself as Unique Self. You experience the Unique perspective of divinity that lives in you, as you, and through you. You awaken to your evolutionary context and you realize that as kabbalist Isaac Luria taught and Jesuit priest Teilhard de Chardin reminded us, evolution is waking up as you. Evolution is becoming conscious of itself in you. Evolution is seeking to advance through you. You feel a powerful sense of responsibility—more powerful than anything you have ever felt before—to live your story, to live the unique God-story that lives only and exclusively as you. Paradoxically, in that self-recognition, union, and embrace with your Unique Self, you feel naturally connected and empathetically identified in love, recognition, union, and embrace with all-that-is. *Love is the natural function of Unique Self. For in Unique Self you are so at home in yourself that all grasping falls away, and the lover that is your True Nature emerges as you.*

Ethnocentric transcends and includes egocentric. Worldcentric transcends and includes ethnocentric. Kosmocentric transcends and includes worldcentric. Each of these developmental levels expresses the same core movement of evolution we have seen from the beginning—in which every evolutionary level results in widening circles of recognition, union, and embrace. The principle of self-organization through self-transcendence, which defined the earliest stages of evolution from the level of quarks and cells, is also at play in the evolution of human development. It is all the play and dance of love climaxing in Unique Self.

Three Core Perspectives

Another way to understand this core teaching of Integral evolutionary mysticism is as the integration of the three core perspectives on reality, first, second, and third person, which reveal the three faces of God, of all-that-is.

To explain this teaching, drawn from the great traditions, evolved, and placed front and center in contemporary Integral Theory, let me first briefly explain what I mean in referring to the three faces of God, or the first, second, and third person of God.

Your inner experience is your first-person perspective. The experience of taste, for example, is a first-person experience. Bliss as well as pain are first-person experiences. Your inner experience of the energy of another person, of the taste of ice cream, the spaciousness of meditation, or the inner feeling-tone of love, are all first-person experiences of reality. Your experience of God in the first person is therefore what we are referring to as the first person of God. To experience yourself as divine love, for example, would be to experience the first person of God.

Your experience in relationship to an other is your second-person perspective. It is relational. Second person is your inner experience of the reality of we, of relationship. Your experience of loving and being loved is a second-person experience. To experience yourself as loved by God is to experience God in the second person.

Your experience of an other as an object of perception—as an "it"—is your third-person perspective. It is neither your inner I-experience nor a relational We-experience. Rather, it is your objective recognition of an aspect of reality as an "it" outside of your inner experience or direct relational field. So, for example, when you recognize your friend's height, weight, hair color, and social or political characteristics, or when you look at the physical Uni-verse and describe how it looks, or go deeper into the principles that define the way things work, you are taking a third-person—an impersonal—perspective on reality.

From a third-person perspective, love is an impersonal energy of eros that animates the evolutionary impulse and process. From a second-person perspective, however, the love that animates the evolutionary impulse is more than just an impersonal process. Rather, the process is also personal and intimate. You are personally addressed by the evolutionary process that knows your name. From a first-person perspective, you are lived as love; the evolutionary process lives in you as love.

In the next few pages, mixing freely my own words and those of the Unique Self mystics of my lineage who experienced their spiritual lives as profoundly evolutionary, as well as with other seminal evolutionary thinkers like paleontologist and Jesuit priest Teilhard de Chardin, Integral philosopher Ken Wilber, and proto-Integral theorist, Charles Peirce, I will outline this utterly pivotal teaching on the evolutionary impulse whose inner quality is love. But this time we will look at the exact same teaching through the prism of the three perspectives.

The essence of the Unique Self transmission that we have been unfolding in this book is the second-person perspective. If we are all only True Selves—that is, we realize that we are impersonally part of the One, and as Whitehead pithily reminded us, the total number of True Selves is one—then there is no room for relationship, that is, no room for second person. Second person and Second Taste imply distinction within the One. Second person breaks the monism of the One. It is utterly personal. This is precisely the teaching of Unique Self. If all is one, then there is nothing personal and no relationship. Although, as we have seen, relationship does not require separate selves, it does require Unique Selves.

Mystical realization correctly points out that the separate self is an illusion: you are not ultimately separate from God or other. But even within your oneness, you are not only a nonseparate True Self, but a Unique Self. You and every other person, as a Unique Self, are an infinitely unique, necessary, and dignified expression of the One. Authentic relationship takes place between Unique Selves.[15] The evolutionary impulse is expressed uniquely in every person. The unique quality of the evolutionary impulse expressed through each individual's perspective is the personal face of evolutionary impulse. The ostensibly impersonal process of evolution reveals itself as radically personal. This is the great realization of what I have called in another work "Nondual Humanism". Moreover, the realization of Uniqueness implies that the allegedly impersonal evolutionary process addresses each person personally.

To describe the evolutionary impulse primarily as an awakened impersonal energy that emerges when you evolve beyond ego is to limit your experience and description of the evolutionary process to a third-person perspective. This perspective, as suggested above, is true but partial. *When you move from the third-person perspective to the first- and second-person perspectives, you realize that the inner fabric of all reality is love—and that you are personally addressed by that love. And that there is ultimately no distinction between impersonal and personal love. Both participate in the same essential energy.*

This teaching of One Love is the nondual transmission that I received from my lineage teacher, Hasidic master Mordechai Lainer of Izbica. It is the core transmission of Rumi, Kabir, Hafiz, and all of Sufism. It may be the essential teaching of the Cathars in mystical Christianity, and of the Hindu devotional tradition. In describing it, I will speak from my original tradition, which is the lineage of Hasidic realizers originating in the master Israel Baal Shem Tov, rooted in the teaching of Isaac Luria.

My teacher, Mordechai Lainer, is of this lineage. Luria and Lainer's enlightened realization, born of radical knowing and practice, is that the ever-evolving divinity that appears externally as matter, is realized on the inside to be nothing less than love.[16] This realization is the central teaching of what I have termed evolutionary Kabbalah.[17] This realization finds expression in many ways, including the ecstatic prayer, chant, and dance practice of Hasidism.

The love that animates the evolutionary impulse is not merely personal in the sense of separate self or personality, but it is also not in any sense merely impersonal. It is rather the inner essence of all-that-is, which expresses itself both as the vast impersonal kosmic love that suffuses and sustains all-that-is, and as the radically personal love in which spirit holds every being, as well as the personal love that exists between all beings who have realized their True Nature. For in your True Nature, you are not separate from the True Nature of all-that-is. *Your True Nature and the True Nature of all-that-is—which is love—expresses itself as the drive to ever higher and more sustained unions.*

The utter identity of the impersonal kosmic love and the personal love between spirit and between all beings is the core transmission with which I was gifted by my lineage, and which I have come to know in my own realization.[18]

Personal love cannot be reduced to the egoic posturing of the unrealized, fearful, and insecure personality, which always seems to be searching and working for love from outside itself. This reduction of love to the level of the grasping of the separate self yields an intimacy of impotence. At the same time, love cannot be magnified to the merely impersonal. Love, distanced into vast impersonal spaciousness, yields an infinity of indifference.

On the Nature of Evolutionary Love

Evolutionary love is the impulse to recognition, consciousness, and union. All forms of caring, concern, and passion are expressions of all three of these qualities. You recognize other, are conscious of the infinite subjectivity of other, and move toward closer intimacy through care, compassion, and passion.

In the words of Teilhard de Chardin, "Love is the affinity that links and draws together the elements of the world. Love, in fact, is the agent of universal synthesis. Love alone can unite living beings so as to complete and fulfill them. For it alone joins them by what is deepest in them. Our most urgent need is to imagine our ability to love developing until it embraces the totality of men and the earth."[19]

Here again is de Chardin, in a famous phrase that I have amended slightly: "Someday, after mastering the winds, the waves, the tides and gravity, we shall harness for and *as* God, the energies of love, and then, for a second time in the history of the world, man will have discovered fire."

In every single moment, aware of it or not, you are drenched in the kosmic love that animates the kosmos, and which is alive in and as all-that-is. Every single corner of you is loved and accepted in that love. It is utterly nourishing, radically enlivening, and profoundly awakening. In this sense love is not hard to find. Love is not difficult to achieve. Rather love is impossible to avoid.

This love described by the Unique Self mystics, in my own teaching and that of my realized lineage masters, in Charles Peirce's essay on evolutionary love, as well as by de Chardin and by many of the great traditions, is absolutely beyond the personal, even as it is radically personal.

Leading-edge scientific thinkers are now searching to identify the animating quality of the evolutionary impulse. Some thinkers describe the complex self-organizing system of the Uni-verse as the great web of life. The leading edge of systems theory, and chaos or complexity theory, deal specifically with the mysterious workings of this force, which is sometimes called the fifth force of the Uni-verse. The fifth force is the energy of attraction (which I would call Eros) that brings things together, called the "fifth" to distinguish it from the four physical forces that govern reality. The first four forces are generally thought to be nuclear, gravitational, magnetic, the strong, and the weak.

The fifth force is the inherent tendency of matter to self-organize, to rise above a chaotic state to more complex forms that are more unified. Seen from the inside by the great realizers, through the eye of the spirit, each level of complexity is innately more conscious, which ultimately means more loving.

A phrase like "fifth force" describes the outside of the reality. Seen from the inside, that same force can be described as love.

When we describe the Uni-verse as the great Web of Life, or use phrases like "fifth force of the Uni-verse," we are taking a third-person view of reality. In third person, we see reality as a complex evolving meshwork of integrated matter—of "its." This is precisely right. This perception of reality comes from deploying particular faculties of perception, namely the empirical and logical eyes of the sense and the eye of the mind. These faculties do not, however, exhaust our ways of knowing reality. Deploying the faculties of perception available through a different "eye of the spirit," a different face of the same reality is revealed. *The eye of the spirit reveals beyond a shadow of a doubt that the inner quality of matter is consciousness, and that the inner quality of consciousness is love.*[20]

It is to this truth that the Hindu mystics pointed in their epigram *sat-chit-ananda*. *Sat* is being. *Chit* is consciousness, which is the inner nature of being. *Ananda* is love, which is the inner nature of consciousness. Evolutionary drive unfolding reality to successively higher and deeper levels of complexity and consciousness is none other than love.

It is to this love that Alfred North Whitehead referred when he said that evolution is really "the gentle movement toward God by the gentle persuasion of love." *Love is the fabric of the Uni-verse, the glue that holds the Uni-verse together. The Uni-verse feels, and it feels love. It is one Uni-verse precisely through the gentle persuasion of love operating throughout the kosmos. It is this precise force of love that also manifests in the realm of the personal as authentic love between human beings.*[21]

Love's Direction

There's a direction to evolution. This is the revelation of the eye of the spirit, which discloses glimmerings of the interior face of the kosmos. That direction is toward Eros, or love. Love manifests in third person as evolutionary emergence powered by a driving Eros. This Eros is now being expressed by leading-edge voices in science like Stuart Kauffman and Erich Jantsch, as an inherent drive in matter toward self-organization and self-transcendence.

Whatever that drive is, one thing is clear: it is the opposite of chance. As I mentioned earlier, the dogma of scientism that claims evolution to be random, chance, or natural necessity is exactly wrong. It is simply impossible to make the probabilities and the numbers and the statistics work. As Ken Wilber likes to say, there is no chance that we went from dirt to Shakespeare by chance, that is to say, based on arbitrarily selected random mutations over billions of years.

Evolution in Second- and First-Person Perspectives

So the evolutionary process, seen from a third-person perspective, is the self-organizing drive to greater levels of complexity. As we have seen, however, we can also describe the evolutionary process in first- and second-person terms. Every time a more complex material form emerges, a greater degree of consciousness emerges as well. This is always true. ***Consciousness increases as the complexity of matter increases.*** And with greater consciousness comes greater integration, cooperation, and union—that is to say, greater love.

We see consciousness increase from the little prehension it has in atoms, up to the emergence of amphibians and life-forms with neural nets, then up into paleomammals with limbic systems, followed by mammals with the capacity to form images and symbols, up to chimpanzees, apes, and gorillas with the capacity to form early concepts, and so on. This continues up to humans, who have a triune brain and the capacity to form complex rules, as well as the capacity to awaken to the source of this entire sequence, which of course is spirit, whether we look at it from first person or second person or third person.

In third person, it is the drive to higher and higher forms of complexity. In first person, it is the drive to higher and higher consciousness. In second person, it is the drive to more and more inclusive forms of love recognition and embrace. For instance, from a second-person perspective, we could say that when molecules form out of atoms, that the molecule is embracing the atom—even that the molecule is loving the atom. (Of course, I'm not suggesting that molecules have conscious personal agency!) From a first-person perspective, we might say that the interior proto-I-ness of the molecule is expanding to include others into its own self.

Cellular Love in Human Beings

When we look at the way love works in human life, we begin to realize that human beings have emerged in part as a higher expression of love. Love is an insistent Eros, an insistent pressure in human beings. One of the major drives human beings have is the drive to love.

To uncover evolutionary love in human guise, let's turn briefly to the studies of the great developmental psychologist Abraham Maslow. Maslow began the developmental study of human beings' motivations. Why does a human being do something? Maslow found that there is a holarchy of needs.[22]

Holarchy means a nested hierarchy, a hierarchy that's inclusive of the levels that come before it, not a dominator hierarchy.[23]

Maslow's empirical research, backed up by other developmental psychologists, shows that as human beings evolve to higher levels of consciousness, they are no longer satisfied by merely meeting their basic needs for safety, community, self-esteem, or even self-actualization.[24] All of these needs are what Maslow called deficiency needs. They emerge to meet a felt sense of lack in the human being, which is fueled by the appropriate strategies of the separate self.

Once those needs are met, however, a new kind of need becomes dominant in the human heart. It is what Maslow called a need for self-transcendence. This need—motivated by the fullness of Eros and love—to include others in one's boundary of self, expresses itself as a profound desire to give, to serve, and to include others in one's own self-definition—is the miracle of We. In the original Hebrew, the word for "love" derives from the root word, *hav*, which means "radical giving." This is the movement of love and Eros, which began at the cellular level and ascends up the evolutionary scale to the leading edges of human consciousness. It is a constant movement toward ever-higher recognition, inclusion, and embrace.

This movement of love and Eros, which is visible in third person from the simplest cellular level to the most advanced human level, is at all times felt in the second person as love. *In the realized human being, love breaks out.* This is, finally, love revealed. Because evolution is the constant increase of complexity—paralleled on the interior by the constant increase of consciousness, whose inner relational quality is love—in the evolved human being who has reached the level of self-transcendence, the operation of love itself breaks into consciousness and becomes a prime motivator for individuals.

In evolutionary mysticism, self-transcendence is what happens when you become so full that you cannot possibly feel sufficient unless you break out of the small self toward True and Unique Self. In True Self, whose personal face is Unique Self, you not only act lovingly, you are lived as love. True Self and Unique Self, having trance-ended the limited identity with separate self, are moved by the infinite spaciousness of True Self, coupled with the infinite fullness of Unique Self, to ever-greater depths of love and Eros.

So, we might recapitulate this entire great movement to evolutionary love and Eros in the following manner:

1. The evolutionary process is the evolution of complexity. This is a third-person perspective.

2. Higher and higher levels of complexity in evolution are paralleled by ever-higher levels of consciousness. Complexity is the view from the outside, and consciousness is the view from the inside.

3. The inner experience of consciousness is none other than love. This is the realization revealed to mystics, over and over again, by the eye of the spirit.* This great perception of the eye of the spirit was transmitted to us by the greatest mystics and realizers from all traditions over all of recorded time. None of them knew each other. In this sense, the practices that open the eye of the spirit and lead to enlightenment, enacted repeatedly by leading-edge realizers all over the world and who did not know each other, may be viewed as a great double-blind experiment of spirit. Over and over again, they report experiences of seeing the kosmos with the eye of the spirit—and recognizing that

---

*A peak experience was made available to the masses through holotropic substances, whose effect in the brain can make possible an open-eyed recognition of oneness and love. In a filmed interview by Dr. Sidney Cohen, a researcher on LSD at the Los Angeles Veterans Administration Hospital in the 1950s, a man identified only as Joe is asked to describe his experience, and he says, "People who appeared dull in my eyes suddenly become so fascinating, so mysterious, so wonderful. Suddenly you notice that there aren't these separations . . . we aren't these separate islands shouting across to someone else . . . this thing is flowing underneath . . . we are parts of a single continent, it's all connected beneath the water . . . and with this flows such delight. The sober certainty of waking bliss." Love by any other name.

the inner face of consciousness is love.

4. The more complexity, the deeper the consciousness, the more we become aware of ever-increasing levels of Uniqueness. Just as the human physiological structure is more complex than that of the previous rungs of evolution, it is also more conscious and more unique. One has only to look at the human immune system to see a display of radical uniqueness.

5. The evolution of love is both the evolution of consciousness and the evolution of one's perception. In the intersubjective context, as we will see in a later chapter, love is a Unique Self perception, a spectacular awakened function in a human being that allows them to perceive and delight in the infinite uniqueness of an other.

6. The same love that drives the evolutionary process from cells to human beings, in ever-increasing levels of recognition, union, and embrace, is the very same love that manifests between people as Unique Self perception. It is that love as Unique Self perception that motivates human beings to transcend separate self and move toward each other in ever-increasing levels of recognition, union, and embrace.

Love, which previously was cloaked in third-person as an impersonal force, becomes obvious in second person and first person. This is the awesome realization that impersonal kosmic love and personal human love at their highest levels are one and the same. One love expresses itself all up and down the great chain of being, and all up and down the evolutionary ladder. We see love in action in our lives and feel love as Source from which we live. More than that, we are capable of articulating our first-person love and sharing it in second-person conversation and third-person reporting. This is the momentous evolutionary leap of love at the leading edge of human consciousness.

CORE RECAPITULATION OF UNIQUE SELF

EVERY EVOLVED CULTURE AND EVERY EVOLVED INDIVIDUAL may realize Unique Self when True Self awakens to its Unique Perspective. Unique Perspective is the prism of postmodern revelation. An early expression of this insight, expressed as True Self + Perspective = Unique Self, is sourced in premodernity in the great teachings of the kabbalists. For these masters, the sacred text of the Torah is the word of God. Yet, paradoxically, in Hebrew mystical teaching it is said that a human being who is deeply grounded in True Self while fully incarnating his or her own uniqueness, also speaks the word of God! Human insight, however, is considered the word of God and given the status of Torah only when it derives directly from the clarified unique perspective of a human being who is connected to the ground of True Self. In this radical teaching the ultimate identity between a human being and the godhead is only realized through the paradoxical portal of radical human uniqueness. Irreducible uniqueness, the full inhabiting of unique perspective or voice, is revealed to be an absolute quality of essence.

In modernity and especially in postmodernity, this early realization of the kabbalists in regard to the primacy of perspective takes center stage. There is an emergent cultural realization, placed front and center in Integral theory, that perspectives are foundational. But in post-modernity, perspectives have too often been used as the key tool for post-modernity's deconstructive project. The sentence used to deny all truth is "that's just your perspective".

Our conclusion in World Spirituality teaching, however, is different from that of the post-modern deconstructive thinkers who were among the champions of this insight. Deconstructive thinkers assume that when perspective is revealed to be part of the process of meaning making there is no longer any real meaning. However, in the World Spirituality teachings, we understand perspective in this way: Every culture and every great tradition of spirit has its own Unique Self and therefore its own unique perspective. Perspective reveals a plenitude of meaning and not a dearth or death of meaning.

All cultures perceive Essence, but each unique perspective gives a particular resonance and cast to Essence. Loyalty to one's religion and culture is not, therefore (as modern and postmodern fashions sometimes suggest), primitive or fundamentalist. Instead, it is *partially true* in that it is how *my* culture intuits essence. The premodern mistake was the failure to realize that every religion has a particular perspective, and therefore not to realize that no religion can claim that its intuition of ultimate truth is the only truth. Now that we understand that every great tradition and culture perceived essence through a particular perspective, we can avoid the tragic mistake of deconstructing the traditions as meaningless. Instead, we understand that every tradition has a particular perspective, a particular instrument in the symphony of spirit that is indeed making sacred music. All of the perspectives come together to create a symphony. And at that point, there is the possibility that the followers of each tradition can begin to realize that their particular religion is not the music, but an instrument of the music.

The kabbalists foreshadow our post- postmodern World Spirituality reconstructive project. Nothing is true, says postmodernity, because everything is contextual. For the kabbalists foreshadowing World Spirituality teaching, the opposite is correct. When you fully inhabit your unique perspective, you enter into Source. You not only speak the word of God, you incarnate the word of God. World Spirituality based on Integral principles, including the first principle of Unique Self, understands that uniqueness reveals essence through a particular prism. Perspective creates not a dearth of truth, but a magnificent kaleidoscope of truth. Every authentic insight deriving from Unique Perspective is true but partial. No part is reducible to the whole, but no part stands alone. It is this insight of Unique Self that is the foundation of the great reconstructive project, which is Spirit's Next Move.

UNIQUE SELF AND WOUNDED SELF

THERE ARE TEACHINGS THAT SUGGEST that when you awaken to and identify with the process of evolution moving in you, your wounds will not matter so much anymore. The core of this teaching is that when you move beyond the personal to the impersonal, only the process matters. If you just identify with some version of your higher self you can leave your psychological problems behind.

This is a true but partial teaching. It suffers from a number of essential limitations, not least of which is the false split between the personal and the impersonal.

First, let's say what's true about the teaching. If you are living within the narrow identity of your skin-encapsulated ego and you have suffered betrayal or abuse in your life, then it is likely that the pain of these wounds will take up an enormous amount of your psychic space and emotional energy. However, if you have evolved beyond identification with ego to a lived identity with your Unique Self, your relationship with your wounds will dramatically shift. Your Unique Self lives and breathes aligned with the larger evolutionary framework, seeking to contribute your Unique Gifts for the sake of the larger whole. In such a large context, the evolutionary perspective of Unique Self naturally puts your wounds in perspective. This means that you will be able to see your wounds from a kosmocentric perspective instead of from an egocentric perspective. Identifying yourself as a Unique expression of the divine, responsible for co-creating the next evolutionary leap toward greater love, inclusion, and embrace—the kos-mocentric perspective—obviously places your wounds in such a wider lens that your personal obsession with the insults of your life is exposed for the narcissism that it is.

But narcissism it is—only in part. Holding your enlightened kosmo-centric realization more deeply, you understand that you are not merely part of the whole, in the sense of being a cog in a machine or a link in a process. Rather your part is the whole itself. Your part—that is to say, you—has infinite value, dignity, and worth. *The pain of your part, your pain, is the pain of All-That-Is. God, the love and compassion that is the substantial reality of All-That-Is, feels your pain.* You and God meet in empathetic embrace within the depth of your wounding, for which God cries.

When we talk about the infinite nature of the divine, we refer not only to the infinity of divine power or the infinity of the divine process, we refer also to the infinity of divine pain for the wounds of every finite being. In Kabbalah this is called the pain of the Shekhinah in exile; in Christianity it came to be called the mystery of incarnation. The momentous insight into the infinite dignity of the individual is a realization of the dignity of the tears of every finite being. This is the great paradox of your wounds. The abuse you suffered infinitely matters. *And from the context of your larger evolutionary Unique Self, you can forgive and move on, held in the sweetness of the evolutionary creativity and Unique Gifts that are yours to manifest and give in this lifetime.*

When we move beyond the personal, we are moving not to the imper-sonal but to the transpersonal. This is an evolutionary and not a regressive move. In taking a dismissive posture in regard to your wounds because you have begun to identify with the impersonal, this teaching commits a classic pre-trans fallacy. A pre-trans fallacy means simply to confuse that which is pre- with that which is trans. For example, the pre-personal that appears before the appropriate development of the healthy personal ego, and the transpersonal that trance-ends and includes the healthy personal ego. For example, a baby and an enlightened sage may both be said to be "not stuck" in personality. However, the baby is pre-personal (and prerational), while the enlightened sage is transpersonal (and transrational). The difference is that while the baby has not yet evolved to the mature individuation of the personal, the enlightened sage has first achieved a mature personal individuation, and only afterward, transcended the personal. But even in that transcendence, the enlightened sage does not exclude the personal, but rather transcends and includes the personal. In a pre-trans fallacy, the prepersonal and impersonal are implicitly lumped together, and then conflated with the transpersonal. That is a colossal mistake. The dignity of the personal is the dignity of your story. *Your Unique Self story is the core of your Eros.* Your story, as we have seen, is not to be confused with the pseudo-Eros and pseudostory of your ego.

When you move from personal to transpersonal, the core rules for the healthy ascension to higher levels of consciousness always apply. You must always transcend and *include* the previous level. A transrational mysticism must transcend and include the rational—there are places where the merely rational cannot go. However, the transrational must never be confused with the prerational, which is superstitious and often antirational. Similarly, the transpersonal must transcend and *include* the personal.

Evolutionary We Space

This understanding of the paradoxical relationship between the transpersonal and the personal, the knowing that the transpersonal must always transcend and include the personal, is precisely the difference between an evolutionary spiritual community and a cult. Enter either one on a Sunday morning, and from the outside, they look strikingly similar. In both, groups of people may be chanting, swaying, meditating, or praying. When you enter the room, you can palpably feel that you are not entering personal but collective space.

To determine whether you are in a cult or an evolutionary We Space, you need to enter the interior face of the group's consciousness. One of the most precise and powerful ways to do so is to check its relationship to the personal. Has the group transcended and included, or has it excluded the personal? It is pretty easy to tell. Decision making and personal autonomy are key litmus tests. Can you legitimately hold a perspective different from the leader? How easy or hard is it to leave? Is the leader held to be perfect and egoless, and everyone else flawed and trapped in ego? Is clearly abusive behavior that flagrantly violates personal boundaries acceptable under the guise of ego-busting?

We need to be very careful here. It is fully possible for a spiritual community to have a strong leader who has a contract with his or her students to rigorously challenge their egoic attachment. That contract may allow for what has been called "crazy wisdom" behavior that would not be acceptable from your boss at work. The hypersensitive self is rooted not in the Unique Liberated Self but in the ego. There are profound systems of guru yoga that challenge the egoic predicament. Whether such a system is in fact motivated by the pure intention and integrity of the leader, or has been subtly hijacked by the sophisticated ego of the leader, is next to impossible to ascertain from the outside.

A critical distinction must be drawn between the dignity of the personal and the ego. They are not the same, and the teacher and student must profoundly honor the former even while challenging the latter. The job of the true teacher is to comfort the afflicted and afflict the comfortable.

The Wounds of Love or The Idolatry of Hurt

Evolution beyond exclusive identification with ego, whether through prayer, meditation, or ethical mindfulness, profoundly transforms your relationship to your wounds. It is essential to any person who wants to live a decent life. Clearly, in the Western context, there has been an obsessive and even narcissistic emphasis on personal hurt. It is further true that when the ego is the center of gravity of your person, then the ego will experience hurt as a terrible insult to your very existence.

Your hurt activates the ritual of rejection, and degenerative patterns of recrimination are activated. In order to assert your power, you seek to hurt the one whom you feel hurt you. By damaging the one who hurt you, your ego is sated. You have proven to your hypersensitive, empty self, and to whoever the spectators might be, that you exist. You have done this in the most degraded way, by inflicting hurt. In the contemporary context of our victim culture, saying "I was hurt" is all too often a justification for the most insidiously motivated malice. "Being hurt" has become an idol who forgives all sin.

It is only through divine communion, in which you access your larger self, that you learn the freedom of staying open as love despite and through the hurt. You practice staying open as love through the pain. You turn the egoic insults to the small self into the wounds of love of the Unique Self.[1]

Expand the context of your consciousness. Widen your circle of caring and concern. The obsession with your wound will begin to dissipate and ultimately disappear as you begin to realize your own liberation.

Let me tell you a story I first read in a Buddhist text some decades back:

> There was a woman—Kiso Gotami may have been her name— who was so broken, to whom life had dealt such a harsh hand, that she simply was unable to get up in the morning. So she went to the Buddha and asked what she could do. She had come to the end. Life was just too painful. The Buddha said to her, "If you bring me a mustard seed from a house that knows no sorrow, then all will be well with you."
>
> She thought, "This will be very simple." Life was hard for her, but so many of her neighbors led such easy, happy lives.
>
> She knocked on the door of her neighbor's house, the couple with the wonderful relationship and seven smiling children. She told them, "The Buddha has told me to bring a mustard seed from a house that knows no sorrow, and all will be well with me. I know you have such a joyous house! Might you please spare me a mustard seed?"
>
> They looked at her almost angrily and said, "You have no idea what is going on in our house. You don't know about . . . " and they began to tell her of the tragedies they had suffered— a tale of secret woe and hidden sorrow the likes of which she had never heard.

We think we know so well what is going on in someone else's reality.

> She hears their story. She decides to stay for a short time and offer comfort. A good while later, she leaves and goes to the next house. She is sure this house is a house of joy with no sorrow. She asks again for a mustard seed. The response is again, "Why did you come to us? You think we're a house with no sorrow?" They begin to tell her their story of sadness and woe.

What can she do? Again, she is so moved, she wants to comfort them. She stays with the second family for a period of time, comforting, soothing, and trying to cheer them.

She goes to a third house and again meets the same story of sorrow. Her compassion is aroused once again. She stays with them and comforts them as well.

So it continues from house to house. She is comforted as she comforts. Her ego falls away as she enters the Unique calling of her life and realizes her liberation.

When you add an alignment with the evolutionary impulse itself to this teaching of compassion, the obsession with wounds begins to take on a sense of the ridiculous. This is good.

Lying About Your Hurt to Support Your Ego

You need to engage in a true-reality consideration to consider how much you have actually been hurt. Is your ego hurt or is your Unique Self hurt? What advantages are you receiving from your hurt? How are you manipulating and even lying about your hurt to prop up your otherwise contracted identity?

It is critical for you to remember that hurt is a "state." All states, whether they be altered, drunken, mystical, or sexual states, are temporary. The state overtakes you and shifts your consciousness. Then, however, you invariably return to what for you is your more natural state of consciousness. At that point, you begin, without even being aware that you are doing it, to interpret your state experience. All states of being are subject to interpretation through many different prisms—cultural, social, psychological, emotional, and developmental. For example, developmentally, states are interpreted through the prism of the stage of consciousness in which the person experiencing the state usually locates.[2]

A stage, unlike a state, is not passing and temporary. It is rather a stable and irreversible level of consciousness. In every line of development, there are clearly discernible stages. For example, in motor development, there is a stage before and a stage after a child is able to ride a bike. In cognitive development, there is a before-reading stage and an after-reading stage. In mathematical development, there is a significant cognitive leap after the multiplication tables. And in moral development, there are four distinct stages that have been identified as egocentric, ethnocentric, worldcentric, and kosmocentric. Each level is based on who is in your circle of felt caring and concern.

States do not yield any information by themselves, but are always interpreted through the prism of stages. It is for this reason that so many aphorisms suggest that a person's true level of consciousness and interior psychological self is revealed when they are drunk. Some people get very kind and open when drunk, and others, surprisingly, seem to get very mean and cruel. Some reveal their open heart, and others reveal their racism. Their ethnocentric stage of consciousness is revealed by the drink.

Mystical states are also interpreted through the prism of stages of consciousness. Let's say you have a genuine mystical experience. If you are at an egocentric level of moral development, you will interpret it to mean that you are enlightened. If you are obsessively egocentric in a highly narcissistic way, you may think that you are the only enlightened being on the planet. If you have the same experience, and you are at an ethnocentric level of consciousness, then you may well believe that your people and no other are the chosen people of God. If you are at a worldcentric level of consciousness, you will be more likely to interpret your experience as a call that obligates you to engage in healing and transformation on a global scale.

If you are at a kosmocentric stage of consciousness, then the level of depth and wisdom with which you approach the global activism sparked by your mystical state will be of a fundamentally deeper quality. Kosmocentric implies an expansive and integral embrace of all systems and forms of knowing available to you. So, for example, from a kosmocentric level of consciousness, you bring to the situation you are engaging an integrated mind, body, and heart, and a whole-systems understanding of the evolutionary possibilities available to meet the moment. Your wisdom merges profound reverence for the past, penetrating insight into the present, and a humble boldness toward the future.

Your state, in this case a mystical state, is always interpreted through your level of consciousness.

Hurt is a state. This is a huge insight. You need to really take it in.

Hurt is not an objective reality that gives you license for cruelty under the cover of "I was hurt." ***Hurt is a state, and it is interpreted through*** *your stage or level of consciousness. As you evolve, your relationship to your wounds naturally shifts. More than any other single barometer, what you do with your hurt reveals to you and others your genuine level of consciousness.* When you feel hurt, the masks of piety and the guises of liberation from ego are stripped away, and your naked heart is revealed to yourself and those with eyes to see.

Once you approach your hurt from this wider context, you can begin to appreciate the next instruction. Here it is in the form of a story:

> The Hasidic master Naftali of Rophsitz told his students a tale of great healers being called to help the king. The king's son was crying desperately. All the wise men of the kingdom, the doctors, the magicians, and shamans (the psychologists of the day) had been to see him, and none could comfort him or stop his crying. Indeed, every attempt at healing seemed to intensify the young prince's woe.
>
> It happened that an old woman from the hinterland of the kingdom was bringing milk to the palace. She passed the boy as he wandered, sobbing, near the kitchen. She approached him, not realizing he was the king's son, and whispered a few words in his ear.
>
> Lo and behold, he looked up at her, and his crying began to abate. In just a few minutes, he was not crying at all. And here Naftali ended his tale.
>
> "Please, holy master," the disciples pleaded with their teacher, "you must tell us. What magic, what amulet, what secret did the old wise woman—who we know must have been the Shekhinah herself—what did she say?"
>
> The master smiled. "It was very simple," he said. "She told the boy, 'You must not cry more than it hurts.'"

If we learn to live wide open even as we are hurt by love, then the divine wakes up to its own True Nature. *To be firm in your knowing of love, even when you are desperate, and to be strong in your heart of forgiveness even when you are betrayed, this is what it means to be holy.*

Hurt is a state. You must always ask what has been hurt—your Unique Self or your ego. Then you must ask how much have you genuinely been hurt, and what license does your hurt give or not give you. People lost in victimhood, making exaggerated or false claims, often inflict a thousand-fold more hurt on their alleged abuser than the actual or imagined hurt they are claiming. We must always protect the abused. We need, however, to be very discerning, for sometimes the abusers disguise themselves as the abused. Lost in the egoic hypersensitive self, the true abusers have failed to align themselves with the larger context of the evolutionary impulse. When you do align yourself with your evolutionary obligation, your Unique Self, you do not ignore your wounds; however your *attachment* to your wounds falls to the wayside.

You can let go of your own hurt as you embrace the wider evolutionary context. But you dare not do so with the hurt of another. Yes, you can and must demand that they not cry more than it hurts. You can and must demand that they not hurt others from the place of their untransformed wound. If they move to inflict hurt in such ways, you must hold them accountable before the bar of integrity and justice. This is absolutely true even if the impulse that moved them to maliciously inflict hurt was the confusion and pain of their own sense of woundedness. All the more so when the objective hurt they inflict exponentially exceeds the subjective and relatively minor wounds they received.

And yet, after all these caveats, and after we align with the larger evolutionary impulse that is beyond the personal—we need to never lose the full intensity of compassion for all personal suffering. Even when it is self-inflicted, narcissistic, and unnecessary. To judge which suffering will receive our love and compassion is a tricky business, with multiple egoic traps along the way.

The liberated prophet Isaiah channels the following divine teaching: *bekol tzaratam lo tzar.* "In all of your pain, God is in pain." This refers not only to legitimate pain. Even petty and self-inflicted pain is felt and held by God.

The Hebrew word *tzar* means both pain and contraction. For the prophetic teaching refers not only to necessary pain. It refers rather to the majority of our pain, which is unnecessary and even frivolous. All of this pain is at its root a result of self-contraction. The prophetic channeling of the divine voice by Isaiah can be literally translated from the Hebrew as "In all of your contraction, God is contracted."

The way to open your heart through the pain is to find the God that is infinitely pained in your contraction. It is that God which leads from the narrow constriction of your pain to walk again in the wide spaces of your heart.

When the ego's heart breaks, then the heart closes and contracts. When the Unique Self's heart breaks, the heart opens through the pain into greater love.

The divine is dependent on us. In the direct language of the Unique Self Kabbalists, "Your actions either weaken or empower God." When you expand, the divine surges with power and ecstasy, and expands with you and as you. When you recoil into your small, petty, egoic self, the divine contracts with you and as you. But in that contraction, God also feels your pain. We may live lives of quiet desperation, but there are truly no lives of lonely desperation, for God is always with us in our pain.

You are invited to *imitatio dei,* the "imitation of the divine." Imitate no one except God. Just as God never forsakes the personal for the sake of the process, so too never let go of your empathy and compassion, even for self-inflicted suffering.

The prophets never close their hearts. When someone hurts, they say, "Oh my God, you hurt so badly! Let me hold you and love you. I know you may have done to this yourself, and I will bust you for it tomorrow. But at this very moment, I do not care. I just want to hold you and make it better."

Facing Through the Fear of Death

The movement taught by all the great teachers from ego to True Self is referred to by some as the hero's journey.

It is called *ratzo* by the great enlightened prophet Ezekiel. *Ratzo* means "to run" or "to desire." *Ratzo* is the ecstatic running toward God, who is the spacious Ground of Being.

At that precise point of realization, however, when you have fallen into the spaciousness of True Self, you are required to do what Ezekiel calls *shov.* You turn. You turn back and face life fully without flinching. You are filled with the courage and freedom born in you from your hero's journey.

You feel your Unique Self arising from the ashes of your ego. You feel the full power and humility of your Unique Self coursing through you. *You have transformed your fate as ego into your destiny as a Unique Self. Every detour in your life has revealed itself to be a necessary destination on the way to your destiny.* You are now ready to begin your second hero's journey as a Unique Self living passionately and fully in deep and joyful service to God and your fellow beings.

When you awaken to this realization, the fear of death—which was only the fear of not having responded to the Unique Obligation of your life—disappears. You may wake up early in life or later. *At any point in which you are moved to respond to your evolutionary obligation, you can heal the past. You can heal the past with sincere right action or sincere right intention. There is no such thing as being too late. The potential for radical awakening and change is present at every moment.* You are then radically shocked and wildly ecstatic when you realize the complete and total identity between your purpose and God's purpose. This is the true meaning of evolutionary alignment with the ecstatic God-impulse that lives in you and calls you to service.

God Is More Than Physical, Not Less Than Physical; More Than Personal, Not Less Than Personal

Your ability to choose your own evolution is the God-impulse in you. The mystery of your free choice, in defiance of every force of inertia and downward gravitational pull exerted by all the painful and traumatic circumstances of your life, is the mystery of God pulsating in you, as you, and through you.

That does not mean, as some evolutionary-spirituality teachers mistakenly suggest, that there is no God *beyond* you. Of course there is. It would be a rather grand narcissism to think that you alone exhaust all of divinity. This incarnation of God in You is not the limit of God. It is but one face of the divine, the first person of God. God discloses in the second person as well. Just look at the Unique Self of your friend. And in third person, just look at the wonders of nature.

It also does not mean that God is also not merely process and principle. The divine is also infinitely personal. This is the infinity of intimacy that lies at the heart of the kosmos. To say God is not personal is much the same as to say that God is not physical.

I once read a spiritually tragic report of Jewish schoolchildren who were asked to draw God. The papers came back either entirely empty or with pallid drawings, empty of life. The children had been raised on the classic sacred teaching of the nonphysicality of God. But the teaching has not been transmitted properly. When we say that God is not physical, we mean to say that God is *more* than physical, not less. We mean to say that the infinite depth of God's realness cannot be exhausted or even approximated by the shallow reality of the physical. It is much the same when we say that God is not personal.

When we say that God is not personal, we mean that the quality of personal that is God is not limited to a particular person. In the language of the Zohar, "There is no place devoid of God." Second, we mean that the personal as we know it cannot begin to exhaust the infinite personal intimacy, caring, and love that is the divine. God is not personal in a human-personality sense. But this is because the limited personal quality of the separate self cannot hold the infinite reality or the infinite tenderness of God's loving embrace.

Yearn for the beloved in whose bosom you may rest and before whom you are privileged to chant in radical devotion and insane joy. Prostrate yourself wonderstruck before the love intelligence that expresses itself as All-That-Is. In all of these, you will feel the God that is both within you and beyond you. Know that where you fall, you fall into the infinitely personal divine embrace. God is process, principle, and personal plus.

It would be a horrific loss to lose our devotion. It would be a violation of deeper truth to lose our ability to bow before God as Thou. It would inflict a great wound in God if we lost our yearning for the beloved God. To lose our passionate attachment to God as second person under the guise of an impersonal evolutionary spirituality or an impersonal Buddhist teaching is to lose our belongingness in the world. When teachers of evolutionary spirituality proclaim, "No one else can save us. There is no God beyond that. Never was, is, not now, and never will be," they are telling only half the story. It is a partial truth. When it is made into a whole, it is distorting, damaging, and destructive. It undermines our ability to evolve and realize higher levels of truth and consciousness.

Nikos Kazantzakis was right. We are the saviors of God. We are responsible for the evolution of God. But that gift was given to us by God in love. The God who gave us that gift is always catching us when we fall. Again and again, wherever we fall, we fall into God's arms. We live in the arms of the beloved. Process, principle, and personal God are all different faces of the One. The divinely evolved ability to hold paradox in our very body and being is the necessary faculty of awakened consciousness.

It All Depends on You Personally

The experience of being personally implicated in the evolution of All-That-Is is central to evolutionary mystical consciousness. Every right act done by a human being was understood by the evolutionary mystics as effecting a *tikkun,* an evolutionary fixing of the kosmos. One of the many formulas deployed by the evolutionary mystics was *leshem yichud,* "This act is for the sake of the unification/evolution of consciousness." This interior realization of awakened consciousness is captured in the simple biblical words "God spoke to Abraham."

God actually spoke to every individual Being, but it was Abraham who *heard.* God did not choose Abraham. Abraham chose God.

To live awake in an evolutionary context is to be personally addressed.

The evolutionary mystics of Kabbalah unveil the esoteric reading of the wisdom maxim: "Know that which is above you," taught by the old wise masters of the second and third centuries. In the evolutionary mystical reading, this maxim is understood to say, "Know that which is above you Depends On You!"[3]

BETWEEN UNIQUE SELF AND AUTHENTIC SELF

I HAVE BEEN ASKED NUMEROUS TIMES TO CLARIFY the relationship between Authentic Self (in the teaching of my colleague and friend Andrew Cohen) and my teaching of Unique Self. The issue has been raised numerous times in at least five public dialogues between different dyads and at least three articles that I am aware of in the last couple of years. Honorable dharmic dialogue rooted in a search for the deepest possible truth which is emergent from a matrix of mutual love and respect is hugely important. We have lost the art of such dialogue because for so many of us, ideas, dharma, worldviews and their implications, have ceased to matter.

Happily, part and parcel of the reconstructive project implicit in Evolutionary, Integral and World Spiritualities is the possibility of a new post metaphysical integral worldview which is embracing, illuminating and evolving. To the extent that worldviews matter, and I believe they matter vitally, fleshing out the core paradigms is of vital importance. I have very briefly addressed this issue in scattered footnotes through out this book. Further conversation in this regard within the context of this work would have taken us far astray from our core purposes. To better serve the task, however, I have written a hundred page essay which outlines, from my perspective, the core parallels, core distinctions—and why they matter—between Authentic Self and Unique Self teachings.

The essay is posted on www.UniqueSelf.com. In this space I offer only a very brief formulaic set of equations, which summarizes in concise form the basic points of that essay. Virtually all citations in the equations are drawn from the most recent official statement of Authentic Self teaching in Andrew's recent book Evolutionary Enlightenment. (pub date Summer 2011) All the subsequent citations in the Unique Self equation are drawn from Marc Gafni, Your Unique Self, The Radical Path to Personal Enlightenment, (initial pub date Summer 2011) All constructive and loving critique, which will further clarify the teachings, is most welcome.

1) The Level of Personal Self in the Authentic Self Teaching

Ego = personal = separate self = individuated self sense = uniqueness = unique self sense = special = narcissist personality = inauthentic - merely personal = personal prism = secondary = external sheath = personal drama = petty personal = not you = personal which is, "if not irrelevant, secondary" to process = personal which is "outer sheath" = relative = past = little or no choice = culturally conditioned = relative

2) The Level of Impersonal Self in the Authentic Self Teaching

You = impersonal I = authentic self = impersonal evolutionary impulse = impersonal process = absolute = truth of impersonality – impersonal creativity = primary = heroic impersonal = courageous = beyond ego = thrilling = future = eros = eros of evolutionary impulse = god = eros of impersonal process = god = metaphor = no god outside of you = you = personal self is an illusion, result of conditioning = choice only at the level of the impersonal = impersonal process = god does not care about your personal self = god = metaphor for impersonal = cares only about your contribution to the impersonal process = your personal needs are irrelevant or at least secondary to the process = you are not special

3. Personal and Impersonal in Unique Self Teaching

Unique Self enlightenment includes both the impersonal {True Self} and the personal face of Essence which is the personal that appears beyond the impersonal. The core distinction is between the personal that appears before the impersonal True Self has been realized, and the Personal that emerges after True Self has been realized, namely Unique Self.

Evolutionary Emergent of Unique Self = Personal Face of Essence = Essence Beyond Ego = Distinction between personal at level of ego and Personal beyond True Self = Personal after Emptiness = there is no impersonal self anyplace in the manifest world = the impersonal is an illusion = the impersonal always appears personally in the manifest world = specialness beyond ego = courageous = God having a Marc experience = uniqueness is an irreducible feature of essence = the personal beyond the impersonal = self beyond ego = Form and Emptiness are one = all four quadrants tetra arise = Individuation beyond Ego = Individuation as Enlightenment = the post egoic personal face of the process = the unique post egoic personal incarnation of the evolutionary impulse = Unique Self = eros of unique self = eros = relationship = evolutionary intimacy = partnership with the divine = second face of god = uniqueness = choice fully emergent at the level of Unique Self = Self beyond Ego

ACKNOWLEDGEMENTS

IT IS MY DELIGHT TO THANK the board and inner circle of Center for World Spirituality for everything that have done and do which enable us to unfold together a humble yet audacious next step in the evolution of love. The Center is a think tank, training institute and community lab which is both my intellectual and spiritual home. I am delighted to thank the board of the Center for World Spirituality for their work in supporting the emergence of the Unique Self and World Spirituality teachings. They include John Mackey and Lori Galperin as Board Chairs. John and Lori, you are great humans. And that is true of everyone on this holy list. A deep thanks to the entire CWS Board. Sally Kempton, Mariana Caplan, Kathleen J. Brownback, Raquel Prieguez, Wyatt Woodsmall, Eben Pagan, Warren Farrell, Terry Nelson, Victoria Myer, Bill Little, Shawn Ramer, Heather Fester, Lesley Freeman, Joe Perez, Chahat Corten, Leon Gras, Mauk Pepier, Tom Goddard, Elizabeth Helen Bullock, Liza Braude, Marty Cooper, Heather Ussery Knight, Mike Ginn, Claudia Kleefeld, Bence Ganti, Richard Sclove, Babs Yohai, John Friend, Carlos Neuman, Betsy and Sandy Sanders. I want to also thank Peter Dunlap and my dear friends Sam and Barbara Alexander. Each of these relationships is unique and irreducible and each have made or are making wonderful contributions to CWS and my life. It is my pleasure to thank Bruce and Mary who at a critical moment deeply supported the development of this work.

Deep appreciation and love to my dear friend and brother, Ken Wilber, for the Integral Theory gifts which have been so important to me and so many others in the last decade, for the depth of presence, love and conversation over hundreds of hours for continued partnership in birthing and evolving the core structures of a World Spirituality based on Integral principles. To Diane Hamilton for everything. To brother in Karma Michael Zimmerman for everything. To my brothers Warren Farrell and Eben Pagan for weekly depth and friendship. To my partner Joe Perez for every day. For W. For Ariel. For Sprite. To all of the inner circle students. To Hans. To Mark Schwartz a rare human being and new brother. To Lady V. To Rocky for friendship in key moments. To Avraham Leader. To Arjunah Ardagh. To Fern. To Chana Ross. To Emanuel Green. To Karen Rosica.

To Men's group which is precious to me, Warren, John, Terry, Mark, Neil, Ken, Rob and Bob. You guys rock!

To the awesome team at Integral Publishers especially Keith Bellamy, Russ Volckmann and Brett Thomas. Russ's creative competence, rigor and love made the actual book a reality. Keith's wisdom birthed and nurtures the relationship and Brett's visionary integral leadership takes it into the world. Also, much appreciation to Kathryn Lloyd for her many hours of dedication to design and detail.

Deep appreciation and love to Mariana Caplan. Our daily family conversation is part of the deep fabric of my life. Deep appreciation and love to Lori Galperin who emerged fully in my life after this book and the first draft of this dedication were written. For everything. To George Ward and Derek Evans for help at key moments. To Chen. To all the people who have been part of my Unique Self world, present and past wherever they might be today. To the new friends entering my Unique Self world today.

Thanks also are due with delight to Sean Esbjörn-Hargens who together with Zachary Stein and Clint Fuhs are the academic co-chairs of the Center for World Spirituality and are important interlocutors for me in the world of Integral Theory, as well as good friends. Sean particularly published and introduced a portion of this work in the Integral academic journal, Journey of Integral Theory and Practice (JITP 6:1, 2011). To Sally Kempton, from whose grace this book and so much that is precious is born.

~ Carmel CA, 2012

INTEGRAL AFTERNOTE:
UNIQUE SELF
AND LEVELS OF
CONSCIOUSNESS

THE FOLLOWING EMERGED from a series of conversations between Ken Wilber and myself, which sought to clarify clearly the term Unique Self. Some of these issues are more fully explicated in the scholarly treatment of Unique Self and in the footnotes there. (Gafni JITP, 6:1 Evolutionary Emergent of Unique Self fn. 3, 13, 17, 21, 26, and 27.

What I am calling Unique Self is primarily a structure stage of consciousness that one awakens to at a particular level of development. That is the primary usage of Unique Self. Unique Self, however, is also accessible as a state of consciousness, for example during an ecstatic flow state, at earlier developmental stages. Unique Self in its fullest expression is also the unique perspective of True Self, and is therefore a fully Self-realized state of consciousness. As I have pointed out over the years, at the level of Unique Self, the integral distinction between states and structure stages of consciousness melts into the larger One. Using the term Unique Self in an entirely different way it is also true that every form has its own intrinsic uniqueness. So in this sense, in early dialogues both Ken and I have said things like, all forms have a Unique Self. But this meaning of the term Unique Self refers not to the Self-realized state or structure stage of consciousness, but rather to the essential uniqueness that form always exhibits once it emerges from emptiness. To avoid the confusion of double-dipping terms, in this book, Unique Self and in Unique Self theory, Unique Self virtually always refers to the structure-stage of Unique Self-realization, which occurs when Unique Self awakens as the unique perspective of True Self. This is the expression of Unique Self as both state and structure stage of consciousness. It would be more accurate *not* to refer to other expression of uniqueness as Unique Self since unique essence as the structure stage of a developed and awakened self-quality does not come online until much higher stages of human development both in terms of states and structure stages. For nuanced discussion of these issues see footnote 1 Ch. 1.)

NOTES

Preface

1. For an extended discussion of false sentence, false core, and false self, see for example, Stephen Wolinsky, *The Way of the Human: The Quantum Psychology Notebooks* (Capitola, CA: Quantum Institute, 1999). Wolinsky focuses on the false core as that one conclusion you can make about yourself that organizes not only your entire psychology but also how you imagine the world sees you; and the false self, which compensates for this false conclusion. Volume 2 contains exercises, demonstrations, and protocols for dismantling the false core–false self complex (unpacking the core teaching of seminal thinker Oscar Ichazo, founder of the Arica school).

2. See Harold Solave, *The Future of Reputation* (New Haven, CT: Yale University Press, 2007).

3. William Blake, "Proverbs of Hell," *The Marriage of Heaven and Hell* (New York: Oxford University Press, 1975).

Chapter 1: The Great Invitation of Your Life

1. It is worth mentioning that the idea of love as an evolutionary catalyst can be traced to the great American philosopher Charles S. Peirce and his famous essay "Evolutionary Love," [*The Monist* 3 (1893): 176–200]. Peirce offers one of the first and best post-Darwinian evolutionary metaphysics, and his ideas foreshadow much of contemporary complexity, chaos, and dynamic-systems theorizing. But his vision, unlike that of most disciplines, was of a universe with depth, and one moving toward love. He was an important Integral progenitor. (According to Zachary Stein in his article "On the Normative Function of MetaTheoretical Endeavors" [*Integral Review* 6, no. 2C (July 2010): 5–22], "Peirce [articulated] a broad evolutionary vision

of the universe where the strivings of humanity are continuous with the evolution of the kosmos. It was a sophisticated and empirically grounded evolutionary ontology where all events are semiotic processes that co-evolve toward increasing complexity, autonomy, self-awareness, and possible harmony. Peirce's pansemiotic evolutionary theory was a unique [postmetaphysical] view insofar as it was explicitly offered as a hypothesis amenable to correction in light of forthcoming empirical data. It greatly influenced Whitehead and continues to intrigue and inspire scholars in the physical and biological sciences and philosophy.")

This understanding of evolution allowed Peirce to bring his overarching normative concerns about the trajectory of academic discourses in line with a venerable philosophical tradition that articulated the radical significance of humanity's cultural endeavors in terms of a cosmic evolutionary unfolding. Ultimately, Peirce, with a look in Kant's direction, envisioned humanity as capable of multitudinous self-correcting intellectual and ethical endeavors, which ought to result in an ideal communication community coterminous with the kosmos. In this postmetaphysical eschatology, the ideals of harmonious love between all beings and unconditional knowledge about all things stand as goals to be approached asymptotically. With this thought, Peirce rearticulates a philosophical motif that can be traced back through Emerson, Schelling, and Kant to the obscure cipher of Böhme's mystical Protestant religiosity and its ancient Hebraic and Neoplatonic roots.

Evolutionary love is later a major motif in the world of Teilhard de Chardin and in many of the contemporary evolutionary thinkers who write in his wake. Notable among them is the work of Brian Swimme, who writes in the wake of Thomas Berry and who speaks of the allurement that is the very glue of the Uni-verse. The contemporary understanding of love at the cellular level augments the understanding of the great traditions, some of which also saw love as the primary motivating force of the kosmos. This is the primary position of the Kabbalists, such as my lineage teacher Lainer of Izbica, rooted in Luria and in the earlier Zoharic texts, as well as of many Christian thinkers like St. Thomas and Dante, who talks of *l'amor che move il sole e l'altre stele*, the "love that moves the sun and the other stars." For St. Thomas the "dynamic pulse and throb of creation is the love of all things for the infinite" (Huston Smith, 78). Spiritual teacher and scholar Sally Kempton points out that in the Hindu text of *Spanda-karikas* and other major texts of the Kashmir Shaivism and other Indian traditions, love is described as the intrinsic motivator of the substance of creation. A text called the *Maharthi Manthari* describes how Shakti, the creative power of the divine, leaping forth in her own bliss, manifests this universe as an expression or even an outpouring of love.

2. Ken Wilber and I, in the final discussions before ISE (Integral Spiritual Experience 2010) and Ken in his keynote at ISE, termed "Unique Self: An Evolutionary Emergent." In earlier discussions in 2005–6 and in one of our first Unique Self Dialogues in 2009 (see Integral Life website, Unique Self, Ken Wilber, Sally Kempton, Marc Gafni), Ken and I talked about Unique Self as resonant if not identical with the Buddhist image of enlightenment captured in the Tenth Oxherding picture. On the Tenth Oxherding Picture as an expression of Buddhist enlightenment teaching, see for example, Lex Hixon, *Coming Home: The Experience of Enlightenment in Sacred Traditions* (Bordett, NY: Larson Publications, 1978), 60–92.

My teaching on Unique Self developed from the Talmudic and Kabbalistic traditions. A. H. Almaas describes what he terms "Personal Essence" in Sufi teaching in terms that are remarkably close to my Unique Self teaching. Having said that, the full implications of individuality have evolved with the advent of modernity and postmodernity, particularly in light of the dignities of modernity, foremost among them democracy and its sociopolitical implications, as well as the contextual realizations of self in postmodernity. The heightened appreciation of the postmetaphysical "ontology" of perspectives that characterizes postmodernity also needs to be taken into account in the formulation of Unique Self. All of these have served to evolve our understanding of Unique Self, which is why Unique Self is termed an evolutionary emergent. It is in this sense, as well, that the Unique Self models World Spirituality as an integration of the best practice of premodern, modern, and postmodern streams of gnosis. (See Epilogue.)

3. My thinking on Unique Self, drawn from Hebrew mystical sources, originated in 1989, which was the first time I taught about what I then termed "soul prints." I still have the video of the first time the term "soul prints" "came down" in a teaching, when I was twenty-six years old, giving a Hebrew dharma talk at the Temple Emeth Synagogue in Delray Beach, Florida. There were five hundred senior citizens at that talk, and I was seeking to communicate to them the Hebrew mystical intuition that their lives were infinitely and uniquely significant, and that therefore they should not spend the last decades of life adrift in the regressive atmosphere of mahjong and card games that dominated the culture of Delray Beach. I said to them, "Not only do you have a fingerprint, you have a soul print," and at that moment something shifted in the subtle energy in the room, and many of us there knew that some deep knowing had been named. This became a core part of my teaching for the next ten years.

In my book *Soul Prints: Your Path to Fulfillment* (New York: Simon and Schuster, 2001), I formally coined both the term "soul prints" and "Unique Self." On the term "Unique Self," see *Soul Prints* (p. 160): "The address of the divine commands us each to realize our Unique Self." In context, this referred to the internal divine voice that lives in and as the interior face of consciousness. The second mention (p. 164) refers to Unique Self as the expression of the human being living in an evolutionary context. I label Unique Self the core human evolutionary mechanism: "The only path to survival is the path of the Unique Self." The third usage of Unique Self in *Soul Prints* (p. 301) is in the context of the obligation to present one's Unique Self in what is termed there a "Soul Print" or "Unique Self encounter." The ethical question in such a meeting is framed as "Have I brought my Unique Self to the table?" In the *Soul Prints* book and teaching, the enlightened nature of post-egoic individuality as an expression of nondual realization is explicit in a number of passages (see for example p. 49 and p. 50) but not sufficiently highlighted.

In what was originally my doctoral dissertation on Nondual Humanism and the Unique Self in the teaching of Mordechai Lainer of Izbica and in the Talmudic and Kabbalistic tradition from which he emerged, the distinction between egoic and enlightened Uniqueness became more dominant as one of the pivoting points of the Unique Self teaching. For Lainer, an essential part of the process of what he termed *berur* might well be understood as precisely this clarification of Uniqueness beyond egoic separate self. See my discussion of *berur* in Gafni, *Radical Kabbalah: The Enlightenment Teaching of Unique Self, Nondual Humanism and the Wisdom of Solomon* (Chapter 10, "The Nature of Berur"). This work originally appeared as my doctorate, taken at Oxford University under the co-supervision of Professor Moshe Idel and Dr. Norman Solomon.

Ken Wilber and I dialogued and debated about the nature of Unique Self enlightenment for some time. When I sent this work to Ken (who had already read my more popular work *Soul Prints* the night after our first meeting), he immediately evolved his position, and in a series of conversations and emails recognized the Unique Self teaching as a significant New Enlightenment lineage that has much to offer the Integral teaching enlightenment. Ken then invited me to give a featured address to a group of some fifty leading spiritual teachers at the Integral Spiritual Center in 2006 on the nature of Unique Self enlightenment. In a series of conversations between Ken Wilber and myself as part of the preparation for the ISC teaching, we sharpened the distinction between egoic individuality and post-egoic individuality.

In the months after ISC, a number of teachers who were moved by the Unique Self-realization began to incorporate it into their teaching. These included John Kesler, Viddeyuva, Sofia Diaz, John Forman, and others. It was, however, my friend Diane Musho Hamilton who began to facilitate the voice of Soul Prints/Unique Self as part of the Big Mind process developed by her teacher, Genpo Roshi. Diane, in conversations with Ken and myself, was pivotal in the full transition in the Integral world from the term "Soul Prints" and its third-person, metaphysical implications, to the term "Unique Self," which more readily expressed Unique Self also as a first-person realization. Her teacher, Genpo Roshi, following her lead, integrated the voice and term "Unique Self" into the Big Mind process and into the official Big Mind book. See Dennis Genpo Merzel, *Big Mind, Big Heart* (McLean, VA: Big Mind Publishing, 2007), 122–24. It was Ken, in a call in January 2006 before the Integral Spiritual Center meeting, who suggested that I prefer the term "Unique Self" over "soul prints" in my upcoming presentation, so that the Unique Self teaching would not be confused with the separate-self soul teaching of exoteric Western religion.

Other teachers, like Sally Kempton, helped identify in their traditions teachings that resonated with the core intuition of Unique Self. The distinction between Unique Self and other teachings like the Authentic Self teaching of Andrew Cohen were clarified in a number of direct engagements with Andrew, beginning with a shared public teaching in Tel Aviv in 2006, followed by an exchange of emails with Andrew after that teaching, and then again in a 2010 dialogue between Andrew and myself, as part of the Future of Love series hosted by iEvolve and Integral Life. This dialogue is slated for publication in *Future of Love: Dialogues on Evolutionary Integral Relationships,* Eds. Marc Gafni and Diane Hamilton (forthcoming). A transcript of that dialogue appears as well in the *Journal of Integral Theory and Practice* 6, no. 1 (Spring 2011). After this Integral Spiritual Center gathering, explicitly drawing on my Unique Self term and teaching, my friend and colleague Terry Patten added a chapter on Unique Self to the almost-complete *Integral Life Practice* book. The chapter is entitled "Unique Self" in integrallife.com (Boulder, CO: Integral Books, 2008).

Unique Self further evolved the Integral space in 2010, when I was privileged to lead an effort, together with Ken Wilber, Robb Smith, Diane Hamilton, and Sally Kempton, to reinvigorate the Integral Spiritual Movement. The focal point of the effort was a series of Integral Spiritual Experiences. Because Unique Self had by that time begun to emerge as a new chapter in Integral Theory, we held the event around the teaching of Unique Self. In a series of dialogues both public and private leading up to the event, the teaching on Unique Self evolved even further. For some of these conversations with Ken Wilber, Sally Kempton, Diane Hamilton, Lama Surya Das, Jean Houston, and Alex Grey, see Marc Gafni, contributors page, *JITP* (Spring 2001). During the months leading up to the event, I wrote the eight stations of the Unique Self, which were featured in the attendee guide for the conference and which form the crux of this book. At this event, in a series of keynote presentations given by myself and Ken, and through Big Mind/Unique Self facilitations by Diane, as well as a True Self/false self plenary by Sally Kempton, the Unique Self teaching deepened once again. For these presentations, see the ISE 1 media package, available at integrallife.com.

4. These include certain schools of developmental psychology and the deconstructive schools of literature, which are rooted in Saussure and ultimately Kant.

5. The modern notion of perspectives is foundational in the Lurianic one-letter tradition of Kabbalah. For a discussion of the Lurianic one-letter tradition and its influence on Unique Self, see Marc Gafni, *Unique Self and Nondual Humanism* (forthcoming), Chapter 4. For an intellectual history of Unique Self within Hebrew wisdom, surveying Talmudic, Zoharic, Lurianic, and Hasidic sources, see Chapters 1–4, 8, 9, and 14.

Chapter 2: The New Enlightenment of Unique Self

1. Living "in you, as you, and through you" means that Unique Self is refracted through all the prisms of your consciousness.

An Integral View of Unique Self

Overview

Unique Self is a liberating realization that promises to integrate the so-called trans-egoic, No-Self teachings of Eastern traditions with the individuality emphasized in the West and the uniqueness that is inherent to all human beings. We would offer Unique Self as a living koan; an inquiry meant to provoke curiosity, exploration, and presence, rather than an attempt to reify or fix our self-understanding.

We understand that Unique Self can and will be interpreted differently according to personal inclination and constitution, cultural orientation, and differences in stages of development. For example, a Benedictine monk, whose realization validates an eternal transcendent soul, may understand Unique Self as an expression of that unique soul. A Zen Buddhist, whose realization does not posit a reified transcendent, may experience Unique Self as the freedom to manifest exactly as we are: complete, whole, empty, and unique. In another example, a secular materialist might understand Unique Self as an expression of one's unique perspective and abilities to succeed and develop.

In each case, we would hope that the Integral practitioner would see that classical enlightenment, in the formulation of the great traditions as a realized state of unity with the oneness of all ever-present reality, is recognition of what might be called "True Self." This realization finds that the total number of True Selves only and always is one. This, however, is only true in unmanifest oneness. There is no True Self anywhere in the manifest world. At the same time, every person's awakening to this oneness arises through their own unique perspective. In this way, True Self plus my own perspective equals My Unique Self.

In developmental-psychology terms, the fullest flowering of Unique Self might best be articulated as a living glimpse into the "Indigo" stage of human consciousness and self-identity: this is the stage of evolution of human consciousness at which my felt ever-present unity of reality—a state of ongoing "flow presence," if you will—and the unique characteristics of my own life and perspective—the unique evolutionary features of my life—clearly intersect and find a cohesive and stabilized integration. At second-tier and third-tier, perspectives are inherent in awareness. It is an inherent aspect of what emerges at Turquoise and Indigo. So even though Unique Self was present from the earlier stages of consciousness, it can seem to emerge at second-tier and third-tier. Perspective is an inherent part of the realization of the Indigo structure. When someone develops to Indigo, they know that they are looking through a particular perspective even as they recognize other perspectives, and are even to some extent able to disidentify from their own. And my own perspective is never absent, even as it is progressively clarified and deepened through the evolution of self to Self. It is important to note, however, that proto-expressions of Unique Self appear in significant ways in earlier stages of consciousness as well.

Our Intent

Our efforts at ISE are meant to provide a vibrant, open, and enlivened look into the emerging potential of the possibility for humanity at this stage in our evolution. In the first-person perspective, Unique Self is a practice of recognizing the profundity of your own life, the preciousness of your specific perspective, history, and talents, and the opportunity to become fully who you already are—I am uniquely this. In the second-person perspective, Unique Self is minimally an opportunity to see and support the Uniqueness of others' gifts and to foster a durable community that supports the evolutionary possibilities of humankind—I see who you uniquely are. At a higher level of intersubjective space the collective intelligence of evolutionary We space becomes possible. This is one of the core features of Unique Self encounters. (See Chapter 21, The Seven Laws of Unique Self Encounters.) And in the third-person perspective, Unique Self can be understood as an evolutionary emergent—a subtle, gentle, yet powerful and compelling whisper from the emerging future of humankind—this is who we can become.

The Foundation of Unique Self

World Spirituality based on Integral principles provides a foundational program upon which to reconstruct spiritual insights and human meaning-making in a modern world that has transcended merely literal interpretations of religious mythology and seeks to transcend the nihilistic and narcissistic assertions of atheistic scientism and postmodern relativism. Unique Self rests squarely on the "postmetaphysical" core of Integral World Spirituality.

Tenet 1: Perspective is foundational.

Integral World Spirituality maintains that the deep structure of reality is composed of perspectives. Whether we take this commitment as "strong" (ontologically real) or "weak" (usefully descriptive), we can still easily understand that all sentient creatures have a perspective.

Tenet 2: Uniqueness is obvious.

All human beings and perhaps all sentient beings will have a unique perspective. This perspective will be unique on the one hand due to different location—all perspectives have a unique angle of perception—but also due to the different psychology, biology, culture, and history of each creature and its context. According to the realization of the eye of the spirit, human uniqueness is essential, and that human beings' location reflects the unique dimension of divinity that literally births the individual. (See Gafni, "Unique Self and Nondual Humanism," Pt. 2, forthcoming.)

Tenet 3: Perspectives evolve.

Going further, we see that all sentient creatures have their being arise in four quadrants—those of subjective experience, biological, cultural, and social dimensions—and that each of these quadrants is holonic in nature. Therefore, each aspect of reality evolves over time and thus perspectives will also evolve over time.

Tenet 4: "Conventional" metaphysics is unnecessary.

There is no necessary metaphysical aspect to perspectives. At the same time, while a metaphysical perspective is not necessary to an engagement with Unique Self, there is nothing about perspective that precludes ontological revelations. Perspectives thus create a common ground up and down the spiral. In the postmetaphysical view they arise, for example, in human beings and evolve over time, inexorably influenced and cocreated by the evolution of all four quadrants. We need not make any necessary reference to any transcendental concepts or extra-evolutionary features to describe Unique Self. At the same time, Unique Self does not exclude communities who hold a set of realizations that they signify as pertaining to the transcendent (e.g., God). Thus every perspective grounded in direct experience supported by a valid community of interpreters has an honored, if partial, place at the Integral table.

Tenet 5: Ego need not be transcended or obliterated.

"Ego" is a term that is used in many ways. We will use "ego" in this context to mean the general patterns of self-understanding and self-identity that developmental psychologists have tested and articulated using Integral's Zone 2 research methodologies (the outside view of an individual-interior reality). Of course, viewed from within our own subjectivity (i.e., Zone 1), these same patterns "look and feel" as purely phenomenological realities. Because this usage of ego is around an enduring line of self-development that extends up and down the first-person holonic spectrum, it is inaccurate to think of ego as being transcended *per se*. Rather, ego expressions become more inclusive, subtle, refined, and expansive with each successive stage of development and envelopment. When the West first ran into the Eastern traditions, particularly Theravada Buddhism, and first met the whole notion of transcending self, the ego was made bad in all ways. You had two columns. In one column was ego, which was equated with the devil, and in the second column was non-ego, which was equated with God. The critical Western insight of ego being the functional organizing center of conventional awareness, which is utterly essential in the finite world, was effaced. This was a disaster because if you get rid of ego in the finite world, you are borderline or psychotic. You're not enlightened.

Tenet 6: We are never outside of a state, and always within a stage.

All "structure-stages" of consciousness get enacted only within the ontology of present-moment states. We are never outside of the now. So states describe a "substrate of awareness" in which the real arises (and gets interpreted), and stages of consciousness can be understood as the large-scale characterizable patterns of these moment-to-moment interpretations. So we can discuss a state of deep presence, flow states, or nondual identity. But as any uniqueness of self comes into the picture, there will always be a stage particularity to the interpretive act. It makes no sense to talk about Unique Self as a state outside of a particular developmental stage. Unique Self is always interpreted through the prism of stage development.

Tenet 7: Unique Self is fully expressed at an "Indigo" stage of consciousness.

After considering all other tenets above, it is clear that Unique Self therefore can best be described as the stage at which general patterns of ego development evidence an integration between stabilized "No-Self" insight (e.g., cosmic identification) and one's own felt-sense of uniqueness in their life, talents, and history (i.e., their four-quadrant evolution). This stage has been empirically mapped and articulated using Zone 2 methodologies as the "Indigo" self.

We might describe the subtle and refined ego of the Unique Self understanding as one that has let go of the exclusive identification of the subject with its separate self. The transcending of the egoic separate self through repeated access to "presence-flow" states is the goal of classical enlightenment teaching. This, however, does not mean that the ego is annihilated. Rather, the exclusive identification with the egoic separate self is overcome. We are able to experience our fundamental identity—not as an ego isolated from other, nature, community, and All-That-Is—rather, as part of a larger whole. Note the similarities of this description with how researchers have characterized the Indigo stage of ego development:

> [They] experience themselves and others as part of ongoing humanity, embedded in the creative ground, fulfilling "the destiny of evolution" and are in tune with their lives and their shared humanity "as a simultaneous expression of their unique selves." (Cook-Greuter 2002)

That is, these individuals are capable of integrating the unity of reality realized only in deep presence-states (the "creative ground") and their own uniqueness as a living expression of a dynamic evolutionary process that continually will call on them for their special contribution ("the destiny of evolution"). We allow for the possibility that glimmerings of this stage of consciousness, where Unique Self has emerged as this integration, can appear up and down the spiral of human development.

A more rudimentary version of the following note was occasioned by a debate between me and Robb Smith from the postmetaphysical nature of Unique Self enlightenment. The original version of this note was coauthored by me, Robb, Diane Hamilton, Ken Wilber, and Sally Kempton. It appeared in the ISE1 attendee guide.

In our discussion of the Indigo level of consciousness, a potential distinction between the premodern realization and postmodern Indigo realization of Unique Self suggests itself. For much of the premodern world (excepting many of the great realizers and their inner circles who founded new schools of thought), Unique Self was a deduction that went something like this: "Since we all view the mountain from a different perspective, we all have a unique perspective." At the postmodern, second-tier, and third-tier consciousness of Indigo, Unique Self is not only a deduction but a realization. Every person at Indigo has direct access to what only the great realizers were able to access in the premodern world.

2. "Seamless but not featureless" originally appears in R. H. Blyth, *Zen and Zen Classics,* 5 vols. (Tokyo: Hokuseido Press, 1970).

3. See Wolinsky, *The Way of the Human: The Quantum Psychology Notebooks.*

4. See Stephen Wolinsky, *Trances People Live: Healing Approaches in Quantum Psychology* (Putney, VT: Bramble Books, 2007).

5. Naturally there can be healthy and unhealthy prisoners in the cave. The West focused on making the prisoner in the cave healthy by clarifying the false self, taking back shadow projections, and so on, in order to have a healthy separate self. The problem with this approach is that the prisoner is still in the cave, which is the source of suffering. The East focused on getting

the prisoner out of the cave by moving from separate self to the realization of True Self. The problem with this approach is that the realization of True Self does not heal all the neurosis or pathological dysfunction of separate self. It is only in Unique Self that we embrace both the individual uniqueness of the self, which naturally requires clarification, and at the same time realize the True Nature of the individual as an indivisible part of True Self, the seamless coat of the Uni-verse.

6. Any experience of formless True Self, when it manifests as any object at all, manifests as the Unique Self. So to repeat, there is no True Self anywhere in the manifest world. There is always a perspective—that is to say, True Self always manifests as Unique Self. That means Unique Self is always the source of awareness, "all the way up and all the way down." Of course, Unique Self is always present as the witness of consciousness at all levels of awareness, because awareness or consciousness is always embodied in form, and therefore always has a perspective. Unique Self, however, becomes progressively more conscious and full in direct proportion to one's level of True Self-realization. The base awareness of Unique Self is True Self. True Self is the actual origin of awareness at all levels of development, even though it only comes online as conscious awareness with the stage of enlightenment, or what Integral Theory has referred to as third-tier growth. The point is that there is no True Self in the manifest world. The True Self is *always* looking through a perspective. So in the manifest world—that is to say, in the only world we know—there is only the Unique Self. Only pure, formless unmanifest awareness is pure perception without a perspective. In this unmanifest state there are no objects, only consciousness without an object, so there is nothing to take a perspective on. This can be said to be unqualifiable True Self. But we live—always—in the world of manifestation. Once the awareness of True Self manifests, it does so through a particular perspective. That is always the Unique Self.

7. With the emergence of second-tier and particularly third-tier structure stages of consciousness, perspectives themselves become noticed. So at this stage the conscious realization of Unique Self fully emerges. It was of course present all along but tended to be confused with True Self because perspectives were not yet fully conscious. But when the full awareness of perspectives emerges, the awareness of Unique Self emerges. Then any experience of formless True Self, when it manifests as any object at all, manifests as the Unique Self.

8. The centrality of perspective was simply not understood in the premodern world the way we understand it in our postmodern context. We used to think we were directly engaging reality as it is. This is why every spiritual system thought that it owned the truth. Every system thought it was seeing

reality itself. This was only half true. At some point we began to realize that there is no reality without perspective—or put another way, reality itself is *fundamentally constructed from perspectives.* There is nothing we see that is not filtered through the prism of perspective. True Self cannot exist independent of your Unique Perspective. Thus, every enlightenment realization is defined in part by the unique perspective of the practitioner.

Of course, perspective itself can be understood from many perspectives. Perspective might imply ontology, methodology, or epistemology. All of these understandings of perspective appear in the old Hebrew texts, which unfold perspective as the central hermeneutic category of textual interpretation, which is the essential spiritual act of the Talmudic *homo religiosus.*

In the matrix tradition of Unique Self, which is that of Talmud and Kabbalah, taking different perspectives on the sacred text is a central spiritual practice. Judaism is first and foremost a textual tradition. The nature of a textual tradition is that competing readings of the text need to be explained, especially if the text is said to be divine. How can it be, it is asked, that different readers of the text, with different and often mutually exclusive readings, all express the word of God?

This question is answered in a number of ways. Each is based on a different reading of the idea of perspectives. The champions of methodological pluralism claim that in fact only one reading of the text is correct, and the other readings are granted equal status simply because we lack an appropriate method to inform us which reading is correct. In this reading, what is emphasized is the limited nature of each perspective on the one hand, and the hierarchy of perspectives on the other; namely, one perspective is better than the others because it more clearly captures the true intention and meaning of the divine text.

On the far other side of the spectrum are the champions of an ontological pluralism, who assert the radical ontology of perspectives as the core tenet to be recognized and affirmed. This position is rooted in both the classic Hebrew legal and mystical traditions, for whom the text was thought to be a living expression of divinity that did not exist independently of the perspective of its reader. "God, Torah, and Israel are One," is an old Kabbalistic dictum, which essentially means, "Reader, God, and text are One."

In one expression of this teaching, this ontology of perspectives is thought to originate at the source event of revelation, the theophany of Mount Sinai. In this teaching, every person standing at Mount Sinai during the time when the divine voice was heard is said to have stood at a different angle in relation to the mountain. As a result, each person heard a different voice of revelation. And in a nondual matrix of realization, each Unique Perspective on the mountain is understood to have yielded a unique voice of God. This is an ancient version of the New Enlightenment teaching of Unique Perspective, which creates Unique Self. For the Kabbalists who assert ontological pluralism rooted in perspectives, the validity of the hermeneutic is based on the unique perspective of the interpreter who is situated at a unique angle toward—and therefore experiencing and incarnating a unique expression of—the divine face. It is this unique angle that dictates a person's Unique Letter in the kosmic scroll. This original insight of perspectives in regard to revelation becomes the matrix for a sophisticated ontological pluralism in Talmudic and Kabbalistic sources.

Related to this pluralism in regard to the voice of revelation, there emerges what has been called the one-letter teaching of Lurianic Kabbalah. In this teaching, each person is regarded as having their own letter in the Torah. In one-letter theory, your letter in the Torah is both the ontological source and purpose of your existence. Your individual existence is both rooted in, nourished by, and intended to realize your Unique Letter in the Torah scroll. Your Unique Letter is your Unique Self, your Unique song whose notes are formed by your Unique Perspective.

9. Echoes of Unique Self appear in the understanding of Agape love penetratingly languaged by Christian mystic Paul Tillich: "Agape seeks that which is concrete, individual, unique, here and now. Agape seeks the person, the other one who cannot be exchanged for anything or anyone else. He cannot be subsumed under abstractions. He must be accepted in spite of the universals which try to prevent his acceptance, such as moral judgments based on general norms, or social differences justifying indifference or hostility, or psychological characteristics inhibiting full community with him. Agape accepts the concrete in spite of the power of the universal which tries to swallow the concrete." Thanks to Dr. Wyatt Woodsmall for this reference.

10. In an email correspondence with Ken Wilber, after much conversation at his loft and over the phone in 2005, I formulated the core understanding of Soul Print/Unique Self as perspective, as emergent from Hebrew mystical sources on the ontology of perspectives. In this understanding emerging from Hebrew mysticism and from deep conversations with Ken, including his radical emphasis on perspective, Soul Print/Unique Self was understood as the perspective attained at the post-egoic enlightenment level of consciousness. I have kept my note to Ken in its original form to capture some of the energy and excitement of these early conversations:

Giga Pandit,

So much love to you! In terms of Soul Print/Unique Self.

It is very important to understand that soul prints do not emerge from the world of ego or soul but rather from radical nonduality. Soul Prints is an expression of the Self with a capital *S*. The way I teach it to my students, Story and non-Story are one. Or in the expression of the great vehicle of

Buddhism, Emptiness is form and form is emptiness. Or in classic Kabbalistic expression, *Keter* is *Malkhut* and *Malkhut* is *Keter*. This is what I refer to as "a nondual humanism" in the fullest sense of the word.

To explain what I mean, let me offer a simple map of the three classic levels of transpersonal consciousness that—as you [Ken] have pointed out—show up one way or another in virtually every system. We can call them Communion, Union, and Identity. Communion, which Scholem felt was critical in Hebrew mysticism, is ultimately dual. God in the second person. Union moves toward nonduality, and full nonduality is achieved in Identity. Or we might use the more classic terms, which you deploy in your wonderful essay "The Depths of the Divine"— psychic, subtle, casual, and nondual. Or we might call them Ego, Soul, and Self. Or we might call them *ani, ayin, ani*. Or we might use Eastern terms in which "psychic" and" subtle" might be roughly equivalent to *savikalpa samadhi*. At the highest edge of *savikalpa samadhi*, the way I understand it, there is already a glimpse of the formless void of the next stage.

This next stage of formless union, what for some Kabbalists would be called *ayin,* the realm of the impersonal, approximates the Eastern state of *nirvikalpa samadhi*. This is a stage of formless awareness that is beyond the personal. You call this stage the causal state.

The highest and deepest stage is, however, beyond even the formless state of *ayin, nirvikalpa samadhi;* this is the nondual that is the very Suchness of all being. It is the Suchness of both emptiness and form, both personal and impersonal. This is the world of One Taste or *sahaj* in Eastern terms, or the *shma* declaration of *hashem echad,* "God is one" in Judaic consciousness.

The way to reach the ultimate nondual realization—for example, according to my teacher Mordechai Lainer of Izbica— is through the prism of soul prints or Unique Self. Soul prints is the absolute and radical uniqueness of the individual, which is the expression of emptiness in form; it is *ein sof,* revealing itself in the only face we know—the face of unique form. It is not only that there is absolutely no distinction between the radically personal and the radically impersonal; it is also that in terms of stages of unfolding, the radically personal is the portal to the embrace and identity of the absolute one. Moreover, the absolute one expresses itself only through its infinite faces, or what have been called its infinite soul prints (or Unique Self).

Another way to say this might be to borrow the image suggested by the Midrash in this regard, that of the ascending and descending ladders on Jacob's Ladder. For the Kabbalists, this is the ladder of nonduality. On the ladder are angels of God. "Angel" in biblical Hebrew refers to a divine entity or to a human being. What they share in common is that each is a radically unique messenger of God. Or said differently, each is a radically unique perspective. One ascends to the divine through soul print, and the divine descends through soul print (Unique Self). Indeed, all human reality as we know it is soul print (Unique Self).

But even this language is insufficient. For in the experience of nonduality, soul print (Unique Self) is the divine. So one ascends to the divine through the divine soul print (Unique Self). And divinity descends to the divine world of form through the divine soul print (Unique Self). All faces of divinity are kissing each other. What the sages of old called *nashkei ar'a verakia,* "the kiss of heaven and earth."

Now, another term for soul print might be "perspective." As we have pointed out many times, the classic image for unique form or soul print in Hebrew consciousness is *panim,* face. "Face" is an expression in Talmudic language for what we moderns and postmoderns might call perspective. This is what the ancient sages meant when they taught: "There are seventy faces to Torah." Torah contains objective God-givens and yet can only be read through the prism of perspectives.

Ultimately in Hebrew mysticism, each human being is the bearer of a Unique Face that is by very definition a unique perspective (Unique Self). This is a radically particular perception of the world, which is shared exactly by no other being. In this sense, the person is the eyes of *ein sof,* of the absolute. The person is the eyes of the absolute in a way shared by no other being on the planet. This is the source of our grandeur, our infinite adequacy and dignity, and occasionally our almost unbearable loneliness, which for this very reason can only be ultimately quenched in the caress of the divine.

How does one get there, to the soul-printed merger with the absolute?

In Hebrew mysticism, through erotic merger with the Shekhinah.

This might take place through many methods of practice, including the concentrated, intense, and ultimately ecstatic study of sacred text (Hasidei Ashkenaz, in the twelfth century, and the Kabbalah of the Vilna Gaon and his school), the intense meditation of sacred chant and song (classic Hasidic practice), the rigorous and uncompromising process of introspection and dialogue, with results in the clarification-purification of motive and desire called *berur,* out of which the Unique Self naturally emerges (Luria, Izbica, Mussar), classical mystical techniques of letter combination, soul ascent, meditation, crying, and more. Total Love, Total Good!

Mega Reb

My note to Ken, emergent from our many conversations, clarifies both the post-egoic nature of Unique Self—that is to say, Unique Self is fully realized only as an expression of True Self—as well as the identification of Unique Self with Unique Perspective. At Integral Spiritual Experience 2010, both Ken and I gave keynotes on Unique Self in which we crystallized many of our conversations, and for myself, twenty years of writing and thinking in this regard. Ken's wonderful formulation in his keynote was "True Self + Perspective = Unique Self."

It is also critical to note that from an Integral developmental view your perspective on the world is largely informed by your level of consciousness, and indeed it is refracted through the entire prism of AQUAL, all quadrants, levels, line types, and states—the core matrix of Ken Wilber's Integral Theory.

11. This realization of love as the motive force—as the very feeling and glue of the kosmos—is the underlying enlightened realization of Unique Self mystic Isaac Luria and his school. Luria's school includes perhaps the most important, profound, and influential teachers of Western mysticism, who inform the core teaching of evolutionary spirituality that would later emerge in the writings of the great German idealist Schelling and his colleagues. This mystical insight is slowly finding its way into the leading-edge discourse of science and spirit.

12. This is the second-person expression of evolutionary love in the intersubjective context. In third-person evolutionary love, will appears as the Eros that coheres and persuades the kosmos toward unfolding. See the discussion of evolutionary love in Chapter 8, "Unique Self and Evolutionary Spirituality."

13. What modernity—beginning with Kant, deepened by Saussure, and driven home by the postmodernists—has realized is the truth of perspective and context. Everything we see is through a perspective. Nothing lives independently of its context. Naturally this does not mean what the extreme postmodernists claimed it did. In their ecstatic confusion, intoxicated as they were with their own revelation of contexts, they thought that reality was only perspectives. This is not the case. There is a reality independent of perspective. But it is always mediated through a perspective. What is true is that perspective really matters.

Now let's apply this insight to the enlightenment teachings of True Self. The same way that the scientist is seeing reality through a particular perspective, so is the spiritual teacher, the church, and everyone else. The enlightened master is seeing reality through perspective just like everyone else. Just like the church and the scientist. In the premodern world the enlightened masters thought that when they realized their True Nature—their True Self—it was reality as it was, not mediated by any prism. Today we realize that this is simply not the case. True Self is always mediated by Unique Perspective, hence there is no True Self that ever appears without Unique Self. Precisely, Unique Self is the nature of True Self in the manifest world.

Chapter 3: Two Visions of Enlightenment and Their Higher Integration in Unique Self

1. It also appears in spiritual liberation traditions like Hinduism and mystical Judaism and Christianity as the communion of the separate self with the divine. Similarly, the Western enlightenment tradition, which affirms the separate self in some versions, affirms the goal of the communion of the separate self with the divine.

2. The mystical understanding of enlightenment, East and West, focuses on what Integral Theory has referred to as *states* of consciousness. Enlightenment is some form of satori, metanoia, redemption, or awakening. It is a state of consciousness that is at once always already present and at the same time requires realization.

   In contradistinction, the exoteric Western deployment of the idea and term "enlightenment," the idea that produced democracy and human rights, is referring not to a state but to a *structure stage* of consciousness. By structure stage, we refer to an internalized worldview that represents a particular level of development, for example, magical, mythic, rational, pluralistic, or integral. These levels of consciousness have been extensively described and evolved in the context of developmental and Integral Theory.

   The West has pushed into what have been termed by developmentalists orange/rational structure stages of consciousness (Graves, 1974), which express themselves in areas like representational democracy and human rights. The Eastern traditions (and some Western mystical lineages) have pressed into the higher states of awakened consciousness, expressed in different forms of satori, awakening, communion, metanoia, and *unio mystica*. While the West acknowledges states and state stages, they are not part of what might be termed the "official" Western orientation. Unique Self is both a state of consciousness, which like classical mystical enlightenment is available—in a flow state for example—at any level or structure stage of consciousness. Unique Self is also a structure stage of consciousness revealed in and as the expression of the second-tier structure stages of consciousness when perspective is revealed as an essential structure of higher consciousness.

3. Bruce H. Lipton, *The Biology of Belief* (Carlsbad, CA: Hay House, 2011), 70.

4. James L. Oschman, *Energy Medicine in Therapeutics and Human Performance* (Oxford, England: 2003), 20.

5. Lipton, *The Biology of Belief,* 86

6. Ibid., 22

7. Ibid., 27

8. Ibid., 53

9. Ibid., 57

10. Ibid., 159. On the surface of our cells is a family of identity receptors that distinguish one individual from another. All of this is part of the unique biological identity that makes each person's cellular community unique: "One well-studied subset of these receptors consists of what are called human leukocyte antigens (HLA), which are related to functions of the immune system. The closer your self-receptors match, the more chance an organ transplant might take. However there are no 100 percent matches." No two individuals are biologically the same.

    It is critical to understand that it is not these protein receptors themselves but what activates them that gives individuals their identity. It is not the identity receptors that are the uniqueness of the cell. It would be more accurate to say that the identity receptors are a key part of the *perspective* of the cell.

11. Ibid., 160. The analogy is not precise for two reasons. First, unlike a television set, which is a "passive play-back instrument," the self is dynamic and affects the environment; and second, the unique structure of DNA as well as the identity receptors of the proteins contain more complex givens of a Unique Self cellular signature than a television set. However, the core analogy suggested by Lipton holds.

12. In fact, in Hebrew the words for "love" and "obligation"—*chovah* and *chibbah*—are derived from the same root.

13. William Butler Yeats, "The Second Coming," *The Collected Poems of W. B. Yeats* (New York: Scribner, 1996).

Chapter 4: Eight Stations on the Road to Unique Self

1. This teaching which I call the "Three Stations Of Love" is the basis of the Integral Spiritual Experience and will form the core of the forthcoming book, *The Three Stations of Love*. I have used the term "stage" here instead of "stations" in order not to confuse the Three Stations of Love with the Eight Stations of Unique Self. In general, however, I prefer the term "station" so as not to confuse the term "stage" which in Integral Theory refers to Levels of Consciousness.

2. The full recognition of the centrality of shadow comes online only in the modern period. The great traditions had what might be termed a proto-shadow awareness that was profound but not developed.

3. William Blake, *Proverbs from Hell* (New York: Oxford University Press, 1975).

4. In Hebrew mysticism, this vow is taken by the hidden realized masters who are said to participate in the soul/root of the prophet Elijah.

5. In a long discussion with my friend and colleague, Richard Schwartz, founder of Internal Family Systems Theory, I shared with him my perspective on the relation of Ego and Unique Self and the larger set of core distinctions that comprise Unique Self teaching. In that conversation, catalyzed by Richard I first used the term, Awakening of the Ego. Richard excitedly concurred and added important empirical validation from his clinical perspective. He sent me this written communication after our conversation. "Many spiritual traditions make the mistake of viewing 'the ego' as the problem. At worst it vilified as greedy, anxious, clinging, needy, focused on wounds from the past or fear in the future, full of limiting or false beliefs about you, the source of all suffering, and something one must evolve beyond in order to taste enlightenment. At best it is seen as a confused and childish, to be treated with patience and acceptance but not to be taken seriously or listened to." My 30 years of experience exploring internal worlds has led to very different conclusions regarding the ego. What is called the ego or false self in these spiritualities is a collection of sub personalities I call parts. When you first become aware of them, these parts manifest all the negative qualities described above so I understand why this mistake is so widespread.

   As you get to know them from a place of curiosity and compassion, however, you learn that they are not what they seem. Instead, they are spiritual beings themselves who, because of being hurt by events in your life, are forced into roles that are far from their natures, and carry extreme beliefs and emotions that drive their limiting or suffering perspectives. Once they are able to release those beliefs and emotions (what I call burdens) they immediately transform into their natural, enlightened states and can join your evolution toward increasing embodiment of your true nature, what Marc Gafni importantly refers to as correctly, your unique Self. Thus, if instead of trying to ignore or transcend an annoying ego, you relate to even the apparent worst of your parts with love and open curiosity you will find that, just like you, they long for the liberating realization of their connection with the divine and provide delightful and sage company on your journey toward enlightenment. In this way you will be relating to these inner entities in the same way that Jesus and Buddha taught us to relate to suffering, exiled people. For a fuller explication of the conversation between us in this regard see our dialogue in Answering the Call series located at UniqueSelf. com.

6. Aurobindo and Abraham Kook talk of an "evolutionary imperative". Contemporary evolutionary mystic, Barbara Marx Hubbard calls this the evolutionary impulse. (Conscious Evolution, 1998)

7. The fourth awakening, together with strong elements of the fifth awakening, is described in the core teachings of Renaissance Hebrew mystic Isaac Luria. Kabbalah scholar M. Kallus characterizes the Lurianic realization as being absolutely nondual, one in which the human being awakens to his or her place as an incarnation of the divine process. This creates an activist posture in which human consciousness is realized to be an expression of evolving divine consciousness. This activist posture, based on the evolutionary impulse living personally in the human being, caused Kallus to characterize Luria's mysticism with the poignant pathos of Nikos Kazantzakis' phrase, "We are the saviors of God." This teaching, partially sourced in Kabbalah had direct influence on German idealists Fichte and Schelling. (Kabbalah scholar Eliot Wolfson [2005] has already pointed to a vast literature showing the Kabbalistic influence on Fichte and Schelling.) In the twentieth century, this impulse was powerfully expressed in the writings of Abraham Kook, Sri Aurobindo, and Teilhard de Chardin, three modern evolutionary mystics.

What it means to be "saviors of God" shifts and evolves as the human being ascends to higher structure-stages of consciousness. For Luria, this teaching has little of the humanist cast that it takes on in Kook and even more dramatically in the teachings of some contemporary evolutionary mystics. Some of these contemporary teachers understand the awakening to be the emergence of the inherent creativity, which is the enlightened creativity of what has been called the Authentic Self. In their teaching one awakens to the impersonal face of the process, which expresses itself in you, as you, and through you. In my reading Lurianic Kabbalah can best be characterized as a form of evolutionary mysticism and a precursor of modern evolutionary spirituality. Clearly, Luria, and the Zoharic authors before him, were writing before science had recognized the existence of evolution within the physical world. It is for that reason that I have chosen to characterize these seminal Kabbalists—in a private dialogue in 2011 with Andrew Cohen and Ken Wilber—as proto-evolutionary thinkers. The topic of this dialogue was the relationship among world spirituality, evolutionary spirituality, and integral spirituality as well as the relationship between Kabbalah and evolutionary thought.

Every evolved culture, and every evolved individual, may realize Unique Self when True Self awakens to its Unique Perspective. Unique Perspective is the prism of postmodern revelation. An early expression of this insight, expressed as True Self + Perspective = Unique Self, is sourced in premodernity in the great teachings of the Kabbalists. For these masters, the sacred text of the Torah is the word of God. Yet, paradoxically, in Hebrew mystical teaching it is said that a human being who is deeply grounded in True Self while fully incarnating his or her own uniqueness, also speaks the word of God! Human insight, however, is considered the word of God and given the status of Torah only when it derives directly from the clarified unique perspective of a human being who is connected to the ground of True Self. In this radical teaching, the ultimate identity between a human being and the godhead is only realized through the paradoxical portal of radical human uniqueness. Irreducible uniqueness, the full inhabiting of unique perspective or voice, is revealed to be an absolute quality of essence.

In modernity and especially in postmodernity, this early realization of the Kabbalists in regard to the primacy of perspective takes center stage. There is an emergent cultural realization, placed front and center in Integral Theory, that perspectives are foundational. But in postmodernity, perspectives have too often been used as the key tool for postmodernity's deconstructive project. The sentence used to deny all truth is "that's just your perspective".

Our conclusion in World Spirituality teaching, however is different from that of the post-modern deconstructive thinkers who were among the champions of this insight. Deconstructive thinkers assume that when perspective is revealed to be part of the process of meaning making, there is no longer any real meaning. However, in the World Spirituality teachings, we understand perspective in this way: every culture and every great tradition of spirit has its own Unique Self and therefore its own unique perspective. Perspective reveals a plenitude of meaning and not a dearth or death of meaning.

All cultures perceive Essence, but each unique perspective gives a particular resonance and cast to Essence. Loyalty to one's religion and culture is not, therefore (as modern and post-modern fashions sometimes suggest), primitive or fundamentalist. Instead, it is partially true, in that it is how my culture intuites essence. The pre-modern mistake was the failure to realize that every religion has a particular perspective, and therefore not to realize that no religion can claim that its intuition of ultimate truth is the only truth. Now that we understand that every great tradition and culture perceived essence through a particular perspective, we can avoid the tragic mistake of deconstructing the traditions as meaningless. Instead, we understand that every tradition has a particular perspective, a particular instrument in the symphony of spirit that is indeed making sacred music. All of the perspectives come together to create a symphony. And at that point, there is the possibility that the followers of each tradition can begin to realize that their particular religion is not the music, but an instrument of the music.

The Kabbalists foreshadow our post- postmodern World Spirituality reconstructive project. Nothing is true, says postmodernity, because everything is contextual. For the Kabbalists, foreshadowing World Spirituality teaching, the opposite is correct. When you fully inhabit your unique perspective, you enter into Source. You not only speak the word of God. You incarnate the word of God. World Spirituality based on Integral principles, including the first principle of Unique Self, understands that uniqueness reveals essence through a particular prism. Perspective creates, not a dearth of truth, but a magnificent kaleidoscope of truth. Every authentic insight deriving from Unique Perspective is true but partial. No part is reducible to the whole, but no part stands alone. It is this insight of Unique Self that is the foundation of the great reconstructive project, which is Spirit's Next Move.

Chapter 5: The Evolutionary Integration of Eastern and Western Enlightenment

1. To be clear, state development, from separate to True Self, is insufficient to heal suffering. We also need structure-stage development, to higher levels of consciousness from mythic rational to pluralistic to second-tier. "Static development" refers to the process of waking up to your True Nature. "Stage-structure development" refers to the process of growing up to higher levels of consciousness, for example, growth from egocentric to ethnocentric to worldcentric consciousness.

2. Lest you think we are misreading *A Course in Miracles,* let's look at the highly popular book *A Return To Love* (New York: HarperCollins, 1992), a popularization of the Course in Miracles by Marianne Williamson (p. 110): "From a course perspective special means different (unique), therefore separate, which is characteristic of ego rather than spirit."

3. See for example Gurdjieff's discussion of the vital forces of the energy body. See also the Vedantic principle and key yogic traditions that understand that your sexual energy is the vital impersonal force itself.

4. New Testament, Corinthians 7:9.

5. I have somewhat edited and reorganized Rollie's writing, but the core content in regard to Christian thought set out in these paragraphs is entirely Rollie's material. I look forward to seeing it under his name in his own books and articles.

6. See Ken Wilber, *Sex, Ecology, Spirituality,* 2nd ed. (Boston: Shambala Publications, 2001), p. 717–734, for a profound unpacking of Nagarjuna's critique of the Theravada No-Self doctrine.

7. The centrality of perspectives, which is the core of Hebrew mysticism and the postmodern context, is not obviously apparent in Nagarjuna.

8. See for example the *Pesikta deRav Kahana* 12:5.

9. Claude Lelouch film *Un homme et une femme,* 1966.

Chapter 6: Ego and Unique Self

1. See A. H. Almaas, *The Pearl Beyond Price* (Boston: Shambala, 2001).

2. To reach enlightenment, you must be able to take a perspective on your story. This is the Hebrew mystical reading of Abraham, who is commanded to leave his land, birthplace, and father's house, that is to say, to step out of his perspective and take a perspective on his perspective. This same teaching is the deeper intent of the Talmudic teaching, "Anyone who says something in the name of the person who said it brings redemption to the world." Let the hint be sufficient to the wise.

3. Humanity emerges from its semi-immersion in the Great Mother. As the human sense of separate self solidifies in what is called by anthropologists "the early farming period," so too does the person's terror of death.

4. See Ken Wilber, *Up from Eden: A Transpersonal View of Human Evolution* (Wheaton, IL: Quest Books, 2007), in which he brings Becker, Norman O. Brown, and others to bear to develop this core line of thought. At this stage of his work, Ken understands the correct intuitions of immortality as applying to what we have referred to in this book as True Self. I am applying the same intuition to Unique Self: In *Up from Eden,* the second person, or what he later called the second face of God, was not yet crystallized in Ken's thinking. In part, the dialogues Ken initiated between himself, Brother David Steindl-Rast, Father Thomas Keating, myself, and others helped evolve the Integral perspective on second person. The understanding of the three faces of God is fundamental to Vedanta and Kabbalah, and after these dialogues was placed front and center in Integral Theory. Within Integral Theory, Unique Self, a corollary of second person, can be seen as part of that Integral evolution, particularly within the very sophisticated context of Integral Perspectival Thought.

Chapter 7: Personal and Impersonal

1. We need to evolve our gender language. The term "man" is clearly inappropriate; yet to use "man and woman" is awkward in this context, and gender-neutral language like "self" does not quite do it either.

2. For an expression of the seamless integration of the personal and impersonal as two faces of the one, see the notion of a monad, central to theosophical teaching. See, for example, the writing of Alice Bailey in *The Rays and Initiations* (New York: Lucis Publishing, 1971), p. 106:

   > This point is conscious, immutable, and aware of the two extremes of the divine expression: the sense of individual identity and the sense of universality. These are fused and blended in the One. Of this One, the divine Hermaphrodite is the concrete symbol—the union in one of the pairs of opposites, negative and positive, male and female. In the state of being that we call the monadic, no difference is recognized between these two because it is realized that there is no identity apart from universality and no appreciation of the universal apart from the individual realization.

   I am indebted to Bruce Lyon for this reference.

3. Cynthia Bourgeault in reviewing this work pointed in a number of key directions which are both supportive of and deepen the general direction of this work in affirmation of the personal heart of the kosmos. Below is a citation from her email. All of these directions need to be carefully considered in the deepening of this critical realization of the personal thou, the infinity of intimacy that lies at and as the heart of the kosmos. Cynthia writes that "in the Gurdjieff work, for example, in Raimon Panikkar, in the meticulous Trinitarian work of Christos Yannaros (PERSON AND ESSENCE, a brilliant and challenging exploration of the notion of personhood at the heart of the Trinity) and in the intricate phenomenology of Robert Sardello . . . a case can be built that transcending the egoic definition of personal does not open us up to the impersonal, but for the first time makes possible the authentic understanding of the personal—the "thou" or pure intimacy at the heart of everything! I also believe that your discussion of the movement from ego self to what you call "your Unique Self" needs also to be grounded more seriously in an exploration of the structures of consciousness supporting that movement (I'm talking about neurology here, the movement from brain perception to heart perception) which makes possible the doing of what you suggest: perceiving particularity without separation. This is my complaint in general with the otherwise good work being done by Ken and the Integral folks: in my opinion (again based on the teachings of the Christian and Sufi esoteric traditions), what Ken calls the higher conscious realms (Christ,

witness, nondual) are not a further extension of the cognitive line of the mind; they require the engagement of the "operating system" of the heart. When you explore the material here awaiting you in the Philokalia, Sufism, and the HeartMath Institute, you can make your case much, much stronger as to why the Unique Self is not simply the ego-self "writ large."

4. From John Donne's poem "The Canonization."

5. This is David Deida's phrase, attributed to "William" in his book *Wild Nights* (Boulder, CO: 2005). David is a person I love, and whose writing and teaching have been highly significant for many people. Among other contributions, David has done important work in evolving the masculine archetype to a place where it could reclaim the sacred energy of masculine forcefulness, ravishing the feminine at a level of consciousness in which the feminine was fully honored and delighted.

6. This form of erotic merger is called by the kabbalists *zivug.*

7. Both Unique Self and Authentic Self teachings, as in the kind expressed by my colleague Andrew Cohen, would, I believe, agree with this critique of the Stepford Wife student, fostered by a teaching that views True Self as the end goal of the enlightenment process. In respectful dialogue, Andrew and I have disagreed about the place of Uniqueness in the enlightenment process. For Andrew, uniqueness is a function of "social, cultural, and psychological conditioning", but it is not an essential function of Authentic Self. Rather, Andrew holds it as an "awakened impersonal function". Unique Self, in my teaching, drawn from the depth of my lineage and my own realization, is ontological in the sense of an ontology of perspectives, and not merely conditioned.

The difference between an irreducible uniqueness and a merely conditioned uniqueness is profound, with vast existential, ethical, and social implications in many areas. Andrew calls Authentic Self "an awakened impersonal function." In other writings and teachings, he argues passionately that "there is no such thing as a unique spiritual experience." He used to call his community an "impersonal enlightenment fellowship." Or in still other statements, which are resonant with the old dialectical materialism of Hegel, he implies that the dignity of the individual is subordinated to the process, in this case the evolutionary process. Uniqueness is seen as being a function of the personal, which is identified at best with social, cultural, and psychological conditioning that needs to be transcended if one is to evolve beyond ego.

In my reading, Andrew fails to distinguish between uniqueness at the post-egoic level of Unique Self and pre-egoic Uniqueness, which is a function of personality, and must be overcome as one identifies with the impersonal field of consciousness, which I refer to in this book as True Self. In my understanding, however, the final stage of enlightenment is when the personal and impersonal are fully merged in Evolutionary Unique Self. The personal comes back online post–True Self as the Unique Perspective of True Self, that is, Unique Self. I said to Andrew that the ultimate proof of Unique Self, which is not an awakened impersonal function but the personal face of essence and the unique perspective of enlightenment, was none other then Andrew Cohen. Andrew laughed and said, "Touché." Indeed, I shared with Andrew that in the introduction to a recent volume of his teaching (2010), the book is described as his "unique perspective." That is a far cry from his 2006 critique of Uniqueness in our recorded dialogue in Tel Aviv and quite a distance as well from his statement of record in his Authentic Self teaching, "There is no such thing as a Unique Spiritual Experience." Indeed, the entire point of the Unique Self teaching is that there is no such thing as a non-Unique Spiritual Experience. What is fair to say is that I agree with Andrew's critique of the hyperinflated egoic individuality at the level of separate self, which is often but a thinly disguised narcissism. That is why I place so much emphasis on the distinction between ego and Unique Self.

So while we have drawn closer on this issue through dialogue, it remains fair to say that our core intuitions are in some profound sense diametrically opposed. In Unique Self teaching, everything is ultimately personal, and the dignity of the individual is in dialectical tension with the process, but is never reducible to the service it renders the process. Unique Self is a function as well of the personal address of a personal God—what we have recently called in Integral Theory the second face of God. For a partial explanation of our respective views, see our dialogue, "Authentic Self and Unique Self," *JITP* 6, no. 1 (March 2011). Andrew asked some of his students to contact me to respond to my critique and clarify his perspective. Their remarks were important and appreciated. I cite them here.

"It is true to say, however, that Andrew does not overly emphasize this dimension of his teaching. In my understanding, this is more of a pedagogical matter than a philosophical one. Andrew's primary concern as a teacher is with helping people to move beyond the postmodern tendency toward narcissism and exaggerated self-importance that has become such an evolutionary cul-de-sac for our culture. In this context, I think he may be concerned that overemphasizing uniqueness either as a path or a goal might reinforce the very tendency he is trying to help people to transcend. As he puts it, 'We tend to be much more familiar with the world of the personal self than we are with the cosmic context and identity of the Authentic Self. In our culture, in which the rights, needs, and significance of the individual tend to be held most sacred, the personal dimension has become imbued with exaggerated importance. We have become conditioned to seek the deepest connection to life primarily through the personal sphere, and, therefore, it is a profound step forward when we gain the ability to see this dimension of our experience in a context that infinitely transcends it.' I think Andrew's experience and teaching is that the flowering of post-egoic autonomy and uniqueness is something that happens naturally by itself when the individual lets go of his or her need to cling to the idea of uniqueness, and therefore it is not something he feels he needs to spend too much time on."

Andrew's editor kindly sent me the following paragraph in response to the points expressed in this footnote. "He has explained that his purpose is not to deny that there is an authentic, post-egoic expression of autonomy and uniqueness. However, he chooses not to emphasize this dimension of enlightenment for pedagogical more than philosophical reasons, because his primary concern is to help individuals to transcend the postmodern cultural tendency toward narcissism. As he writes in his new book, *Evolutionary Enlightenment:* 'Both [the personal sphere and the impersonal process] are real, but they are different dimensions of the self and we tend to be much more familiar with the world of the personal self than we are with the cosmic context and identity of the Authentic Self. In our culture, in which the rights, needs, and significance of the individual tend to be held most sacred, the personal dimension has become imbued with exaggerated importance. We have become conditioned to seek the deepest connection to life primarily through the personal sphere, and, therefore, it is a profound step forward when we gain the ability to see this dimension of our experience in a context that infinitely transcends it.' "

This wonderful paragraph is a marked evolution of his earlier teaching and its radical emphasis on the impersonal. I am delighted by this. However, it still identifies the personal with what I would call personality or separate self. This deployment of the term personal to refer to the separate self, ego or personality level of consciousness is consistent in virtually all the citations throughout the book. The point of Unique Self teaching is that the personal itself is a quality of the infinite. Divinity, the ground of being, the suchness of All-That-Is the infinitely personal love intelligence and love beauty that knows your name. This is the level of the personal beyond impersonal. In this sense the impersonal does not only infinitely transcend the personal but rather the personal is an interior face of the impersonal, what in Unique Self teaching we call the personal face of essence. Andrew and his student have leveled the critique that Unique Self is easily hijacked by ego. The same is true, however, of the evolutionary impulse which lies at the heart of the evolutionary teaching which I share with Andrew. Discernment is always essential. Finally Andrew and his student have suggested that Uniqueness is a natural expression which emerges authentically after evolution beyond ego. While that is certainly true for some people, for most, clarification of Uniqueness, including Unique perspective, Unique Gifts and Unique Obligation is a lifelong spiritual journey.

8. Sexual intimacy in the context of a dual relationship between teacher and student, when specific contexts and conditions are met, may well be appropriate and ethical. This point was made by Ken Wilber as well in a recorded dialogue at the German Integrales Forum in 2010, and has been made by numerous feminist writers including bell hooks, Christina Hoff Sommers, Laura Kipnis, Daphne Patai, and many others. I also discuss this issue in an article, "Spiritually Incorrect: Sex, Ethics, and Injury" (see marcgafni.com and *Integrales Magazine*, 2011. However, as I and all of the aforementioned writers point out, sexual intimacy between teacher and student may also potentially endanger both the teacher and the student. It requires a particularly evolved student and a particularly evolved teacher to successfully navigate this territory. In this sense, one might argue that if the Unique Self teaching is to be lived out in its entirety, it requires a particular kind of student and teacher, who are both able to hold the complexities of dual or multiple relationships without falling into the classical egoic traps. This is rare, for all people are geniuses at self-deception.

It is for this reason that I generally recommend proscribing sexual relations between the student and teacher. The exceptions are in the realm of the postconventional, and therefore by definition need to be looked at individually and cannot be taught in public articles or teachings.

Chapter 8: Unique Self and Evolutionary Spirituality

1. On the distinction between Being and Becoming, see Alfred North Whitehead, who first formulated this nomenclature. I refer to this distinction in my original work on Soul Prints, which pre-dates by some five years my first encounter with my dear friend and Integral mentor Ken Wilber and the contemporary community of Integral evolutionary mystics.

The dialectic between Being and Becoming is a perennial philosophical theme running back to Zeno and Heraclitus. It figured prominently in the philosophy of Plotinus and in some of the debates of the medieval philosophers. Kant, Hegel, and Marx took up the issues, as did Emerson and the American pragmatists. More recently, Whitehead provided a synoptic view of the history of the debate by way of distilling the main theological implications of a thoroughgoing evolutionary worldview.

I heard the specific term "ecstatic urgency" from my friend and colleague, spiritual teacher Andrew Cohen, after I gave a talk at his Foxhollow center on Soul Prints and kabbalist Ibn Gabai's evolutionary teaching, which I have termed "God Needs Your Service," as well as during my conversations with him on evolutionary spirituality during a weekend that we cohosted and cotaught in Israel in December 2005.

It is my delight to credit him with the term. Andrew has done a great deal to evolve and teach the evolutionary worldview. The root source of

Andrew's teaching, beyond his own realization, seems to be at least in part Hindu mystic Aurobindo. The source of my teaching, beyond my own humble realization, is the kabbalistic lineage in which I live. Some of our differences in nuance and emphasis, particularly in terms of the relationship between the relative and the absolute, the personal and impersonal, may be rooted in the different original sources of our teaching.

2. See Abraham Kook, adduced in this chapter. This footnote in its entirety is adduced from , *Language, Eros, Being: Kabbalistic Hermeneutics and Poetic Imagination* (New York: Fordham University Press, 2005), 392–393. The reason I cite it in its entirety is to ground in scholarship my claim, which I have put forward in public teaching for many years, that evolutionary spirituality is not rooted in the Friedrich Schelling school of German idealism. It seems to me more accurate to root evolutionary spirituality in the core matrix of Zoharic and primarily Lurianic Kabbalah, which greatly influenced Schelling and his colleagues.

On the influence of kabbalistic sources on Schelling, see Scholem, *Major Trends in Jewish Mysticism,* p. 409–19 and p. 412–77; Idel, *Kabbalah,* p. 134 and 200; Schulze, "Schelling und die Kabbala," p. 65–99, 143–170, 210–232; Idel, *Kabbalah: New Perspectives,* p. 264; A. Olson, *Hegel and the Spirit,* p. 42–44; Schulte, "Zimzum in the Works of Schelling," p. 21–40; E. Beach, *Potencies of God(s),* p. 1–2, 6–13, 25–45, 22–230; Drob, *Kabbalistic Metaphors,* p. 83–85; Gibbons, *Spirituality and the Occult,* p. 12–13; Kosolowski, *Philsophien der Offenbarung,* p. 565–771.

3. This is a core teaching of evolutionary mystic Abraham Kook.

4. As kabbalist Abraham Kook indicates, the core kabbalistic category of *tikkun,* which is usually translated as "to fix or to heal," is actually better translated as "to evolve." The entire goal of Kabbalah is what scholars have referred to as "theurgy," that is to say, to effect a cosmic *tikkun* through personal action, which means to evolve God. The nature of Hebrew mysticism is evolutionary. Kabbalah interprets all of life as taking place in an evolutionary context. Indeed, the Lurianic and post-Lurianic is best characterized as a kind of proto-evolutionary mysticism. I use the term "proto" because to the best of my knowledge, Luria does not discuss evolution in the biosphere, although the possibility is clearly implicit. This is not a vague idea retrojected onto old sources. For those who know how to read the sources, this is the very lodestone on which Kabbalah rests. In the kabbalistic realization, the entire world exists within the divine. Every human act is for the sake of *tikkun,* to evolve the Godhead, that is to say, all of reality. Every human action is for the sake of the whole and impacts the whole. Every human being is necessary, born to fulfill a particular function in the evolution of All-That-Is.

The Kabbalists had significant influence on Fichte and Schelling, who are often listed as the originators of evolutionary spirituality. On the influence on Kabbalistic sources on Schelling, see Eliot Wolfson, *Language, Eros, Being: Kabbalistic Hermeneutics and Poetic Imagination* (New York: Fordham University Press, 2005), 392n2. This influence is not a minor fancy of some scholar, but a major insight of the most respected scholars in the field.

5. In Kabbalah, both the first *ani* before *ayin* and the second *ani* after *ayin* are three-letter names of God. For the teaching of my teacher on Unique Self in the context of these two names, see Mei HaShiloach, vol. I, *Likkutim, Vehineh.* That both expressions of *ani* are names of God is one of the esoteric hints that the ego prefigures Unique Self.

6. In my teaching I refer to Kook both as a Unique Self mystic and as an evolutionary mystic. Both are correct. Kook's understanding of Unique Self, which informs my own, locates Uniqueness firmly within an evolutionary context. More than that, Kook explicitly sees the personal address of evolution inviting, even obligating, every person to live their unique life, to give their Unique Gift. It is to be lived as a Unique verb of God—according to Kook's Kabbalah, which is rooted in Luria—which is the very essence of one's life and the purpose of one's birth at a particular place in time. The realization that one is needed by God, by All-That-Is, by the great evolutionary process, all of which are one, is the greatest source of human joy, which is the joy of all the kosmos.

For more on Kook's evoutionary mysticism, see for example Yosef Ben Shlomo's study of Kook, *The Song of Life,* Chapter 12, and the relevant footnotes there that give a nuanced accounting of the evolutionary mysticism that lay at the core of Kook's teaching, and which was rooted in his Kabbalistic lineage. Ben Shlomo points out the striking parallels between Kook's thought and that of Teilhard de Chardin and Henri Bergson. Most important, however, it is critical to realize, as Ben Shlomo does, that Kook's evolutionary mysticism is a natural expression of the Lurianic matrix of thought that formed Kook's mental and spiritual furniture. Luria's concepts of *yichud, zivug,* and *tikkun* are all infused by a proto-evolutionary mysticism.

7. Kook, *Orot HaKodesh,* Vol. 2, p. 507. The first and second quotes are also from Kook, *Orot HaKodesh,* Vol. 2, p. 532.3, 548.

8. The precise Hebrew word used is "Yichud," which in many texts is deployed in a virtually identical manner to the term "*tikkun.*" *Tikkun,* as I discuss elsewhere, is often translated as "to evolve."

Chapter 9: Evolutionary Spirituality Reloaded

1. See Ken Wilber's discussion of parts and wholes in *Sex, Ecology, Spirituality,* p. 25.

2. I have heard different oral versions of this story over the years. I was told that it was a well-known story told by American Yiddish writers at the turn of the century but have been unable to locate a precise source.

3. "Love is as powerful as death," cries out the Song of Songs. Interpret the third-century Babylonian wisdom masters, "Charity saves from death." "What could that mean?" ask the disciples.

Chapter 10: True Self and Unique Self, Parts and Wholes Reloaded

1. Letter can be found in Alice Calaprice's *The New Quotable Einstein* (Princeton, NJ: Princeton University Press, 2005), 206.

2. Thanks for this formulation to the anonymous reviewers of my scholarly articles on Unique Self.

3. Unique Self-realization in this sense of the Unique being the portal to the universal one undermines the postmodern rejection of all universals. This is a standard first-tier pluralistic stance that recognizes only particulars. It cannot see patterns that connect and create what Wilber has called "good-enough universals" (Wilber, personal communication). As Wilber has pointed out, we recognize universals all the time in the physical world: 208 bones, two kidneys, two lungs, one heart, and so on. This is not an imperialistic colonial statement. It is simply the truth. Of course, the postmodernists assert with no awareness of contradiction or even irony the most dramatic universal, the assertion that there are never universals.

4. Book of Proverbs

Chapter 11: Eros and Unique Self

1. I first wrote and gave major teaching on Eros around the year 2000, and it appears in part in my audio series *The Erotic and the Holy* (Boulder, CO: Sounds True, 2006) and my book *The Mystery of Love* (New York: Simon & Schuster, 2003). I stand by this work 1,000 percent. At the same time, my understanding of the pain of Eros as well as the identity between personal and impersonal Eros has evolved since that time, and will be included (I hope) in a new version of this material to be published under the title *On the Erotic and the Holy*.

2. Pierre Delattre's book *Tales of a Dalai Lama* (Sandpoint, ID: Lost Horse Press, 1999), 89.

3. See Mihaly Csikszentmihalyi, *Flow: The Psychology of Optimal Experience* (New York: Harper and Row, 2008).

4. The unpacking of this teaching will be the subject, God willing, of my next book, tentatively titled *The Erotic and the Holy*. For now, it is enough to

point out that Judah in Kabbalah is a symbol for Shekhinah. A careful reading of many Shekhinah passages reveals the identity between Shekhinah and Eros. Judah is also in Mordechai Lainer's unpacking of a certain set of Zoharic passages on the incarnation of Unique Self. The entire teaching might then be stated as the following set of equations:

$$\text{Judah} = \text{Unique Self}$$

$$\text{Judah} = \text{Shekhinah}$$

$$\text{Shekhinah} = \text{Eros}$$

$$\text{Eros} = \text{Unique Self}$$

Abraham Kook, who was directly influenced by Lainer, views the original sin of the Garden of Eden—replayed in every human life—as the alienation from one's *ani*, one's Unique Self story. See Kook, *Lights of Holiness*, vol. 3, sec. 140. On Lainer's direct influence on Kook, see Marc Gafni, *Nondual Humanism and the Unique Self*, particularly the section on Abraham Kook.

5. This quote was attributed to Emerson by Dev S. Pathak in his book *Promotion of Pharmaceuticals: Issues, Trends, Options.*

6. Plato, *Phaedrus,* from Christopher Rowe's translation (New York: Penguin Classics, 2005).

7. On the mystical nature of Hebrew language, see for example Joseph Dan, "The Language of Creation and Its Grammar," in *Jewish Mysticism* (Northvale, NY: 1998), 129–154.

8. See for example Gershom Scholem in "Isaac Luria and His School," in *Major Trends in Jewish Mysticism* (New York: Shocken, 1941), 224–286.

9. This is the essential teaching of Hebrew mysticism. See Joseph Dan's scholarship on Kabbalah, which deals extensively with this issue. I paraphrased the formulation of this sentence from Terence McKenna.

10. Clearly, the individual embedded in the mother church is a more evolved level of consciousness than the individual embedded in the typhonic level of mother nature. Nonetheless, mother church—what Spiral Dynamics theory calls the blue level of consciousness—still stands in the way of the fuller versions of healthy separate-self ego that emerged with the Renaissance and the Enlightenment—what Spiral Dynamics theory calls the orange level of consciousness. This is evolved into a still-fuller expression of the healthy separate-self ego in the multicultural, pluralistic meme of consciousness, what Spiral Dynamics labels as green consciousness.

11. For discussion of this and other ancient sources that shed light on the emergence of war as a human institution, see Ken Wilber, *Up from Eden* (Wheaton, IL: Quest, 2007), 163–166, 296–297.

12. What I term in *Mystery of Love* as pseudo-Eros, Ken Wilber terms in *Up from Eden* as the Atman project. While *Mystery of Love* was written before I was aware of Ken and Integral Theory, my later understanding of pseudo-Eros was greatly enriched by Ken's Atman project. Ken weaves together and evolves the core teachings of Norman O. Brown, Becker, and many others in a highly important and helpful way.

Chapter 12: The Story of Story

1. The sections "The Grace of the Story" and "The Loss of Memory" are a free mixing of my Soul Print teaching and language in part IV of my book *Soul Prints* (New York: Atria, 2002), as well as oral teachings on story that I have been giving since around 1996. Other formulations come from Jean, including the phrase, "A myth is something that never was but is always happening." (I don't recall if that phrase is Jean's or Joseph Campbell's.) I wrote *Soul Prints* in Israel several years before I came across Jean's teaching. When we did our first public dialogue (in Ashland, Oregon, April 2006), we were both struck by our shared passion for story.

2. On the compelling moral context of the evolutionary worldview in both Abraham Kook and Jesuit Teilhard de Chardin, see Hugo Bergman, *Teilhard de Chardin and the Idea of Evolution,* in Abraham Uderachim as cited in Yosef Ben Shlomo, *Poetry of Being: Lectures on the Philosophy of Rabbi Kook* (Mod Books, 1997).

3. For the implicit identity of *axis mundi,* radical Kabbalah's Unique Self, and Goddess, see my book *Unique Self and Nondual Humanism.* In the Zohar, Judah is the Goddess. In the Evolution of this Zoharic identification, Mordechai Lainer identifies the Judah-goddess archetype with what I have called Unique Self. Indeed, this evolutionary reading of the Zohar by Mordechai Lainer is one of the primary Kabbalistic lineage sources for my teaching of Unique Self.

4. King James Bible, John 1:9.

5. Rabbi Kook, *Orot HaKodesh,* section 3:221 (Jerusalem, 1995).

6. The superior man is the language used by Franklin Jones to describe the righteous enlightened person. See Franklin Jones (Adi Da), *Love of the Two-Armed Form* (Middletown, CA: Dawn Horse Press, 1978).

7. See my dialogue with Spiral Dynamics founder Don Beck on the five movements against story. Available on iEvolve.org.

8. See for example Jack Engler's essay "Being Somebody and Being Nobody: A Reexamination of the Understanding of Self in Psychoanalysis and Buddhism," in *Psychoanalysis and Buddhism: An Unfolding Dialogue,* ed.

Jeremy A. Safrar (Boston: Wisdom Publications, 2003), 35–79. See also Adyashanti, "Awakening," in *Emptiness Dancing.*

9. See Deitrich Bonhoeffer on Cheap Grace.

10. Cited in Huston Smith, *The Forgotten Truth,* Ch. 1.

11. *Collected Letters of St. Therese of Lisieux,* trans. F. J. Sheed, 1949, p. 303. Second citation p. 254.

12. Martin Buber, *Good and Evil* (New York: Charles Scribner and Sons, 1953), 111.

Chapter 13: Sacred Autobiography

1. Even from a postmodern perspective, the physical is at least a metaphor for the spiritual. From a Kabbalistic perspective of realization, the vessel is actually ossified light, making the physical much more than a mere metaphor for spirit.

2. See Richard Mann, *The Light of Consciousness* (Albany: State University of New York, 1984).

3. I am currently writing a full work on the evolutionary masculine and feminine with my dear friend Warren Farrell.

4. Abraham Kook, *The Lights of Holiness* 3:140.

5. Recovering the Uni-verse story is one of the essential projects of the emergent world. Spirituality based on integral principles. See, for example, the work of Thomas Berry.

Chapter 14: Unique Self and Loneliness

1. See Joseph Soloveitchik, *Lonely Man of Faith* (New York: Doubleday, 2006).

2. Cited in Leo Buscaglia's *Love: What Life Is All About* (New York: Ballentine Books, 1996).

3. Talmud, Ethics of the Fathers 4:1.

Chapter 16: Joy and Unique Self

1. Talmud, Tractate Shabbot, 30.

2. Talmud, Tractate Sanhedrin, 34 and 47.

3. The original Hebrew word is *hevel,* usually translated as "vanity," as in "vanity of vanities, all is vanity." However, the literal Hebrew word *hevel* means something closer to "insubstantial." It is in this sense that the mist created by our breath on a cold day is called *hevel.* It is with this same sense

of the word that I have re-translated Solomon's famous verse as "illusion of" instead of the more standard, illusionary "vanity of vanities."

Chapter 17: Shadow Integration and Unique Self

1. J. Ruth Chandler, *The Book of Qualities* (New York: Harper Paperbacks, 1988).

2. I am not suggesting that Bly actually believes that the baby is the ideal. Rather, Bly is committing the classical pre-trans fallacy typical of many neo-romantic thinkers, who confuse pre-personal radiance with transpersonal maturity and realization. See Wilber's *The Marriage of Sense and Soul* (New York: Random House, 1998).

3. See *Two Letters to Gandhi* by Martin Buber and Judah Magnes.

4. The word *tikkun,* which to a certain degree has become common parlance, is generally understood as meaning "fixing," "repair," or "emendation." This usage is most likely based on the Lurianic writings, or possibly on the Talmud, where the phrase *tikkun olam* is used to describe rabbinic edicts that were not necessarily based on *halakha,* but rather to ensure the general well-being of society.

   In the Zohar, however, the meaning of *tikkun* is generally quite different (although there are instances of the more familiar usage). Particularly in the epic *Sifra deTzniuta, Idra Rabba,* and *Idra Zuta* sections, we find lengthy discussions on the *tikkunim* of Atiqa Kadisha, the Holy Ancient One, who is the first and most elevated manifestation of the Godhead, who is perfect unto itself and certainly not in need of repair.

   The Aramaic word *tikuna,* which is the Zoharic way of saying *tikkun,* means either "garment" or "adornment" (jewelry). For example, in the *Idra Rabba* section of the Zohar (vol. 3, 132b), we find: "The beard of the High Priest is set in eight *tikkunim,* which is why the High Priest had eight garments (*tikkunim*)." Yet another example, also from Idra Rabba (140b): "These are the honored garments (*porfira*) of the king, as is written (Psalms 104): 'You wore glory and beauty,' (that is), the garments (*tikkunim*) that You wear."

   We may therefore conclude that when, for example, the Zohar speaks about the "Thirteen *Tikkunim* of *Atiqa Kadisha,*" we are referring to how divinity reveals itself in the world. "Clothing" or "garment" is the perfect metaphor for this idea, since it hints at the seemingly contradictory act of revelation by means of concealment. I cannot go out into the world (revelation) if I am not dressed (concealment). Similarly, the Infinite cannot interface with a finite world unless its infinity is concealed or tempered.

   Additionally, this movement on the part of the Infinite toward the finite implies a certain change in the immutable divine, yet another paradox, and it is at this junction that we may begin to speak of divine evolution. In the

Zoharic sense of these texts, when the divine reveals itself in the human realm, when the Infinite expresses itself in the creative process, there is an actual evolution that takes place within divinity. Something new emerges that—paradoxically—was not there before. All this is expressed by the word *tikkun* or *tikuna*.

I would also note that the root *t'k'n'* is also used as a verb, for example, *lehatkin* or *itkan*. In a strange twist of fate, the best possible translation of this verb might be "to install" in a computer sense, as it refers to introducing some new factor into the greater system, either to the aspect of the divine or to that of humanity.

5. From the biblical book of Job, Chapter 19, as read by many Hasidic masters.

6. This footnote is in part drawn from the scholarship of Avraham Leader, as it emerged in our joint study in 2005.

7. These last three paragraphs are a paraphrase of a personal communication that Dr. Mark Kirschbaum sent me in regard to the biological uniqueness of the body. Mark is chief of developmental therapeutic service at the Nevada Cancer Institute, and one of the leaders in cell and cancer research in the United States. For a partial list of Kirschbaum's publications, see cityofhope. org/directory/people/kirschbaum-mark-h/Pages/selected-publications.aspx.

8. A version of this story is told by Alan Cohen in "The African Song of the Soul."

Chapter 19: Shadow and Unique Self Reloaded

1. Love at its core, however, is not intersubjective; that is, it is not limited to the interpersonal context of love between people or beings. Love lives in first, second, and third persons. In all of these perspectives, love at its core is a realization of the True Nature of what is. Love is not merely a realization. Love is. Love is the innermost nature of All-That-Is. It is in this sense that we pray to God—the second person—to be "lived as love." My colleague David Deida has made this a signature phrase of his teaching. Some version of this phrase is also central in the teaching of Hindu teacher Muktananda.

2. While the masculine acts as a pure mirror reminding you that you are seen, that is to say, pure consciousness, it is the feminine that adds the radiant affirmation that you are loved.

3. In all of the goddess traditions, there is a second face of the divine feminine that is apparently destructive, but is in fact deconstructive.

4. Song of Songs 8:3.

5. A living master who is teaching these practices today is Sally Kempton.

6. A teaching phrase used by my colleague Andrew Cohen.

7. This is the core teaching underlying the meditation taught by Hasidic master Nachman of Breslov, referred to as the BeOdee meditation. BeOdee is mystically translated by Nachman to mean, "Sing to God with whatever point of goodness you can find in your self about which you are absolutely certain. From that place of knowing your absolute goodness, expand into God."

8. See Michael Lerner's book, *The Left Hand of God* (New York: HarperCollins, 2005).

9. David Gordon and Maribeth Meyers-Anderson, *Phoenix: Therapeutic Patterns of Milton H. Erickson* (Capitola, CA: META Publications, 1981).

10. See Cormac McCarthy's *The Road* (New York: Vintage Books, 2007) in which it is the boy who engages the snake. Thanks to Haven Iverson for this reference.

11. In Hebrew, every letter has an equivalent numerical value. The Hebrew words for "messiah" and "snake," although comprised of different letters, add up to the same numerical amount. This, in the code of Hebrew numerology, points to an underlying linkage between them.

12. Abraham Kook, *Lights of Holiness* 3:140.

Chapter 20: Sex and Unique Self

1. Rob Brezsny, *Pronoia Is the Antidote for Paranoia* (San Rafael, CA: Televisionary Publishing, 2005), 141–143.

Chapter 21: The Seven Laws of Unique Self Encounters

1. I am indebted to my friend and colleague Craig Hamilton, who gathered these key quotes. See Craig Hamilton, "Come Together: Can We Discover a Depth of Wisdom Far Beyond What Is Available to Individuals Alone?", *What Is Enlightenment,* May/June 2004.

Chapter 22: Parenting and Unique Self

1. Rainer Maria Rilke, *The Notebooks of Malte Laurids Brigge* (New York: Random House, 1983).

Chapter 23: Malice

1. Joseph Berke, *The Tyranny of Malice: Exploring the Dark Side of Character and Culture* (London: Summit Books, 1989). See also the updated edition, *Malice through the Looking Glass* (London: Teva Books, 2006).

Chapter 24: Death and Unique Self

1. Rabbi Kook, *Orat Hatshuma*, 1972.

Epilogue: Unique Self, Global Spirituality, and Evolutionary We Space

1. The distinction between waking up and growing up was originally published by John Welwood in *Toward a Psychology of Awakening*, p. 231. Mariana Caplan (2009) points out that Chögyam Trungpa used to have people practice by saying "om mani padme hum,"—grow up. The om mani phrase expresses the enlightened state of consciousness called the Jewel in the Lotus. In effect, Trungpa was saying wake up and grow up. In a conversation with John (2011), I suggested that Trungpa, who was his teacher, was the inspiration for his core distinction between wake up and grow up, which John readily acknowledged. Trungpa understood intuitively that the western work of growing up, which for him meant psychological work, and the eastern work of waking up were two distinct lines of development, which needed to be integrated. In this tense, Chögyam Trungpa is an important forerunner of World Spirituality. Thanks to Sally Kempton for referring us to John's work. John, however, uses the term "growing up" to refer to healthy psychological growth and resolution of psychological issues within a given level of consciousness, while in the context of world spirituality we are using the term to refer to growing up to higher levels of consciousness. This recasting of these core terms was suggested by Ken Wilber who has consistently used waking up and growing up to refer to state and stage development respectively. Dustin Diperna, in his new book, *The Heart of Conscious Evolution* (Integral Publishing House, San Francisco, 2011, p. 238) suggests calling shadow work "cleaning up." I prefer the term lighten up because of its dual connotation and elegance. He also suggests using the terms "showing up" and "opening up," but in a different way then I have deployed them. I have adopted the terms much like we adopted "waking up" and "growing up" from Trungpa and changed their core meaning to reflect the new evolutionary emergent of Unique Self. Similarly, I deploy the terms open up and show up as ways of expressing the core teachings of Unique Self enlightenment. Each of these terms is taken to express a different dimension of Unique Self. If, however, you combine my Unique Self teaching and Global Spirituality understanding, in conjunction with Ken's re-deployment of Welwood's terms to refer to states and stages, and together with Dustin Diperna's first clustering of all these terms into one package—all originally sourced in Trungpa's insight—then you have the genealogy of this wonderful and pithy formulation. Together with Ken, we are just now in the process of standardizing these usages within the world spirituality teachings that we are co-creating.

We are also adding a new category which we are calling Storying Up which refers to the essential post-postmodern endeavor of constructing a new world view or big picture, a new universe story which creates a context of meaning.

Appendix I: Evolutionary Love: One Love—Kosmic and Impersonal, Intimate and Personal

1. This chapter is an early draft of a chapter on evolutionary love in an upcoming book on world spirituality based on Integral principles coauthored by Ken Wilber and me. In this draft I have begun to integrate our voices. Several formulations in the chapter belong directly to Ken. Others belong to me. Since this is in essence a first draft of what is to be a chapter in a coauthored book on World Spirituality, based on Integral principles, I have tried to integrate my voice and Ken's in this chapter and thus have not placed my own or Ken's formulations in separate quotation marks. Ken has not formally reviewed this chapter and I bear full responsibility for it at this stage. It will undoubtedly evolve as we reengage, deepen and expand the presentation of this material in a more structured and formal way for the world spirituality book.

2. On the evolutionary impulse that throbs in each person and in all the kosmos, see Aurobindo, *The Future Evolution of Man: The Divine Life Upon Earth* (Twin Lakes, WI: Lotus Press, 1964). See also Abraham Kook texts, cited below in chapter on evolutionary spirituality, p. 141. See also the reference to the evolution of God.

3. This position is evinced by many teachers. One powerful and compelling expression of this position is taken by Andrew Cohen. See http://www .andrewcohen.org/blog/index.php?/blog/post/i-just-called-to-say-i-love-you/.

    As some of the talkbacks indicate, this blog was in part emergence out of a wonderful conversation I had with Andrew in the Future of Love Dialogue series.

    When I read the blog, I realized once again both the respect I have for Andrew as a teacher of dharma, and how sharply—in regard to love and generally the place of the personal, my dharma, realization and essential intuitions—were suggesting a different model in path. I wrote Andrew and we agreed to do a dialogue based on his blog post. The dialogue was excellent and will be published on the Center for World Spirituality website. In the dialogue I tried to share the core positions expressed in this section of the book.

4. See for example the teachings of the currently popular teachers, Adyashanti or Stephen Bodian: Adyashanti, *Emptiness Dancing* (Boulder, CO: Sounds True, 2004); Stephen Bodian, *Wake Up Now* (New York: McGraw Hill, 2008).

For an older version see Jean Klein, *I Am* (Tempe, AZ: Third Millenium, 1989). This teaching is rooted in the seminal texts of Vedanta such as eighth-century philosopher Shankaracharya's texts, *Viveka Chudamani* ("The Crest Jewel of Discrimination") and *Atma-Bodhi* ("Self-Realization").

5. My colleague and friend Andrew Cohen is a sophisticated dharma thinker and does not formally blur these categories. However, in his writing and recordings, the two are sometimes blurred—both in the writing and in the mind of the reader. More then one passage implicitly equates the personal with personality. On a formal level, Andrew and I agree on the distinctions. Our disagreement is a matter of emphasis and path. I respectfully honor the integrity of Andrew's position, even as I profoundly and even fiercely disagree with any implicit undermining of the infinite integrity and absolute nature of the personal. In this emerging out of my lineage, I explicitly reject the split between the absolute and the relative, and particularly the emphasis on that split, which is so dominant in Eastern teaching.

6. For Maezumi Roshi, see for example his book *Appreciate Your Life: The Essence of the Practice* (Boston: Shambhala, 2002). Maezumi Roshi's "free functioning human being" seems to be a restatement of the Tenth Oxherding picture in Buddhism. This intuition was confirmed by discussion with two lineage holders in Maezumi Roshi's line, Michael Mugaku Zimmerman and Diane Musho Hamilton. In this image, the enlightened person returns to the marketplace, where their nondual realization is incarnated in full engagement with life.

7. The Authentic Self as awakened impersonal function is a teaching, rooted at least in part in Aurobindo's teaching, given by Andrew Cohen. Andrew's transmission of the teaching of Authentic Self has in my understanding been of great benefit to many of his students and reflects an important—if in my view partial—spiritual truth. It shares in common a core intuition of the Unique Self, namely that True Self—the realization of classical enlightenment, in which one becomes identified with one's True Nature beyond the Separate Self—is not the end of the enlightenment path. It also shares with the Unique Self a strong sense of the evolutionary context within which the awakened Unique Self lives, as well as a shared centrality given to the evolutionary impulse with which the Unique Self aligns and even incarnates. Unique Self teaching is firmly rooted in my Kabbalistic transmission, which is evolutionary at its very core—even if still in a proto-modern sense.

Both Authentic Self and Unique Self recognize True Self as an absolutely pivotal realization, even as they both view True Self as a prelude to the next ultimate step, in which True Self creatively engages life. The essential difference is that Unique Self teaches that engagement with and incarnation of the evolutionary impulse is irreducibly personal and Unique—an awakened personal function, while Authentic Self teaches that the ultimate step is an impersonal realization. The implications of this difference are wide and deep.

8. See Future of Love Dialogues 2010. The dialogue is slated to be published in an upcoming volume, *Integral Dialogues on the Future of Love,* eds. Marc Gafni and Diane Hamilton.

9. The most succinct and lovely expression that I know of describing what Charles Peirce called Evolutionary Love, which is the core position of the Unique Self mystics, de Chardin, and many more, was expressed by Ken Wilber for the first time in our dialogue in Dialogue One of the Future of Love series and then again in his opening keynote address at Integral Spiritual Experience 2. The dialogue is slated to be published in an upcoming volume, *Integral Dialogues on the Future of Love,* eds. Marc Gafni.

   The following several paragraphs are Ken's words with my slight emendations and additions. Because of those emendations, the paragraphs are not in quotation marks but I want to—with delight—clearly attribute the core formulations to Ken.

10. God, if you come from a theistic tradition, and the Absolute if you take a nontheistic perspective, such as the point of view of Vedanta.

11. Love as the motivation Eros of manifestation and spiritual evolution is a core teaching of Luria. The clearest accessible expression of this teaching on love that I know of for the English reader would be the short book, *The Way of God,* by a post-Lurianic Kabbalist, Moshe Chaim Luzzatto.

12. See Eric Jantsch, *The Self-Organizing Universe: Scientific and Human Implications of the Emerging Paradigm of Evolution* (Pergamon, 1985).

13. On the move from ego to ethno to world to kosmocentric see Lawrence Kohlberg.

14. Modern and postmodern cities and nations often lack this overall ethnocentric sense of mutuality and connection, but operate as clusters of egocentric individuals, as collections of different ethnocentric groups occupying the same physical space but lacking the ability to identify with one another.

15. The third-person perspective on reality reveals a web of separate objects and selves. Billions of separate selves. This is the perspective of matter. It is the third person of God, the third face of God, the face of I-It. The first-person perspective on reality reveals True Selves, billions of True Selves, whose total number is one. This is the first person of God, the first face of God, the face of I Am. The second perspective on reality reveals Unique Selves, billions of unique selves, which are distinct within the context of Union. This is the second person of God, the second face of the divine, what Hebrew mystical philosopher Martin Buber called I and Thou.

As we all sought to evolve Integral thought back in the first years of this new millennium, 2003–2005, Thomas Keating, David Steindl-Rast, and I had many conversations with Integral philosopher Ken Wilber about what Ken later described as the second-person of God. Some of the conversations were passionate, loving contestations. I remember one in particular where we all laughed because the recorder at Ken's loft broke, we thought from the intense heat of the conversation.

In these conversations I shared my and my lineage's realization of this second face of God, which is revealed by the eye of the spirit—through enactment—that is sustained practice, which leads to realization. The second person, infinitely personal realization of God that we shared with Ken at that time is mythic, but mystical: it is not dogma, but dharma.

As noted above, the second face of God is not the mythic God who has died; it is not the God given to us by the dogmas of churches. Rather, the second face of God is born no less than the first face of God of the dharma of realization. The mystical realization of *tat tvam asi*, "Thou Art That, "called by the Buddhists "I Am," and the Hebrew mystical realization of what Martin Buber called "I and Thou," the personal face of the infinite, are simply two different faces of the divine. Because Thou Art That, you do not become less Thou. The personal and impersonal are two faces of the same one.

Unique Self and True Self are one. And even separate self is included in the one. How could it not be? To evolve beyond ego is never the goal. Developmental thought confirms the spiritual traditions that remind us that ego will always be present, even at the highest level of development. The goal is to evolve beyond exclusive identification with the ego.

16. See Marc Gafni, *Radical Kabbalah: The Enlightenment Teaching of Unique Self, Nondual Humanism and the Wisdom of Solomon*, section on Love and Nondual Humanism, part three. This teaching is hidden in thousands of mainstream Hasidic texts. To cite but one example, see Netivot Shalom, Rebbe of Slonim, vol. 2 essays, on Passover, Jerusalem 1994.

17. See the short essay and sources for evolutionary Kabbalah at marcgafni.com.

18. See Zohar on the verse in Exodus, "Is God in our Midst or naught [*ayin*]?" The Hebrew word for "naught" is *ayin*, which in later Kabbalah was understood as a description of the human being who has realized True Self. In the Zohar, the biblical question is reread to mean, Are we separate personal selves who love and are loved by God, or True Selves whose true first-person nature is the kosmic love referred to as *ayin*?

19. Teilhard de Chardin quote can be found in Marion Woodman's *Bone: Dying Into Life,* (Penguin, 2001).

20. The different faces of the spirit revealed by the various eyes of the spirit, deploying very different faculties of perception, are complementary. They

are equally real. They are both scientific in the precise sense that both faces of spirit are revealed by repeating time and again an experimental process that consistently yields the same results. This is the essential scientific definition of valid knowing: an experiment is performed. In the case of the eye of the mind and the eye of the senses, the experiment involves testing empirical measurable realities that can be seen through the senses or the mind. The great knowings of chemistry, biology, physics, and math are all advances made through these kinds of third-person experiments.

The eye of the spirit, however, deploys first- and second-person perspectives. The eye of the spirit might deploy meditation, prayer, chanting, ecstatic or devotional practices, and the like in their experiments. These experiments of the eye of the spirit performed independently by different groups of advanced scientists of spirit, in all parts of the world, in every generation of recorded time, have all yielded the same result.

21. Third-person science is one way to interpret moment-to-moment existence. If we interpret moment-to-moment existence in third-person terms, we'll see it as a great evolving net of processes and a great web of Life. First-person meditation is another way to interpret moment-to-moment reality, and its experiments will reveal reality as unqualified awareness—pure awareness and pure attention. Consciousness. When we interpret the very same reality through the great experiment of second person—using second-person methods of enactment—that is to say, the relational technologies of ecstatic and devotional practices, including prayer, chant, and much more, then we are able to access the inner feeling of the Uni-verse. As my teacher transmitted to me, a genuine mystic does not ask, "What is God?"; that is the job of the philosopher, which they can never answer. The mystic, by contrast, asks, "How does God feel?" Second-person reality is the inner, personal, feeling face of the kosmos, in relationship with you and all that is. From the perspective of the second-person eye of the spirit, the Uni-verse feels, and it feels love. The feeling of God is called by some of the Hasidic masters, "Hargasha," literally translated as "feeling." See Derekh Hamelek (Warsaw 1970).

22. A holarchy of needs.

23. Holarchy emphasizes the fact that every new level transcends and includes, and actually envelops, the previous level. That's how love tends to work, because that's how you get higher wholes.

If you look just at the evolution of atoms to molecules, molecules to cells, cells to organisms—in each case, the higher level transcends and includes the previous level. Molecules, for example, transcend and include atoms. Molecules actually include atoms. They love atoms. They *embrace* atoms. They don't hate them. They don't repress them. They don't oppress them.

They love them. Love is the inside second-person animation of this third-person reality. We might also give the first-person explanation of what's going on, which is that the interior proto-I-ness of the molecule is expanding to include others into its own self.

The Unique Self mystics of Kabbalah and Sufism utterly identified personal and impersonal cosmic love. The process is identified as the Shakti by Hindus, the Shekhinah by Kabbalists, the Beloved by Sufis. It is this love that mysteriously birthed life.

At this point, let's recapitulate the process. But this time with a deeper understanding of three faces of love dancing before us. Love in third person appears as the Eros of evolution driving all of reality to ever-higher levels of complexity, consciousness, recognition, and uniqueness. Love in second person animates the space between sentient beings in their most evolved expressions, as human beings love each other and all of reality. Love in second person lives as evolutionary love, living in and as the form of your Unique Self expressed in part as the drive to interpersonal love. Love in first person incarnates as the evolutionary impulse calling to evolve both the interior face of the kosmos through your own evolution, and the exterior face of the kosmos through the power of your mind, heart, and body. The Eros of evolutionary love that lives in you, as you, and through you, calls you to give your Unique Gifts, which are themselves no less than the next step of God's unfolding, the evolution of all that is.

"One of the truly remarkable leaps of evolution happened one day when several molecules were hanging out. They were large, complex molecules but still separate molecules: Several of them bumped into each other, and the love that animated them basically said, 'Hey, let's get together and form a union.' And a cell was born. Life was born from love. All these molecules were wrapped by an actual boundary that kept them all together as one unit—increased their complexity enormously and brought life into being." That was a major move of love, a major move of consciousness, reaching out and embracing others into a single union. That single union marked the beginning of prokaryotic cell life on the planet, which still exists today.

The next major step is that some of these prokaryotic cells were then incorporated into subsequently more complex cells. It was the same process—transcend and include, transcend and include. What that simply means is that, at each level, more is included. Single-celled organisms include themselves and more cells to become multicelluar organism. Multicellular organisms include themselves and more to become organelles. Organelles include themselves and more to evolve to higher complexity. The essential process, all the way up to human beings, is this transcend and include, transcend and include.

24. Abraham Maslow's work is dedicated to measuring the motivation of individuals. He found that individuals had several different types of motivation,

including safety, belongingness, self-esteem, and self-actualization. As Maslow looked at these carefully, he found that over time, these needs were organized in a hierarchy and tended to emerge in one direction. In other words, there was a developmental sequence of levels of need. When a more basic need was met in a sustained way, then the next need, a higher form of need, came online. Maslow found that these levels of need went from safety needs, to belongingness needs, to self-esteem needs, to self-actualization needs, to self-transcendence needs.

But the momentous evolutionary leap is between the first four kinds of needs and self-transcendence. The difference between the first four needs and these is so startling that late in his life Maslow gave them different names. The first four needs he called deficiency needs. The final set of needs he called self-transcendent needs. These needs are motivated not by lack but by fullness, Eros, abundant love, and overflowing. It was not a feeling of lacking something, but of being so full of something that you are motivated to share it with others.

In the original Hebrew text, the word for love is *ahavah*. The root word is *hav*, which in biblical Hebrew connotes radical giving. Radical giving, which emerges from the recognition of other and your willingness to suspend your egoic needs for the sake of an other's evolution, is the second-person expression of the third-person evolutionary force of love.

Appendix III: Unique Self and Wounded Self

1. On the wounds of love and the ritual of rejection, see Franklin Jones, *Dawn Horse Testament*, Chapters 21, 22, 23.

2. See Ken Wilber, *Integral Spirituality* (Boston: Shambala, 2007).

3. Kabbalist Hayyim of Voloshin, 19th century.

INDEX

Abulafia, Abraham ben Samuel 15
A Course in Miracles 61–63,
    152–153, 464–465
Adam 275–276, 301–303, 348–349,
    394–395
Adyashanti 476, 481–482
Agape 455
age of enlightenment 16
Agnon, S. Y. 193
aham 117, 172–173
ahava 185, 487
Alexander, Barbara 439
Alexander, Sam 439
alienation xxviii–xxix, 101–102,
    139–140, 157–158, 161–163, 200,
    210–211, 252–253, 260, 363, 366,
    474–475
Almaas, A. H. 445, 465
ananda 414
angel 457–458
ani 28, 37–38, 117, 136–137,
    172–173, 276, 456–458, 472,
    474–475
answering the call 22, 24, 42, 462
antar atman 15–16
AQUAL 458
Aquinas, Thomas 113, 319–321, 343,
    406–409, 444
Aramaic 24–25, 162–163, 199–200,
    202–203, 213–214, 217, 234,

256, 263, 268–269, 282, 293–294,
    477–478
Ardagh, Arjunah 440
Ariadne 192
Arica school 443
Aristotle 121–122, 228–229
Arnon, Dalit xxxi
Ashkenaz, Hasidei 457–458
Assagioli, Robert 33
Atiqa Kadisha 477–478
atma-bodhi 482
atman 15–16, 28, 114, 164, 350–352,
    475
atman project 350, 475
attachment 37–38, 73, 90–93,
    144–146, 160–161, 191, 209–211,
    424, 429–430, 432–433
Aurobindo, Sri 39, 176, 322, 462,
    471, 481–482
authentic friendship 77
authentic self 40, 49–53, 107–108,
    403–409, 447, 462–464, 467–469,
    482–483
autonomy 16, 31–32, 64, 75–76, 143,
    144–146, 250, 370–371, 423–424,
    444, 469
avra kedabra 162–163
awakening to your Unique Self xxv–
    xxvi, 24, 37–38
axis mundi 176–177, 475–476

ayin 37–38, 50–53, 69, 115–117, 122–123, 136–137, 172–173, 456–458, 472, 484–485

Baal Shem Tov, Israel 185, 235–236, 304, 353–355, 412
Bailey, Alice 466
Bashō 334
Beach, E. 471
Beck, Don 475
Becker, Ernest 166–167, 174, 350–352, 465, 475
bekol tzaratam lo tzar 429–430
Bellamy, Keith 440
Bell, John Stewart 64
Ben Shlomo, Yosef 472, 475–476
BeOdee 479
Bergman, Hugo 475
Bergson, Henri 472
Berke, Joseph 338–345, 479
Berry, Thomas 444, 476
berur 160–161, 446–447, 458
berur teshuka 160–161
Bible 90–93, 188–189, 200, 235, 275–276, 475–476
big mind 35, 114, 122–123, 136–137, 446–448
bittul hayesh 69
Blake, William xxxi, 41, 233, 443, 461
Bly, Robert 228–229
Blyth, R. H. 452–453
bodhichitta 136
bodhisattva 38, 42, 287–288, 303–304, 396–397, 399–401
    bodhisattva sexing 287–288, 303–304
Bodian, Stephen 481–482
Bohm, David 128
Böhme, Gernot 444
Bonhoeffer, Deitrich 476
book of life 190–191, 209–211, 252–253
Bourgealt, Cynthia 466–467
Braude, Liza 439
Brezsny, Rob 479
Brownback, Kathleen J. 439, 505

Brown, Norman O. 166–167, 465, 475
Buber, Martin 182–183, 476–477, 483
Buddha xxx–xxxi, 16, 36, 60, 69, 113, 123, 136–137, 164, 183, 225, 425, 462
Buddhism xxiv, 5, 11–12, 15–16, 18, 28, 38, 42, 50–53, 64–66, 68–69, 72–73, 113–114, 136, 153, 180–182, 191, 294, 303–304, 340–342, 355, 376–378, 425, 432–433, 445, 448, 451, 456–458, 475–476, 482, 484
Bullock, Elizabeth Helen 439
Bunim, Simcha 225
Buscaglia, Leo 476

Calaprice, Alice 473
Campbell, Joseph 175–176, 475–476
Caplan, Mariana 439–440, 480
Castenada, Carlos 191
Center for World Spirituality 392–395, 439–440, 481, 503–504
certainty of being 331
Chandler, J. Ruth 477
charity 129–133, 473
Chaucer, Geoffrey 343
cheshbon hanefesh 353
chibbah 460
chisaron 238–239
chit 414
chiyut 224–225, 254–256
chovah 460
Christ 1, 15–16, 36, 66–68, 70, 108–109, 136, 342, 466–467
    Christ Consciousness 15–16
Christianity 5, 12, 15–16, 65–68, 70, 108–109, 319–321, 376–378, 385–386, 412, 422–423, 459
    mystical Christianity 5, 412
classical enlightenment xxiv, 16–18, 26–27, 34, 37–38, 46–47, 50–53, 144–147, 294–295, 364–366, 448, 451–452, 482
Cohen, Alan 478
Cohen, Andrew 40, 447, 462–464, 467–470, 478–479, 481–482, 505

Cohen, Sidney 417
communism 100, 125–126
conflict 91–93, 97, 141–142, 147, 354–355, 378, 385
conscious pleasure 292–294
Cook-Greuter, Suzanne 452, 505
Cooper, Marty 439
Corten, Chahat 439
cosmic axis 176–177
Cosmic Scroll 387
Csikszentmihalyi, Mihaly 473–474

daimon 224
Dalai Lama 153–156, 180, 210–211, 473–474
Dan, Joseph 474–475
Dante 4–5, 104, 406–409, 444
de Chardin, Teilhard 176–178, 322–323, 406–409, 411–414, 444, 462, 472, 475–476, 483–485
deep trance phenomenon 313
de Fermat, Pierre 197–198
Deida, David 467, 478–479
Delattre, Pierre 473–474
democratization of enlightenment xxiii, xxv–xxvi, 21–22, 24, 176–177, 366–367, 379, 387
derek hataninim 263
destiny of evolution 452
devekut 105, 301–303
dharma 27, 48–49, 55–58, 123, 148–150, 233, 238–239, 304, 340–342, 383, 445, 481–482, 484
Diaz, Sofia 446–447
Dickens, Charles 190–191
Diperna, Dustin 480–481
divine communion 294–295, 300–303, 323–324, 424–425
DNA 19, 20–21, 239, 241–242, 277, 332, 460
Donne, John 103, 303, 467
Dov Ber of Mezritch 234
Dovid of Lilov 191, 192
Drob, Sanford L. 471
dual citizen 368–369, 373, 384–385
Dunlap, Peter 439

Eastern enlightenment xxiv, 49–53, 365–366, 464
Eastern spirituality 56
echad 301–303, 456–458
Eckhart, Meister 67–68, 240
egocentric consciousness 408–409
ego story xxxi, 32–33, 73–74, 82, 200
eight stations 31, 44–48, 71–72, 447–448, 461
ein sof 69, 456–458
Einstein, Albert 146–147, 196–198, 473
ekyeh asher ekyeh 214
Emerson, Ralph Waldo 157–158, 240, 322, 357, 444, 470, 474–475
Engler, Jack 475–476
enlightened realization 8, 412, 458
enlightenment of emptiness xxiv, 50–53
enlightenment of fullness xxiii, xxv, 50–53
enlightenment teaching xix–xx, xxxi, 4–5, 18, 27, 48–53, 69, 86–87, 144–147, 366, 386–387, 392–395, 403, 445, 451–452, 454–455
enneagram type 10–12, 34, 85–87
environmental signals 19, 20–21
epigenetics 19
erekh 143
Erickson, Milton H. 479
eros of evolution 4–5, 23–24, 404–409, 486
eros of life 359
Esbjörn-Hargens, Sean 440, 505
essence of enlightenment 23–24, 61
ethnocentric consciousness 408–409
eudaimonia 224
Evans, Derek 440
Eve 275–276, 301–303
evolutionary emergent 5, 11–12, 164, 374, 378, 386–387, 441, 445, 449, 480–481
evolutionary imperative 39–40, 380–381, 462
evolutionary integrity 47–48, 124–126, 178, 326
evolutionary love 13–14, 403–409, 413–417, 443–444, 458, 481, 483, 486

evolutionary mysticism 4–5, 121–122, 127–128, 137–140, 146, 177, 210–211, 217, 409, 417, 462–464, 471, 472

evolutionary Unique Self xxi–xxii, 38, 40, 47, 53, 380, 422–423, 468–469

evolution of consciousness xxiii, 3, 42, 76, 89, 121–122, 125–126, 138–140, 151–153, 166–167, 234, 323, 359–361, 364, 367–368, 377–379, 381, 386–387, 418, 433

evolution of love 3–5, 18, 23–24, 139–140, 151–153, 371–372, 379, 387, 418, 439

Exile of God 9

expanded mind 15–16, 267–268

eye of the spirit 49–53, 56, 119–120, 370, 405–409, 414–415, 417–418, 450, 484–485

faces of Eros 156, 158, 160, 161–163

false self xxviii–xxix, 10–14, 32–34, 45–46, 48, 101–102, 137, 332, 443, 447–448, 452–453, 461

Farrell, Warren 439–440, 476

fascism 125–126

Fellini, Federico 169

Fester, Heather 439

Feynman, Richard 198

Fichte, Johann Gottlieb 462, 472

first taste 114

first-tier 381, 390–395, 398–401, 473

fixation 33–34, 86–87

Forman, John 446–447

Freeman, Lesley 439

Freud, Sigmund 31–33, 98, 217, 277, 302–303, 329–330, 342, 378, 381

Friend, John 439

Fromm, Erich 199–200, 333

Fuhs, Clint 440

Future of Love 404, 447, 481, 483

Gabai, Ibn 470

Galperin, Lori 439–440, 505

Gandhi, Mahatma 232

Ganti, Bence 439

garden of eden 157–158, 275–276, 348–349, 465, 474–475

Gebser, Jean 390–391

Gibbons, Brian 471

Gibran, Kahlil 331

giga pandit 455

Ginn, Mike 439

glimmerings 28, 33, 35–36, 85–87, 172–173, 278, 414–415, 452

Global Spirituality xxii, 480–481

Goddard, Tom 382, 439

goddess 109, 156, 164–167, 177, 267–269, 275–276, 304–307, 475–476, 478–479

God-spark 7, 9, 165–167, 361

Goethe, Johann Wolfgang von 214, 291

Gordon, David 479

Gras, Leon 439

Graves, Clare 390–391, 459–460

great invitation of your life 3, 179–180, 443

great mother 45–47, 166–167, 349, 465

great story 76, 166–167, 174–176, 387, 404–409

greed 73, 230, 339–345

green consciousness 180–182, 474–475

Green, Emanuel 440

grenvy 339–345

Grey, Alex 447–448

ground of being 16, 46–47, 68–69, 72–73, 99, 106–108, 122–123, 151–153, 430–431, 469

group-think 31–32, 146

growing up 21–22, 51–53, 131–133, 276–277, 331, 380–382, 464–465, 480–481

Gurdjieff, George Ivanovich 464–467

Gyatso, Tenzin 153

Hafiz 29, 205, 236, 412

hakna'ah 232–233, 348

halakha 477

Hamelek, Derekh 485

Hamilton, Craig 479
Hamilton, Diane xx, 392–395, 440, 447–448, 452, 483
Hamilton, Diane Musho 446–447, 482
hamtaka 233, 353–355
hamtakat hadin 353–355
Hasidic masters 53, 125–126, 136, 234, 280–281, 320–321, 412, 428, 478–479, 485
hav 416–417, 487
havdalah 233, 349–355
Hayyim of Voloshin 487
Heard, Gerard 375–376
HeartMath Institute 467
heart sutra 68–69, 172–173
Hebrew mysticism 12–13, 45–46, 69, 117–118, 130–133, 137, 177, 254–255, 348–355, 445–458, 461, 463–465, 471, 474–475, 483–484
Hegel, Georg Wilhelm Friedrich 125–126, 467–471
Heisenberg, Werner 11
Heraclitus of Ephesus 470
Hesse, Hermann 111, 236
hevel 476–477
Hinduism 11, 12, 15–16, 28, 36–38, 96, 109, 117, 136, 153–156, 164–167, 172, 176–177, 186, 210–211, 213, 288, 293–294, 322, 377–378, 412, 414, 444, 459, 471, 478, 486
hitboddedut 122–123
Hitler, Adolf 188–189, 232
Hixon, Lex 445
Hobbes, Thomas 16
holarchy 416–417, 485
holding heart 267
holonic 450–451
holons 140, 394–395
holy of holies 158, 219, 299, 354–355, 359–361
homo religiosus 454–455
Hopkins, Gerard Manley 1
Houston, Jean 173–174, 176, 447–448, 475–476
Hubbard, Barbara Marx 39, 462
hubris 177–178, 341–342

Hume, David 11
Huxley, Aldous 375–376

Ichazo, Oscar 33, 443
Idel, Moshe 446–447, 471, 503
identity receptors 19, 20–21, 460
iEvolve 447, 475–476
imitatio dei 133, 430
impersonal love 103, 404–409
impersonal man 89–94
impersonal sexing 103
impersonal tantra 294–295, 299, 300–303
indigo 449, 451–452
injustice 76–78, 179–180, 340–342
Inner Self 15–16, 28
integral-aperspectival 390–391
Integral Life 445–447
integral perspectival thought 465
integral principles xx, xxii, 13–14, 104, 367, 371–372, 392–395, 440, 449, 464, 481, 503–504
integral theory xx, xxii, 12–13, 49, 251, 392–395, 404–412, 419–420, 440, 447–448, 453, 458–459, 461, 463–465, 468–469, 475, 503, 505
Integral World Spirituality xxiv–xxv, 381, 449, 450
integral worldview 372
internal family systems theory 461
intimate communion 105, 294–295, 300–303
Isaac, Levi 53, 125–126, 274
Isaac the Blind 275–276
Islam 12
itcafya 282
ithapcha 282
itkan 478
Iverson, Haven 479

Jabès, Edmond 320–321
Jackson, Phil 322
jacob's ladder 176–177, 297–299, 457–458
jagadguru 176–177
Jantsch, Erich 406–409, 415, 483

Jerusalem 130–133, 202–203, 241, 281, 320–321, 475–476, 484–485
Jesus 11–12, 66–68, 108–109, 176–177, 182–183, 462
jewel in the lotus 480–481
Jewish mysticism 322, 471, 474–475
John Forman 446
Jones, Franklin 475
Journal of Integral Theory and Practice 447–448, 468–469, 503, 505
Joyce, James 358, 359
Judah xix–xx, 391, 474–477
Judah archetype xix–xx, 391
Judaism 12, 109, 376–378, 385–386, 454–455, 459
judgment 59–60, 66, 157–158, 179–180, 339, 347–348, 351–355
Jung, Carl Gustav 230–231, 327, 378, 381
justice 77, 92–93, 130, 179–180, 251, 294, 340–342, 369–370, 429–430

kabbalist 13–14, 64, 124–126, 130, 185, 225, 277, 409, 470–471
Kafka, Franz 193
Kallus, M. 462
Kama Sutra 293–294
Kant, Immanuel 11, 444, 448, 458, 470
karma 92–93, 245–246, 288, 339
Kashmir Shaivism 5, 172–173, 360–361, 444
Kauffman, Stuart 415
kavvanot 124–126, 185
Kazantzakis, Nikos 150, 432–433, 462
Keating, Thomas 392–395, 465, 484
Kegan, Robert 33
kein 357
Kelly, Neville 505
Kempton, Sally xx, 172, 392, 439–440, 444–445, 447, 452, 478, 480
kensho 36
kesef 349
Kesler, John 446–447
keter 456–458
Khoikhoi 344

King David 113, 188, 344–345, 361
Kipnis, Laura 470
Kirschbaum, Mark 237–238, 478
Kleefeld, Claudia 439
Klein, Jean 482
Koestler, Arthur 127–128, 140
Kohlberg, Lawrence 408, 483
komat ha'adam 277
Kook, Abraham 39–40, 118–119, 176–178, 189, 217, 276, 282, 352, 406–409, 462–464, 471–472, 474–476, 479–481
kosmic scroll 5, 10, 69, 455
kosmocentric consciousness 380–381
kosmoscentric 52–53
Kosolowski, Peter 471
Kundera, Milan 338–339
kung fu 153–156

labels 317–319, 321, 446–447, 474–475
Lainer, Mordechai xix–xx, 63, 238–239, 352, 391, 412, 444, 446, 456, 474–475, 505
Lama Surya Das 447–448
lataif 164
Leader, Avraham 234, 440, 478
lehatkin 478
Lelouch, Claude 70, 465
Lennon, John 357
Lerner, Michael 479
leshem yichud 38–40, 433
levado 201
liberation 15–16, 34, 37, 42–45, 61, 97, 124–126, 136–137, 147, 171, 209–211, 268–269, 325–326, 425–426, 428, 459
Lipton, Bruce H. 152, 460
Lipton, Robert 20
Little, Bill 439
living your story xxi–xxii, 151, 189, 252–255, 279–281
Lloyd, Kathryn 440
Locke, John 16
Loevinger, Jane 390–391
Luria, Isaac 1, 5, 38–39, 64, 124, 160, 176, 201, 409, 412, 444, 458, 462, 471–472, 474, 483

Lurianic Kabbalah 146, 235, 330, 448, 455, 462–464, 471–472, 477, 483
Lurianic mysticism 330
Luzzatto, Moshe Chaim 483
Lyon, Bruce 466

Mackey, John 404–409, 439, 505
Maharshi, Ramana 15
Maharthi Manthari 444
Mahayana 68–69
Maimonides, Moses 178, 319–321
malkhut 456–458
manifestation of consciousness 27
Mann, Richard 476
Marx, Karl Heinrich 39, 462, 470
Maslow, Abraham 390–391, 416–417, 486–487
McCarthy, Cormac 479
McKenna, Terence 474–475
Mei HaShiloach 472
Mendel, Menachem 219, 335
Merzel, Dennis Genpo 447
metanoia 459–460
methodological pluralism 454–455
Meyers-Anderson, Maribeth 479
midrash 457–458
Milton, John 200–201
mispar 186–191, 198, 223–224, 276–277
mitzvah 208, 217–219, 222
mitzvah temidit 208
Mizrahi, Victor 196–198
mochin degadlut 15–16
modernity 12–13, 24–25, 39–40, 193, 374, 377–378, 382–385, 445, 458, 463–464
Moses 66, 100–102, 187–188, 214, 319–321
mosif coach le-maleh 361
Mount Sinai 69, 454–455
Muktananda, Swami 117, 136, 186–187, 478–479
Mumford, Lewis 181–182, 371–372
Mussolini, Benito Amilcare Andrea 232
Myer, Victoria 439
mystery of creation 123

Nachman of Breslov 479
Naftali of Rophsitz 428
Nagarjuna 68–69, 465
narcissism 35, 81, 86–87, 99, 101–102, 124–126, 175–176, 192, 219, 318, 326, 341–342, 348–349, 422–424, 427–433, 449, 468–469
nashkei ar'a verakia 457–458
nazism 125–126, 188–189
nekudah achat 123
Nelson, Terry 439
Neuman, Carlos 439
new age 109, 337, 340–342
new enlightenment xx, xxxi, 11–12, 14, 17, 28, 37, 69, 86–87, 123, 143, 177–178, 241, 263–264, 287, 299–303, 392–395, 446–448, 454–455
new enlightenment of Unique Self 7–8, 123, 143, 241, 448
new integral enlightenment 14, 69
Newton, Sir Isaac 196–198
Nietzsche, Friedrich 169, 264
Nijhout, Frederik 19
Nin, Anaïs 327
nondual humanism xix–xx, 391, 411–412, 446–448, 450, 456–458, 474–476, 484–485, 503, 505
nondual sweetness 353–355
nonexistence xxxi, 115, 163–167, 324
normal consciousness 25, 364
no-self 68, 114, 152–153, 180–182, 294–295, 299, 448, 451, 465
numerology 275–276, 479

ohr hakadosh baruch hu 185
olam haba 353–355
olam hazeh 353–355
Olesha, Yuri 279
Olson, Alan M. 471
om mani padme hum 480–481
one taste 113–115, 122–123, 219, 353–355, 456–458
Ono, Yoko 357
ontological pluralism 454–455
original face 68–69, 72–73, 122–123, 353–355, 393–395
Oschman, James L. 460

Pagan, Eben 439–440
pain trance 312–313
Panikkar, Raimon 466–467
panim 157–158, 457–458
Patai, Daphne 470
Pathak, Dev S. 474
pathologize 173–176
Patten Terry 447
Paul, Charles Randall 385
Peck, M. Scott 338–339
Peirce, Charles 411–414, 443–444, 483
Pepier, Mauk 439
perennial philosophy 245, 374–375, 386
Perez, Joe 439–440
Persia 29, 192, 236
personal face of essence xxv, xxvi, 7, 23–24, 29, 53, 94, 379–380, 468–469
personality sexing 287–294, 299
personal love 79–80, 106–108, 267–268, 404–409, 412, 469
personal man 89–94
personal sexing 290
personal tantra 300–303
Peter Pan 276–277
Philokalia 467
Plato 10–12, 66, 90–93, 186–187, 238, 474–475
pleasure sexing 287–288, 292–294
Plotinus 470
pole 176–177
pole, feminine 187
pole, masculine 187
postmodernity 12–14, 181–182, 193, 371–372, 374, 379, 383, 445, 463–464
pregnancy 142–143, 242, 370
premodernity 12–13, 368, 377–378, 463–464
prerational 166–167, 422–423
pre-trans fallacy 422–423, 477
Prieguez, Raquel 439
pseudo-eros 164–167, 248–249, 252–253, 264, 289–291, 348–352, 423, 475
pseudofriendship 77

quantum physics 64, 107–108, 137, 235, 405–409

racism 145–146, 427–428
Ramer, Shawn 439
Rauschning, Hermann 188–189
rebbe of thieves 236
receptor proteins 20–21
Reich, Wilhelm 342
reincarnation 27
religious diplomacy 385
Renaissance 38–40, 124–126, 384–385, 389–391, 462, 474–475
Reznikoff, Charles 189
Riding, Laura 192
rigpa 15–16
Rilke, Rainer Maria 264, 333, 479
Rinpoche, Chögyam Trungpa 111, 480
Roshi, Genpo 392, 446–447
Roshi, Maezumi 403, 482
Rosica, Karen 440
Ross, Chana 440
Rousseau, Jean-Jacques 16
Rowe, Christopher 474–475
Rumi 29, 53, 216, 406–409, 412

Safrar, Jeremy A. 476
sahaj 456–458
samadhi 12, 36, 456–458
Sanders, Betsy 439
Sanders, Sandy 439
Sangha 123
Sanskrit 27, 172–173, 393–395
sapir 186–187, 190–191, 198, 245–246, 276–277
Sardello, Robert 466–467
sat-chit-ananda 414
satori 36, 459–460
Saussure, Ferdinand de 11, 448, 458
savior of God 150
Scheherazade 192
Schelling, Friedrich Wilhelm Joseph 39–40, 116, 444, 458, 462, 471–472
Scholem, Gershom 456–458, 471, 474–475

Schrödinger, Erwin 394–395
Schuhon, Fritz 375–376
Schulte 471
Schuon, Frithjof 386
Schwartz, Mark 440, 505
Schwartz, Richard 461, 505
Sclove, Richard 439
second taste 114–115, 123, 411–412
second-tier 381, 390–395, 398–401, 449, 452–453, 460, 464–465
secularization 384–385
Seer of Lublin 214
sefira 162–163, 276–277
sefirot 162–163, 276–277
self-contraction 9, 86–87, 93, 106, 137–140, 175–176, 183, 324–326, 393–395, 429–430
self-creation 4–5, 102–103
selfishness 219, 228–229, 343
self-love 137, 183, 216–217, 219, 265–266, 281, 357
self-realization 15–16, 35–36, 38, 42, 48–49, 52–53, 85–87, 148, 191, 198, 222, 241, 323–324, 442, 446–447, 453, 473, 482
separateness and uniqueness 55–60, 81, 92–93, 148, 365–366
separate-self sexing 288–290, 302–303
seventy faces to Torah 457–458
shad-ai 239–240
shadow integration xxii, 227–231, 242, 245–246, 252, 254, 256, 263–264, 266, 381, 477
shadow of the impersonal 99–100, 107–108
shadow qualities 245–261, 266, 277–278
Shakespeare, Richard II 327
Shakespeare, William 227–229, 342, 345, 415
Shakti 156, 267–268, 322, 444, 486
Shalom, Netivot 484–485
Shankara, Adi 15
Shankaracharya 482
Sheed, F. J. 476
Shekhinah 11–12, 156, 158–159, 164–167, 213–214, 216, 260,

275–276, 297–299, 322, 422–423, 428, 457–458, 474, 486
shevirat hacaylim 234
Shiva Nataraj 153–156
shma 354–355, 456–458
shma mantra 354–355
showing up 8, 21–22, 41, 85–87, 103, 144–146, 158, 238, 242, 250, 273, 293–294, 310–312, 342, 379, 382, 398–401, 456–458, 480–481
sin 24–25, 66, 158, 162–163, 182, 343, 424–425, 474–475
sippur 186–187, 190–191, 198, 245–246, 276–277
Skeels, H. M. 201
Smith, Huston 375–376, 386, 444, 476
Smith, Robb 447–448, 452
Socrates 157–158, 344–345
sod ha-yichud 304
Solave, Harold 443
Solomon, King xix–xx, 122–123, 156–157, 233–235, 267, 304, 446–447, 484–485
Soloveitchik, Joseph 476
Sommers, Christina Hoff 470
Songs of Songs 353–355
soul prints 50–53, 199–200, 445–447, 455–458, 470, 475–476
source code 125–127, 140, 363, 387
spanda-karikas 444
spiral dynamics 180–182, 390–391, 474–476
stage-structure development 464–465
Stanich, Rollie 67
states of consciousness 57–58, 299, 379, 392–395, 459
static development 464–465
Steindl-Rast, David 392–395, 465, 484
Steiner, Rudolf 322
Stein, Zachary 440, 443, 505
Stevens, Wallace 327, 359–361
St. John of the Cross 239
Stoddard, William 375–376
storying up 481
structure stage of consciousness 441–442, 459–460
substrate of awareness 451

Sufism 5, 28, 37–38, 53, 114, 164–167, 176–177, 231, 360–361, 407–409, 412, 445, 466–467, 486
sunyatta 50–53, 69, 136–137
superstition 145–146, 343
Sweeney, Patrick 392
Swimme, Brian 444

Talmud 129–130, 146, 191, 221–224, 294, 352, 376, 445–448, 454–455, 457–458, 465, 476–477
tantric Kabbalah 231–233
tantric kabbalist 233, 235
Tao 8, 114
tat tvam asi 15–16, 59–60, 484
teacher-student 105–108
teleological factor 329–330
Ten Commandments 188–189
ten oxherding pictures 38, 445, 482
Teresa of Avila 157
teshuva 352
Teutonic myths 188–189
textual tradition 454–455
Thanatos 165–167, 348–352
Theravada 68–69, 180–182, 191, 340–342, 451, 465
Theseus 192
the three stations of love 461
third-tier 449, 452–453
Thomas, Brett 440
thou art that 15–16, 53, 59–60, 484
three faces of God 53, 409–412, 465
three stations of love 461
Thucydides 207–208
Tibet 154–156, 179–180
Tibetan Buddhism 15–16
tikkun 38–40, 96, 116, 124–126, 162–163, 191, 234, 238, 287–288, 303–304, 376, 433, 471–472, 477–478
tikuna 477–478
Tillich, Paul 455
Tolkien, J. R. R. 178
Torah xix–xx, 1, 12–13, 69, 185, 191, 454–458, 463–464
transformation of identity 3–5, 21–22, 251, 256, 264, 282

transpersonal man 91–93
transpersonal sexing 302–303
transrational 422–423
true nature of self 15–16
true self-realization 35–36, 85–87, 453
true self sexing 287–288, 302–303
true self tantra 294–295, 299–303
turiya 392–395, 397–401
turiyatita 392–395, 397–401
turquoise 449
twin towers 207–208
tzadik hador 176–177
tzar 429–430
tzedaka 130
tzim tzum 333

unio mystica 459–460
unique being 29, 42, 75–76, 169, 358
unique destiny 189, 222, 357
unique expression of essence 23–24, 27
unique face 68–69, 72–73, 159, 457–458
unique gift 23–24, 38, 40–43, 47–48, 50–53, 71, 76, 92–93, 119–120, 124–126, 130, 161, 246, 326, 361, 366–367, 379, 382–383, 387, 421–423, 469, 472, 486
unique letter xxii, 1, 69, 455
unique obligation 42–43, 50–53, 71, 92–93, 130, 431, 469
Unique Self distortion 239, 245, 255, 266, 278–279, 337, 339–342, 381
Unique Self encounters xxii, 156, 213, 300–303, 309–314, 317–321, 323–324, 326, 337, 446–447, 449
Unique Self enlightenment xxi–xxii, xxiv–xxvi, 16, 21–24, 26–27, 38, 43, 50–53, 71–72, 89, 94–95, 156, 196–198, 232, 234, 249, 256, 265, 319, 365–366, 378, 404–409, 446–447, 452, 480–481
Unique Self orgasm 303
Unique Self perception xxvi, 200, 212–215, 265, 331–332, 337, 339–342, 381–382, 418

Unique Self personal tantra 300–303
Unique Self principle 21–22, 67–68
Unique Self sexing 287–288,
 293–294, 300–303
Unique Self story xxxi, 32–33, 73–74,
 82–84, 161, 180–182, 189,
 199–200, 423, 474–475
Unique Self tantra 299–303
Unique Self theory 329–330, 332,
 442
Unique song 455
unique story 70, 182–183, 187, 246,
 387
unlove 102, 138–140, 252–253, 281,
 323–326
Upanishads 53, 121–122, 213
Ussery Knight, Heather 439

Vajrayana Buddhism 5
vanity 476–477
Vedanta 464, 465, 482–483
via negativa 319–321
Viddeyuva 446–447
viduy 353–355
Vilna Gaon 457–458
vital sexing 287–288, 292–294
Volckmann, Russ 440
voodoo 145–146

waking up 21–22, 44–45, 51–53,
 62–63, 70, 74, 116–117, 120, 142,
 164, 178, 224, 363, 379–380, 382,
 409, 431, 464–465, 480–482
Ward, George 440
Welwood, John 480
we space 321, 323, 364, 366–367,
 379, 423–424, 449, 480
Western enlightenment xxiii, xxiv, 16,
 55, 166–167, 365–366, 383–385,
 459, 464
Western spirituality 56, 58–60
Whitehead, Alfred North 4, 10, 104,
 121, 411, 414, 444, 470
Wilber, Ken xix, 25–27, 49, 104,
 119–120, 174, 340–342, 350–352,
 367, 382, 389, 404, 411–412,
 415, 440–441, 445–448, 452, 455,
 458, 462–465, 470, 472–475, 477,
 480–481, 483–484, 487, 503–504
Wilde, Oscar 1, 121
Williamson, Marianne 464–465
Winkler, Rabbi Gershon 503
Winnicott, Donald 331–332, 334
Wolfenden, John 333
Wolfson, Elliot R. 462, 471–472
Wolinsky, Stephen 313–317, 443,
 452–453
Woodman, Marion 484–485
Woodsmall, Wyatt 439, 455
worldcentric 51–53, 116–117, 140,
 175–176, 373–374, 380–381,
 408–409, 427–428, 464–465
world to come 137–140, 353–355
world tree, the 176–177

Yannaros, Christos 466
Yeats, W. B. 372, 460
Yeats, William Butler 460
yesh 115–116, 122–123
yichud 38–40, 148–150, 304, 433,
 472
yichudim 185
Yochai, Shimon bar 406–409
Yoga Vasistha 37–38
Yohai, Babs 439
Yom Kippur 125–126, 344–345

Zarathustra 264
zeman simchatenu 351–352
Zen 26–27, 29, 36, 69, 191, 334,
 393–395, 403–409, 448, 452–453
Zeno of Verona 470
Zimmerman, Michael 440
Zimmerrnan, Michael Mugaku 482
zivug 467, 472
Zohar 157–158, 217, 231, 234, 406–
 409, 432–433, 444, 448, 462–464,
 471, 474–478, 484–485
Zushya, Reb 66

ABOUT THE AUTHOR

DR. MARC GAFNI is a cutting-edge evolutionary visionary; a provocative spiritual artist; and a teacher, academic, author, social activist, and lover of people. He holds a doctorate, written on nondual humanism in Kabbalah, from Oxford University under the co-supervision of professor Moshe Idel. He received Rabbinic Ordination as a "Rav Yishuv" from the Chief Rabbinate of Israel, as well as private Rabbinic Ordination from his colleague Rabbi Gershon Winkler. He serves as the founding director of the Center for World Spirituality, a guest editor of academic Integral Spirituality series of the *Journal of Integral Theory and Practice*. Gafni also serves as scholar-in-residence at Pacific Coast Church, as the founder and lead teacher at Shalom Mountain Wisdom School and teacher-in-residence at the Venwoude Spiritual Community in Holland.

Marc Gafni has seeded and inspired leading-edge spiritual contexts from seminars, to teachings, to communities his entire life. He initiated the Center for World Spirituality (CWS), where Ken Wilber is active as the leading voice in the wisdom council, as a scholar at Integral Institute. CWS is a think tank as well as an international spiritual movement and community committed to the evolution and fostering of a World Spirituality based on Integral principles. CWS is dedicated to spiritual and social activism, and to the development and deployment of a shared language of spirit, which will positively inform the future of our reality.

To study with Dr. Gafni as a private student, in telecasted communities, or at live events, email marc19@hushmail.com.

To learn more about the Center for World Spirituality, visit centerforworld spirituality.org.

Unique Self Scholars Project

This work on Unique Self is part of a larger intellectual cultural project on World Spirituality that seeks to evolve the nature of enlightenment and human potential.

There are nine primary components to this exploration in regard to Unique Self.

1. A three-volume work entitled *Radical Kabbalah: Unique Self and Nondual Humanism, The Teachings of Mordechai Lainer of Izbica* by Marc Gafni, PhD

2. *Journal of Integral Theory and Practice.* Executive editor Sean Esbjörn-Hargens. This journal is the first of a series of academic journal issues on Integral Spirituality. This volume was guest edited by Dr. Marc Gafni. This journal's topic is "Unique Self;" it includes two articles by Marc Gafni and additional important articles and dialogues discussing Unique Self with Suzanne Cook Greuter, Andrew Cohen, Dustin Diperna, Zak Stein, and Neville Kelly. The editor's foreword, written by Sean Esbjörn-Hargens, and Marc Gafni's guest editor introduction set the context for the Unique Self conversation within Integral Theory.

3. The book you are holding: *Your Unique Self: The Radical Path to Personal Enlightenment.* This is a broader statement of Unique Self within the context of World Spirituality.

4. *The Unique Self Process* (in preparation)

5. *The Unique Self Index* (in preparation)

6. Unique Self in Education, Kathleen J. Brownback

7. Unique Self and Psychology, White Paper and Modules with Lori Galperin, Mark Schwartz and team.

8. Unique Self and Conscious Capitalism (White Paper with John Mackey)

9. Unique Self and Internal Family Systems (White Paper) Prof. Richard Schwartz

ABOUT
INTEGRAL PUBLISHERS

INTEGRAL PUBLISHERS was established to provide works on emerging developmental psychology, transdisciplinarity, integral and other theoretical and philosophical frameworks. It is our objective to ensure that both new and established, integrally informed authors be given the opportunity to be published and distributed.

We have published, and plan to continue to publish, works that contribute to and build the future. It is our desire to make a significant contribution to the knowledge base and improve the communication between integral practitioners, leaders and followers across the globe.

We are committed to earning a reputation for integrity, intelligence, quality, fairness and support for all stakeholders who contribute to and receive benefit from this enterprise.

trilogy of love and evolutionary healing for humanity. Read and be restored.

"Gafni makes these psychologists believe once again that psychology needs spirit. Particularly the notions of self presented in the emergent Buddhist psychotherapy conversation seem inadequate to integrate the core sense of individuality which is so essential to any western paradigm. Gafni's integral unfolding of eastern and western enlightenment opens up the conversation in a whole new way. The treatment modules that are now emerging from the Unique Self work have the potential to become a significant approach to psychological healing and transformation"

— Lori Galperin, former Clinical Co-Director, Masters and Johnson Institute; Clinical Co-Director, Castlewood Treatments Centers

"My dear brother and Rebbe, Marc Gafni has written a love letter from his heart to ours. I have experienced myself his heart transmission of the Hasidic Master, the Baal Shem Tov, and know of its profound power and authenticity. Truly the best way to characterize Marc is as a Hasidic sage who has moved beyond the confines of one tradition, dancing among us, weaving the strands of a World Spirituality. Like the Hasidic Rebbes of old, Gafni merges ecstatic brilliance with an awakened heart and a deep caring for every individual being. He takes us back through the layers of illusion to enlightenment and then to the unique manifestation of that realization through each one of us. *Your Unique Self* is an invitation to live a truly authentic life as love in each of our unique forms. For many people, this book will be the portal to awakening"

— Eli Jaxon-Bear, author of *From Fixation to Freedom: The Enneagram of Liberation*

"Dr. Marc Gafni's *Your Unique Self* presents a new "universal spirituality for the 21st century." It is a true synthesis of the enlightenment teachings of both East and West. It appeals to both the head and the heart and is highly practical. It is a must read for all spiritual seekers."

— Dr. Wyatt Woodsmall, author of *The Future of Learning and People Pattern Power*

"One of the great problems with so much of modern 'new age spirituality' is that it lacks depth. Dr. Gafni, in his new book *Your Unique Self*, has written an emotionally moving and intellectually stimulating book that moves the reader to ponder deeply many of the very core elements of their faith and practice. His discussion of enlightenment within a modern context is worth the price of the book alone! I heartily recommend this book to all serious pilgrims on the religious or spiritual road."

— Rabbi Avram Davis. Ph.D. author of *The Way Of Flame.* Founder, Chochmat Halev Educational Center

"Dr. Marc Gafni's writing on the Unique Self, in both academic and popular form, has opened up a prism into spirituality that is far beyond much of the material coming from the New Age and Human Potential movements. It is particularly noteworthy that he speaks to students who are beginning to ask if a larger identity beyond ego is possible, and whose lives are surrounded by mixed messages on love, Eros and addiction. They hunger for an understanding of God that energizes and challenges them. Grounded in serious scholarship, *Your Unique Self* offers a set of immensely powerful insights that have the rare ability to transform a student's perspective in a way that is grounded, authentic and inspired. A must read for every teacher and every student."

— Katherine J. Brownback, Senior Faculty, (former) Dean of Students,
Exeter Academy

"Drawing on his vast knowledge of Jewish mysticism, which he leavens with insights from many other spiritual traditions, Marc Gafni has provided readers with a comprehensive and compassionate understanding of what makes each of us unique, namely, the "I" that is in fact a particular manifestation of Divinity. Grounded as it is in decades of research and first-person spiritual and psychological exploration, Gafni's book makes an enormous contribution to contemporary understanding of what is possible for human beings."

— Prof. Michael E. Zimmerman, author of *Eclipse of the Self: The Development of Heidegger's Concept of Authenticity.*

"If there is a spiritual teaching that the Millennial Generation could get behind, this is surely it. *Your Unique Self* is the most important book to appear on the Integral scene since Wilber's Integral Spirituality. In a world where one's spiritual options are limited to dogmatic religion, atheism, New Age mysticism and Self Help, Gafni's *Your Unique Self* realization is a breath of fresh air. The teachings about the difference between separateness and uniqueness are worth the price of this book alone."

— Michael Richardson, author of *Suicide Dictionary*
and Founder of the C-CAM Collective

"Dr. Marc Gafni is simply one of the great brilliant overflowing heart minds of the generation. I heard his teaching on Unique Self at the first Integral Spiritual Experience and it blew my mind and melted my heart. This book is a *must read*. For anyone who wants to fulfill their purpose on this earth, Marc is one of the great new voices in the Translucent Revolution."

— Arjuna Ardagh, author of *Awakening into Oneness* and *Leap Before You Look*

"Marc Gafni is an important and exciting new spiritual guide. With humility, genuine warmth, and enormous power, Gafni merges ancient wisdom with his profound insights to lead us back to ourselves."

— Richard Carlson, author of *Don't Sweat the Small Stuff*

"Marc Gafni's wisdom and insight moved my heart and inspired my mind. This new teacher of spirit... is sure to become an important voice in helping to chart our soul paths in the new millennium."

— Barbara De Angelis, PhD, author of *Real Moments*

"*Your Unique Self* is picking up on this new emerging sense of self which emerges at the second tier of consciousness. It's very powerful, this teaching of Unique Self, because it has to escape a very heavy communal pressures of the 'we' who suggests that after spiritual practice you realize that there is no essential individuality at all. Well, that's not true. Thank God for this Unique Self teaching; that's where creativity is. In your genius you've hit upon what the very unique properties are of this seventh station understanding of self. It's just in the nick of time my friend. Thank you very much for it."

— Don Beck, developmental theorist, co-author of *Spiral Dynamics*

"Spiritual traditions have long denied the importance of our unique self, but Gafni brings out in living color how this aspect of the divine is necessary for evolution to occur. Even more, it's necessary for love to occur, with love as the evolutionary force that pulls us into the kosmic co-creation of our future, an important contribution to the evolutionary conversation—one we can't do without."

— Anodea Judith, PhD, author of *Waking the Global Heart*,
Eastern Body-Western Mind and *Chakra Balancing*

"Marc's Gafni's spiritual democracy is the evolutionary unfolding of love and intelligence in our era. This book is dangerous because it contains ideas if put into practice could bridge the long-time dichotomy between Western and Eastern spirituality and provide a revolutionary method to transcend your ego-binding separateness while still retaining your specialness—is a radical willingness to be your unique self. *Your Unique Self* is dangerous for a second reason as well: Not only is this volume way brilliant, it breaks through your head and opens your heart. In the age of the ruling elites, be they spiritual or political is over—the future of our world depends on your enlightenment. For all of our sake, please read on..."

— Sharon Gannon, founder of the Jivamukti Yoga Method

"It appears that the rumors of God's death have been greatly exaggerated! There may be no better way to understand the Divine in the coming decades than what is expressed in this book, where ancient traditions are cast in a new light and brought into a new century. You will be compelled to respect the unparalleled rigor and depth of scholarship while at the same time swooning from the beauty of the ideas. A work like this comes along once in a generation."

— Zachary Stein, expert in metrics research; Integral scholar, Harvard University

"*Your Unique Self* is a profound and powerful evolutionary teaching on how the realization of the unique human soul transforms the core experience of one's life. *Your Unique Self* is simply essential reading for everyone who wants to step into the fullness of their being."

— Richard Barrett, Chairman and founder of the Barrett Values Centre, author of *The New Leadership Paradigm* and *Love, Fear and the Destiny of Nations.*

"*Your Unique Self* marks a beautiful integration of Eastern and Western perspectives on what it means to be fully human. In Gafni's Unique Self teaching, through our own relentless practice, each of us has the opportunity to stabilize our awareness beyond the confines of separateness. Anchored in this deeper vantage point and with a heart overflowing with a commitment to both service and evolution, the realization of wholeness has no choice but to shine through the fractilization of its uniqueness. Gafni's teaching of Unique Self provides one of the vital keys needed to unlock a World Spirituality based on Integral Principles."

— Dustin DiPerna, author of *Integral Religious Studies Volume 2: The Heart of Conscious Evolution - An Advanced Guide to Integral Spiritual Development*

"If you're reading this, there's a 100% chance this unforgettable book is for YOU. *Your Unique Self* is unequivocally one of the most brilliant and sorely needed treasures of our time. In an age of small self hijacking soul, of ego masquerading as God, this stunning new work ushers in a genuine miracle; the big Self that is uniquely YOU."

— Stuart Davis, songwriter, rock star

"In this brilliant and spiritually expansive book, Marc Gafni has transcended previous interpretations of the mystical texts upon which Unique Self is based, through his intense study and interaction with this material, which led him to imbibe the material at the level of *ruah ha-kodesh*, the holy Spirit. It is Rabbi Gafni's insights on this level that let us understand this work as a detailed map of the process of liberation in the Hebrew mystical path.

"A great and luminous work has come before my eyes, a vast and deep sea of illuminating wisdom embodied in clear and accessible writ. Rabbi Marc Gafni did step daringly into the void created by the dearth of enlivening and invigorating teachings of our tradition, and blessed us with this brilliant beyond measure and transformative work. This work is a true masterpiece of the sort our people have not witnessed for many centuries.

"Rabbi Gafni introduces us to the great lineage from which he drinks and which inspired him to bring the great teaching of Unique Self into the world of world spirituality. We see the lineage of Unique Self rooted grandly in the hidden teachings of

Mordechai Lainer which Mordechai Gafni, reveals, shares a broadens, deepens and evolves from the matrix of his own profound enlightened consciousness."

— Rabbi Gershon Winkler, author of *The Soul of the Matter: A Jewish-Kabbalistic Perspective on the Human Soul Before, During, and After Life*

"So often in our firm's work, we see a pattern where high achieving CEOs struggle to reconcile the transcendence of their spiritual life with the practicalities of their organizational work. Dr. Gafni's enlightened point of view offers leaders a highly accessible framework for expressing their Unique Selves through their organizations. This book is truly groundbreaking and should be in the hands of all aspiring conscious leaders."

— Rand Stagen, Managing Director of Stagen

"My first reaction, upon reading the table of contents for *Your Unique Self* was a realization that my entire core conversation—inner and outer—about God, Self, Life and spiritual practice was about to change in profound ways. What I could not anticipate from those initial pages is the astonishing breadth and depth of this profound work of love. In a single work, Dr. Gafni has painted a portrait of the emerging face of consciousness, using as his paint the worlds of spiritual traditions, psychology, physics and biology. He articulates, as nobody has done before, a sweeping notion of enlightenment that honors, simultaneously, the Great Unity and the Great Uniqueness that is the human experience. While the entire book is a treasure chest of deep wisdom, I feel confident in saying Dr. Gafni's treatment of 'Shadow' will change the way humanity thinks about shadow integration from now on. I'll no doubt be reading this book many times, as a textbook for living, loving and being."

— Thomas G. Goddard, J.D., Ph.D., Chief Executive Officer
of Integral Healthcare Solutions

"This book contains a profound healing and integration of East and West enlightenment paradigms. The individual self is not only transcended but also crucially resurrected as a point of unique fire in the universal life we all share. Marc's articulation of this core realization as the heart of an emergent and synthetic world spirituality is nothing less than utterly essential."

— Bruce Lyon, Tantric teacher

"Marc's development and articulation of the Unique Self teaching lays down the most original and important statement that we have of a genuine of an Integral evolutionary enlightenment. Unique Self, with stunning clarity and power merges in higher Integral embrace the best of premodern, modern and postmodern gnosis. This exciting new chapter in Integral Theory is simply invaluable."

— Barbara Alexander, M.A., M.Div., Spiritual director, teacher and coach

"In response to a culture wandering and aimless, Dr. Gafni has produced nothing less than a context of meaning that can draw us into the heart of Spirit's next creative move."

— Sam Alexander, Presbyterian Minister

"I predict that history will note *Your Unique Self* as being a seminal work in helping to accelerate the evolution of the consciousness of the planet in the 21st century. In a truly momentous book of integrated philosophy by Marc Gafni, the Tantric view that we are in essence unique reflections of the Supreme Self is presented in an unprecedented way. For the masses to make an inspired personal choice to glorify the Universal as singularly diverse individuals will be the legacy of this great book."

— John Friend, founder of Anusara Yoga

"The profound teachings in this book do not only bring together East and West in a way that both are honored, but also transmit a whole system for evolving our Unique Selves. It is rare to find a spiritual developmental evolutionary map that holds together from multiple vantage points, all the way up, all the way down. This is one of those works! In *Your Unique Self* you will find profound gems polished over a lifetime of study elegantly expressing the ineffable. I highly recommend it!"

— Joanne Hunt, CEO, Integral Coaching Canada, Inc.

"Marc Gafni's concept of 'Unique Self' is extraordinary. His deep inquiry into how every person on this planet has at their fingertips the ability to have a unique 'enlightenment' experience is not only revolutionary, it is also highly practical. This book is a transmission from a loving and compassionate teacher whose intentions are nothing more than helping people live to their highest and fullest potential. Is it possible to attain enlightenment without having to sit in a cave for 30 years in deep meditation? Marc Gafni says YES, and that having an 'enlightenment' experience is not only possible for every single person on this planet, it is also unique and personal for each one of us. This book will meet you wherever you might be in your life, and provides you with incredible transmissions of wisdom, understanding and compassion. I highly recommend this book to anyone who is interested in becoming the best person they can be."

— Todd Goldfarb, founder of The Global Tipping Point Series

"*Your Unique Self* stands forth as a masterwork of our times. Its message is vibrant and accessible—an altogether stunning articulation of what it is to live as a spiritual being who's irreducibly and inseparably a synthesis of transcendence and immanence, perspective and presence, fullness and freedom. Dr. Marc Gafni, from my perspective, is simply one of the few—if not the only teacher—who's ceaselessly strived to ground his work deeply in the Integral approach, while simultaneously innovating it in service of one of the most significant and robust spiritual visions I've ever encountered."

— Clint Fuhs, founder of Core Integral and Chairman of Integral Institute

"Marc Gafni's book gives us an essential guide for embracing all of who we are, warts and all, and for coming out of the closet of our self into our fullest and highest Unique Self. It maps an Integral spiritual path urgently needed today by anyone struggling with self-acceptance, for it is a powerful call to love every part of the self that has until now escaped the generous embrace of Love. Moreover, it does this in an intellectually rigorous and original fashion that stands out as unique among contemporary spirituality authors, establishing in the process a foundational piece of an intellectual framework capable of bringing about a revolution in our understanding of what it means to be integrally, fully human."

— Joe Perez, author of *Soulfully Gay*

"Dr. Marc Gafni's latest book offers a profound and vital insight on the nature of spiritual growth. This understanding is essential for both our personal awakening, and our capacity to transform our relationship with the planet. By clarifying that the traditional notion of spiritual awakening (letting go of our sense of separateness), is only one aspect of spiritual development, Marc frees us to understand the vital next step for 21st century spirituality. The other pole of the equation is the evolution of our "unique self," the particular gifts that each of us has to offer to the world. Developing those gifts and bringing them forward in a way that simultaneously honors our interconnection is the essential step towards an embodies spirituality that can be embraced by the entire human family."

— Rev. Michael Pergola, MA, MBA, JD, co-founder and former
Executive Director of One Spirit Learning Alliance

"Marc Gafni has written a magisterial work. Like Gafni himself, it combines depth of intellect with integrity of heart and has much to teach us both from a scholarly perspective and as a contemporary transmission of what Gafni calls Evolutionary Kabbalah, in this case wisdom of Mordechai Lainer's Izbica school of Kaballah. In some sense this work can also be seen as Gafni's spiritual autobiography. This is a seminal contribution to the next stage of Spirit's unfoldment."

— Sally Kempton, author of *Meditation for the Love of It*

"This magisterial work by Dr. Marc Gafni, *Radical Kabbalah,* makes a seminal contribution to a number of fields. Particularly the fields of transpersonal psychology, theology and integral studies are here offered a crucial building block as they attempt to fashion a model of consciousness that is grounded in traditional wisdom but still open to the next creative synthesis that is now emerging. I am reminded in reading Dr. Gafni's work of the legitimate excitement that was generated by Elaine Pagels and others as they opened the parallel tradition of the Gnostic Gospels that had been expunged from the Church's teachings. I expect Gafni's to gradually emerge as one of the significant intellectual figures of our time and to make a significant contribution to the evolution of consciousness."

— Prof. Richard Mann, Editor Transpersonal Series, SUNY Press

"It appears that the rumors of God's death have been greatly exaggerated! There may be no better way to understand the Divine in the coming decades than what is expressed in this book, where ancient traditions are cast in a new light and brought into a new Century. You will be compelled to respect the unparalleled rigor and depth of scholarship while at the same time swooning from the beauty of the ideas. A work like this comes along once in a generation."

— Zachary Stein, expert in metrics research; Integral scholar, Harvard University

"As I wrote in my forward to the *Journal of Integral Theory and Practice*, 6:1, Dr. Marc Gafni has played a foundational role in emergence and development of Integral Spirituality. Gafni is involved in an ongoing process of ecstatic teaching and scholarship. That his work is birthing new forms of evolutionary spirituality is evidenced in his emergent articulations of World Spirituality and Unique Self. Unique Self, a term coined and a concept and realization developed by Marc over the last fifteen years, represents a truly world-centric, planet-centric and kosmocentric evolutionary mysticism. It changes the way we think about enlightenment by integrating the enlightenment traditions of the premodern East and modern West in a higher integral embrace. In mystical hermeneutics, according to Kripal, the reading of mystical texts is engaged with such devotion and transcendental openness that the very act of reading becomes an injunction of mystical practice and revelation. Such is the nature of the work before you."

— Sean Esbjörn-Hargens PhD co-author of *Integral Ecology*
and editor of *Integral Theory in Action*

"In this brilliant and spiritually expansive book, Rabbi Mordechai Gafni has transcended previous interpretations of Lainer's work through his intense study and interaction with this material, which led him to imbibe the material at the level of *ruah ha-kodesh*, the holy Spirit. It is Rabbi Gafni's insights on this level—meaning the level of divine inspiration rather than prophetic revelation, which ended at the fall of the First Temple—that let us understand this work as a detailed map of the process of liberation in the Jewish path.

"Rabbi Gabriel congratulates Rabbi Gafni for his ability to draw out the essence of the mystical teachings of Lainer in a way that goes beyond academic interpretations. Rabbi Gabriel's feeling is that Mordechai Lainer had the direct apperception of the truth of self-realization, and that his teachings initially developed through following of the Joseph archetypal path before he evolved/woke up into the Judah archetypal path of liberation. Rabbi Gafni's holy understanding of this great teacher is absolutely vital and compelling for our times, and it can open us up to the Divine urge. These teachings bring us back to Avraham sitting in his tent in the heat—the spiritual passion—of the day. This inspired interpretation of Lainer by Rabbi Gafni's reading of Lainer offered in this treatise is a pioneering work transmitting Judaism as it was originally intended—as an inspired path to full liberation."

— Dr. Gabriel Cousens, author of seven books; founder, Tree of Life Center

"I have only found one... blessed individual, a man who on his own volition, and out of his soul-deep passion for the wisdom of Torah, took it upon himself to endeavor where no one else rose to the occasion, and to expend his time and energy, even amid great personal suffering and against overwhelming obstacles, to gift us with a massive compendium of long-neglected wisdom destined to lift our eyes above the stagnating ways in which we have been seeing for far too long, so that we might see anew, and our hearts become thereby opened wider to enable the removal of the many layers of ignorance and oblivion that have obscured our vision in the fog of our lengthy exile.

"This work is a true masterpiece of the sort our people have not witnessed for many centuries, shaking us out of our stupor toward reclaiming life again, reclaiming our goddess heritage and teachings, and the bond with the ancient spark of Eros of our so-called pagan ways of many of our aboriginal sisters and brothers, a bond we had begun to forge under Solomon and are destined to forge once again in the time to come. But Rabbi Gafni in his fine and original reading of Mordechai Lainer purifies the spark of its prepersonal ethical taint. In a Lurianic act of exalted scholarship and love he raises the spark of paganism and sets it in new evolved ethical context so that the passion for the goddess expresses itself, not in irresponsible abandon, but in the infinitely sacred details of judicial procedure and fairness.

"The erotic goddess is channeled into justice and small claims court becomes the arena of the goddesses revelation. This is in Gafni's reading the major wonder of Izbica and it is also the major goal of Gafni's own life and work. It is Gafni's particular sensitivity and evolving passion for the ethical that reveals these strains in Izbica.

"Much of this sacred work will raise brows, even more of it will challenge the way in which we have grown accustomed to think. And all of it, I pray, will finally restore us to our primal mindset, our original way of perceiving and encountering the divine in both its immanent and transcendent dances, so that the thousand songs and dances of the Pharaoh's daughter will no longer be for us the antithesis we had presumed it was, and instead become the sacred rite of divine connection it was intended to be.

"For those who will approach this challenging and daring work with trepidation or with skepticism—or worse with criticism—be forewarned that Rabbi Gafni's work is fully supported by an enormous legion of ancient and medieval classical text sources from the earlier writings of teachers who are revered by the most traditional amongst us. He is not attempting in this book to introduce anything new to our eyes, but rather to introduce our eyes to what has been there all along, veiled from our sight by our own blindness. His work is a gift, a blessing, and most importantly a rare opportunity for all of us to reclaim the authenticity of our true selves, and to breathe the breath of Life back into our souls."

— Rabbi Gershon Winkler, author of ten books of Jewish teaching
and scholarship, a master of original Jewish texts and a highly beloved
and respected teacher of Jewish sources and practice

"It is a pleasure to help launch this remarkable piece of scholarly and religious analysis. In Dr. Gafni's fascinating exploration of the teachings and personal path of Mordechai Lainer of Izbica, there is an affirmation of the individual as a reliable moral agent, albeit an individual who has been through a mystical unity with the divine and has been purged of self-orientation. The parallels with the ethical teachings of Eihei Dogen Zenji, the founder of the Soto school of Zen, are intriguing.

"While Rebbe Lainer's theism contrasts with Dogen Zenji's non-theism, and their cultural contexts give their teachings a radically differing flavors, beneath the differences is a strikingly similar evocation of the potential for each of us to rely on our ability to make sound ethical choices in our daily lives without wooden adherence to convention. Each teaches that if we engage in the practices they advocate, we can find within us a non-dual awareness empty of self, yet simultaneously fully present to all that is manifest in each moment. From this place, reliably ethical action springs.

"Dr. Gafni's provocative study of Mordacai Lainer of Izbica, and his dialogue with various of Lainer's analysts, will leave the reader enriched, both from the scholarly discourse, and from an internal dialogue first with the Sage of Izbica, then with Dr. Gafni and the others who have written on the subject, and finally with the self, the one who is called upon to make decisions and take action."

— Michael D. Zimmerman, former Chief Justice, State of Utah;
Zen Sensei, Boulder Mountain Zen Center

This is a great work of inspired and audacious scholarship. Professor Moshe Idel's letter of recommendation to Oxford University, and Professor Richard Mann's words (comparing Marc's work on Kabbalah to Elaine Pagels' work on the Gnostic gospels), which introduce these volumes, speak for themselves. Similarly, the statements by Michael Zimmerman from the perspective of a chief justice of an American supreme court and by Sally Kempton, Dr. Gabriel Cousens, and Rabbi Winkler as scholars and teachers of enlightenment show something of the broad relevance of the volumes, as do the remarks by Sean Esbjörn-Hargens and Zachary Stein.

I read Dr. Gafni's masterwork on Radical Kabbalah in its first drafts almost seven years ago. It was then over a thousand pages long, and I read it over two or three days with great excitement. I sent Marc a series delighted emails, after reading every few chapters. The breadth, depth and the sheer importance of the work moved me. I immediately recognized it as a seminal work, identifying a critical lineage of enlightenment from the tradition of Kabbalah, which needed to be incorporated into the Integral model.

We have done this work of integration in a special issue of the Journal of Integral Theory and Practice, under the leadership of Sean Esbjörn-Hargens, dedicated to this new chapter in Integral Theory, Unique Self. (JITP 6:1) This issue was guest edited by Dr. Gafni. Marc has further elaborated on this work in his book entitled, Your Unique Self: The Radical Path to Personal Enlightenment, published by Integral Publishers.

All this writing and discussion on Unique Self, including our first Integral Spiritual Experience Retreat on the same topic, was to a significant extent informed and catalyzed by Marc's scholarly work, teaching and leadership. This is the kind of work that the Center for World Spirituality, of which I am an active member, exists to bring forth, drawing on every great tradition, pre-modern, modern and post-modern. All this will inform the emergence of a genuine framework for a world spirituality based on Integral principles, which is one of the critical needs of this moment in time.

— Ken Wilber, Integral Philosopher and Author

CPSIA information can be obtained at www.ICGtesting.com
Printed in the USA
LVOW061622030413

327445LV00003B/410/P